D0554423

The Devil's Adjutant

To Marie-Berthe and Edouard de Harenne

THE DEVIL'S ADJUTANT

JOCHEN PEIPER, PANZER LEADER

by

Michael Reynolds

The story of one of Himmler's former Adjutants and the battle which brought this senior commander in Hitler's SS Bodyguard to the foreground of history.

SPELLMOUNT
Staplehurst

SARPEDON
New York

British Library Cataloguing in Publication Data:
A catalogue record for this book is available
from the British Library

Copyright © Michael Reynolds 1995, 1997
Maps © Jay Karamales 1995, 1997

UK ISBN 1-873376-41-3

First published in the UK in 1995 by
Spellmount Limited
The Old Rectory
Staplehurst
Kent TN12 0AZ

Revised and Updated 1997

and in the United States by Sarpedon Publishers
166 Fifth Avenue
New York, NY 10010
USA ISBN 1-885119-15-1

Library of Congress Cataloging-in-Publication data available

3 5 7 9 8 6 4 2

Typeset in Palatino by Rowland Phototypesetting Limited
Printed in Great Britain by Mackays of Chatham plc

Contents

Author's Note

This story has been written with events in strict chronological order. If, however, the reader wishes to follow what happened in a particular place without interruption, for example in La Gleize, it is possible to do so by reading Chapters XXI, XXVI, XXXIII and XXXVI immediately after Chapter XIX.

List of Maps

between pages 301 and 320

List of Plates

17. Panther number 131, commanded by Oberscharführer Strelow, immobilized in an air attack 18th December 1944. Note Cheneux bridge in background. (Courtesy Gérard Grégoire)
18. Gustav Knittel, Commander 1st SS Panzer Reconnaissance Battalion and Fast Group Knittel. (Author's collection)
19. Jupp Diefenthal, Commanding Officer, 3rd SS Panzer-Grenadier Battalion, 2nd SS Panzer-Grenadier Regiment – part of KG Peiper. (Courtesy Gérard Grégoire)
20. Otto Holst's Jagdpanzer IV/70 in the Amblève river after collapsing the Petit Spai bridge, 21st December 1944. (Courtesy Gérard Grégoire)
21. Hal McCown, Commanding Officer 2/119 Infantry – Peiper's prisoner 21st–24th December 1944. (Author's collection)
22. David Knox, Officer Commanding L Company 3/119 Infantry. (Courtesy Mrs Betty Knox)
23. A Sherman of C Coy 740th Tank Battalion knocked out at the La Venne crossroads on the morning of 23rd December 1944. (Courtesy Gérard Grégoire)
24. Jim Gavin, Commanding General 82nd Airborne Division. (US Army)
25. George Rubel, Commanding Officer 740th Tank Battalion. (Courtesy Gérard Grégoire)
26. Jochen Peiper in April 1944, newly promoted to Obersturmbannführer and wearing Oakleaves to his Knight's Cross. (Author's collection)
27. Peiper shortly before the Ardennes offensive. (Author's collection)
28. Panther number 002 abandoned in La Gleize after the battle. The number would indicate it was a command tank of Peiper's KG HQ. (Coutesy Gérard Grégoire)
29. Werner Poetschke, Commanding Officer 1st SS Panzer Battalion. (Author's collection)
30. Otto Skorzeny, Commander 150th Panzer Brigade. (Author's collection)
31. Tiger II number 204 near the Petit Spai bridge after the battle, January 1945. (Author's collection)
32. Panther number 221, commanded by Hauptscharführer Knappisch, in La Gleize after the battle. It was damaged during the attack on Stoumont. (Courtesy Gérard Grégoire)
33. US engineers of the 291st uncovering bodies at the Baugnez crossroads, mid January 1945. (US Army)
34. Victims of The 'Malmédy Massacre', showing body tags and the Café Bodarwé in the background. (US Army)
35. Peiper branded as a war criminal at Schwabisch Hall. (US Army)
36. Ursula Dietrich followed by Sigurd Peiper arriving at the Dachau Trial, 1946. (US Army)
37. Some of those accused at Dachau 16th May 1946: Dietrich (11),

Acknowledgments

I am indebted to many people for their help in producing this book and I place the cast in order of appearance rather than importance! First, I must mention Lieutenant Colonel Peter Crocker, because he was my original partner and without his enthusiasm and persuasion I would never, at a very busy period in my own military career, have bothered to pursue the story of Battlegroup Peiper. I am also indebted to him for his meticulous research in the early days of our joint interest.

Next I must thank my very dear Belgian friends Marie-Berthe and Edouard de Harenne to whom this book is dedicated. We first met in 1975 when Edouard was the Mayor of La Gleize; within a short time they had welcomed me into their home and treated me almost as one of their family. With incredible generosity they have allowed me to take literally hundreds of NATO officers and NCOs to visit them and, depending on the very unpredictable Ardennes weather, to have picnic lunches in their Château or garden. Nearly every year since 1975 I have spent several weeks at the Château de la Vaulx Renard and have been able to delight in the beauty of the Amblève valley and the haunting forests which surround it. I have listened to the local legends, enjoyed 'les scandales' of the various village communities and been able to feel the atmosphere of the area where this incredible story happened. I have come to know and love it more than anywhere else.

Then I come to my first American in the cast – Colonel Dave Pergrin. His cheerful enthusiasm and lovely sense of humour, as well as his deep Christian beliefs, have always been infectious. I am greatly indebted to him for introducing me to members of his famous 'Damned Engineers' and to some of the survivors of The 'Malmédy Massacre'; and for painting vivid pictures for me of how it felt to be a 26-year-old Commanding Officer during those frightening and 'misty days of WW II'.

In 1985 I met Wolf Dietlef Mauder, a young German reservist panzer colonel who had not been born in 1944 but who has a deep knowledge of the Battle of the Ardennes. Through him I met and came to know a number of former members of Die Leibstandarte Adolf Hitler and it was to him and another Bundeswehr regular officer, Lieutenant Colonel Hans-Dieter Bechtold, that I turned when I had a detailed query concerning the German side of the battle. They never let me down and I am very grateful.

And then, again on the Belgian side of the cast, come Serge Fontaine and Joseph Dejardin, both residents of Stavelot, and Gérard Grégoire of La Gleize. They were all young men in the Ardennes in December 1944. Their loving and very detailed research into what happened during the battle, particularly to the local people, is exemplary and I thank them for the very generous way in which they have shared their research with me.

My friend Georges Balaes was a former Chief Commissioner for Criminal Intelligence in the Belgian Department of Justice and he arranged an introduction to the French police in Dijon and worked his way through the voluminous files on the 'Traves Murder' for me. I would be much the poorer without his generous friendship.

During my first visit to Dave and Peggy Pergrin's home in Pennsylvania in 1987 I met John Bauserman – a high school teacher with a passionate interest in finding out what really happened at the Baugnez Crossroads on 17th December 1944. He and I have spent many hours discussing the subject and have written scores of letters to each other about it. He and Joy have had me to stay several times at their home in Virginia and we have spent many happy hours under the watchful eye of Miss Washington in the Suitland National Archives. John has shared with me everything he found there and his book *The Malmédy Massacre*, published by the White Mane Publishing Company Inc., is a definitive work on this tragic event. It was in John's company at Suitland that I first met Jay Karamalis, another military history enthusiast and a wizard with a computer. When he came to Europe I showed him the 'Peiper Trail' and we went on to visit some of the 1916 Somme battlefields and study those of Mortain and Falaise 1944 in detail; we even called in to see the Field of Agincourt 1415! He too has written a book; his co-author is Al Vannoy and it is called *Against the Panzers*. All those interested in the 1944 battles of Normandy and the Ardennes will wish to read it. Jay took my hand-drawn maps and, using his personal computer and at his own expense, turned them into the highly professional end-products which appear in this book – I am forever in his debt.

My thanks must also go to two Englishmen, the French wife of a British officer and a Belgian lady. First, Brigadier Tony Baxter, an old friend and Sandhurst comrade who, without hesitation, offered to read and correct my typescript; and then Brigadier John Moore-Bick and Mrs Francoise Murcott who over the years generously translated many foreign documents for me – so did Mademoiselle Marie-France Grégoire and she also patiently interpreted the many conversations I enjoyed with her father.

And finally I would like to thank the people of La Gleize, Cheneux, Stoumont, Trois Ponts and Stavelot who have always made me feel so welcome – especially Georges and Chantal de Harenne and their sons Charles and François at the Château Froidcour, where I have also taken numerous NATO visitors and friends; also Georges and Susie Balaes in their enchanting home above La Gleize, Simone at the Echo des Campagnes café and Louis and Maggy at the Aux Ecuries de la Reine restaurant where I spent so many happy evenings. Happy memories indeed!

Sussex, England   MFR
May 1995

Anyone writing a detailed history of a modern military operation is bound to receive letters from veterans pointing out what they consider to be errors, or adding to the story. I have been fortunate with *The Devil's Adjutant* in that virtually all those I have received since June 1995 have been complimentary and a number have been useful in adding to the accuracy of the overall picture. This revised edition includes a number of important corrections and further details which I have received from American, British, Belgian, Dutch and German veterans and historians. I am particularly grateful to Lyle Bouck, Leon Kent, Danny Parker, William Tucker, Joseph Dejardin and Neill Thomson.

Sussex, England   MFR
July 1997

Introduction

In 1970 my wife brought home a book from the American Library at the NATO Headquarters in Holland where I was serving at the time. It was Janice Holt-Giles's *The Damned Engineers* and it was about the German offensive in the Ardennes in 1944, better known as 'The Battle of the Bulge'. The author's husband had been a sergeant in an American engineer battalion in the battle and she told a fascinating story. That book changed my life.

Living as we did at that time, close to where the fighting had taken place, it was not long before Anne and I set out to visit some of the places mentioned in the story and, while she picked flowers or read her book after a picnic in the beautiful countryside of the Ardennes, I became more and more excited as I read that a Tiger tank had come round this or that corner or that some combat engineers had blown up this particular bridge just before the Germans could cross it.

The Damned Engineers led on to other books about the Ardennes Offensive and soon I began to realise that the lessons to be learned from this battle, especially those involving leadership, were as valid in 1970 as they had been nearly a quarter of a century earlier. And so when I became the Commanding Officer of a mechanised infantry battalion in the British Army of the Rhine shortly afterwards, I asked three of my young officers to study the exploits of one particular German armoured battle-group in this battle, Kampfgruppe Peiper, and six months later to conduct all my officers and sergeants through the battle, drawing appropriate lessons as they did so. It was a two-day affair and, apart from its being of great military value, we had a thoroughly enjoyable time.

I decided to continue with this idea and as a Brigade Commander I repeated these battlefield studies in 1975 and 1976, calling them 'Exercise Pied Peiper'. One of the three officers I chose at that time to conduct the tours was a young captain named Peter Crocker. He 'caught the bug' just as I had done but he did a lot more research than his predecessors. In 1978 we found ourselves serving together again, this time in the main British Headquarters in West Germany. When Peter suggested that we should do some more 'Pied Peiper' tours I readily agreed but, since I could hardly expect him to do it all by himself, I offered to help. And so began my personal research into this fascinating story.

My first breakthrough came in 1982 when I met Colonel Dave Pergrin, the Commanding Officer of the Engineer Battalion about which Janice Holt-Giles had written in 1970; then in 1985 I had the luck to meet and accompany some important former members of the 1st SS Panzer

Division when they retraced their 1944 steps through the Ardennes. They ranged in appointment from Regimental to tank commander. I was able to join a similar group in 1991.

Since I retired from the Army in 1986 this subject has been my main interest and I have continued to appear as a guest speaker on 'Exercise Pied Peiper'. I have been able to tell the essentials of this story, on the ground where it actually happened, to nearly two thousand NATO officers and NCOs and interested civilians; I have conducted the generals of NATO's Military Committee and, perhaps more surprisingly, even some 1st SS Panzer Division veterans, along the 'Peiper Trail'.

So why have I decided to write this book now? It is simply because I have become irritated by the plethora of inaccurate accounts about this battle and because in recent months I have been angered by the propaganda being put about by neo-Nazis and Nazi sympathisers who have the clear aim of glorifying or excusing the events of December 1944. It has always surprised me when talking to German veterans, and even some researchers, that they have little interest in what the Americans say happened – and, to be fair, vice versa. Perhaps it takes someone less prejudiced to listen to both sides of the story and, when the two sides are in dispute, for a former soldier to apply military experience and knowledge to work out what probably happened. Harsh and unheroic reality may be less exciting than a film or television version but we owe it to those who died to present it. This is, I believe, the first book to juxtapose the various accounts of what each side says happened. By seeking out original sources whenever possible and not merely giving a different twist to the accounts of previous writers and historians, I believe my account to be the most accurate yet written.

It is now nearly a quarter of a century since I first heard the name Jochen Peiper; my quest for the truth about this man and the battle which brought him into the foreground of history has given me great pleasure and taken me all over Belgium and to France, Germany and America. Hardly a week, and certainly a month, has gone by without a letter, telephone call or meeting with a veteran or fellow researcher. It has been one giant jigsaw puzzle and there are inevitably some pieces still missing. Some may yet turn up but I should like my account of what I think happened to be read by those who took part – before they join their fallen comrades of fifty years ago. As an excited fourteen-year-old schoolboy in 1944 I never dreamed that one day I would meet and become a friend of some of the heroes of this book, Dave Pergrin, or Bill Merriken, a survivor of The 'Malmédy Massacre', and certainly not that I would one day have dinner with Ralf Tiemann, the December 1944 Chief of Staff of the 1st SS Panzer Division, or General von Manteuffel, the Commander of the 5th Panzer Army. The book Anne brought home for me in 1970 did indeed change my life.

Guide to Abbreviations

AA	anti-aircraft
AAA	anti aircraft artillery
AAR	After Action Report
Amb	ambulance
AP	armour piercing
Armd	armoured
Arty	artillery
AT	anti-tank
bazooka	US hand held rocket launcher
Bn	battalion
Bty	battery
Capt	Captain
CCA/B/R	Combat Command A/B/R
Coy	company
CP	command post
Cpl	Corporal
DR	Das Reich (2nd SS Pz Div)
Engr	engineer
ETHINT	European Theatre Historical Interrogations
FA	field artillery
GI	US infantryman
H hour	time an attack begins
HJ	Hitlerjugend (12th SS Pz Div)
HMG	heavy machine gun
HS	Hohenstaufen (9th SS Pz Div)
Hy	heavy
Inf	infantry
LAH	Leibstandarte Adolf Hitler (1st SS Pz Div)
Lt	lieutenant
M/Sgt	master sergeant
MG	machine gun
MP	military police
NCO	non commissioned officer
Pfc	Private 1st class
PG	panzer-grenadier
Pl	platoon
Pnr	pioneer (German engineer)
Pvt	private

Pz	panzer
PZ JG	panzer jäger (tank hunter)
PZ-Gren	panzer-grenadier
RCT	regimental combat team
Recce	reconnaissance
Regt	regiment
S-1/G-1	personnel branch
S-2/G-2	intelligence branch
S-3/G-3	operations branch
S-4/G-4	supply branch
Sgt	Sergeant
SP	self-propelled
StuG	armoured assault gun
T/3	corporal
T/4	sergeant
T/5	staff sergeant
T/Sgt	technical sergeant
TD	Tank Destroyer
TF	task force
Tk	tank
V-G	volks-grenadier
V1/V2	German rocket weapon

CHAPTER I
The Man and His Regiment

Much has been written about the main character in this World War II odyssey and yet it is unlikely that he would have been heard of outside Germany but for the infamous massacre near Malmédy in Belgium with which his name will be forever associated. Initially shunned and even despised in the years following Germany's surrender, Jochen Peiper is now revered by his former comrades and generally accepted as a brilliant soldier. Even Hollywood, with its fantasy *The Battle of the Bulge*, has played its part in immortalizing this good-looking darling of the Third Reich. But what is the truth about this man who after the war became known as 'GI enemy number 1' and who was murdered in France thirty-one years later?

Joachim (Jochen) Peiper was born in Berlin on 30th January 1915 to Woldemar and Charlotte Peiper. His father reached the rank of captain in the First World War, serving in both Turkey and France in an undistinguished military career. He worked in a lottery business between the wars and claimed, amongst other things, to have been the manager of a tank factory during World War II.[1] Peiper had two brothers, both of whom were in the SS. Hasso, a member of the Totenkopfverbände (Death's Head units employed as concentration camp guards) was killed in 1942, and the other, Horst, died in 1941. Peiper said the cause of death was tuberculosis but there have been suggestions that he committed suicide after being sterilized by the Nazis for homosexuality.

After primary school Peiper went to the Goethe Oberrealschule in Berlin. He left in 1933, allegedly before taking his final exams. After the war his father said[2] that Peiper had been keen to become a cavalry officer and had therefore taken riding lessons at a Herr Beermann's riding school. One evening a high-ranking SS leader had arrived at the school and announced that everyone there was henceforth an automatic member of the SS Reitersturm (SS Cavalry). Whatever the truth, Peiper's records show that on 12th October 1933,[3] only two weeks after its formation, he was indeed a member of the 1st SS Reitersturm, 7th SS Reiter Standarte (Regiment), and four days later at the age of eighteen he was an official candidate for the SS-Verfugungstruppe (SS-VT). These Special Purpose Troops consisted of the 'Leibstandarte Adolf Hitler' (Hitler's Bodyguard) and three Standarten or Regiments: the

21

'Germania', 'Deutschland' and 'Der Führer'. Later, in 1935, Hitler decreed that these Standarten would form part of the Army in time of war; thus, by 1943, the Leibstandarte had become the 1st SS Panzer Division, the Deutschland and Der Führer Standarten had formed the 2nd SS Panzer Division 'Das Reich' and the Germania was part of the 5th SS Panzer Division 'Wiking'. Peiper joined the SS-VT for full-time service on 23rd January 1934 and reached the rank of corporal in October. He entered the SS training unit at Jüterbog in January 1935 and on 24th April the same year Peiper was selected for training at the SS Officer's School at Braunschweig. As a staff sergeant and potential member of Hitler's Bodyguard, Peiper was one of those who swore allegiance to the Führer in a torchlight ceremony held in front of the hallowed Feldherrnhalle War Memorial in Munich on 9th November. He was already under the spell of the leader of Nazi Germany. After SS officers' training, including an eight-week platoon commanders' tactical course at Dachau, Peiper was commissioned[4] on 20th April 1936, Hitler's birthday, as an Untersturmführer (second lieutenant) in the 11th Sturm (company), 3rd Sturmbann (battalion), Leibstandarte SS Adolf Hitler (LSSAH). The commander of this elite guard, and Peiper's close military superior for the next nine years, was Sepp Dietrich, himself an ex-personal bodyguard and intimate associate of the Führer.

What sort of regiment was this that Peiper had joined? In early 1933 Hitler had ordered Sepp Dietrich to form an headquarters guard to supplement the existing Führer Bodyguard which had been formed in February 1932. All SS units were requested to provide three dependable young men who were to be under 25, at least 1.8 metres tall, in good health, without criminal record and to have joined the SS before 30th January 1933. These regulations were later expanded to almost ludicrous extremes, such as filled teeth being unacceptable, demands for well proportioned bodies with no disparity between body and legs and lower leg and thigh, proof of ancestry back to 1800 for soldiers and 1750 for officers and even racial investigation of prospective wives.

At the end of February 1933 Dietrich personally selected 117 men for the 'Stabswache Berlin' as it was called and they assembled on 17th March in the Friesenstrasse Kaserne. A Prussian State Police battalion, also stationed in the barracks, provided administrative support and basic instruction. In April the retitled 'SS-Sonderkommando Berlin' moved into the famous Berlin Lichterfelde Kaserne, opened by Kaiser Wilhelm I in 1873 as an officer cadet school for the Prussian Army. It consisted of an Headquarters, 1st Company and Motor Company. Its first public appearance was as an Honour Guard to Hitler on 8th April at the Sports Palace in Berlin when he addressed a 'Sturm Abteilung' (SA) rally, and shortly afterwards the first twelve-man guard under Wilhelm Mohnke took post at the Reich Chancellery. Ironically twelve years later Mohnke was again commander of the Chancellery Guard, but this time as an SS major general, with Hitler dead and the Russians at the very gates of the building.

The remainder of 1933 saw the new Guard expand rapidly. Two training units, a music corps and a cavalry unit were formed, and on 9th November 835 men swore their oath of allegiance to the Führer in Munich. 'Adolf Hitler' banners were presented, the Führer's name was embroidered on their cuff bands and the unit was renamed 'Leibstandarte Adolf Hitler'. The letters 'SS' were inserted shortly afterwards. It was organised into two battalions, the first with two guard companies and a machine gun company and the second with two guard companies and a motor company.

On 30th June 1934 the Leibstandarte took part in the infamous 'Night of the Long Knives', when Hitler finally took action against Ernst Roehm, the Chief of Staff of the Sturm Abteilung (SA) and other senior members of the organisation that had helped him to power and that had been purposely designed for political indoctrination and strong-arm activities. Six members of the Guard, led by Sepp Dietrich himself, executed six SA men in Munich, and in the Lichterfelde Kaserne in Berlin three more senior members of the SA were shot by eight Leibstandarte NCOs and the Drum Major. The following day a further eleven senior SA men were shot. There has never been any suggestion, however, that Peiper was involved in these executions. It is perhaps noteworthy that in the semi-official history[5] of the Leibstandarte it is stressed that as far as Dietrich was concerned it was unimaginable that Hitler could ever give him an order which was not right and proper. If Hitler said the men were guilty of high treason then that was sufficient and he was merely executing a legal sentence. It has also to be said that many more than the twenty mentioned above died on the 'Night of the Long Knives' and the day following it.

During 1935 and 1936 the expansion of the Bodyguard continued. It led the Army in its occupation of the Saarland on 1st March 1935 and provided the Honour Guard at the Winter Olympics in February 1936. It took part in the occupation of the Sudetenland in October 1938 but was not involved in the notorious 'Kristallnacht' in November of the same year which saw the first open intimidation of the Jewish population.

Perhaps surprisingly there was a remarkable degree of informality within and between ranks in the Leibstandarte, and members addressed one another as 'Kamerad' when off duty; as time went on first names were frequently used. Much emphasis was placed on trust, even to the extent of forbidding locks on personal wardrobes. The fact that all officers had served in the ranks did much to foster the feeling of kinship.

By the time the war started in 1939 the LSSAH was a full regiment with three infantry battalions, an artillery battalion and anti-tank, reconnaissance, motorcycle, heavy infantry gun, engineer and signals sub units. A fourth battalion had been formed strictly for guard duties. It should be made clear, however, that the LSSAH was completely separate from both the Allgemeine, or general, SS and the Totenkopf Standarten which had been formed for concentration camp duties and from which grew the 3rd SS Totenkopf Division. This is not to say, though, that it was not reinforced from these elements as the war progressed. Similarly if a member of the Leibstandarte became unfit for combat he was fully eligible for transfer to the non-combatant parts of the SS.

This then was the Regiment into which Jochen Peiper had been commissioned; but what sort of man was this new young officer in his striking black uniform, high shining boots, white accoutrements and cuff titles bearing the name of the man who had already mesmerized the nation? Despite leaving school without formal qualifications, Peiper was an officer in an elite 3000-man force and is said to have been a literate, courteous and charming person with a good sense of humour and a passable knowledge of French and English. He was a natural soldier and enjoyed the company of both men and women, which was hardly surprising in view of his dashing looks. Being only 1.78m in height and of slight build, he was the antithesis of the normal Anglo-Saxon conception of a typical SS man.

Life in the Leibstandarte at this stage was extremely pleasant, if at times a little boring. It was after all a guard unit with all that implies, though duties such as Honour Guard at the 1936 Winter Olympics had its compensations. Being known as the 'asphalt soldiers' to their compatriots in the Wehrmacht certainly did not worry the swaggering occupants of the Lichterfelde Kaserne. They were close to their hypnotic leader and revelled in providing the many Honour Guards, culminating in those in Austria in 1938 following the Anschluss and on Hitler's 50th birthday in 1939 when he opened the new 7km-long Tiergartenstrasse in Berlin by driving its entire length; his Bodyguard stood as Honour Guard at the beginning and end of this magnificent street. In fairness, however, it must be said that whilst one battalion of the LSSAH always provided the necessary ceremonial guards, the remainder of the force was undergoing normal military training as a potential combat formation. Many exaggerated stories have been written about the toughness of this training, including the ridiculous one that a recruit was required to stand still while a grenade was exploded on his helmet! In reality, training was very similar to that carried out in the Army but with more emphasis on sport.

Between 1936 and 1938 Peiper took leave in Sweden, Norway and Denmark; they were perhaps lucky to see him only as a tourist. Shortly after the Anschluss with Austria in April 1938 Peiper was promoted to the rank of SS Lieutenant and for the first time he left the LSSAH. He had been selected[6] by the Reichsführer SS, Heinrich Himmler, to join his personal staff as a Liaison Officer to the SS-VT. Peiper's reaction to this appointment is unknown but he must have filled it well because his trial period of three months was extended to a full tour. It seems reasonable to assume therefore that he enjoyed himself in the appointment, although it would seem equally natural that he would, as a professional soldier, have felt some disappointment at being absent from his parent unit just as it went to war.

On the evening of 3rd September 1939 Peiper joined Himmler's entourage at the Stettin railway station in Berlin.[7] There he found three special trains – Hitler's, Hermann Göring's and Himmler's, appropriately named 'Heinrich'. It had fourteen cars and comprised a mobile Gestapo and SS Headquarters, anti-aircraft coaches and ample space for staff and secretaries. During the night the trains moved into Silesia and halted close to the German–Polish border. From there Peiper monitored the advance of his Regiment as it took part in the first, highly successful, 'Blitzkrieg' operation of the war.

On 29th June, just before the start of the Polish campaign, Jochen Peiper had married Sigurd Hinrichsen,[8] one of Himmler's secretaries. She was two and a half years his senior and her two brothers, like Peiper's, were in the SS. 'Sigi', as he called her, and he were to have two daughters, Elke and Silke and one son, Hinrich.

It is hardly surprising that there are few references to Peiper during his time on Himmler's personal staff – in 1939 no one could possibly have foreseen that within a few years he would have earned an international reputation for himself. However, it is known that in late January 1940 he accompanied Himmler to Przemysl in Poland,[9] where the Reichsführer SS welcomed the last few of more than a hundred thousand ethnic Germans who had been living in the section of eastern Poland now in Soviet hands. During the trip Peiper allegedly told another member of the staff, Ernst Schaefer, that Hitler had entrusted Himmler with the extermination of the Polish intelligentsia and that Himmler had already taken part in one execution himself. Whilst there can be no certainty that such a conversation ever took place, it is inconceivable that Peiper did not know about the resettlement programme in Poland, involving the expulsion or elimination of 'undesirables' and the settlement of Germans from the Baltic States and eastern Poland.

In early May 1940 Peiper was released from his duties with Himmler so that he could rejoin the Bodyguard and 'win his spurs' on active service. His Regiment had already taken part in the successful invasion of Holland and he found his comrades on 18th May at Bilzen. Although only a lieutenant, and perhaps due to Himmler's influence, Peiper was given command of the 11th Company in his original Battalion. The LSSAH moved through Belgium, via Huy on the Meuse, and crossed into France on the 20th. Ironically Huy was to be Peiper's main objective in the 1944 Ardennes campaign.

Peiper's baptism of fire began with the action to seize the Wattenberg feature, near Dunkirk, on 25th May. This involved an assault crossing of the Aa canal. Despite being slightly wounded by shell splinters in the back of the head,[10] Peiper distinguished himself in this successful attack and for this and the actions which followed it near Vichy, he was awarded[11] the Iron Cross, both 2nd and 1st Class. He was promoted to SS Captain on 1st June. Peiper remained with his company for the completion of the French campaign but on 21st June he received orders to return to Himmler's personal staff, again as Adjutant and Liaison Officer to the Waffen SS.[12] Thus, although he was to miss the invasions of Yugoslavia and Greece, his short period of active service with his Regiment had proved unusually successful and there must be the inevitable suspicion that Himmler's influence played its part in the recognition Peiper received.

It is significant that alongside Peiper in France at this time were all the important commanders who would be with him again in the Ardennes four and a half years later – Mohnke, a battalion commander in 1940, would be his Divisional Commander; Max Hansen and Rudolf Sandig, brother company commanders, would be commanding Kampfgruppes (battlegroups); Werner Poetschke would be Peiper's armoured commander and Jupp Diefenthal his infantry commander; Gustav Knittel, a reconnaissance platoon commander, would be commanding the Divisional Reconnaissance Group; Franz Steineck, commanding a heavy gun company, would be the Divisional Artillery commander and Karl Böttcher would be commanding a panzer-grenadier battalion. Unlike in other western armies, it was unusual for Waffen SS officers to leave their units, and this continuous service together paid big dividends as the war progressed. It is amazing that although most of them were wounded at least once they survived so much fighting.

Another event which occurred at this time is pertinent to our story. On 28th May at Wormhoudt, again near Dunkirk, some eighty, perhaps more, British soldiers died in suspicious circumstances at the hands of the LSSAH. Peiper's company was certainly not involved but his future commander in the Ardennes campaign, Wilhelm Mohnke, has been named in more than one book – and even in the British Parliament – as the officer responsible for this atrocity. The following statement, dated 1994, concerning this incident appears in the British Public Record Office at Kew, near London:

This crime was thoroughly investigated after the war but a number of people, including Mohnke, were not in British hands and despite considerable efforts, it did not prove possible to bring anyone to trial. The case was reopened in 1988 by the German authorities at the request of one of the survivors who had discovered that Mohnke had returned from Russian captivity and was alive in Germany. [Author's note: he had in fact been released by the Russians on 10th October 1955 and had been living quite openly in West Germany.] The British records of the post-war War Crimes investigations were closed but were made available to the German Prosecutor, who came to this country to further his investigations. . . . He has now concluded that there is insufficient evidence to bring charges against Mohnke.

Nevertheless, the first of many blemishes had appeared on the reputation of the Regiment.

On 1st November 1939 Peiper had been made First Military Adjutant to Himmler. This was an important step in his career for it indicates that he had found particular favour with the Reichsführer SS. As personal Adjutant he would have been privy to virtually everything in Himmler's office and he could not have failed to be aware of Hitler's and Himmler's policies for the ethnic cleansing of the Greater Reich, the organisation and establishment of concentration camps and the overall policy for the genocide of the Jewish race. Indeed, there is photographic evidence of Peiper with Himmler at Mauthausen during a visit to this, the most deadly of all the existing concentration camps, at the end of May 1941. Furthermore it was Peiper who summoned the first and best known Commandant of Auschwitz, Rudolf Höss,[13] to Himmler's presence in the summer of 1941 for him to be told that the Führer had ordered the 'final solution' of the Jewish problem and that Auschwitz had been earmarked as a major centre for this purpose due to its good position with regard to communications and because the area could be easily isolated and camouflaged!

On 25th June 1941, just after the beginning of the invasion of Russia, Himmler moved his personal train to Angerburg in East Prussia so that he could be near Hitler's 'Wolf's Lair' at Rastenburg.[14] His Adjutant naturally went with him and from this forward position Peiper was able to monitor the progress of the campaign. He was also able to assist his 'master' in his joint responsibilities of overseeing the Waffen-SS troops operating under Army command but still under Himmler's authority, and more particularly in directing the police and Einsatzgruppen (extermination squads) tasked with the elimination of as many Jews and other undesirables as possible from the areas conquered.

By the middle of July 1941 German forces were nearing Leningrad in the north of the Soviet Union and Kiev in the south. In the centre

Smolensk, only two hundred miles from Moscow, had been captured. It appeared that the war in the East would shortly end in total victory. Whether Peiper persuaded Himmler to release him or Himmler decided it was time for his Adjutant to win a few more medals and honours before the fighting finished is unknown! Nevertheless, Peiper returned to the LSSAH in August and as it turned out this was the end of his personal service with the Reichsführer SS.

Peiper found the Regiment heavily engaged in securing Cherson and the right bank of the Dnieper river. He was soon given command of the 11th Company in the 3rd Battalion and with it he took part in the bitter fighting from the Dnieper to the Don river and the pursuit of the Soviet Army along the Sea of Azov. Peiper was again slightly wounded, in the right knee,[15] and he suffered ruptured ear drums and concussion during this period. By 21st November III Panzer Corps, of which the LSSAH was now part, had secured Rostov. In three days the Corps had captured 10,000 prisoners, 159 artillery pieces, 56 tanks and two armoured trains. But by now the dreaded Russian winter had come to the rescue of its peoples and the LSSAH was exhausted. Its vehicles were worn out and it was at half strength due to appalling casualties. It was time to go on the defensive. But the LSSAH had won its spurs and all talk of 'asphalt soldiers' had ceased. On the contrary, the Bodyguard was well on its way to a new title, that of 'The Führer's Fire Brigade'. On 26th December 1941 the Corps Commander, General von Mackensen, wrote to the Reichsführer SS as follows:

I can assure you that the Leibstandarte is held in high regard, not only by the officers but also by its fellow comrades in the Heer (Army). Every unit wants to have the Leibstandarte as its adjacent unit, both in the attack and defence. The unit's internal discipline, its refreshing eagerness, its cheerful enthusiasm, its unshakeable calmness in crisis no matter how great, and its toughness are examples to us all. Its members' feeling for their fellow soldiers, I would like to emphasize, is exemplary and unsurpassed. . . . This truly is an elite unit.[16]

The average age of its soldiers was 19.35 years.

In July 1942, after a year in Russia, it was decided to rest the Bodyguard and restructure it into a full Division. It was transferred to France and took part in a ceremonial parade through Paris in front of Field Marshal von Rundstedt. Between August and December the restructuring into a Panzer-Grenadier Division took place. On 14th September Peiper was given command of the 3rd (Armoured) SS Panzer-Grenadier Battalion of the 2nd SS Panzer-Grenadier Regiment, 1st SS Panzer-Grenadier Division, Leibstandarte Adolf Hitler (LAH). For unknown reasons the letters 'SS' were no longer used.

In January 1943 the LAH entrained for the Ukraine where it was urgently needed to help stem the Russian winter offensive. SS General Hausser's SS Panzer Corps, of which the LAH was to form part, also included the Das Reich and Totenkopf SS Divisions; its task was the defence of the Donetz river and the city of Kharkov. Peiper had been promoted to the rank of SS Major on 30th January and for his part in the desperate fighting to defend and later recapture Kharkov and the actions around Belgorod he was awarded[17] the Knight's Cross on 9th March and the German Cross in Gold on 6th May. He was not forgotten by his old superior, Heinrich Himmler, who sent him a congratulatory telegram over his Knight's Cross addressed to 'My dear Jochen'.[18]

At this time the LAH was placed in reserve and given a badly needed rest period. It had lost 44% of its strength in the recent savage fighting – 167 officers and 4,373 men. It had also been accused of major atrocities in Kharkov. As late as 1976 the Soviets produced charges[19] alleging that some 300 wounded Russian soldiers had died when the Leibstandarte had burned down a hospital in Kharkov and that a further 400 or more officers had been shot in their beds in an army isolation hospital. These claims were never substantiated but there can be little doubt that the savagery of the fighting resulted in both sides committing numerous acts of barbarism. The LAH history highlights a number of examples of the mutilation of German dead and alleges that some of these mutilations were inflicted before death.

The rest period lasted until the end of June and was used not only for leave, which the Führer had reinstated after the recapture of Kharkov, but for re-equipping and also for complete restructuring. Sepp Dietrich, known as 'Obersepp' to his men, had been awarded 'Swords' to his Knight's Cross for the recent fighting and when he returned from the award ceremony with Hitler on 21st March he brought astounding news. All the officers for a new SS Panzer Corps Headquarters and all the regimental, battalion and company commanders of a new division to be known as the 12th SS 'Hitlerjugend' were to be found from the LAH! This meant that Dietrich himself, after ten years in command, was to hand over to Teddy Wisch in order to become the new Corps commander and many other famous and highly experienced officers were also to go: Fritz Witt, a member of the original 117-man Stabswache, Kurt 'Panzer' Meyer and Max Wünsche, all holders of the Knight's Cross, to mention only a few. As if this was not enough, the entire Panzerjaegerabteilung (anti-tank battalion), a complete medical clearing station from the Medical Battalion and eleven senior NCOs and 125 men were also to be transferred to the 'Hitlerjugend'. Peiper himself was to remain. So were his fellow commanders in the future 1944 Ardennes campaign, Max Hansen, Rudolf Sandig, Gustav Knittel, von Westernhagen, Jupp Diefenthal and Karl Rettlinger. Wilhelm

Mohnke had already gone, having lost a foot in Yugoslavia, but he would be back as Peiper's superior. During April and May the battle casualties and the transfers were made good. The replacements, however, included 2,500 Luftwaffe personnel who had not volunteered for army, let alone Waffen SS, service and there were even a number of non volunteers from Waffen SS replacement units. The 'purity' of the LAH was at last being diluted. But incredibly all these 'Yankalongs', as they were known, were transformed into worthy and enthusiastic members of the Division in the few weeks available before Operation Zitadelle, the gigantic armoured battle of Kursk.

In only ten years the Leibstandarte Adolf Hitler had become a Regiment with a spirit and fighting reputation second to none. In this short period it had achieved what most regiments and armies strive for but take decades and even centuries to attain; moreover, it had gone even further and formed something rarely achieved in any army, a division of all arms – infantry, armour, artillery, engineers etc., but with the same badge, spirit and sense of 'family' as a regiment. To this was added the advanced military thinking current in the Wehrmacht generally at this time, thinking which had developed the tactics of 'blitzkrieg', produced the necessary equipment to practise it and maintained a cooperation on the battlefield between different ground elements, and even between air and ground elements, unheard of in the Allied nations. Indeed, it took another thirty years for most of their military establishments to reach the same levels of operational efficiency, and many have still not achieved it as this book is being written!

How did the LAH create its remarkable spirit? The fact that it was the Guard unit of the national leader must be one factor, constant active service another. The LAH spent over five and a half years at war and from June 1941 enjoyed only ten months away from front line service – even then it was based in occupied countries and often faced resistance forces. It never served at home after leaving Germany in May 1940, although of course Guard elements protected the Führer in Berlin right to the end.

But there was something else which gave the LAH its unique character. A hint of it appeared in von Mackensen's letter of December 1941. The LAH, and other premier Waffen SS divisions like Das Reich, had developed their own unique philosophy of soldiering. It glorified fighting for fighting's sake. Its members had little regard for life, either their own or that of anyone else. As one American officer put it in 1944 'These men fought in a way I had never seen before. It was as though they loved fighting, almost glorified it. They obviously preferred to die on the battlefield than in bed.' This, to modern thinking, alien attitude is well described by a Leibstandarte captain:

It was those defensive battles in Russia which I shall always remember for the sheer beauty of the fighting, rather than the victorious advances. Many of us died horribly, some even as cowards, but for those who lived, even for a short period out there, it was well worth all the dreadful suffering and danger. After a time we reached a point where we were not concerned for ourselves or even for Germany, but lived entirely for the next clash, the next engagement with the enemy. There was a tremendous sense of 'being', an exhilarating feeling that every nerve in the body was alive to the fight.

This then was the spirit and atmosphere which had surrounded Peiper from the age of 21. It is hardly surprising that by the end of 1944 he was an arrogant and ruthless officer who gloried in his Regiment.

By the time Operation Zitadelle was halted on 13th July 1943 the LAH had lost over a third of its armour and suffered 2,753 casualties including 474 killed.[20] One of the reasons given for Hitler's decision to call off the Kursk offensive was the Allied invasion of Sicily and his worry about his southern flank. Consequently at the end of July the LAH handed over its remaining tanks to the Das Reich and Totenkopf Divisions and moved to northern Italy. It then spent the first part of August disarming the Italian army in the Po river valley, following the collapse of Mussolini's fascist dictatorship, before undertaking the defence of northern Italy and Croatia.

In September Peiper's 3rd SS Panzer-Grenadier Battalion was stationed in the Province of Cuneo, south of Turin, where an incident occurred which was to have far reaching effects. On the afternoon of the 19th Italian police reported that Italian soldiers had kidnapped two of Peiper's NCOs in the small town of Boves. He immediately ordered their company commander to rescue them but when the officer radioed that he had been attacked by superior forces and needed help, Peiper reacted characteristically by personally leading his Battalion to the rescue. On arrival he shelled the town with 150mm self-propelled infantry guns. This had the required effect. Peiper later reported:

> I am of the opinion that our action to free our encircled comrades in Boves nipped in the bud the Italian army's attack, for the army fell apart and no attack ever took place on Cuneo or Turin. However regrettable the consequences of our action was for the affected residents of Boves [author's note: 34 of them died], it should not be overlooked that our one-time intervention prevented further immeasurable casualties which would have resulted from continued Italian attacks.[21]

Twenty-five years later in 1968 Peiper and two of his officers were accused, by the Italian authorities in a Stuttgart court, of murder for their actions at Boves. The finding was that 'there is insufficient suspicion of criminal activity on the part of any of the accused to warrant prosecution'. In the same year, however, the Osnabrück Assize Court convicted five ex-members of the Leibstandarte for the murder, or aiding and abetting with the murder, of Jews living in several towns along Lake Maggiore in northern Italy.[22] This had occurred at the same time as the Boves affair. Although these proceedings were dropped because the prosecution had exceeded the statute of limitations, the reputation of the Bodyguard was again shown to be tarnished.

After a few more weeks in the relatively peaceful surroundings of northern Italy it was time for Peiper and the 1st SS Panzer Division to return to the Ukraine for another six months' bitter fighting. On 21st November he was appointed commander of the 1st SS Panzer Regiment. This contained all the Division's tanks, which at full strength numbered 160. Other very capable officers like Max Hansen were senior to him, but it was a sign of his superiors' trust, or perhaps the fact that he had extremely powerful friends, that at the age of 28 Peiper was given the best command in the Division. On 27th January 1944 he was awarded Oakleaves to his Knight's Cross for his leadership in the actions around Zhitomir; by then he was also the holder of the Close Combat Badge in Silver,[23] which indicated that he had been in close combat a minimum of thirty times.

The winter campaign in the Ukraine was harder than ever. The Division even had to fight its way out of its detraining stations. In the weeks which followed the LAH took part in many desperate actions to stem the Soviet advance, including a breakthrough to two surrounded Army Corps in which 32,000 German soldiers were rescued out of a total of 50,000. But by 28th February it had been reduced to little more than a Kampfgruppe (Battlegroup) with only three tanks and four armoured assault guns operational.[24] Two weeks later, after retreating into Galicia, the Division had ceased to exist as such – its strength was 41 officers and 1,188 NCOs and men. Field Marshal von Manstein wrote: 'Our forces had finally reached the point of exhaustion. The German divisions . . . were literally burned out. . . . The fighting had eaten away at the very core of the fighting units. How could we wage effective counterattacks, for example, when an entire Panzerkorps had only twenty-four panzers ready for battle?'[25] On 18th April, when the pathetic remnants of the 1st SS Panzer Division left the Eastern front, Sandig's 2nd SS Panzer-Grenadier Regiment, the only part of the LAH for which figures are available, had suffered 2,714 casualties out of a strength of 2,925;[26] 417 men were dead. Once more Peiper and the few remaining veterans of the old Division would be the nucleus around which a new Leibstandarte would be built.

By 25th April the LAH was complete in the Turnhout area of Belgium and Peiper had been promoted to the rank of SS Lieutenant Colonel. The 1st SS Panzer Division was part of the strategic reserve and subordinated to Sepp Dietrich's I SS Panzer Corps. New men, known as 'Young Marchers', and brand new equipment arrived during May to join the 'Old Hares' as the veterans were called. Although the speed of this restructuring was impressive, the lack of training of the new recruits was of great concern. There was a desperate shortage of experienced tank commanders and many of the appointed drivers had never been in a moving tank. Hard work, *ésprit de corps* and enthusiasm soon began to overcome these problems but if the old hands had been hoping for a rest period they were to be sorely disappointed. On 6th June, following the Allied invasion of Normandy, the Leibstandarte was alerted for operations. The Division was ordered to move, not to Normandy where the 12th SS Panzer Hitlerjugend and Panzer Lehr Divisions were released for action under I SS Panzer Corps, but to an area east of Bruges where it could counter attack any landing at the mouth of the Schelde. Hitler still believed a second and larger landing might be made in and to the east of the Pas de Calais. After an exhausting drive to the area around Ursel, Maldegem and Ardenburg the LAH set about painting its new tanks in camouflage colours.

On 12th June Hitler demanded that the Division be united with the 12th SS Hitlerjugend Division in the Caen area under I SS Panzer Corps. The move by train began on the 17th but it was 6th July before the LAH was complete in Normandy. Allied air attacks forced diversions via Reims, Soissons and Laon, from where units had to complete the journey by road at night – part of the 2nd SS Panzer-Grenadier Regiment for example took five nights to move from near Reims to just south of Caen.

This disjointed move resulted in the LAH being committed piecemeal to battle – the 1st SS Panzer-Grenadier Regiment, less the 3rd Battalion, was the first element into action when it joined the Hitlerjugend Division on 28th June near Caen. It was during this fighting that Max Hansen was wounded for the ninth time. Strong elements of the Leibstandarte fought against the British and Canadians to the west of Caen in 'Operation Charnwood' between 6th and 9th July; and then, after a short period in reserve, the LAH as a Division inflicted appalling tank casualties on the British Guards, 7th and 11th Armoured Divisions on the Bourguebus ridge over the period 18th to 21st July during 'Operation Goodwood'. This was immediately followed by two weeks' bitter fighting against the Canadians around Tilly-la-Campagne.

In 1976 Peiper told the French police that he had been wounded whilst fighting the Canadians around Caen and consequently evacuated, first to Paris and later to recuperate in Tegernsee, Bavaria – close to where Sigi and the children lived in Rottach am Tegernsee.[27] It is perhaps not without significance that Himmler's wife also lived on the Tegernsee, at Gmund, and the SS Officers' School at Bad Tölz was only 15km away.

A medical document,[28] dated 30th January 1945, signed by SS Major Dr Kurt Sickel, the medical officer of Peiper's Regiment and witnessed by his Adjutant, SS Captain Hans Gruhle, shows that Peiper was wounded twice in 1944 – once with splinters in the left thigh and secondly with a bullet graze on the left hand. Exact dates are not given. It also shows that he had jaundice that year, with connected damage to his gall bladder. There is separate evidence to show that Peiper was indeed evacuated to a field hospital on 2nd August 1944 and sent to Tegernsee Reserve Hospital in Bavaria on 6th August.

Whether Peiper was wounded, which sounds more heroic, or ill with jaundice, which is perhaps more likely, makes little difference – what is important is that he missed the Mortain counter-attack and the ghastly killing grounds of the Falaise pocket, which together saw, yet again, the virtual destruction of the Leibstandarte. What remained of it was withdrawn behind the river Seine between the 21st and 24th August. There are no firm figures for the casualties the LAH received in the Normandy fighting but estimates put the losses in the region of 5,000 men. On 27th August orders were received for a move to the Laon/ Marle area and the next day Field Marshal Model ordered the creation of a single combat unit from the remains of the LAH, Das Reich and Hitlerjugend Divisions.

After a fighting withdrawal made through Marle and Vervins, small groups of the LAH were still resisting around Maubeuge and Philippeville as late as 3rd September. A day later the Division was ordered back to Germany for 'total rest and recuperation'.

NOTES

1. Woldemar Peiper's petition to US authorities for pardoning his son, 30 Aug 1946.
2. Ibid.
3. *Service Record I SS Reitersturm*, 3 Jan 1935.
4. Peiper's *SS Personalangaben*.
5. Lehmann, *The Leibstandarte I*, p. 28.
6. Peiper's *SS Personalangaben*.
7. Breitman, *The Architect of Genocide*, p. 69.
8. Peiper's *SS Personalangaben*.
9. Breitman, *The Architect of Genocide*, p. 95.
10. Peiper, *Bestätigung der Verwundungen*, 30 Jan 1945.
11. Peiper's *SS Personalangaben*.
12. Ibid.
13. Broszat, *Commandant of Auschwitz, Autobiographical Notes of Rudolf Höss*, p. 153.
14. Breitman, *The Architect of Genocide*, pp. 168–169.
15. Peiper, *Bestätigung der Verwundungen*, 30 Jan 1945.

16. Lehmann, *The Leibstandarte II*, p. 199.
17. Peiper's *SS Personalangaben*.
18. Himmler, copy of his radio message of 9 March 1943, stamped '12 Mar 43 SS Personalhauptamt'.
19. Lehmann, *The Leibstandarte III*, pp. 185–190.
20. Ibid., p. 249.
21. Ibid., p. 292–3.
22. Ibid., p. 294.
23. Peiper's *SS Personalangaben*.
24. Lehmann & Tiemann, *The Leibstandarte IV/1*, p. 51.
25. Manstein, *Verlorene Siege*, p. 601.
26. Lehmann & Tiemann op. cit., pp. 95–6.
27. Brigade Récherches Vesoul Procès Verbal No.336, 22 Jul 1976.
28. Peiper, *Bestätigung der Verwundungen*, 30 Jan 1945.

CHAPTER II
The Plan

When SS Lieutenant Colonel Jochen Peiper rejoined the 1st SS Panzer Division in the Minden, Lübbecke and Osnabrück area in early October he would have been appalled at the state in which he found it. It was a Panzer division in name only. Sepp Dietrich had always sent his officers into battle with the words 'Bring my boys back!' but time and time again this had proved impossible. Russia and France were the final resting places of many of Peiper's comrades. And then there was a new commander. The previous General, Teddy Wisch who had been Peiper's friend and brother officer since 1936, had been wounded at Falaise on 20th August and his replacement, SS Brigadier Wilhelm Mohnke, had taken over on the 31st. Mohnke had spent nearly a year recuperating after the loss of his foot in Yugoslavia in 1941 but in March 1942 he returned to duty as commander of the LAH Replacement Battalion in Berlin. Just over a year later he saw his chance to return to active duty with the formation of the new 12th SS Hitlerjugend Division, and in July 1943, despite his incapacity, he was given command of its 26th SS Panzer-Grenadier Regiment. The Hitlerjugend saw its first action against the Canadians in June 1944 and when members of his Regiment were later accused of killing Allied prisoners of war in cold blood in Normandy, Mohnke's name was once again associated with war crimes.

In late September the LAH, along with the other three SS Panzer Divisions of the I and II SS Panzer Corps, had been released by Feldmarschall von Rundstedt, C-in-C West (Ob West) for reorganisation, re-equipping and retraining back in Germany. The towns and villages east of Osnabrück in which the 1st SS Panzer Division was stationed by mid October will be familiar to all British soldiers who served after the war in the British Army of the Rhine. The LAH headquarters was in the lovely hillside town of Lübbecke and other units of the Division were to be found in the nearby towns of Wehrendorf, Hille, Bunde, Vlotho, Ostercappeln, Herringhausen and so on.[1] Peiper's Headquarters was in Rahden. Tanks were received direct from the factory and in a short time the Division was re-equipped in readiness for Hitler's last great offensive. Some 3,500 personnel replacements were posted in but they were very young and included many ethnic Germans from the eastern territories. Once again they were not all volunteers.

On 9th November orders were received for the LAH to move to a new concentration area west of Köln. The move was completed by the 18th and the Division was delighted to find that the commander of the 6th Panzer Army, of which it was part, was its old much loved leader, General Sepp Dietrich. Peiper's panzers were located in the area of Weilerswist while other elements of the Division were in and around Jülich, Mechernich, Zülpich and Düren. Whilst stationed there men of the LAH helped with the rescue of civilians injured, buried alive and killed as a result of Allied carpet bombing raids which by this stage of the war were reaching a climax of intensity. After the war Peiper said:

> I recognise that after the battle of Normandy my unit was composed mainly of young, fanatical soldiers. A good deal of them had lost their parents, their sisters and brothers during the bombing. They had seen for themselves in Köln thousands of mangled corpses after a terror raid had passed. Their hatred for the enemy was such, I swear it, I could not always keep it under control.

As far as Peiper was concerned the location of his Division in the Köln area made sense. An Allied thrust across the Rhine and into the Ruhr seemed imminent and the 6th Panzer Army was therefore well positioned as a counter-attack force. This was in fact exactly what Hitler wanted both his own forces and the Allies to think and why the whole plan for the Ardennes offensive was code-named 'Watch on the Rhine'. The code-name for the offensive itself was 'Autumn Mist'.

After the war Peiper told his American interrogators[2] that Dietrich's Chief of Staff, Fritz Kraemer, asked him on the 11th December what he thought about the possibilities of a German attack against the Americans out of the Eifel region into the Ardennes. Peiper was not averse to playing games with his interrogators and telling stories which bolstered his ego. But if this is true he would certainly not have been surprised when orders came for him to move his Regiment during the night 12/13th December to a new concentration area further south. In fact the whole of the LAH and indeed the whole 6th Panzer Army side-stepped south during that night and the following two. The move, which went entirely undetected by the Americans, was carried out without lights and under radio silence.

Peiper's first detailed knowledge of the Ardennes offensive came at 11 o'clock on 14th December when he attended an Orders Group[3] given by the Divisional commander, Mohnke, at his Headquarters in Tondorf on the edge of the Blankenheim forest. It was therefore only 42 hours before 'H' hour that he was given details of his role, organisation and proposed routes in the great offensive.

The basic plan and strategic goals of the offensive were entirely Hitler's own. They were first mentioned by him in mid September and although many objections were raised by his senior commanders and staff officers, the final plan was virtually unchanged when it was issued in late November. It has been described in many previous books and there is no need to go into it again in detail. Essentially it called for three Armies under the command of Field Marshal Model, the commander of Hœresgruppe (Army Group) B, to break through the American front in the Ardennes and Luxembourg and, with the main weight on the right flank, cross the Meuse river south of Liège and then exploit to the great port of Antwerp (Map 1). This, it was hoped, would cut off the British and Canadian 21st Army Group and the American 9th Army from the rest of the Allied front, causing mass surrenders and depriving the Allies of their most important port. Indeed, Hitler saw it as the basis for another 'Dunkirk', particularly for the British. A huge force of seven panzer and thirteen infantry divisions was to be used in the initial assault, with a further two panzer and seven infantry divisions ready to be thrown in later. In all some 1,460 tanks, assault guns and self propelled anti-tank guns and 2,600 artillery pieces and rocket launchers were to be made available.

Hitler decreed the utmost secrecy in relation to his plan and Dietrich's 6th Panzer Army did not receive details of it until 29th November and the divisional commanders until 6th December. Mohnke and other senior commanders were briefed by the Führer himself at the Adlerhof, near Bad Nauheim, on 11th December. Hitler is said to have been rational and clear in what he said. He reminded his audience of the ill-founded doubts which had been expressed before the 1940 offensive in the same area and made it clear that he considered the fulfilment of this mission as being vital to Germany's success in the war. So how did Peiper fit into his grand design?

The 6th Panzer Army was destined by Hitler to gain the major honours in the forthcoming campaign. Its objective was Antwerp and the other two Armies, the 5th Panzer under General Hasso von Manteuffel, and the 7th under General Erich Brandenberger, were seen as very much in support. Dietrich was given three corps to command: the

LXVII Corps with two Volks-Grenadier Divisions, I SS Panzer Corps with two SS Panzer, one Parachute and two Volks-Grenadier Divisions, and II SS Panzer Corps with two more SS Panzer Divisions. Peiper and the LAH, together with the 12th SS Panzer Division Hitlerjugend, were part of SS Lieutenant General Hermann Priess's I SS Panzer Corps. The plan called for these two crack divisions, both bearing the Führer's own name, to form an all-powerful wave which would surge to and across the Meuse river south of Liège. II SS Panzer Corps, under SS General Wilhelm Bittrich of Arnhem fame, comprising the 2nd Das Reich and 9th Hohenstaufen SS Panzer Divisions, would then exploit north-west and seize Antwerp. The infantry divisions would form a hard shoulder on the right flank of this advance (Map 2).

To achieve his mission Wilhelm Mohnke divided his Division into four Kampfgruppes (KGs) or Battlegroups. He placed Peiper in command of the most powerful and therefore the most important KG, which was based on his own 1st SS Panzer Regiment. A second very strong KG was given to SS Lieutenant Colonel Max Hansen, again based on his own 1st SS Panzer-Grenadier Regiment. Following these two groups were a third KG commanded by SS Lieutenant Colonel Rudolf Sandig, based on his 2nd SS Panzer-Grenadier Regiment and a Schnelle Gruppe, or fast reconnaissance group, under the command of SS Major Gustav Knittel, based on his 1st SS Reconnaissance Battalion. Unallocated artillery, engineer and anti-aircraft elements of the Division would follow up behind the KGs. Amazingly, despite all the casualties, these four commanders were still together in the LAH after four and a half years of savage fighting. It was no wonder that they trusted one another and knew instinctively how each would react in battle. The 12th SS Panzer Division Hitlerjugend, again with commanders who had fought together for years, was organised into KGs in a very similar way and it would seem that this organisation was imposed by Corps, if not Army, Headquarters.

The plan as it affected Peiper was essentially a very simple one. After a heavy artillery bombardment the two Volks-Grenadier Divisions and single Parachute Division of I SS Panzer Corps would break through the thin American defences between Hollerath and Krewinkel (Map 3). The armoured KGs would then pour through the breaches thus created and strike hard for the Meuse in an operation described in the 6th Panzer Army order as: 'ruthless and rapid penetration'. Peiper and the other KG commanders were expected to bypass opposition whenever possible. It was envisaged that the panic this would create, as in previous 'blitzkrieg' campaigns, would cause the entire American defence to collapse. As far as timings were concerned it was expected that the Meuse crossings would be secured in three days as had happened in 1940.

In front of the two Leibstandarte KGs of Peiper and Hansen, the 12th

Volks-Grenadier and 3rd Parachute Divisions were expected to make the necessary breaches in the areas of Losheimergraben and Manderfeld respectively.

To aid the two Panzer Divisions in their dash for the Meuse two special operations were ordered, both the brainchildren of Hitler. They have become very well known and gained a fame quite unwarranted by their actual achievements. The first was called Operation 'Greif' and was commanded by a favourite of the Führer, SS Lieutenant Colonel Otto Skorzeny. He was a member of the Leibstandarte and had made his name in the daring rescue of Mussolini in 1943. In essence he was to form two English-speaking groups who would wear American uniforms and use captured American equipment. The task of the first group, comprising about fifty men in teams of four or five, was to penetrate US lines and then sabotage important installations and generally cause confusion. The second much larger group, some 3,000 men, was to be equipped with armoured vehicles; its task was to move at night, in three KGs, on parallel lines to the advancing panzer spearheads and seize bridges over the Meuse.

The second special operation was known as 'Stoesser'. Its commander was Luftwaffe Colonel Freiherr Dr von der Heydte. He was a parachute commander who had been awarded the Knight's Cross for his part in the Crete invasion. In December 1944 he was commanding a parachute school at Aalten in Holland. On 8th December, much to his surprise, he was told by General Student, the commander of Heeresgruppe 'H', to form an airborne force of some 800 men for use in a forthcoming undesignated operation. On 11th December he learned that his task was to drop at night, before the 'H' hour (attack time) of the ground forces, and seize an important road junction in the area of the Baraque Michel north of Malmédy (Map 3).

In concert with 'Autumn Mist' Hitler ordered an air offensive code-named 'Bodenplatte'. He had seen the devastating effects that Allied air power had achieved on his forces in Normandy and he hoped to avert a similar disaster in the Ardennes. He aimed to achieve this by launching his offensive in a period of bad flying weather and, paradoxically, at the same time by launching 622 of his own aircraft against eighteen Allied airfields in Holland and Belgium with the task of destroying his enemy's aircraft on the ground.

Much has been written about the routes to be used by the KGs of I SS Panzer Corps and they are shown in nearly every book written about the Ardennes offensive. Unfortunately there have been many misunderstandings over these routes and thus over the actions of Peiper and indeed the whole of I SS Panzer Division. It is therefore important to examine this subject in some detail.

Five basic routes, to be shared by the LAH and Hitlerjugend Divisions, were allocated to I SS Panzer Corps by 6th Panzer Army. Looking at them from north to south, Routes A, B and C were given to 12th SS, and D and E to the LAH. 12th SS was given the extra, northern, route for use by a panzer-grenadier battalion which was destined to link up with von der Heydte's parachute operation and provide flank protection for the armoured KGs. The misunderstandings over these routes have arisen because of statements made by senior German officers after the war, and because of a map held in the Bundesarchiv which is said to be the situation map of the Commander-in-Chief West (Ob West) for 18th December 1944.

When looking at transcripts of the interviews with the German officers it should be remembered that the routes drawn, or described, were completed from memory, a considerable time after the event and on large scale maps.

In his interview with Robert Merriam in August 1945 Major General Fritz Kraemer, the Chief of Staff of the 6th Panzer Army, said:

> Although the actual directive from higher headquarters stated that the Army was to cross the Meuse south of Liège, I preferred to cross to the north at the bend in the river near Herstadt . . . we gave the corps commanders instructions to move across the river wherever they could find a crossing but I issued instructions that plans be made for a northern crossing as well as a southern one . . . as a result of this map study and my personal knowledge of the terrain, I selected the five routes you have on the map before me.

Merriam then adds a note:

> A captured German map with five routes labelled A to E: Route A from east of Rocherath through Elsenborn to Polleur; B separating from A at Rocherath, south to Wirtsfeld and then west to Sart; C from Losheim, through Malmédy to Spa; D from Losheim to Stavelot, and E from Krewinkel west to Trois Ponts.

Kraemer went on:

> These roads were to be directional only. If the divisional commanders wanted to take others, they were at liberty to do so . . . these five routes led to the general line Verviers–Spa–Stavelot and from that line new orders were to be given according to the situation at the time.[4]

As well as being entirely logical from a military viewpoint, this statement firmly quashes the often quoted myth that KG commanders had to stick to their assigned routes under pain of death. The whole offensive was based on the principle of 'blitzkrieg' and it would have made no sense to tie commanders to rigid routes.

The interview given in March 1946 by SS Lieutenant General Hermann Priess, Commander I SS Panzer Corps, has given rise to further confusion because he goes much further than Kraemer in that he extends the routes all the way to the Meuse, giving the impression that they were firmly fixed. Many writers have, however, ignored the fact that Priess went on to say: 'The Corps and, under Corps command, the divisions had freedom of movement within this area. Thus, march routes did not have to be rigidly adhered to. Each division had express permission to deviate from prescribed routes whenever the situation demanded, such as weak spots in enemy positions etc.'[5]

In September 1945 Peiper was interviewed by Major Ken Hechler of the US Army.[6] He outlined what he said was his complete route to the Meuse, and this again gave rise to the erroneous idea that he was required to stick to a precise route. An analysis of the route, however, reveals that it is a mixture of three of those mentioned. Peiper also specified a main route for his running mate, Kuhlmann, in 12th SS Panzer Division and again this is in fact another mixture. This mixing of routes by Peiper may well have been a deliberate attempt to confuse his interrogators or it may have been quite simply nothing more than confused memory. Whatever else it does, it indicates that he saw the routes as directional, not fixed, and for use as the situation demanded. In the event this was certainly how he used them!

In summary it can be said that all the relevant commanders saw the so-called 'Five Routes' as directional and as ones which could be used as needed to achieve the mission.

And the Ob West map? Although it is difficult to see the exact routes due to the scale, it certainly shows five routes leading to the same initial objectives specified by Kraemer. On the other hand it would be entirely logical for a map, dated two days after the offensive started, to show the routes actually taken as well as those planned; certainly the route shown from Losheim to Lanzerath is the actual route taken by Peiper. The routes shown beyond the initial objectives are the most logical ones leading to the Meuse and can reasonably be accepted as those used for planning purposes by the Ob West staff.

Further light is shed on the routes to be used by a map marked 'Attack Plan 6th PZ Army, Ardennes Offensive' prepared by a Captain GM Tuttle, Historical Sec, US Army in October 1945 and annotated 'Approved by Gen Kraemer, C of S, 6th PZ Army.' This shows the five infantry divisions of the 6th Panzer Army holding a line from Liège east to Roetgen. Beneath this 'Blocking Line' the 1st and 12th SS Panzer Divisions are shown advancing west. And for the first time each Division is shown having a 'Main Route' and a 'Flank Protection' route. These routes equate closely with the well known Routes B, C, D and E. It would seem therefore that in Kraemer's mind at least, Peiper's KG was to advance on Route D with flank protection provided by KG Hansen on Route E and similarly, the tank-heavy KG of 12th SS was to advance on Route C with flank protection provided by a reinforced panzer-grenadier KG on Route B. Route A, as already described, was for the link-up with von der Heydte.

A map study carried out today reveals that the obvious initial and vital objectives for any offensive in this area are Polleur, Spa, Trois Ponts and Vielsalm. Not quite the same as those mentioned by Kraemer but with only Vielsalm added. The fact that in the event KG Hansen actually took the route to Vielsalm may well indicate that this was indeed his assigned route and that Kraemer's memory after the war had been slightly at fault.

When considering the best route for Peiper, it seems inconceivable that, with the strongest KG in I SS Panzer Corps, he should not have been allocated the best route to get him on his way. That route was Losheimergraben to Büllingen and certainly not the appallingly difficult Losheim–Merlscheid–Buchholz–Honsfeld–Hepscheid route given to him by most commentators. It is highly significant that just before 'H' hour on the day of the attack, Peiper moved to the Headquarters of Major General Engel's 12th Volks-Grenadier Division.[7] This Division had as its axes of attack the Losheim–Büllingen road and railway line, and its immediate objective was Losheimergraben. It therefore seems logical to assume that Peiper was expecting to advance via the good road Losheim–Losheimergraben–Büllingen. The fact that, due to American resistance, he was forced to divert from Losheim to Lanzerath has given rise to the view that this was really his assigned route. Further reasons for thinking this are the statement by Priess and the Ob West map, which both allocate Büllingen to 12th SS Panzer Division. Nevertheless a careful look at the map or the ground itself shows that there were, and are, two quite separate and easily identifiable routes through Büllingen, one from Mürringen running through the northern part of the town and emerging on the Bütgenbach road; the other being the main Losheimergraben–Büllingen N-32 road which has a left fork at the west end of the town leading south-west to Point 616 and Heppen-bach (Map 8). The fact that two major routes may have gone through Büllingen is no stranger than the fact that most commentators have two routes passing through Trois Ponts.

So taking all these factors into account, what firm conclusions can we come to regarding the actual routes planned for Peiper and the other KGs? (Map 3). Clearly Peiper's planned Route D was Losheim–Losheimergraben–Büllingen–Moderscheid–Ondenval–Ligneuville–Stavelot–Trois Ponts–Werbomont–Hamoir–Tinlot–Meuse crossing at Huy or Ombret Rawsa. It will be remembered that Peiper and the LAH had previously crossed the Meuse at Huy in May 1940! The planned

Route C for the strongest KG of 12th SS Panzer Division, KG Kuhlmann, was Mürringen–Büllingen–Bütgenbach–Malmédy–Spa–Remouchamps –Esneux–Meuse crossing. Peiper's flank running mate, KG Hansen, on Route E was expected to move via Krewinkel – Amel–Recht–Vielsalm –Lierneux–Werbomont, and 12th SS's flank KG (Müller) on Route B via Elsenborn–Sourbrodt–Polleur–Louveigné.

Hitler gave orders for his great offensive to begin at 0530 hours on Saturday 16th December 1944. Peiper would be ready, but sadly for him the 3rd Parachute and 12th Volks-Grenadier Divisions would not.

NOTES

1. Tiemann, *Die Leibstandarte IV/2*, p. 23.
2. *An Interview with Obst Joachim Peiper I SS PZ Regt (11–24 Dec 1944) 7 Sep 1945*, (US Department of the Army History Branch, ETHINT 10, US National Archives).
3. Ibid.
4. *An Interview with Genmaj (W-SS) Fritz Kraemer Sixth Pz Army (1 Nov 1944–4 Jan 1945) 14–15 Aug 1945*, ETHINT 21.
5. *Commitment of I SS Pz Corps during the Ardennes Offensive (16 Dec 1944–25 Jan 1945), Gruppenführer Herman Priess*, MS # A-877 dated March 1946.
6. ETHINT 10.
7. Ibid.

CHAPTER III

The Machines and the Means

In order to exploit to the full the well proven tactics of 'blitzkrieg', the Germans had designed, developed and produced highly advanced equipment. In virtually every sphere they were ahead of the Allies, even to the extent of being able to put into practical use basic infra-red optical devices and jet-engined aircraft. So that the part played in the Ardennes offensive by KG Peiper and the 1st SS Panzer Division can be better appreciated, it is necessary, without going into too much technical detail, to look at the weaponry available to them. Their most important weapons were of course the tanks. Peiper had three types – Type IVs, Type Vs better known as 'Panthers', and Type VI Bs, better known as 'King Tigers' or 'Tiger Royals'. The Type IV was numerically the most important German tank of the Second World War and certainly the most reliable. It weighed 25 tons, had 80mm frontal armour, a range of about

200km, a high velocity 75mm L/48 gun and two 7.92mm machine guns. It was marginally inferior to the American Sherman it met in the Ardennes. The Panther was almost certainly the best tank produced by any nation in World War II. It weighed 45 tons, had 100mm sloped frontal armour, a range of 200km, again a high velocity 75mm L/70 gun but three 7.92mm machine guns. The King Tiger was the largest production tank of the war, weighing a massive 69 tons. It mounted the famous 88mm high velocity L/71 gun and three machine guns and its frontal armour was 180mm thick. It had a range of about 150km but was mechanically unreliable. The ranges quoted apply to road movement in good conditions and these figures need to be halved when applied to movement on the icy, twisting roads and tracks of the Ardennes or when travelling cross-country. All German tanks used petrol rather than diesel fuel, which was reserved mainly for submarines, and all German tanks had a crew of five: commander, driver, gunner, loader and radio operator. All three types carried about 80 rounds of main armament ammunition.

The Leibstandarte, as an SS panzer division, should have been equipped with two batteries of 105mm self-propelled 'Wespe' guns, one battery of 150mm self-propelled 'Hummel' guns and two battalions of towed guns. But after the huge losses in Normandy the self-propelled equipment no longer existed and all the guns were towed. Again the LAH had three types: the 105mm light field howitzer which fired to a range of about 12km, the 150mm heavy field howitzer firing a little further and the 100mm Kanone with a range of nearly 25km. Rates of fire were six, four and two rounds per minute respectively.

In the field of anti-aircraft weapons the Germans had learned the lessons of Normandy and by December 1944 the LAH had, as well as the standard battalion of 88mm guns, both self-propelled and towed 20mm and 37mm anti-aircraft guns. A four-barrelled version of the 20mm weapon was mounted on a Type IV tank chassis and was known as the 'Wirbelwind'; it was often used in the ground role with devastating effect. It was a large vehicle weighing 22 tons and had a crew of six. The 37mm gun, when turret-mounted on a tank chassis, was even heavier at 25 tons and was called the 'Möbelwagen' or 'furniture van'!

In the self-propelled anti-tank sphere the 1st SS Panzer Division was equipped with the Jagdpanzer IV/70 which was, in effect, a tank with a limited traverse gun. It weighed about 24 tons, mounted a 75mm gun, had 80mm frontal armour and a crew of four.

The panzer-grenadiers of the LAH were armed with extremely effective machine guns with a very high cyclic rate of fire, which completely out-classed anything in use by the Americans and British. The best known were the MP 38 and 40 sub machine guns and the 7.92mm MG 42. This gun, when used with a bipod or tripod, had ranges of 600 and 2000m respectively, firing 750 rounds a minute. Mortars were the 80mm and 120mm with ranges of 2400m and 6000m and the infantry hand-held anti-tank rocket was the familiar 'panzerfaust', effective to 150m. Battalions were also equipped with towed 75mm infantry light guns. These had a rate of fire of up to 12 rounds a minute and a range of 4500m; also within each SS Panzer-Grenadier Regiment was a Heavy Infantry Gun company with six 150mm self-propelled guns called 'Bison'. Like their animal counterparts they were ugly beasts but they fired out to 5km and gave an infantry commander his own artillery.

There is a popular misconception that all panzer-grenadiers were carried in armoured half-tracks. The truth is very different. In December 1944 only one of the Leibstandarte's six panzer-grenadier battalions was so carried, all the others being truck mounted. The standard German half-track was the Schutzenpanzerwagen (SPW) 251. It was a splendid vehicle with many variants. Its only disadvantages were that it was open-topped and had relatively narrow tracks which restricted its cross-country performance. In its basic mode as an infantry carrier it held a commander, driver and ten men, and mounted two 7.92mm machine guns, one fitted in a shield on the front and the other on a pintle mount at the rear. The major variants were the 251/6 command vehicle, 251/2 80mm mortar carrier, 251/7 engineer equipment vehicle carrying a small assault bridge, demolition kit and inflatable rubber assault boats, 251/8 ambulance, 251/9 75mm anti-tank vehicle, 251/10 platoon commander's vehicle mounting a 37mm gun and the 251/17 with a 20mm anti-aircraft weapon. The SPW weighed about 9 tons, had a range of 200km and had 6 to 14.5mm of armour. As well as the armoured panzer-grenadiers of the LAH, Peiper's own engineer company and one of the three companies in the Divisional SS Panzer Pioneer Battalion should also have had SPWs but a shortage of vehicles meant that only two platoons in each company had them. In the German army, including the Waffen SS, engineers were called pioneers and were highly trained in house-to-house fighting. They were therefore often used as infantry for operations in towns and villages and, as we shall see, this was certainly how Peiper used them in the Ardennes.

The only major equipments not so far mentioned are the 'Puma' eight-wheeled armoured cars of Knittel's SS Reconnaissance Battalion. He had only a few of these highly sophisticated vehicles which could travel either forward or backwards at 80 kph, but they are also interesting in that they were the only vehicles in the entire Division to use diesel fuel. This was an obvious logistic error. They mounted a 50mm gun and a 7.95mm machine gun, and had two drivers.

A word must now be said about communications, for, without the means to give orders and convey intentions quickly, armoured warfare, and 'blitzkrieg' in particular, normally grinds to a halt. The German armoured forces therefore made great use of radio, particularly in the advance and, unlike the British and Americans, it was rare for them to assemble commanders in a physical group to give orders. The basic radio in use in the LAH in 1944 was the Funk G5, which had a range of about 5km in good conditions and was fitted in all Peiper's tanks and command vehicles. The Divisional and artillery radio nets used the Funk G8, which had a maximum range, again in good conditions, of 10km for voice and 20km when using morse. The basic problem for commanders of all ranks in the Leibstandarte was that, in the hills and twisting valleys of the Ardennes, these ranges were seriously degraded and very often the only method of communication was by relaying messages from one vehicle to another, with all the consequent perils of distortion and misunderstanding.

These, then, were the tools available to Mohnke, Peiper, Hansen, Sandig and Knittel. How would they try to use them?

The tactics of 'Blitzkrieg' work best under conditions of air superiority, in relatively open country and with good visibility. These parameters had applied in France in 1940 and in the early days in Russia when the Germans had achieved their greatest successes. None of them was to apply in the Ardennes.

Although the Allies had virtual air superiority by this stage of the war, the Luftwaffe was far more active and effective than is generally realised. It used some 1,600 aircraft to support the Ardennes offensive and until the 24th December, when the weather improved, it actually achieved a higher battlefield sortie rate than the Allies; for example on the 18th the comparison was 849 German to 519 Allied sorties. Even so this was a far cry from the early days of the war when close air support had often proved a battlefield winner for the Germans.

Topographically the Ardennes, with its thick forests, numerous streams and rivers, deep gorges and steep hills, obviously favoured a defender rather than an attacker. To compound this problem the severe winter of 1944 had turned the rivers into major obstacles and made off-road movement impossible for wheeled vehicles and almost impossible for tracked vehicles. Although the temperature hovered around zero for much of December 1944, heavy rain in the period immediately before the offensive meant that, beneath a thin crust, the ground was a quagmire. To this had to be added the frequent mists and fogs of the region, often cutting visibility to a matter of metres rather than kilometres and negating many of the advantages of armoured forces.

As if all this was not enough for Peiper and the LAH, there was also the problem of inexperience within the attacking force. A large number of the SS 'Schutzen', privates, were only teenagers, some as young as sixteen. Certainly they were enthusiastic but they had no experience of battle. There was also the question of leaders, for in this the fifth year of the war, the majority of the battle-hardened NCOs and many of the officers of the early Leibstandarte lay dead in Russia and France. There was therefore a curious mixture of highly experienced, but often battle weary, senior commanders leading very young and fanatical soldiers who had yet to hear their first shot fired in anger.

All these factors: the terrain, the weather, the visibility, the state of the ground and the inexperience of the majority of the men, had an effect on the employment of the machines; in other words on the tactics. The lack of good roads and virtual impossibility of cross-country movement precluded tactical manoeuvre and meant that the KGs usually had to advance on a one-vehicle front. It also made the deployment of artillery extremely complicated as gun positions were difficult to find and the forward movement of artillery was generally a nightmare. Brute force rather than finesse and quick frontal attacks rather than complicated envelopments were to be the order of the day. Peiper and the other KG commanders may have had superior machines but they faced enormous problems in finding the best means of using them.

CHAPTER IV

The Organisation[1]

Peiper and his fellow Regimental Commanders in the 1st SS Panzer Division were officially briefed by their Divisional Commander, SS Major General Wilhelm Mohnke, at 1100 hours on 14th December.[2] He gave them their tasks, routes and details of how the Division was to be organised for the offensive. Before looking at this in detail however, it is useful to look at the general organisation of the 1st SS Panzer Division as a whole, for the casualties in both men and equipment had by this time necessitated many changes from the official SS Panzer Division establishment.

One of the most significant changes was in Peiper's own 1st SS Panzer Regiment. This should have had two panzer battalions, one with 76 Panthers and the other with 76 Type IVs, both organised into four companies of 17 tanks each. In fact the serious shortage of tanks meant that Peiper had only one mixed battalion, consisting of two companies of Panthers and two of Type IVs. This composite Battalion was commanded by SS Major Werner Poetschke. Poetschke, born in Brussels in 1914, had already been awarded the Iron Cross 1st and 2nd Class and the German Cross in Gold when he transferred to the Leibstandarte in

1943. He earned the Knight's Cross in Russia later that year and, in July 1944, took command of Peiper's 1st SS Panzer Battalion; he was everyone's idea of a typical SS man – well built and blond.

To make up for the deficiency in tanks the LAH had been allocated I SS Panzer Corps' 501st SS Heavy Panzer Battalion with its 45 King Tigers, under the command of SS Major Hein von Westernhagen, another old comrade of Peiper's. The rest of the 1st SS Panzer Regiment was more or less intact apart from a lack of some equipments, such as a platoon's worth of pioneer SPWs and one or two anti-aircraft vehicles. Its personnel strength of just over 2,300 was about right but private soldiers made up for the lack of 458 NCOs!

Both the 1st and 2nd SS Panzer-Grenadier Regiments of the LAH were up to strength with about 3,500 men each and their equipment was up to scale, except for a few anti-aircraft weapons.

SS Major Gustav Knittel's 1st SS Reconnaissance Battalion had been forced into a total reorganisation. Apart from an Headquarters and a Supply Company it now had only three reconnaissance companies instead of four; the 1st Company had no vehicles at all and was left behind in Germany. Of the others, the 2nd Company's four platoons were equipped with SPW 251s, the 3rd had a mixture of forty-four VW schwimmwagens (amphibious jeeps) and six Puma armoured cars, and the 4th 'Heavy' company was equipped with 120mm mortars, 150mm infantry guns and three anti-tank SPWs. Despite this ad hoc organisation it was still a powerful unit with over 1,000 men.

The Divisional Panzerjäger (Anti-Tank) Battalion was more or less correctly equipped with twenty-one Jagdpanzer IV/70s, but with eleven towed instead of twelve self-propelled 75mm guns. It had 640 men.

The 1st SS Panzer Pioneer Battalion was just over 100 men short of its planned total of 1,138. Only one of its three companies, the 3rd, was mounted in SPWs and due to a shortage of these vehicles one of its platoons was carried in trucks. The other companies were truck mounted.

The organisation of the Leibstandarte's Panzer Artillery Regiment was complicated and this has led to confusion in understanding the allocation of artillery to the KGs, not least because after the war Peiper himself forgot the reorganisation[3] which took place in June 1944 in Flanders. At that time the 2nd SS Panzer Artillery Battalion, which had two Wespe self-propelled batteries, numbers 4 and 5, and one Hummel self-propelled battery, number 6, was renumbered to become the 1st Battalion, and its batteries renumbered accordingly to 1, 2 and 3. As if this was not confusing enough, the 1st Battalion became the 2nd but with only two towed batteries, numbers 4 and 5, and the 3rd Battalion's three towed batteries were renumbered 6, 7 and 8. There was no 9th battery. Since there were no Wespes or Hummels available in December

1944, the five batteries of the 1st and 2nd Battalions were all equipped with 105mm towed guns and the 6th and 7th batteries of the 3rd Battalion were towed 150mm. The 8th battery had four 100mm Kanon. The two other artillery units were the heavy Werfer (mortar) Battalion and the heavy Flak Battalion. The 1st SS Werfer Battalion was up to strength with three batteries of six 150mm towed mortars and one battery of towed 210mm. Similarly the 1st SS Panzer Flak Battalion was correct with three batteries of six towed 88mm guns and two batteries of nine towed 37mm. It was a big battalion with nearly 1,200 men.

The remaining elements of the Division were the Signals, Supply, Repair and Maintenance and Medical services, organised generally into battalion-sized units.

The total strength of the LAH on 16th December 1944 was over 19,000 officers and men and some 3,000 vehicles.

One additional unit was given to Mohnke to help with the air threat. Its strength and organisation is not fully known but part of the 84th Luftwaffe Flak Battalion under a Major Wolf was certainly allocated to the Division. It seems to have had a mixture of about eighteen 20mm and 37mm guns.

So how did SS Major General Mohnke divide up his resources? The main striking power of the Division was placed in the hands of Jochen Peiper. He kept all seventy-two of the LAH tanks and was given the forty-five King Tigers of I SS Panzer Corps's 501st SS Heavy Panzer Battalion; he had his own 10th SS Panzer Anti-Aircraft Company and was given part of the 84th Luftwaffe Flak Battalion under Major Wolf; for infantry he was given the 3rd SS Panzer-Grenadier (Armoured) Battalion of Rudolf Sandig's 2nd SS Panzer-Grenadier Regiment, commanded by another old comrade, SS Captain Jupp Diefenthal. Diefenthal had been born in Euskirchen in 1914 so he knew the Eifel and Ardennes well; he moved back there after the war. After commanding a motor-cycle reconnaissance platoon in 1941, he had been both a battalion and regimental adjutant to Teddy Wisch before commanding an infantry company and then, in July 1944, taking over Peiper's old panzer-grenadier battalion from the days in Russia and Italy. The Battalion was specially designed to operate with tanks, being the only one in the Division equipped with SPWs.

The 13th SS Panzer Heavy Infantry Gun Company also came from Sandig's Regiment with its six 150mm guns; and for further artillery support Peiper was given the three towed 105mm batteries of the 1st, not the 2nd as he said after the war, SS Panzer Artillery Battalion under SS Captain Kalischko.

Peiper therefore had everything he needed for his task except one vital element – bridging for his tanks. His own 9th SS Pioneer Company had no bridging at all and the 3rd SS Pioneer Company carried only infantry assault bridges. This was no oversight though; it was quite deliberate. The whole essence of 'blitzkrieg' is surprise and there was no intention of bridging any of the rivers in Peiper's path. The existing bridges were to be captured intact.

KG Peiper had 117 tanks, 149 SPWs, eighteen 105mm and six 150mm guns, between thirty and forty anti-aircraft weapon systems, roughly 4,800 officers and men and a total of just over 800 vehicles. It was a very powerful force.

The second most powerful KG was that of SS Lieutenant Colonel Max Hansen who was older than Peiper, being born in 1908 in Holstein. He never left the LAH from the day he joined in 1934, and by the time of the offensive had been awarded the Knight's Cross, German Cross in Gold and Iron Cross 1st and 2nd Class. He had commanded at every level up to and including Regiment and Kampfgruppe and had been wounded nine times. He was idolized by his men. Hansen kept the whole of his own 1st SS Panzer-Grenadier Regiment which consisted of three truck-mounted Panzer-Grenadier Battalions, each with four strong companies. He also had his 13th SS Panzer Heavy Infantry Gun Company with five Bisons, the 14th SS Panzer Anti-Aircraft Company with twelve 20mm guns, and the 15th SS Panzer Pioneer Company with infantry assault bridging and assault boats. For armour Hansen was given the whole of the 1st SS Panzerjäger Battalion with its twenty-one Jagdpanzer IV/70s, and for artillery support he was allocated the 4th SS Panzer Artillery towed 105mm Battery and the entire 1st SS Panzer Werfer Battalion with its twenty-four heavy rocket launchers. KG Hansen had over 4,500 men and 750 vehicles.

Following KG Peiper on the northern of the LAH's two routes was KG Sandig. Before he was commissioned in 1939 Sandig was known, even in the Leibstandarte, as a very 'hard' NCO. He had been one of the original twelve sergeant-majors, or 'Lances' as they were known, at the Jüterbog Training centre in July 1934. Small in stature and with a good sense of humour, by December 1944 he too was the holder of the Knight's Cross, German Cross in Gold and Iron Cross 1st and 2nd Class. Sandig's 2nd SS Panzer-Grenadier Regiment had been weakened to provide Peiper with infantry and heavy infantry guns but Sandig still had his two truck-mounted SS Panzer-Grenadier Battalions and his own Anti-Aircraft and Pioneer Companies for a total of about 3,000 men and 400 vehicles.

'Schnelle Gruppe' (Fast Group) Knittel planned to move, at least initially, behind KG Hansen on Route E. SS Major Gustav Knittel had, however, been given the option of changing routes if he thought it would help him achieve his mission, which was to race ahead of the other KGs as soon as the opportunity presented itself and seize bridges over the Meuse. To help him do this his own SS Reconnaissance

Battalion was to be reinforced by the 5th SS Panzer Artillery towed 105mm Battery and the truck mounted 2nd SS Panzer Pioneer Company. This would give Knittel nearly 1,500 men and 150 vehicles.

After allocating the vast majority of the fighting troops to the KGs, Mohnke was left some 6,000 men and 1,000 vehicles, mainly from the Divisional support and service units, but including some vital combat elements. The 1st SS Panzer Artillery Regiment was under the command of SS Lieutenant Colonel Steineck, another old comrade from pre-war days who had ended up commanding the remnants of the Division when Teddy Wisch had been wounded at Falaise. His Regiment still had its 3rd Battalion with two towed 150mm batteries and the four long ranged 100mm Kanons of the 8th Battery. This powerful force was therefore available to support any of the KGs on an as-required basis, provided it could get its weapons into range. This was bound to prove difficult with the few roads and bad ground conditions. To provide anti-aircraft cover for the logistic units of the Division, five batteries of the 1st SS Panzer Flak Battalion under SS Major Ullerich were following up; and still in reserve and standing ready to provide engineer support were the 1st SS Panzer Pioneer Company and the Divisional armoured bridging column.

There was one other small combat force attached to I SS Panzer Corps which must be mentioned. It will be recalled that Otto Skorzeny's main force of about 3,000 men, using captured American or disguised German equipment, was to operate in three KGs with the aim of moving ahead of the armoured KGs in order to capture at least two of the Meuse bridges.[4] This force had the collective title '150th Panzer Brigade'. One of these KGs, code-lettered 'X', under the command of SS Lieutenant Colonel Willi Hardieck, was to advance immediately behind KG Peiper. It consisted of a tank company with five disguised Panthers and a single captured Sherman, two infantry companies each with about 120 men and a Heavy Company with mortar, anti-tank, pioneer and panzer-grenadier platoons; in all about 500 men. Once Peiper had achieved a breakthrough it was hoped that Hardieck's KG would break free and race for the Meuse – this was to prove a very forlorn hope! The other two Skorzeny KGs were due to move behind the 12th SS Panzer and 12th Volks-Grenadier Divisions respectively. The detailed organisations of the 1st SS Panzer Division's KGs and Skorzeny's 150th Panzer Brigade for the Ardennes offensive are shown at Appendix 1.

Before turning to the opposition the Leibstandarte would face in the Ardennes, a word must be said about its 'son' in the attacking force, the 12th SS Panzer Division Hitlerjugend. It will be recalled that when it was formed in 1943 most of its officers had come from the LAH, and despite the terrible casualties suffered in Normandy, this was still so. Its commander and all the Kampfgruppe commanders were ex-Leibstandarte. SS Colonel Hugo Kraas had only been appointed to command the Division a month before the offensive. He joined the LAH a year before Peiper and was the first soldier in the 1940 campaign in France to win the Iron Cross 1st Class. He remained in command of the 'Hitlerjugend' until the end of the war in May 1945. His strongest KG was commanded by Herbert Kuhlmann who had taken over temporary command of the 1st SS Panzer Regiment in Normandy when Peiper had been incapacitated for whatever reason. His KG consisted of a mixed SS Panzer Battalion of thirty-eight Panthers and thirty-nine Type IVs, I SS Panzer Corps's 560th SS Heavy Panzerjäger Battalion with twenty-five Jagdpanzer IV/70s and seventeen Jagdpanthers, an SS Panzer-Grenadier Battalion and an SS Panzer Artillery Battalion. It was therefore almost the exact equivalent of KG Peiper. Similarly, the 'Flank' KG Müller mirrored KG Hansen with an SS Panzer-Grenadier Regiment less a battalion, the 12th SS Panzerjäger Battalion with twenty-two Jagdpanzer IV/70s and SS Panzer Artillery support; while KG Krause equated to KG Sandig and 'Fast Group' Bremer to Knittel.

The two SS Panzer Divisions, each with their four strong Kampfgruppen, were therefore well structured for their mission of slicing through the thin American defences in the Losheim Gap, causing panic in the rear areas and achieving 'bounce' crossings over the Meuse river. Conversely the Volks-Grenadier and Parachute Divisions charged with making the breaches for these elite SS Panzer Divisions were neither equipped, manned nor, in many cases, trained to play their part successfully in the grand design. Their Corps Commander, SS Lieutenant General Hermann Priess, knew this. In March 1946 he told an interviewer:

> The area assigned the Corps for attack was unfavourable. It was broken and heavily wooded. Wartime experience had tended to show that particularly good troops were needed for woodland fighting and that, as a consequence of the state of training of the infantry divisions, a rapid breakthrough in terrain such as this was very doubtful. . . .
> Therefore the following requests were made by the Corps to the Army:
> 1. To transfer our attack sector further to the south because the territory in that region was more open and because more and better roads were available.
>   The request was refused.
> 2. In the event of a disapproval of request 1, the commitment of the two SS Panzer divisions, or at least parts of these, to the actual breakthrough itself in order to force this as quickly as possible.
>   The request was disapproved.[5]

The organisation of a Volks-Grenadier division is shown at Appendix 2.

NOTES

1. All organisational and strength details are taken from *Die Leibstandarte IV/2* by Ralf Tiemann, supplemented by interviews with LAH veterans and strength returns for I SS Pz Corps for December 1944 held in the Bundesarchiv.
2. ETHINT 10.
3. Tiemann op. cit., pp. 556–9.
4. *An Interview with Obstlt Otto Skorzeny, Ardennes Offensive*, ETHINT 12 dated 12 Aug 1945.
5. MS # A-877 dated March 1946.

CHAPTER V

The Opposition[1]

It is a misconception that most American soldiers in Europe in December 1944 thought the war would be over by Christmas. November and early December had seen some of the bloodiest fighting since the June and July battles in Normandy. After the victorious and swift advance across eastern France, Belgium and Holland, Eisenhower's armies had ground to a halt through lack of supplies, and late September and October had been spent building up thousands of tons of ammunition, fuel and other essentials, improving the road systems, rebuilding bridges and replacing the many casualties in men and vehicles. Once this had been achieved he ordered the British and Canadian 21st and American 12th Army Groups to close up to the Rhine. It proved a costly business. The British did not even clear the Meuse until 4th December, the US 9th Army could not close to the Roer river, let alone the Rhine, and the US 1st Army became involved in a World War I type of slogging match south of Aachen. General George Patton's 3rd US Army took two weeks and many casualties to capture Metz in the south. The unpalatable truth was that the Allies had run up against the German 'West Wall' with all its inherent problems for an attacker and advantages for the defender.

It was true that no one from general to private believed that the Allies could lose the war or that the Germans were capable of anything more than defensive actions which might prolong matters for a few more months. Even so very few Allied soldiers were prepared to take risks. This attitude contrasted strongly with that of the Germans who, particularly after the calls for unconditional surrender, realised that they had little to lose and possibly something to gain by continuing the war. Many of them were prepared to die rather than surrender, especially in the defence of sacred German soil and this applied particularly to members of the SS who knew they could expect little mercy if the war were lost.

After two weeks' painful fighting in early December the American 1st and 9th Armies had advanced only 15km – to the Roer river (Map 1). The problem here was that the Germans had built dams at the headwaters of the river which could release floodwaters capable of inundating, or at least isolating, the American troops in the Roer valley. Attempts by the Allied air forces to destroy the dams had failed and it was decided to give the job of capturing them to Lieutenant General Courtney Hodges's 1st US Army.

The most costly part of the entire front had proved to be the Hurtgen Forest south of Aachen, where the US 1st Army had seen three of its divisions cut to pieces. Two of them, the 4th and 28th Infantry were so badly mauled that they had to be withdrawn from the Front and sent to quiet areas in the Ardennes and Luxembourg to recover and refit. They had been replaced by two brand new divisions, the 99th and 106th, neither of which had seen action but would soon bear the brunt of the forthcoming German onslaught. Looking at it from north to south, the situation in the area through which Sepp Dietrich's 6th Panzer Army was to assault on 16th December was as follows (Map 4): the 99th Infantry under Major General Walter Lauer, as the right-hand division of the US V Corps, defended a 25km front from Monschau to Losheim; there was then a 10km gap before the left-hand division of Major General Troy Middleton's VIII Corps, the 106th Infantry, could be found occupying a 20km front reaching down to the northern tip of the Duchy of Luxembourg. This gap, known geographically as the 'Losheim Gap', was Middleton's responsibility and he had given the job of covering it to Colonel Mark Devine's 14th Cavalry Group. They moved in on 10th December. Thus the most vulnerable part of the Allied front, the gap between two corps and an historical attack route, was occupied by only 450 men of the 18th Cavalry Reconnaissance Squadron in village outposts supported by a company of 3" anti-tank guns. This gap and the area just to its north, occupied by the US 99th Division, were the precise initial objectives of Priess's I SS Panzer Corps.

Behind this thin American crust Major General Walter Robinson's 2nd Infantry Division had begun its task of capturing the Roer dams on 13th December. It attacked through the 99th Division's lines and was supported by CCB, an armoured combat command, of the 9th Armored Division. The rest of Major John Leonard's 9th Armored Division was resting in reserve behind the 106th Division to the south. Other relevant formations which would soon become involved were the 30th Infantry and 82nd Airborne Divisions and an armoured Combat Command of the 3rd Armored Division. Taking these in turn, Major General Leland

Hobbs's 30th Division, which had earned for itself the unofficial nickname 'Roosevelt's SS' during the fighting in Normandy, was resting near Aachen after some hard fighting in the Roer river sector. Its organisation, which followed the standard pattern for an infantry division, is shown at Appendix 3. Major General Jim Gavin's 82nd Airborne Division was near Reims in France, resting and preparing for a further airborne operation after the ill fated 'Market Garden' operation in Holland. Combat Command B (CCB) of the 3rd Armored Division, commanded by Brigadier General Truman Boudinot was also resting in the Aachen area to the north.

There were other much smaller units which were to play vital parts in our story, such as the combat engineers of Colonel Wallis Anderson's 1111th Engineer Combat Group, the anti-aircraft gunners of the 110th and 143rd AAA Battalions and the 526th Armored Infantrymen and anti-tank gunners of the 825th Tank Destroyer Battalion, both stationed well to the rear as 1st Army troops. They, like everyone else, were completely unaware that their relatively peaceful routine was about to be shattered and their Christmas in Belgium ruined.

These then were the American units; let us now examine their equipment and men.

American equipment was provided on a lavish scale but it did not always compare favourably with the enemy's. Tanks were a good example. The M4 Sherman with its low-velocity, short-barrelled 75mm gun and only 50mm of frontal armour was highly vulnerable to the Panther, King Tiger and Panzerfaust. Few units saw the up-gunned high velocity 76mm gun version before they crossed the Rhine in 1945. The frequency with which the M4 caught fire after being hit had won for it the dreadful nickname 'The Ronson Lighter'. The only things in its favour were its ease of maintenance and reliability. The M3 Stuart light tank and M8 Greyhound armoured car, both with a 37mm gun, were virtually useless other than for liaison, light recce or escort duties.

American anti-tank guns were known as Tank Destroyers (TDs). Most TD units were equipped with towed 3" guns but at the time of this battle one platoon in each of the companies of the 30th Infantry Division's 823rd TD Battalion had just re-equipped with a self-propelled version, mounted on an open-topped Sherman chassis, known as the M-10.

In the field of artillery the US 105mm and 155mm guns equated well with their German counterparts but the Americans had no heavy rocket launchers or equivalent to the German 150mm heavy infantry gun.

The US M3 half-track was a good vehicle and like the German SPW, which it closely resembled, had been adapted to many different uses.

The most important thing to be said about US equipment was its scale of issue. Again taking tanks first; the Leibstandarte, as an elite and specially reinforced Division, had only 117 tanks. An American armoured division like the 3rd Armored, had 263 tanks, including 164 Shermans. A German Volks-Grenadier Division such as the 12th had no tanks supporting it and only half a dozen armoured assault guns to make up for this deficiency. The US 30th Infantry Division on the other hand had a tank battalion of 54 Shermans and 17 light tanks operating permanently with it and an anti-tank battalion with 36 tank destroyers as part of its Table of Organisation and Equipment. The detailed organisation of the 743rd Tank and 823rd TD Battalions, both attached to the 30th Infantry Division, are shown at Appendix 4.

Turning now to the men, there was a big difference in the standards of training and performance between divisions, within individual regiments and between various arms. The Ardennes campaign was to highlight these differences – for example, the difference between the 1st and 106th Infantry Divisions, between the 1st and 3rd Battalions of the 119th Infantry Regiment in the battle of Stoumont, and between artillery and engineer units on the one hand and armour, cavalry and infantry on the other. These differences appear to have been mainly caused by varying standards of leadership and it is a sad fact that most American Ardennes veterans seem to hold little respect for their officers. This is hardly surprising, though, in view of the rapid turnover rate, particularly at battalion level. In the 30th Infantry Division for example, four of the battalions had three different Commanding Officers in eleven months of fighting and one had four. But frequent officer changes and poor leadership were not the only problems. Heavy casualty rates placed great strain on the reinforcement system, particularly for the infantry. Again using the 30th Infantry as an example, the combat losses[2] in eleven months amounted to nearly twice the Division Table of Organisation strength!

But lack of specialised training was also a problem, especially for armoured units. Colonel William Duncan of the 743rd Tank Battalion, part of the 30th Infantry, wrote in 1990:

> We received many reinforcements who had never seen a tank before, so I used my light tanks for training in the rear when possible; then I would shift them up into my command tanks. It was a case of unpreparedness by my country but the boys did a good job.[3]

So what was the attitude of the average GI in mid-December 1944 in the area facing the German 6th Panzer Army?

The part of Belgium in which many of the Americans found themselves had a depressing effect on their morale. Few knew or cared anything about European history or geography. Those in the rear areas were happy enough. They were living in the Walloon, or French speaking, part of the country where the people treated them as heroes for freeing them from the hated Nazi occupation. The soldiers were invited

into their homes and they had hot baths and were able to dance with
pretty girls. John Stevenson of C Company of the 202nd Engineers, in
a letter to the author, described what it was like in Stavelot:

> My squad was staying in a large mansion-type house. We had no
> specific assignment as far as I knew. We all thought the war was far
> away and almost over. I remember men going to the local photogra-
> pher to have their portraits taken and to the local cobbler to have their
> shoes repaired.[4]

Some of the luckier officers were invited by the landowners to join them
for a day's shooting in the forests where deer and boar abounded or for
fishing in the trout-filled rivers.

In the forward areas the picture was very different, for this was the
German-speaking part of the country. Hardly any of the GIs realised
that before 1919 the places in which they now found themselves – such
as Bütgenbach, Elsenborn, Büllingen, Honsfeld, Amel and Manderfeld
– had all been part of Germany (Map 3). It was only after the First World
War that this region had been handed over, quite arbitrarily, to Belgium
as part of war reparations. Then in 1940 Hitler had reclaimed it as part
of the Third Reich, re-established the original frontier and compelled
the menfolk of military age to join the Wehrmacht.

Another factor affecting the Americans was the depressing Ardennes
weather. It was worst of all for the poor infantrymen in their fox-holes
on the forest edge, shivering in zero and below zero temperatures and
often unable to see more than 20m in the mist. It was no wonder that,
with little expectation of being attacked, they and the cavalrymen of
Colonal Devine's command left their positions and vehicles whenever
they could to seek the shelter and warmth of local houses and farms.

Finally it has to be said that the American soldier was not used to
being on the defensive, nor had he been trained for it. The basic tactic
of the US Army since General Ulysses S Grant in the American Civil
War was, and still is, 'Find 'em, fix 'em, destroy 'em!' This is what the
Americans had been trying to do to the Germans ever since they had
landed in Normandy and their deployment in the Ardennes still
reflected it. For example, the 99th Infantry Division (Map 4) was holding
a 25km front, with all three Regiments 'on line' and battalions responsible for frontages as great as 3,000 metres. The only reserve in the
whole Division was a single, relatively immobile, battalion of infantry.
It therefore came as a particularly nasty shock when the Germans, suddenly and unexpectedly, struck back. It was something for which the
American soldiers were both tactically and mentally unprepared.

NOTES

1. Based on *Ardennes Campaign Statistics 16 Dec 44–19 Jan 1945*, Office of the Chief of Military History, Department of the Army 1952 and other statistical documents held there and in the US National Archives.
2. These and other casualty figures are taken from the Historical Evaluation and Research Organisation USA and from Unit AARs and 30th Infantry Division G-2 Periodic Reports 16–24 Dec 1944.
3. Letter to author dated 16 Jan 1990.
4. Letter to author dated 8 Feb 1990.

CHAPTER VI
The Scene on the German Side

Jochen Peiper left his Divisional commander, Mohnke, at about midday on the 14th December and returned to his own Headquarters 10km away in the Forsthaus Blankenheimer Wald.[1] There he gave a preliminary briefing to the commanders of the various components of his Kampfgruppe: Hein von Westernhagen of the 501st SS Heavy Panzer Battalion, Werner Poetschke commanding his composite 1st SS Panzer Battalion, Jupp Diefenthal of the 3rd SS Panzer-Grenadier Battalion, Erich Rumpf of the 9th and Franz Sievers of the 3rd SS Panzer Pioneer Companies, Karl Heinz Vögler commanding the 10th SS Panzer Anti-Aircraft Company, Ludwig Kalischko of the 1st SS Panzer Artillery Battalion, Luftwaffe Major Wolf of the 84th Flak, SS Major Unger of the Regimental Supply Company and SS Lieutenant Ratschko with the Regimental Workshop. Also there were of course Peiper's own staff officers, including his Adjutant Hans Gruhle, Communications Officer Krause, and Senior Medical Officer and old friend SS Major Kurt Sickel, who at thirty-seven was by far the oldest officer present. Peiper himself was only twenty-nine and few of his company commanders were over twenty-five.

Their units were scattered around Blankenheim under cover of the forest and local villages. It was an area of outstanding beauty untouched by war (Map 4). Sepp Dietrich had his Army Headquarters only a few kilometres away at Marmagen, Priess his Corps HQ at Schmidtheim just down the road, the Hitlerjungend were to Peiper's north, Sandig's KG to his north-east around Tondorf, Hansen's to the south around Alendorf and Knittel's Fast Group near Stadtkyll. Dietrich's 'boys' were all around him.

It was some 30km from the KG Peiper's Assembly Area, and 20km from its Start Point on Route 51 south of Schmidtheim, to the Siegfried Line near Scheid where Peiper would leave Germany and begin the adventure which would radically affect the remaining thirty-one years of his life. The area behind the Siegfried Line was crammed with troops and equipment. Quite apart from the 12th Volks-Grenadier and 3rd Parachute Divisions with all their supporting elements, there were the 391 guns and werfers, many of them horse-drawn, of Volksartillerie Corps 388 and 402 and Volkswerfer Brigades 4 and 9 with all their attendant vehicles. All these would have provided juicy targets for the Allied air forces if only they had known of their existence.

It is interesting to speculate on Peiper's state of mind before the offensive. He was certainly elated to find himself commanding the 'schwerpunkt' of the Division, indeed one of the two from I SS Panzer Corps; he had after all been given all the Leibstandarte's tanks and the King Tigers of the Corps. He knew about the two special operations of Skorzeny and von der Heydte and the air offensive being launched in tandem with 'Autumn Mist'. After the war Peiper said[2] he thought that if all had gone as planned he could have reached the Meuse on the very first day of the offensive. This would seem to indicate that in 1944 he believed the plan had every chance of success. At a higher level Peiper had been briefed, perhaps even brain-washed, about the various 'V' weapons, jet aircraft and snorkel U boats. As far as he was concerned the war was far from lost and provided they could gain time for their beloved Führer he would, like Frederick the Great, gain the final victory.

In the meantime, though, there were more mundane things to be sorted out. The remaining few hours before 'H' hour on the 16th were going to be very busy. Before issuing detailed orders Peiper had discussions with Major General Engel commanding the 12th Volks-Grenadier Division and SS Lieutenant Colonel Hardieck in charge of Skorzeny's KG 'X'. Engel thought he could achieve success in the break-in battle by about 0700 hours on the 16th and this gave Peiper a planning time on which to base his advance. Hardieck explained how he hoped to operate behind US lines. At 1100 hours on the 15th Peiper was required to attend a conference at Corps Headquarters[3] attended by Divisional and KG Commanders and Skorzeny. Priess gave a 'pep' talk explaining the importance of the mission and his Chief of Staff repeated the basic attack order and then stated that two train loads of fuel had not arrived. No reason was given. This was serious news indeed – Peiper's objective was 150km from his assembly area and his tanks had enough fuel for only 100km at best. Details of known American fuel dumps were given and all commanders told to seize as much as they could until resupply could be organised. After the war Peiper described the roads he had been told to use as 'not for tanks, but for bicycles'.[4] But we shall discover much of what he said after the war had little in common with the facts as later revealed and can often be seen as excuses for things which did not work out. One of Peiper's claims was that he himself obtained extra ammunition for his KG from Euskirchen on the 15th. Be that as it may, it does appear that his tanks at least started with enough ammunition for four or five days at intense combat rates.

Peiper calculated that his column, which would have to advance on a one-vehicle front owing to topographical and weather conditions, would be about 25km long. It would therefore take about one hour to pass a single point. By this stage of the war both the Germans and Americans had virtually given up using reconnaissance vehicles to lead an advance. They seem to have adopted Clausewitz's dictum that one should 'point with the fist, not the finger!' Despite Peiper saying after the war that 'in order to provide maximum speed and power, I decided that my armoured half-tracks would proceed as fast as possible until they met resistance, and then the tanks would come up to destroy the resistance, following which the half-tracks would again advance,'[5] he did nothing of the sort. His order of march was as follows: the column was led by a 'Spitze' (Point) consisting of two Panther tanks from SS Lieutenant Kremser's 1st SS Panzer Company, five Type IV tanks from the 6th SS Panzer Company and the SPW-mounted 1st Platoon of the 9th SS Panzer Pioneer Company. It was commanded by SS Lieutenant Werner Sternebeck of the 6th SS Panzer Company.[6] There is a story that Peiper gave command of the 'Spitze' to Sternebeck as a punishment for getting drunk in a Gasthaus just before the offensive!

Following the 'Spitze' came the 'Spitze Company Group' under the command of SS Captain Georg Preuss. It comprised his own 10th SS Panzer-Grenadier Company, the Anti-tank Platoon of the 12th (Heavy) Panzer-Grenadier Company, probably the remainder of the 6th SS Panzer Company under SS Lieutenant Benno Junker and the second SPW-mounted Platoon of the 9th Panzer Pioneer Company. Ten minutes later came Peiper himself and his Command Group. With him were his armoured and infantry commanders, Poetschke and Diefenthal, each with their Adjutants, Fischer and Flacke respectively. Peiper, Poetschke and Fischer were in Panthers, Diefenthal and Flacke in SPWs as was Buchheim, Poetschke's Communications Officer. Peiper's personal staff officer, Neuske, started the operation as a Liaison Officer to Mohnke. Following the Command Group, again with a planned interval of about ten minutes, came the main fighting group with the rest of the panzer and panzer-grenadier companies, and Koch's 13th SS Infantry Heavy Gun Company, all interspersed with panzer pioneers and the anti-aircraft vehicles of the 10th SS Panzer Anti-Aircraft Company and 84th Luftwaffe Flak Detachment. After the main fighting group was the 1st

SS Panzer Artillery Battalion and then, right at the rear due to their immense size, the King Tigers of von Westernhagen. Peiper's Adjutant, Hans Gruhle, with SS Lieutenant Krause, the Regimental Communications Officer, were at the rear of the main fighting group in a Panther and SPW respectively, with the KG's rearward radio facilities to Mohnke and the Divisional HQ.

Peiper issued his detailed orders during the afternoon of Friday the 15th. He gave the overall plan and stressed its importance. He affirmed that his KG would be the first to reach the Meuse! He gave the preferred route, order of march and outline timings including time past the Start Point near Schmidtheim. He assigned radio frequencies. The one thing he could not give much information about was the enemy. Active patrolling had been forbidden immediately before the 16th to preserve secrecy and so there was little information about possible minefields or even forward American positions. As it turned out the Germans even lacked information about their own minefields which had been laid during their retreat to the West Wall. With regard to US formations opposite I SS Panzer Corps all they knew was that there were about one and a half divisions in forward positions, reserves in the Elsenborn area and an armoured division thought to be north of Spa (Map 3).

Following Peiper's orders his unit commanders went off to brief their company and platoon leaders; it was therefore the evening of the 15th or even the early hours of the 16th before many of the soldiers knew exactly what was expected of them. Not surprisingly very few of Peiper's men got any sleep the night before the advance – and they were to get precious little in the coming ten days.

A word should now be said about simple but important matters such as food and maps. Despite great advances in tactical thought and equipment development, the German system of feeding their armoured troops was archaic. Individual tanks and SPWs were not issued with separate rations and had no equipment for cooking, so, if the company supply sergeant did not reach them with hot or even cold food, vehicle crews went without or had to scrounge whatever they could wherever they could find it. It goes without saying that this is what happened in the Ardennes and few of Peiper's men had a hot meal throughout the entire battle.

Maps were not only in short supply but were nearly always printed in black and white to a scale of, at best 1:50,000, and often 1:100,000. This made them difficult enough to read in daylight let alone in a tank at night! Their scale of issue was very restricted.

Turning now to the 12th Volks-Grenadier Division commanded by Major General Engel; it was a veteran division which, as the 12th Infantry Division, had fought with distinction in Poland, France and Russia. It moved to the western front in September 1944 and was involved in the battle of Aachen before being redesignated 12th Volks-Grenadier in October and then withdrawn to the Blankenheim area for refitting on 2nd December. It was at about 80% strength when the offensive started on the 16th. It had no integral armour but was given six 75mm StuG armoured assault guns in lieu. The task of the Division (Map 5) was to seize Losheim and Losheimergraben and then advance along the axes of the N-32 and the railway line to capture Büllingen. Its further objectives were Nidrum and Weywertz, followed eventually by Verviers (Map 2).

The 3rd Parachute Division, under Major General Wedehn, had been formed in France in October 1943. It had been involved in the Normandy battles and suffered badly at St Lô and in the Falaise pocket. It had recently been brought up to about 75% of its official strength at Oldenzaal in Holland but most of the new men were Luftwaffe ground personnel with only minimal combat training. On the 16th December one of its three Regiments, the 8th, had not even arrived in the final assembly area. It had no armoured vehicles in support. The task of the Division was to seize Krewinkel, Lanzerath and Manderfeld and then advance via Holzheim to take Schoppen and Eibertingen (Map 6). Its final objective was just to the east of Liège!

At 0500 hours on Saturday 16th December Jochen Peiper moved to the Headquarters of Major General Engel near Hallschlag so that he could watch the progress of the 12th Volks-Grenadiers and know precisely when to launch his Kampfgruppe. His Corps Commander had said to him 'If you only get to the Meuse with one damned tank, Jochen, you'll have done your job!' He did not plan to disappoint anyone.

The German artillery barrage was due to start at 0530 hours. Dawn would break at about 0745 hours and it would be dark again by 1700 hours. Low cloud covered the Ardennes, mist enveloped the forests and the temperature hovered around zero. Occasional snow flurries further restricted visibility but except on the highest ground, such as the Baraque Michel where von der Heydte and his paratroopers were due to drop, little snow fell and what did soon turned to sleet and rain. Thin ice covered the puddles and men sank into thick clawing mud the moment they stepped off the roads. The metal of armoured vehicles was so cold it was painful to touch; inside they were as cold as refrigerators, making sleep unthinkable.

NOTES

1. ETHINT 10.
2. Ibid.
3. Ibid.
4. Ibid.
5. Ibid.

6. Tiemann, *Die Leibstandarte IV/2* and conversations with Werner Sternebeck, Arndt Fischer and other LAH veterans.

CHAPTER VII
The Scene on the American Side[1]

The 99th Infantry Division, with its Headquarters in Bütgenbach, had been occupying its positions opposite the Siegfried Line for a month when the Germans struck (Map 4). It had been a quiet period with few patrols and only very slight artillery activity. Although the Americans never guessed it, this was of course deliberate on the part of their enemy. The men had improved their living conditions and even built quite elaborate huts for use when they were not in their fox-holes. Marlene Dietrich was due to give a concert in Bütgenbach in a few days time but her namesake would in fact be nearer to the town than she would.

One of the 99th's three Regiments, the 394th Infantry commanded by Colonel Don Riley, was deployed from Neuhof to just north of Losheim, thereby covering the initial part of Peiper's planned route. The other Regiments of the Division would be facing the 12th SS Panzer Division Hitlerjugend and need not concern us further.

The 1st Battalion of the 394th Infantry, commanded by Lieutenant Colonel Robert Douglas, was sitting on the 12th Volks-Grenadiers' primary objective – Losheimergraben (Map 5). The 2nd Battalion under Lieutenant Colonel Wertheimer was on its left flank and the 3rd Battalion, commanded by Major Norman Moore, less a company on loan to another Regiment, was in reserve in the area of Buchholz. Available to fire in support of the Regiment were three 105mm artillery battalions and one 155mm battalion. The Divisional 801st Tank Destroyer Battalion had two of its 3″ guns with the 3rd Battalion in Buchholz and nine more deployed around Honsfeld where a Regimental rest centre had been established. About 125 men were enjoying its facilities on the morning of the 16th. The seventeen men of the Regimental Intelligence and Reconnaissance (I&R) Platoon under Lieutenant Lyle Bouck had taken up a position near the small but important village of Lanzerath, which was in fact outside the Divisional southern boundary.

It held a commanding position, however, and it was not surprising that when Bouck arrived there, on 10th December, he found four TDs and a reconnaissance platoon of the 820th TD Battalion already established in the village under the command of Lieutenant John Arculeer. They were attached to Colonel Mark Devine's 14th Cavalry Group which was responsible for the 'Losheim Gap', but there was little contact between the two groups. Devine's 1,550-man Cavalry Group had two Squadrons, the 18th and the 32nd. These were battalion-sized units, each comprising three 137-man reconnaissance troops equipped with M8 armoured cars, half-tracks and jeeps, a 95-man light tank troop with seventeen Stuart tanks and an 85-man assault gun troop with six 75mm guns mounted on light tank bodies. Only the 18th Squadron was in position and its B Troop was detached to the 106th Infantry Division. The 32nd Squadron had arrived in Vielsalm (Map 3) on the 15th December after attachment to the 28th Infantry Division and was refitting. In support of the 18th Squadron were the twelve towed TDs of Captain Stanton Nash's A Company 820th TD Battalion and the eighteen self-propelled 105mm howitzers of the 275th Field Artillery Battalion positioned 4km to the west of Manderfeld. The cavalry and TDs were deployed as follows: Squadron HQ, the six 75mm SP assault guns of E Troop and Captain William Fitzgerald's seventeen Stuart tanks of F Troop were back in Manderfeld; two TDs were in Merlscheid; four TDs in Berterath; the three cavalry platoons of C Troop had positions in Krewinkel, Weckerath and Afst; two more TDs, under the command of Sergeant Joe Fiscus, and two cavalry platoons of A Troop were in Roth and the other platoon was in Kobscheid. Each cavalry platoon had artillery observers from the 275th Field Artillery Battalion with it – at least during the hours of daylight. Many of these troops were therefore stationed directly in the path of Max Hansen's KG and would consequently need removing by the 3rd Parachute Division. The defensive 'crust' was, however, painfully thin and consisted mainly of cavalrymen whose real role was reconnaissance, rather than static defence for which they were neither trained nor equipped.

The only other combat troops in the forward areas through which the Leibstandarte was due to advance were a platoon of TDs from the 801st TD Battalion near Büllingen and the much more important Combat Command B of the 9th Armored Division. Dealing with Büllingen first; this important road centre on the route of both Peiper, and Kuhlmann of the Hitlerjugend, was the support centre for the 2nd and 99th Infantry Divisions (Map 8). At the west end of the town was a fairly large fuel dump which Peiper certainly knew about and throughout Büllingen there was a host of administrative units such as quartermaster companies and artillery service batteries. Nearby, the V Corps's 254th Engineer Combat Battalion was in bivouac and on the south-west edge of the town there were two air-strips on each of which were based a dozen L-5 observation aircraft from each of the two infantry divisions and a couple from the 9th Armored.

CCB of the 9th Armored Division was commanded by Brigadier General William Hoge. His task was to support the 2nd Infantry Division in its mission of capturing the Roer dams. He had under command the 14th Tank Battalion with Shermans, the 27th Armored Infantry and the 16th Field Artillery Battalions, plus some armoured engineers, cavalry and self-propelled anti-aircraft guns. It was a powerful group and its assembly area to the south of Faymonville meant it was ideally placed to confront Peiper (Map 6).

Behind the forward combat troops there were scores of administrative and supply units. The 1st Army map depot was for example located in Stavelot; and in Malmédy, as well as a Reinforcement Unit, there was the 44th Field Evacuation Hospital. The 1st Platoon of the 47th Field Hospital was in Waimes and the 3rd Platoon in the school in Bütgenbach. Huge fuel dumps could be found north of the Amblève river in Stavelot and south of Spa where Lieutenant General Courtney Hodges's 1st US Army Headquarters was located in the Hotel Britannique. Rear supporting elements of the HQ were a little further north at Chaudfontaine.

Scattered throughout the whole area east of the Meuse a series of 90mm anti-aircraft gun batteries had been sited with the task of shooting down German V1 'buzz bombs' targeted on the many supply dumps and units in and around Liège. The Headquarters of one of these Anti-Aircraft Brigades, the 49th commanded by Brigadier General Edward Timberlake, was located in the luxurious Hôtel du Moulin in Ligneuville.

Also working throughout the area were the engineers of Colonel Wallis Anderson's 1111th Engineer Combat Group. His Headquarters was in the Hôtel Crismer in Trois Ponts and he had under his command three battalions of combat engineers and some supporting sub units. The 629th Engineer Light Equipment Company was based near Bütgenbach and the 962nd Engineer Maintenance Company in Malmédy with B Company of Lieutenant Colonel David Pergrin's 291st Engineer Combat Battalion.[2] Pergrin had part of his A Company in Werbomont, with outstations in Grand Halleux and Born, and C Company living in the huge Château Froidcour near Stoumont, home of the de Harenne family,[3] and the nearby railway station. The companies were working sawmills across the V Corps area in places like Trois Ponts and Stavelot and cutting timber in the forests for the Army winterisation programme. Over the two months they had been there Pergrin's men had come to know the area and its people extremely well. Since October his own headquarters had been set up in the Château Godin at Haute Bodeux, only 7km from Colonel Anderson at Trois Ponts. On 15th December Pergrin had been ordered to provide a company to support CCB of the 9th Armored Division and he had instructed his A Company to concentrate at Born the following morning. The other Battalions of the 1111th Group were the 51st, which was working thirty-eight sawmills in the vicinity of Marche to the south-west, and the 296th around

Sourbrodt, which was assigned primarily to road building and maintenance in the forward areas of V Corps. Another important engineer unit
in our story was a company of the 202nd Engineer Battalion which had
just been transferred from the US 3rd Army and attached to Anderson's
1111th Group. On 16th December its C Company, under Lieutenant Jo
'Blinky' Chinlund, was resting in Stavelot with the occasional bit of road
maintenance to keep it occupied. Chinlund was really the 1st Platoon
commander, but the company commander had been injured and he was
temporarily standing in.[4]

Life for these rear-based troops was really quite pleasant. After the
German withdrawal in September things in Belgium quickly reverted to
normal; the Walloons and Americans got on well together and the ten-
sions of the occupation soon eased. There was still food rationing for
the civilians and unimaginative army food for the soldiers but 'blackout'
restrictions were virtually forgotten and by early December everyone
began to plan Christmas parties. Soldiers were granted leave and some
of the luckier ones, particularly senior officers, managed to get to Paris
and London. Nobody, least of all the generals, thought the Germans
were capable of taking offensive action.

The story of the almost total failure of Allied intelligence has been
told many times and there is no need to repeat it. The simple facts are
that although the Allies knew about the 6th Panzer Army, they did
not realise it had moved south and therefore still considered it to be a
counter-penetration force ready for any thrust towards the Rhine.
ULTRA, the British decrypting organisation, had failed to detect either
the scale or the reason for the build-up or the move south, because
the Germans banned the use of radio and relied instead on telephone
communications. In fact a number of important intelligence indicators,
including the interception of messages between Luftwaffe Headquarters
and bases ignoring the radio ban, should have alerted the Allies. The
problem was that senior officers did not wish to believe their intelligence
staffs when they came up with warnings based on these indicators.
Evidence that a strongly held belief is seldom analysed cannot be better
illustrated.

With the exception of the men of the 2nd Infantry Division and their
supporting troops charged with capturing the Roer dams, most Americans and Belgians went to bed contentedly on the night of 15th
December and slept soundly, at least until 0530 hours on the 16th.

NOTES

1. All geographical locations and combat organisations are based on AARs and/
   or personal letters and conversations.

2. All references to the 291st Engineer Combat Battalion in this and subsequent Chapters are based on conversations with Colonel Dave Pergrin, his officers and men, *The Damned Engineers* and *The GI Journal of Sergeant Giles* by Janice Holt-Giles and *First Across the Rhine* by David E. Pergrin with Eric Hammel.
3. All references to the de Harenne family are based on conversations with members of the family who suffered the events of 1944.
4. Letter from Colonel W. N. Doyle, platoon commander C/202 Engineer Combat Battalion to author dated 16 Jan 1990.

CHAPTER VIII

Saturday 16th December 1944

Break-in

Hitler's last offensive began with two major failures. Due to poor visibility Operation 'Bodenplatte', designed to cripple the Allied air forces on the ground, had to be postponed. It was eventually launched, to the dismay of the Luftwaffe generals, on 1st January 1945. Although it inflicted heavy casualties on the Allies, they could afford them, unlike the Germans who lost nearly 300 aircraft and some 200 pilots in the raids.[1]

The second failure was Baron von der Heydte's Operation 'Stoesser'.[2] The plan was for his parachute force of 870 men to fly from airfields at Paderborn and Lippspringe in sixty-seven JU 52 troop carriers and drop at 0430 hours on the morning of the attack on the Baraque Michel area (Map 3), north of Malmédy. Dummies were to be dropped at the same time in the regions of Elsenborn, Eupen and Spa to create confusion. The aim of the operation was to form a blocking position on the right flank of the 6th Panzer Army and so prevent US units from the north interfering with the advance. It was also of course designed to cause panic behind US lines.

Unbelievably, when it was time to move the paratroopers from their barracks to the mounting airfields there was insufficient transport to lift them. The whole operation had to be aborted. It was resurrected 24 hours later but resulted in failure. After a scattered drop, due to high winds and both friendly and enemy flak, von der Heydte eventually assembled about 300 of his men at Baraque Michel on the Hautes Fagnes by last light on the 17th. They achieved little and at midday on the 20th he disbanded his force telling his men to make their way back to German lines as best they could. He himself was captured near Monschau on the 22nd by men of the 99th Infantry. In some respects, though, the operation was a success. Because of the dispersed drop the Americans

67

gained the impression that there had been a very large parachute operation, with the result that hundreds of men wasted their time looking for mythical paratroopers instead of getting on with their proper jobs. It is also a fact that many veterans and indeed many Belgians, together with most After Action Reports, talk about seeing or getting involved with German paratroopers. Those who landed in Belgium and the dummies certainly produced a remarkable effect.

The artillery barrage by the massed guns and rocket launchers of I SS Panzer Corps opened up precisely at 0530 hours. One German artillery officer described the moment thus:

> It was all so peaceful as it can only be in the hills where fir woods quietly whisper, here and there dropping some of their mantle of snow. A few stars shone out of a black sky; a low cloud layer hovered in the west. And then as far as the eye could see the sky lit up! The mortars sang their eerie song and sent their cones of fire into the heavens. Thunder filled the air and the earth shook under the impact of the blows. At first I was dumb but then I couldn't contain myself any longer, I shouted and danced and laughed![3]

He goes on to say that at 0535 hours the anti-aircraft searchlights switched on, piercing the sky and bouncing light off the low clouds. They were designed to guide the attacking infantry and blind the Americans. At 0545 hours the fire lifted to the second line of suspected US positions and continued until 0555. It lifted again to a third line from 0600 and 0615 and finally to a fourth from 0620 till 0630 hours. Many US units say that in fact the barrage lasted until 0700 hours. In the sector of Major Moore's 3rd Battalion of the 394th Infantry, the Battalion Intelligence Officer had briefed on 15th December that there were only two German horse-drawn guns opposite them. As the Battalion Executive Officer put it later: 'The Germans sure worked those horses to death.' Amazingly, although most US units talk about 'very heavy artillery fire' it seems to have done remarkably little damage, other than to disrupt communications by severing telephone lines. All units were inter-connected with the network of telephone wires hastily laid from wire trucks along roads and through crossroads. A typical crossroads would have had as many as fifty wires running in all directions. Inevitably the German artillery targeted most crossroads with the result that many lines went dead and many units were cut off from their higher headquarters.

The effect of those shells and rockets which did land on troop targets was largely negated by the overhead protection provided for most of the American fox-holes. Certainly casualties were minimal.

In the 394th Infantry Regiment's sector (Map 5) the first major assault came against the 1st Battalion of Lieutenant Colonel Robert Douglas holding the Losheimergraben crossroads and customs post. All day Colonel Wilhelm Osterhold's 48th Regiment, part of the 12th Volks-Grenadiers, struggled to open up Peiper's main axis, but when darkness fell it had failed to take the position. On the 48th Regiment's left flank the 27th Regiment had moved easily through Losheim, which was undefended, and continued on up the railway track leading to Buchholz. There Major Norman Moore's 3rd Battalion, with only two rifle companies, was established in the area of the small railway station. The Germans arrived just as Moore's L Company was lining up for breakfast, seemingly unconcerned despite the artillery barrage. A swift fire-fight developed but the Germans did not persist in their attack and moved off into the forest with the aim of advancing later on Hünningen. The day's fighting had cost both sides about 100 casualties and the Germans had completely failed to make a breach for Peiper's tanks. The 394th Infantry had had a good day but its casualties on this and the following day amounted to 959, including 34 killed and an astonishing 701 missing. Although they had held their positions, the Americans were severely shaken and that evening Colonel Riley ordered four platoons from Major Moore's 3rd Battalion to reinforce the 1st Battalion at Losheimergraben. Moore was left with only two rifle platoons defending the Buchholz–Honsfeld road.

It was during this first day's fighting that we get our first references by the Americans to Tiger tanks. In a recorded interview on 29th January 1945[4] with Lieutenant Colonel Douglas and two of his company commanders we hear that, soon after the German artillery barrage finished, a Tiger tank approached the Battalion position at Losheimergraben and was knocked out by a 57mm anti-tank gun. Actually only forty-five King Tigers, or Tiger IIs, were committed in the entire Ardennes offensive on 16th December and they were those of the 501st SS Heavy Panzer Battalion under Peiper's command. At this stage they were of course nowhere near Losheimergraben. But every American soldier had heard about the dreaded Tiger and expected to see one every time he heard tank noises. Unfortunately vehicle recognition was not a well taught subject in the US Army, even, it seems, to artillery and anti-tank units. In fairness it has to be said that the Panther and Tiger II were similar in appearance. Even so, few Americans ever saw a Tiger in the Ardennes; over half of Peiper's broke down before they reached Stavelot and less than one third crossed to the north side of the Amblève river. References to Tigers in personal interviews or unit After Action Reports should therefore be treated with caution. Similarly most German tank guns are described as '88s'.

In the Losheim Gap the Americans did less well. The 9th Regiment of the 3rd Parachute Division, under Colonel von Hoffmann, with its 1st Battalion leading, advanced along the axis Hüllscheid–Hergersberg–

Merlscheid–Lanzerath. It took 113 casualties, including 33 killed,[5] before securing Lanzerath at the end of the day. The crews of the two TDs of A Company 820th TD Battalion in Merlscheid and the four of Lieutenant Carl Johnson in Berterath inflicted numerous casualties on the paratroopers with their machine guns before they withdrew at about 1030 hours, the Merlscheid group to high ground 800m to the west and later to Manderfeld and the Berterath platoon to Fockert. They had to abandon their TDs, which had been useless against the paratroopers anyway. By the end of the day, after a further withdrawal from Manderfeld, A Company 820th TD Battalion had lost nine guns and suffered four men wounded and thirteen missing, eight of whom were prisoners of the 9th Parachute Regiment.

The main opposition, however, came from Lanzerath. The fifty-five men of the 2nd Reconnaissance Platoon and four TDs of A Company 820th pulled out by 0940 hours, but Lieutenant Bouck's 394th I&R Platoon and Lieutenant Warren Springer and his three man observation party from C Battery 371st Field Artillery Battalion, fought on from their foxholes on the edge of the woodline, 200 yards north-west of the village. All except one of this group survived until dusk before being overwhelmed and captured. Their last message, timed at 1550 hours, read:

> We are holding our position. Enemy strength 75. They are moving from Lanzerath W to railroad. We are still receiving enemy artillery fire. Ammo OK.[6]

The artillerymen received Silver Stars in 1945 but it was not until 1981 that the exploits of the I&R Platoon were recognised with a Presidential Unit Citation. Lyle Bouck and three of his men got DSCs and the other fourteen Silver or Bronze Stars. This made the Platoon the most decorated in the history of the US Army – probably of any army!

The 5th Parachute Regiment's line of advance was through Afst and Krewinkel to Manderfeld. These villages were held by men of the 18th Cavalry Squadron, commanded by Lieutenant Colonel Damon. Following the German artillery barrage Colonel Mark Devine, commanding the 14th Cavalry Group, ordered his other Squadron, the 32nd under Lieutenant Colonel Paul Ridge, to move forward from Vielsalm and join him in Manderfeld. It began its move at 0930 and by 1200 it had elements in Holzheim and Andler, with the bulk of the Squadron in Manderfeld. By then the 18th Squadron was in disarray – the 1st and 2nd Platoons of C Troop had withdrawn from Afst and Krewinkel respectively and further south A Troop, in Roth and Kobscheid, was surrounded by men of the 18th Volks-Grenadier Division, part of the 5th Panzer Army.

At 1230 hours the Operations Officer of 32nd Squadron, Major Mayes, was ordered to retake Lanzerath using C and E Troops supported by three of the TDs which had withdrawn from the village earlier that morning. Devine was unaware that Bouck and his I&R Platoon were still present there. But Mayes did not get far; after 2km he was stopped in his tracks by Hoffmann's paratroopers firing from the Merlscheid area. Some reports say they used the abandoned TDs of the 820th! By 1420 hours the Mayes force was back in Manderfeld and an hour later Devine ordered C Troop 18th Squadron to withdraw to the general line Holzheim–Herresbach. He then went to see Major General Alan Jones, the commander of the 106th Infantry Division at St Vith (Map 6) to whom he was attached. But Jones's Division was in crisis and he refused to see Devine! At 1800 hours Devine ordered C, E and F Troops of 18th Squadron back to Wereth where they arrived around 2200 hours. The 2nd Platoon of A Troop in Roth, under Captain Stanley Porche, had surrendered at 1600 hours with ninety-two of its ninety-five men being taken prisoner and, at about the same time, sixty-one men of the Platoon at Kobscheid, commanded by Lieutenant Lorenz Herdrick, destroyed their equipment and walked out towards St Vith. In the course of the day 18th Squadron had lost 159 men.

Lieutenant Reppa of A Troop 32nd Squadron, finding himself isolated and without orders, decided to leave Holzheim at about 2100 hours and move to Honsfeld, a decision he would have much cause to regret since it placed his Troop directly in the path of Kampfgruppe Peiper! The rest of 32nd Squadron was at Herresbach, Andler and Heuem. Sadly, Colonel Devine, whose Headquarters was now at Meyerode, was beginning to lose control of his Group and just as the 9th Parachute Regiment had cleared a potential path for Peiper, so the 5th Regiment had cleared one for Hansen. The break-in had been achieved but it was twelve hours late and by no means as planned.

After four and a half years of fighting Peiper knew that the best laid plans usually go wrong. He also knew, like his Corps Commander, that this was not the best laid plan and he would not have been particularly surprised therefore when he heard that the infantry were not progressing as quickly as had been hoped. He could tell from the radio nets of the 12th Volks-Grenadiers that things there were not going at all well and his chances of advancing up Route 421 (now 265) to Losheimergraben in daylight were decreasing with each hour that passed (Map 5). Peiper rejoined his Kampfgruppe round about 1400 hours. His tanks and SPWs and the vehicles of KG Hansen had been crawling forward on the few roads and tracks available to them. From just outside Stadtkyll all the KGs would be on one road, and an appalling one at that, as it twisted through Kronenburg and then on to Hallschag, where Hansen and Knittel would turn off to Ormont while KG Peiper, followed by Sandig, would continue due west to cross the dragon's teeth of the Siegfried Line. But Peiper had more than just one poor road to contend

71

with; on that same road and on all adjacent tracks in the forward area there were the vehicles, horses and equipment of two infantry divisions and a mass of artillery. It was a chaotic situation and one which could not be sorted out quickly. Many stories have been told about Peiper ordering his tanks to push out of the way anything obstructing them, including horses. But it was not like that and actually it took Peiper's armoured Spitze till last light at 1700 hours to reach Route 421. The Scheid bridge had also proved a problem. Much has also been made of the fact that this bridge over the railway between Scheid and Route 421 had been demolished by the Germans during their retreat in September and, not having been repaired, created a major barrier for Peiper's tanks. It is said that he cleverly solved the problem by making a detour. Whilst this is true, it did not really demand much initiative because 50m to the north of the bridge site the railway cutting flattens out and it was a very simple matter for Peiper's tanks to drive over without waiting for pioneers to bridge the gap.

The failure to capture Losheimergraben and open up Peiper's planned route to the west presented I SS Panzer Corps with a serious problem. Priess solved it by ordering Peiper to divert through Lanzerath which the 9th Parachute Regiment had secured by last light. This was not as simple as it sounded though, as an old German minefield, completely forgotten by the German planners, barred the way just to the west of Route 421 on the line of the Our valley. The oversight was discovered when one of the two Panthers of the Spitze hit a mine and was immobilized. Once more there are stories that Peiper ordered Sternebeck, the Spitze commander, to drive straight through the minefield regardless of casualties. Needless to say nothing of the sort happened.[7] The pioneers of Rumpf's 9th SS Panzer Pioneer Company went forward and laboriously cleared the mines. In the darkness this took time and inevitably they missed some. Five hundred metres further on the second Spitze Panther hit another mine and not long afterwards Sternebeck's Type IV was similarly brought to a halt near Merlscheid. Luckily there were no casualties and by 2200 hours the reduced Spitze reached Lanzerath and halted at the north edge of the village where the forest begins. There is another story that the commander of the second Panther deliberately drove his tank on to a mine in order to avoid further participation in the battle. It continues that his Commanding Officer, Poetschke, ordered him into SS Captain Georg Preuss's SPW and demoted him to rifleman as a punishment. This may or may not be true but it is certainly true that not all SS men were keen soldiers!

Peiper himself had waited anxiously at Losheim, closely monitoring this painfully slow progress. It was 2300 hours when he entered Colonel Hoffmann's temporary Headquarters in the Café Scholzen in Lanzerath. By this time Priess had assigned the sector to him and he was unimpressed when told by Hoffmann that there were Americans in the woods to his front and that he believed a dawn attack with artillery support was necessary before further advances could be made. There have been many reports of a furious row between the Luftwaffe Colonel and the arrogant SS Lieutenant Colonel who allegedly demanded the use of one of the parachute battalions. Whatever the truth, Hoffmann's men certainly joined Peiper's KG for the advance from Lanzerath to Honsfeld. There seems little doubt that Corps ordered their subordination to the armoured KG.

KG Hansen had experienced a similar problem with mines and, while Leibstandarte pioneers helped those of the 3rd Parachute Division to clear a route, Rettlinger's 1st SS Jagdpanzer Battalion at the head of the KG waited at Ormont. Fast Group Knittel was concentrated by the road Glaadt–Stadtkyll, and just west of Dahlem (Map 4) Skorzeny's 150th Panzer Brigade waited, hoping to follow Peiper once he got going. KG Sandig was still in its assembly area near Tondorf.

Midnight on Day One of Hitler's great offensive found Peiper, Hansen and Mohnke angry and frustrated – it had been a very long day, certainly twenty hours in Peiper's case, and as far as they were concerned they were still in Germany. Priess and Dietrich were equally furious, for the Volks-Grenadiers attempting to make breaches for 12th SS Panzer Division Hitlerjugend had been even less successful!

On the American side nobody in the higher echelons of command seemed to appreciate the seriousness of the German attack except perhaps the Supreme Allied Commander himself. It was fortuitous that General Omar Bradley, Commander 12th US Army Group, happened to be in Paris conferring with Eisenhower on the 16th December. He was there to discuss the general problem of replacements. When, that afternoon, they received a message from Bradley's Headquarters in Luxembourg City giving word of a German attack in the Ardennes, Ike suggested to Bradley that he should perhaps, as a precaution, move the 7th Armored Division down from the north and the 10th Armored up from the south.[8] Bradley agreed and at 1730 hours Brigadier General Bob Hasbrouck's 7th Armored Division at Heerlen in Holland received a warning order for a move south (Map 1). Two hours later its advance party moved out with a planned assembly area in Vielsalm (Map 3).

Also it seems that fairly early on the 16th Hodges, commanding 1st US Army, telephoned Lieutenant General William Simpson of the 9th US Army to discuss the overall situation. The result was a reinforcement from north to south starting the same day and continuing into the 17th December; this included the 26th Infantry Regiment of the uncommitted 1st Infantry Division, which was alerted as early as 1100 hours, and starting at midnight moved south to Elsenborn. Simpson's further offer of the 30th Infantry Division was to have a profound effect on the forthcoming battle. One puzzling decision however, was Hodges's refusal to call off the 2nd Infantry's attack towards the Roer dams.

Of more immediate importance for Peiper was Hodges's decision to release CCB of the 9th Armored Division from its task of supporting the 2nd Infantry Division and attaching it to the increasingly troubled 106th Infantry Division of Major General Alan Jones. Although the fateful day for this Division would be the 17th, it was already clear that two of its regiments were in great danger of being cut off in the Schnee Eifel by the Volks-Grenadiers of General von Manteuffel's 5th Panzer Army. It was destined to become the biggest disaster of the whole war for the Americans in the European theatre. Brigadier General Bill Hoge, commanding CCB, reported to Jones in St Vith at 1800 hours and was told to recapture Manderfeld early the next morning.[9] At midnight that order was cancelled and Hoge was told to move to Steinebruck for an attack on Winterspelt (Map 1). At this time Hoge had his 27th Armored Infantry Battalion deployed on a security line running from Amel to Büllingen including Honsfeld, his 14th Tank Battalion in Ligneuville and the guns of the 16th Field Artillery Battalion in Schoppen and Moderscheid (Map 6). CCB was therefore lying directly across Peiper's path. Fortunately for him the combat elements would all be gone within four hours.

Just after 0700 hours on the 16th December four mammoth 310mm shells, fired from German railway guns, fell on Malmédy killing sixteen civilians and causing considerable damage. Naturally this puzzled and frightened both the Belgian people and the men of B Company 291st Engineers stationed in the town but nobody understood its significance. It is a good example of one of the most surprising things about the American side on the 16th December; although Eisenhower, Bradley, Hodges and Simpson were reacting to events, and the 99th and 106th Infantry Divisions were engaged in serious combat throughout the day, between the two there was an almost complete void of information. There is not a single entry in the log of Colonel Anderson's 1111th Engineer Combat Group on the 16th December to indicate anything unusual; the engineers of the 291st and 296th Battalions, Brigadier General Timberlake in Ligneuville and even the medical teams of the 47th Field Hospital as far forward as Bütgenbach and Waimes were, apart from a few rumours, seemingly unaware that they were about to be engulfed in a wave of terror and death.

NOTES

1. Exact figures for German losses are impossible to obtain. *The Battle of the Bulge Then and Now* by Pallud pp. 433–6 says 214 pilots were lost, of which 151 were killed or missing; *Die Leibstandarte IV/2* by Tiemann p. 183 says 227 aircraft were lost.

2. Pallud, op. cit., pp. 86–89.
3. War diary of an anonymous German artillery officer.
4. US Army official interview with Major George Clayton 29 Jan 1945.
5. Chronicle 9th Para Regt. This and a 2nd Bn casualty return name 43 men killed or wounded in the battle for Lanzerath.
6. G-3 Log, HQ 99 Div, 16 Dec 44.
7. Sternebeck to author loc. cit., 1 Oct 1985.
8. Merriam, *The Battle of the Ardennes*, p. 111.
9. Reichelt, *Phantom Nine*, pp. 95–6.

CHAPTER IX

Sunday AM 17th December

Breakthrough

The 17th of December 1944 was the most significant day in the whole of Peiper's life. As a result of what happened on that fateful Sunday he would be sentenced to death by hanging, serve nearly eleven years imprisonment as a war criminal and eventually be murdered.

The advance from Lanzerath towards Buchholz did not begin until about 0330 hours (Map 6). This additional four-hour delay was due to the acrimonious discussions with Colonel Hoffmann and the difficult task of assembling and organising the paratroopers who were scattered throughout the houses and barns of the village and in most cases asleep. Few if any of them had ever worked with tanks before and the last thing they expected that night was to be riding into the unknown on a King Tiger. The conditions were totally inappropriate for an armoured force since the only route was a narrow, pot-holed road which twisted its way through thick pine forest. Visibility on this pitch-black night was further reduced by freezing fog. The plan therefore was for the tanks and SPWs to be led at walking pace by men of the 9th Parachute Regiment with more paratroopers moving through the edges of the forest as flank protection. The remainder of Colonel Hoffmann's Regiment, mainly his 2nd Battalion, would ride on the tanks, including the King Tigers, with basically a platoon to a tank. Ironically the Shermans and half-tracks of CCB, 9th Armored Division, the only formation which could have given Peiper a real problem that day, moved away at almost exactly the same time towards St Vith.

To everyone's great relief and Hoffmann's embarrassment there were no Americans in the woods. In fact the only Americans to be overcome were two TDs of A Company 801st TD Battalion which the unit After

Action Report claims were positioned near Buchholz, and two platoons, about sixty men, of Major Moore's K Company who were certainly in the area of the hamlet's gasthaus and railway station and a nearby farm. The remainder of Moore's 3rd Battalion was reinforcing the 1st Battalion at Losheimergraben and another Regiment of the Division away to the north. It is not clear what happened to the TDs but if they were ever there at all, which is doubtful, they did not open fire. Unfortunately the men of K Company were asleep and while the Spitze continued towards Honsfeld, Preuss's 10th SS Panzer-Grenadier Company quickly mopped them up without trouble. A radio operator did manage to report what was happening and that German tanks were passing his position.

The KG's next objective was Honsfeld, which contained a large number of American troops and which was officially defended by two reconnaissance platoons and five more TDs of A Company 801st. Two guns were deployed to the south of Honsfeld on the Holzheim road, two more just east of the village on the Buchholz road and one on the edge of the village itself facing east. One reconnaissance platoon of the 801st was in Holzheim and another somewhere to the west. It will be recalled that Honsfeld was a rest centre for the 394th Infantry. After the fighting on the previous day, the 125 men in the centre were formed into some sort of Defence Company but if they did prepare any defensive positions, which is open to doubt, they were certainly not occupying them in any strength that night. It will also be remembered that A Troop 32nd Cavalry Squadron had decided to move to Honsfeld from Holzheim starting at about 2100 hours on the 16th. This decision was entirely that of its commander, Lieutenant Bob Reppa. On arrival in Honsfeld the Troop did not take up tactical positions. Another TD unit had arrived in Honsfeld at about 0400 hours. This was B Company, commanded by Captain John Kennedy, and the 1st Reconnaissance Platoon of the 612th TD Battalion. They had been attached to the 99th Infantry from the 23rd Infantry Regiment and had received orders to move to Honsfeld and 'take up a position of readiness'. Since it was dark and impossible to site the guns the men were told to rest and the guns were not even unlimbered. One of the gunners, W. T. Hawkins, wrote in 1989:

> We were instructed for each platoon to take over a house and for everyone to go to sleep with the exception of leaving a guard posted on the front door and also on the back door which we did. The 1st Platoon took over a house on the right of the road and the 2nd Platoon did the same on the left almost directly across from each other. The house our Platoon was in was a two storey with an attic.[1]

Peiper's Spitze entered Honsfeld at about 0515 hours. The TDs on the east side of the village were unmanned and two captains and a lieutenant were captured in the first house. In fact the leading panzers were able to drive straight through Honsfeld without opposition. W. T. Hawkins continued his description of events in Honsfeld as follows:

> I was sleeping in the attic with three or four other buddies when I was awakened about daylight by one of our other men and told to get up as the Germans had us completely surrounded. I kicked the man down the stairs and told him not to bother us anymore as I thought that he was pulling a prank on us. Immediately one of our sergeants came up the stairs two at a time and informed us that this was no prank but the real thing, at which we all jumped up and began looking out of the various windows and saw that German soldiers were everywhere we looked.

Lieutenant Bob Reppa of A Troop 32nd Cavalry told a similar story of his capture by German paratroopers.[2]

It was only later, after daylight, that the Americans in the houses and farms on the edge of Honsfeld began to offer some resistance. Sporadic fighting lasted for the rest of the morning, mainly involving the paratroopers on the Tigers bringing up the rear of Peiper's column. They suffered thirteen killed and thirty-four wounded before the last Americans surrendered.[3] It also seems that two Panthers of SS Lieutenant Christ's 2nd SS Panzer Company were hit during this period. It is just possible that they were engaged from the area of Hünningen but this appears unlikely as the range would have been at least 1000m. One TD of the 1st Platoon A Company 801st, sited near Hünningen (Map 5) and commanded by the Company Commander himself, claimed to have knocked out four Type IV German tanks and an SPW during the morning before it in turn was knocked out, but there is no mention of this on the German side. It seems more likely that the Panthers were lost to bazookas, or perhaps to fire from two guns of the 612th TD Company which were rushed into action once they could see. One, commanded by Sergeant Fayne Haynes, claimed to have hit three enemy vehicles.[4]

Honsfeld was a disaster for the Americans. Peiper claimed to have captured fifteen TDs and about fifty reconnaissance vehicles.[5] 9th Regiment claimed 150 prisoners. A Troop 32nd Cavalry Squadron lost all its vehicles and equipment and only one officer and forty-three men escaped. B Company 612th TD Battalion lost nine guns and had two of its platoon commanders and 108 men taken prisoner; the 1st Reconnaissance Platoon 612th lost one officer and eighteen men; A Company 801st TD Battalion lost eight guns and most of its vehicles and had twenty-one men taken prisoner; both reconnaissance platoons of the 801st were lost; and as late as 30th January 1945 the 394th Infantry had still heard nothing of their 125 men at the rest centre, so it can be assumed that most of them became prisoners as well. It was later alleged that, in three separate incidents, fifteen US prisoners of war and three Belgians were shot by

Germans in the village.[6] Whatever may have happened to the rear elements of Peiper's column, there was no opposition or delay caused to the forward fighting groups. Peiper was anxious to get on to Büllingen where he had been briefed there was a fuel dump. He was not worried about a possible clash with the advance elements of 12th SS Panzer Division Hitlerjugend, because he knew from the Divisional command net that their advance was completely bogged down in the woods east of Krinkelt and Rocherath.

The thick forest south of Honsfeld was now left behind and, leaving Hoffmann's paratroopers and his own King Tigers to clear up, Peiper ordered Sternebeck's Spitze and Preuss's Spitze Company Group to get on as quickly as possible. Only one parachute company stayed with Peiper after Honsfeld,[7] whether by permission or not is unclear, and certainly a number of other paratroopers continued to move with the Kings Tigers after this point.

It was shortly after 0600 hours when the Spitze left Honsfeld for Büllingen (Map 8). Within a few minutes eight 2½-ton American trucks ran straight into it and were captured; they had been on their way to Honsfeld. It will be recalled that Büllingen was a major support centre for both the 2nd and 99th Infantry Divisions and that an Engineer Combat Battalion, the 254th, was in bivouac just outside the town. At midnight on the 16th it was released by V Corps to the 99th Infantry Division and ordered to form a defensive line to the south and east of the town. The CO was told that all roads leading into the town were blocked with TDs and light tanks and he was to protect these blocks. In fact there were no TDs or tanks in position around Büllingen! The only other combat troops in the vicinity were a reconnaissance platoon of the 644th TD Battalion in the town and four guns of 3rd Platoon, C Company 801st TD Battalion near Bütgenbach in a mobile reserve role.

The 254th Engineers had to deploy in a hurry. A Company found a position just to the east of town covering the N-32 Losheimergraben road at 0400 hours. C Company was to the south-west on the Heppenbach road by about 0500 and B Company took up a position about 2km out on the Honsfeld road at about the same time. They did not have to wait long for action as the panzer Spitze hit B Company around 0630 hours. What happened next remains unclear. In 1985, when retracing his steps of 1944, Sternebeck remembered it as only a minor incident with no tanks being lost or damaged. He stated that Peiper was angry at the small delay and told him in no uncertain terms to get on.[8] The American engineer version claims that B Company beat off three separate attacks, killed forty to fifty Germans, knocked out one tank and damaged two more. It goes on to say that because of flanking movements by the Germans the whole Battalion was instructed to fight a delaying action as it fell back on Bütgenbach. It is clear that while A

Company withdrew north towards Wirtzfeld, the remnants of B Company pulled back to the Bütgenbach road where C Company had already taken up a position. Sternebeck did admit to losing a Type IV tank on the outskirts of Büllingen. The following account by a Sergeant Grant Yager, written in 1986, describes how it happened:

I was a sergeant in the service battery of the 924th Field Artillery Battalion. . . . I was a section chief in our ammunition train and our group was staying in a house just south of the main part of the town on the road to Honsfeld . . . before seven in the morning of December 17th we were ordered to set up a road block south of the town . . . Sergeant Zoller gave myself and Privates Romaker and Maldonado a bazooka and a few hand grenades and sent us on our way. The three of us proceeded south half a mile or so . . . we were about a hundred feet from the edge of the roadway and had a good view. We had been there a minute or so deciding what to do when we heard heavy equipment coming up the road from Honsfeld. As our equipment had been on the road all night we gave it little thought until I looked up and saw a tank with a cross painted on the front. It was German. The tank was buttoned up and the machine gun firing and the turret was turning looking for targets. . . . I made ready the bazooka and had Romaker load and arm it. As the first tank passed in front of us I was ready to fire but found the sights broken and the tank went on by. Then I made up my mind that I could fire without sights by looking alongside the barrel. This I did and fired and hit the second tank as it was directly in front of us. Apparently my shot hit the tank in the track as it turned part way around and stopped.

He then goes on to say he fired at the crew with his carbine as they bailed out but he and his comrades were soon forced to surrender to infantrymen from a German half-track.

At the southern entrance to Büllingen the Honsfeld road splits, with one fork leading into the main part of the town while the right fork runs slightly north-east and then climbs out of the easterly part of Büllingen in the direction of Wirtzfeld and Rocherath. In 1986, when describing the battle of Büllingen, Sternebeck[9] told how, despite it now being daylight, he had mistakenly taken the right hand fork and so ended up on the northern road. He put this down to the general confusion caused by enemy fire and the difficulty of finding your way through a town in a tank! Preuss's Spitze Company Group however, had moved into the main part of the town and in equally confused fighting had received a number of casualties, including two platoon commanders, Sergeant-Majors Otto and Knobloch,[10] both shot in the head. Despite these losses Büllingen was soon overrun and many Americans made prisoner. Once again they had been surprised; the men of the 2nd Infantry Division's

Quartermaster Company were lining up for breakfast when the Germans appeared. Sergeant Yager's Battery had fifty-eight men captured out of sixty-nine, including Captain James Cobb the Battery Commander; and all members of the Reconnaissance Platoon of the 644th TD Battalion in Büllingen that day became prisoners.

Preuss's mopping-up operation included the airstrips but all except one of the 99th Division's pilots managed to take off before the Germans arrived. They were all later awarded the Distinguished Flying Cross. In the case of the 2nd Division's planes the reverse was the case and two aircraft of the 16th Field Artillery Battalion of CCB 9th Armored Division were also lost. In the meantime Sternebeck had continued out on the Wirtzfeld road where, after about a kilometre, he lost yet another Type IV tank to TD fire.[11] He had run into the guns of the 1st Platoon, C Company 644th TD Battalion positioned on the southern outskirts of the village. The Platoon claimed four German tanks and an SPW in its After Action Report. The loss of the Type IV obviously convinced Sternebeck that he was on the wrong road and he turned back with his now much depleted Spitze and retraced his steps into Büllingen. He was reduced to only two Type IV tanks and two 9th SS Pioneer Company SPWs.

It is quite possible that the claims made by the 254th Engineers in the battle of Büllingen are not as exaggerated as they first appear and that confused fighting led to a confused After Action Report. The Germans have described how the Americans were pulling back at exactly the same time as they were advancing into the town and that the two sides were therefore intermingled. Since the 254th suffered the highest number of battle casualties of any American unit there, it is likely that its soldiers were those who inflicted most of the damage on the Germans. The Battalion suffered four killed, twenty-eight wounded and fifty-five missing, mainly from B Company. For his unit's actions that day the CO was rewarded by Major General Lauer, initially with the General's own lunch back in Bütgenbach, and later with the Bronze Star.

The US fuel dump in Büllingen was located in the market square in the south-west corner of the town and it was there that some of Peiper's tanks and SPWs were able to refuel.[12] Intermittent artillery fire fell on Büllingen after the American withdrawal but this did not hold up the Germans and by 0900 hours Peiper's men were ready to resume the advance. The survivors of the 254th Engineer Combat Battalion had taken up a defensive position on the Bütgenbach road near a manor house known to the Americans as 'Dom' Bütgenbach. There they were joined by stragglers from other units and HQ personnel of the 99th Division. A platoon of four TDs from C Company 801st TD Battalion is also said to have been in the area.

Peiper's chosen route out of Büllingen surprised and relieved the defenders of Dom Bütgenbach. Instead of advancing on the main road in their direction, the Spitze Company moved off south-west towards Amel. It is worth noting that had Peiper chosen, or been ordered, to advance to Bütgenbach he would have put at risk the 99th and 2nd American Infantry Divisions and almost certainly caused a crisis of confidence which would have led to their retreat. This in turn would have cleared the way for the 12th SS Panzer Division Hitlerjugend and prevented the Americans creating the strong position running from Bütgenbach through Malmédy to Stavelot which became known as the 'North Shoulder' and which led eventually to the stabilisation of the situation (Map 7). Peiper, however, knew nothing of the overall situation at 0900 hours on the 17th and he had his firm orders to strike hard to the west. It would seem that I SS Panzer Corps did not appreciate the possibilities sufficiently well to give the necessary orders. This supposition must therefore remain one of the interesting 'ifs' of history.

Sternebeck was no longer leading Peiper's column. He was still trying to find his way back through Büllingen and once more ended up on the wrong road, this time the main one to Dom Bütgenbach. Although the TDs of the 801st claimed three German tanks that morning, Sternebeck again had a different story.[13] He remembered no anti-tank fire but said that when he was just short of Dom Bütgenbach an American doctor came forward and offered to surrender his medical unit at that location. At that moment Sternebeck was recalled on the radio and turned south to fall in behind the Spitze Company. It seems an unlikely story but there is no evidence of any German casualties at that time in that area and there was a medical unit of the 47th Field Hospital in Dom Bütgenbach.

By the time Peiper's column moved off from Büllingen the weather had improved enough for flying and in response to urgent requests for help by the 99th Division, thirty-nine P-47 aircraft flew sorties in the Büllingen area between 0900 and 1100 hours. The aircraft were from the US 389th, 390th and 391st Squadrons of the 366th Group based at Asch in Belgium.[14] They were all part of the IXth Tactical Air Command, commanded by the dynamic and brilliant Major General 'Pete' Quesada who had probably done more than any other Allied officer to originate and refine the techniques of air to ground co-operation and put them into practice. His headquarters at this time was only 30km away in Verviers and he himself was living in the Villa des Fleurs in Spa, close to General Hodges whose 1st Army he was supporting. The first sortie by eleven Thunderbolts reported that it 'bombed and strafed a convoy' between 0900 and 1000 hours. This was obviously the Kampfgruppe and Peiper said after the war that he lost one Tiger. One Thunderbolt was shot down and one damaged. The second strike by sixteen P-47s did no damage and was 'jumped' by German ME 109s, neither side suffering any casualties. An hour later twelve more aircraft said they bombed and strafed in the Büllingen area before being attacked by an equal number of ME 109s, resulting in the loss of a further P-47. Overall these air strikes seem to have had little effect on the KG.

When it reached Point 616 (Map 8), 2km south-west of Büllingen, Peiper's Spitze Company Group proceeded straight across the Amel road and took the narrow dirt track which led to Moderscheid. Peiper was back on his assigned Route D.

It was at about this time that an incident happened which began the connection between Peiper and a group of American combat engineers who were to frustrate him in his drive for the Meuse and lead, indirectly, to his prosecution as a war criminal.

On the morning of 17th December Lieutenant Frank Rhea, a West Point officer commanding 3rd Platoon, B Company 291st Engineer Combat Battalion stationed in Malmédy, had some men working on road maintenance between Waimes and Bütgenbach (Map 6). He had no idea that a major German offensive had started but on his way to visit his men early that morning he was puzzled by the heavy volume of US traffic moving west. After visiting his work detail he decided to go on to Bütgenbach to the 99th Division Headquarters and find out what was happening. He could hardly believe it when a Military Policeman told him German tanks had broken through just east of Bütgenbach; he wasted no time in reporting back to his company commander, Captain John Conlin, in Malmédy. This alarming news was immediately passed on to Conlin's CO, Lieutenant Colonel David Pergrin. It was at about the same time that Pergrin's superior, Colonel Wallis Anderson, commanding the 1111th Engineer Combat Group, heard from his Liaison Officer at V Corps that German tanks had been in the vicinity of his 629th Engineer Light Equipment Company at Bütgenbach earlier that morning but had been repelled. Although this was inaccurate information Anderson naturally decided to take action. He instructed Pergrin to go to Malmédy, assume command of all 1111th engineer units there and take defensive measures. Rather belatedly at 1325 hours he ordered the Light Equipment Company to withdraw to Malmédy.

Lieutenant Colonel Dave Pergrin, aged 27, was a civil engineer by profession and a keen soldier by inclination. After graduating from Penn State College in 1940 he had joined the military and by June 1943 was a major and the Executive Officer of the 291st Engineer Battalion at Camp Swift, Texas. He was appointed Commanding Officer in September 1943 and as such had brought his battalion through England and Normandy to the Ardennes. He had worked hard to make his battalion as highly trained as any in the Corps of Engineers.

On his drive to Malmédy, Pergrin met an armoured column of the

7th Armored Division moving through Trois Ponts and another passing through Malmédy. They were both heading south to help the 106th Division at St Vith. This, coupled with the report of German tanks near Bütgenbach, made him uneasy. There was little he could do, though, except recall his A Company which was out on a limb, take defensive measures on the approaches into Malmédy and order a jeep reconnaissance out on the road towards Waimes. These proved wise precautions.

The next part of Peiper's route, from Point 616 to Moderscheid and then on to Schoppen and Ondenval, was the only section where his tanks and some other tracked vehicles attempted to move cross-country. They soon regretted it as vehicle after vehicle sank into the soft ground and even tanks had to be towed out of trouble. As a result of this and the fighting in Büllingen, Peiper's column was soon in a state of confusion with individual vehicles, platoons and even companies muddled up. An indication of the problem is that between Büllingen and Thirimont the KG averaged only 7km per hour. It was during this part of the advance that four jeeps of the Reconnaissance Company of the 32nd Armored Regiment, part of the 3rd Armoured Division, containing two officers and nine men, ran into the KG and were captured. They were acting as Military Government Police and their job was to patrol the roads and generally police the area immediately behind the forward battle zone. One of the jeeps was ordered to lead the column while the others fell in further back. Owing to the difficulties of the terrain, however, the transmission on the lead jeep soon failed and the two officers and the senior NCO were made to ride on one of the lead tanks.[15] Further on down the route another American jeep was captured containing either a signals lineman or perhaps a lieutenant colonel. Peiper himself said after the war that the man was a lieutenant colonel and that he got into the jeep to interrogate him.[16] He learned two things – one, that there was an American Headquarters of considerable importance in Ligneuville and two, that the Americans had no idea how far his Kampfgruppe had penetrated. Peiper's own Panther had broken down in Büllingen and so from that point on he switched to Diefenthal's command SPW.

The 291st Engineer jeep patrol towards Waimes had spotted Peiper's column just short of Thirimont at around midday. The news that the Germans had penetrated this far and not been held short of Bütgenbach came as a considerable shock to Pergrin. Peiper on the other hand must have been in excellent spirits. His order of march was disorganised and he was twenty-four hours behind his planned schedule but none of this mattered. He had made his breakthrough. He could sort the column out later and the only thing that mattered at noon on the 17th was to keep going. He would have been even more elated if he had known that, apart from Pergrin's few engineers in Malmédy, there was not one single American combat unit deployed to oppose him.

On Peiper's southern flank Max Hansen's Kampfgruppe had been having a rather easier time of it. During the night the minefield east of Krewinkel had been successfully breached and shortly after first light the Kampfgruppe moved off with the twenty-one Jagdpanzer IVs of SS Captain Karl Rettlinger, carrying the 1st SS Panzer-Grenadier Battalion, in the lead.[17] SS Captain Unterkofler's 2nd SS Battalion followed and then came the 3rd SS Panzer-Grenadier Battalion of SS Captain Böttcher together with Rettlinger's eleven towed 75mm anti-tank guns.

Hansen's planned route was Krewinkel, Manderfeld, Herresbach and on to Werth (Map 6). Barring his way was B Troop of the 32nd Cavalry Squadron near Andler, commanded by Captain Lindsey, C and E Troops at Herresbach and the seventeen Stuart tanks of F Troop, under Captain Horace Bair, at Heuem. C, E and F Troops of the 18th Cavalry Squadron were concentrated at Wereth, A Troop having been wiped out by Peiper at Honsfeld and B Troop detached to the 106th Division. These forces, although lightly armed, should have been able to cause considerable delay to Hansen. At 0700 hours B Troop 32nd at Andler reported being attacked by a company of infantry and one assault gun. At 1100 hours Captain Lindsey decided to withdraw, first to Schonberg, then to Heuem, where he claimed to have defended his position until 1300 hours, and finally, taking the seventeen Stuarts with him, to a position north-east of St Vith. It is not at all clear who, if anyone, attacked him at Heuem but it was certainly not Hansen's men. In the meantime C and E Troops 32nd Cavalry had vacated Herresbach and moved to join Colonel Devine's Headquarters at Meyerode, where they arrived about midday; the remains of the 18th Squadron had preceded them en route to Born where they arrived at 1130 hours. None of these troops had fired a shot. The way was therefore clear for Hansen; but, faced with thick forest and extremely broken and hilly country between Honsfeld and Andler and only one reasonable road through it, Hansen split his force. The 1st SS Panzer-Grenadiers and the Jagdpanzers moved via Andler to Herresbach which they reached at noon.[18] The 2nd SS Panzer-Grenadier Battalion took the route Holzheim–Honsfeld to Heppenbach, which it also reached at midday. The 3rd SS Panzer-Grenadier Battalion turned north in Manderfeld and took the circuitous route through Lanzerath to Honsfeld and so on west. There is in fact a German report which says that in taking this route the Battalion group was lost. They were certainly a considerable distance behind their comrades. Hansen's leading elements were however, only a few kilometres behind Peiper at midday on the 17th and only 5km to his south.

Rudolf Sandig and his Kampfgruppe spent the whole of the 17th in his assembly area in Germany. His route forward was completely blocked by KG Hansen, Fast Group Knittel, Skorzeny's 150th Panzer Brigade and the artillery and other essential elements of I SS Panzer Corps. Knittel had been able to move close behind Hansen's 2nd Battalion on the route Manderfeld, Holzheim, Honsfeld and Heppenbach, because the 3rd SS Panzer-Grenadier Group had conveniently moved out of his way in Manderfeld.

Otto Skorzeny had been unable to launch any of his Kampfgruppes.[19] KG 'X', which was trying to follow Peiper, was held up just to the west of Losheim and its commander SS Lieutenant Colonel Hardieck had been killed when his vehicle had run on to a mine in the vicinity of Merlscheid. Nevertheless Skorzeny decided to wait another twenty-four hours before calling off 'Operation Greif'. On the other hand some of his four-man commando teams, using US jeeps and uniforms, had successfully penetrated American lines and by last light on the 16th one group had even reached Huy on the Meuse. After the war Skorzeny said forty-four of his men got through successfully. Whatever the exact number, there is no doubt that they achieved some success in that they made the Americans very jittery and security conscious. The story of their exploits has been told many times. Eighteen of these commandos were executed by the Americans for contravening the rules of war by wearing enemy uniforms.

NOTES

1. Letter to author dated 23 Mar 1989.
2. MacDonald, *A Time for Trumpets*, pp. 202–3.
3. Chronicle 9th Para Regt.
4. Haynes at 1994 Unit Reunion in USA.
5. ETHINT 10.
6. US Prosecution at Dachau Trial 1946.
7. Chronicle 9th Para Regt.
8. Sternebeck to author loc. cit., 1 Oct 1985.
9. Ibid.
10. Tiemann, *Die Leibstandarte IV/2*, p. 58.
11. Sternebeck to author loc. cit., 1 Oct 1985.
12. Letter from Arndt Fischer to author dated 29 May 1985.
13. Sternebeck to author loc. cit., 1 Oct 1985.
14. Details of all strikes against Peiper's column on 18 December 1944 by US aircraft are to be found in the Office of Air Force History at Bolling Air Force Base – specifically OPSUMs 79 Pt IV, 85 Pts I–IV, 134 Pt IV, 192 Pts II–IV, 193 Pts II–IV and OPSUM 200 Pt I.
15. Letter from S/Sgt Henry Zach, one of those captured, to John Bauserman dated 19 Jan 1988.
16. Tiemann op. cit., p. 63.
17. Tiemann and LAH veterans to author loc. cit., 2 Oct 1985.
18. Ibid.
19. Skorzeny, *Skorzeny's Special Missions*.

CHAPTER X

Sunday Afternoon 17th December

Prelude to Tragedy

Although there were no American combat units deployed to meet Peiper on the morning of 17th December, Headquarters 1st Army took further precautionary actions at about 1100 hours. Unfortunately General Hodges had few available troops on which to call. The 7th Armored Division was already moving south from Holland to help the 106th Infantry. It was using two routes (Map 6), with Combat Commands A and B moving through Stavelot, Trois Ponts and Vielsalm and Combat Command R and the artillery through Malmédy and Ligneuville. The only uncommitted troops in 1st Army at this stage were nicknamed 'The Praetorian Guard'. They were the 99th Infantry Battalion (Separate), the 526th Armored Infantry Battalion, less C Company which was guarding General Bradley's Tactical Headquarters in Luxembourg City and A Company 825th TD Battalion, all based to the west of Spa. These three units were alerted between 1100 and 1300 hours, just about the same time that CCB 7th Armored was arriving in Vielsalm. Having been offered a full division of infantry by General Simpson the previous day, Hodges realised he now needed it badly. He therefore asked for the 30th Infantry to move to the area Stavelot–Malmédy as soon as possible.

In Malmédy there had been something of a panic that morning, with the evacuation, perhaps most aptly described as a 'bugout', of all the administrative units, including the 500-strong Reinforcement Depot which had been ordered back to Liège, leaving only Pergrin and his B Company with the 962nd Engineer Maintenance Company. At about midday, one of the serials in the 7th Armored Division column, B Battery of the 285th Field Artillery Observation Battalion, arrived outside Pergrin's Tactical Headquarters in Malmédy, situated in the Renz house on the St Vith road. In the leading jeep were two officers who told Pergrin they were heading south behind CCR of the 7th Armored. Pergrin warned them that German armour had been seen just to the east of their proposed route and advised them to divert via Stavelot and Trois Ponts to Vielsalm. They decided to stick with their assigned route and moved off around 1230 hours on the N-23 in the direction of Ligneuville, where Brigadier General Timberlake had just ordered the

Headquarters of his 49th Anti-Aircraft Brigade to evacuate to the west. He stayed, with two of his officers and three enlisted men, in the Hôtel du Moulin to enjoy 'a well prepared lunch'.

Shortly after B Battery of the 285th left Malmédy, the leading serial of the 7th Armored's artillery, the 440th Armored Field Artillery Battalion, came through and, after refusing Pergrin's request that they should stay and help him defend Malmédy, took his advice about the dangers of the N-23 and headed off towards Stavelot. Coming the other way from Bütgenbach, the 3rd Platoon of the 47th Field Hospital was less than an hour ahead of Peiper's Spitze when they passed through the Baugnez crossroads (Map 9) on their way to Malmédy. The 1st Platoon had an even narrower escape and only avoided the Germans by returning to their base in Waimes.[1]

In 1944 the road going to the west out of Thirimont split, with the main, right-hand fork running north towards Waimes and Malmédy and the left one going more or less due west to join the main N-23 Malmédy–St Vith road 2km north of Ligneuville. Today the right-hand fork is the main road and the left-hand one little more than a lane, deteriorating into an unsurfaced track. Now, as then, the lane to the west is the direct and shortest way to Ligneuville but it descends sharply into a valley through which runs a small stream. The track therefore has to cross a culvert before climbing steeply to the main road. There is still no proper bridge.

Peiper knew there was some sort of American headquarters in Ligneuville[2] and he was keen to capture it in order to obtain information on enemy dispositions. As the Spitze Company Group left Thirimont it therefore took the shortest possible route. Its commander, Georg Preuss, had become separated during the battle in Büllingen and had not yet caught up. The acting commander soon had reason to regret the decision to take the short route as his leading SPWs and Type IV tanks became hopelessly bogged in the marshy stream at the bottom of the valley. There was now only one way to Ligneuville and that was to go north to the N-32 Malmédy–Waimes road, turn left to the small hamlet of Baugnez and then south on the N-23. Peiper gave immediate orders for Sternebeck's depleted Spitze, which was following Preuss's Group, to take this route. In doing so he sealed the fate of B Battery 285th Field Artillery Observation Battalion and ensured that his own name would be remembered with ignominy, particularly in America.

What happened next has been told in a host of books written by American, German, British, Belgian and French authors. Few versions have been accurate since no one today knows exactly what happened – not even those who were there, be they American or German. The secret lies with the dead.

NOTES

1. Graves, *Front Line Surgeons*.
2. ETHINT 10.

CHAPTER XI

Sunday Afternoon 17th December

The 'Malmédy Massacre'[1]

Although no one will ever know for sure what happened at the Baugnez crossroads on the afternoon of 17th December 1944, it is possible to establish certain facts. On 16th December 1944, the day Hitler's Ardennes offensive started, Captain Leon Scarbrough, the officer commanding B Battery 285th Field Artillery Observation Battalion, was told that his Battery would be released from VII US Corps at 0600 hours the following day and that he was to report to Headquarters VIII US Corps Artillery at St Vith for duty. Before leaving Schevenhutte, Germany, where the Battery had been located since 2nd December, he instructed Lieutenant Ksidzek, his Executive Officer, to bring the Battery down to the VIII Corps area on the 17th. Scarbrough took five members of the Battery with him. A route-marking vehicle, commanded by Lieutenant Gier, was to precede the Battery by about two hours with a further five men. On reaching Headquarters VIII Corps Artillery at 0900 hours on the 17th, Scarbrough was told to report to the Headquarters of the 4th Division Artillery in Luxembourg; he was first to check in with the 16th Field Artillery Observation Battalion where he would receive survey data and other information relating to the new area. He left instructions with the Battalion to redirect his Battery on to Luxembourg.

B Battery left Schevenhutte at 0800 hours on 17th December. The convoy of thirty vehicles, jeeps, weapons carriers and 2½-ton trucks, was divided into two serials – the first led by Lieutenant Virgil Lary and the second by Lieutenant Perry Reardon. For reasons unknown the Battalion Executive Officer, Captain Roger Mills, accompanied the Battery and travelled in Lary's jeep. It is also a mystery why the Battery Executive Officer, Lieutenant Ksidzek, did not lead the Battery as instructed by Scarbrough but travelled in one of the four vehicles at the rear of the column. The fact that he left the Battery on 20th December suffering from 'battle neurosis' may provide some explanation.

The initial part of B Battery's route lay through Raeren in Germany and then through Eynatten and Eupen in Belgium. Just to the north of Malmédy it passed through the Baraque Michel, the designated drop zone for von der Heydte's parachute force. It is sadly ironic that had his men landed there as planned B Battery would have been forced to take a different route and the 'Malmédy Massacre' would never have occurred! The Battery reached Malmédy at about 1215 hours. Various serials of Combat Command 'R' of the 7th Armored Division and the Battery route markers vehicle had already passed through on their way to St Vith.

As already mentioned, the Tactical Headquarters of the 291st Engineer Combat Battalion, commanded by Lieutenant Colonel Dave Pergrin, was located in a house at the east end of Malmédy on the main N-23 St Vith road. When Captain Mills's and Lieutenant Lary's jeep reached this point Pergrin stopped it and warned both officers that one of his patrols had spotted a German armoured column only a few miles away to the south-east. He advised them to head west through Stavelot to Trois Ponts and then to turn south to St Vith via Vielsalm. After a short discussion, and knowing they had at least two Battery route markers on their assigned route, they decided to proceed as planned. Four vehicles of the column did not follow immediately. Owing to the sickness of a corporal who appeared to have food poisoning, Lieutenant Ksidzek in the Battery Commander's car, the Battery Maintenance truck, the Wire truck and the route markers pick-up truck diverted to the 44th Evacuation Hospital in the town to obtain medical treatment. These four vehicles carried a total of twenty-seven men.

Preceding the B Battery convoy on the N-23 was an ambulance of the 575th Ambulance Company. It was returning to its base in Waimes after leaving the 44th Evacuation Hospital in Malmédy. Following the convoy were four more ambulances – three from the 575th Medical Company at Waimes and one from the 546th Company.

The junction of the N-23 and N-32, 4km to the southeast of Malmédy, is known to the Belgians as the Baugnez crossroads. In 1944 the Americans called it Five Points since it is in fact the intersection of five roads. At 1245 hours on 17th December T/5 John O'Connell of B Battery was standing at the crossroads acting as a route marker; with him was a Military Policeman named Pfc Homer Ford, positioned there to direct serials of the 7th Armoured Division. The only buildings of any significance in the region of the Baugnez crossroads in December 1944 are shown on Map 20.

It was approximately 1245 hours when the leading jeep of B Battery was waved through 'Five Points' on to the N-23 Ligneuville–St Vith road by Ford and O'Connell. The visibility was good, the temperature above zero and there was no snow on the ground except for a light covering in protected areas which never saw the sun.

After the Battery vehicles had passed the crossroads and were heading south on the N-23, they suddenly came under fire from the east. The head of the convoy was at this stage in the area of House 10 and the rear B Battery vehicle near the Café Bodarwé, with the ambulances behind it. This initial firing came from the two Type IV tanks of Sternebeck's Spitze as it proceeded north up to the N-32 at Bagatelle.[2]

They saw the American column some 800m to their west and naturally opened fire with their main tank guns, about five or six rounds each. After they moved on there was further firing at the head of the American convoy by tanks of the 7th SS Panzer Company[3] on the Thirimont–Bagatelle road and possibly even panzer-grenadier mortars from the Thirimont area.

It is uncertain how many B Battery vehicles were destroyed by the German tank fire – probably not more than half a dozen. Survivors described how some were hit and set on fire whilst others crashed into each other or drove into the ditches at the side of the N-23. All serviceable vehicles were commandeered by the Germans and driven away soon after the incident.

Peiper, who was following closely behind the Spitze, boarded the Panther of his armoured commander, Werner Poetschke, and ordered the firing to cease. As he said after the war, 'I was annoyed at having these beautiful trucks which we needed so badly all shot up!'[4] Sternebeck, in the lead tank, then drove as fast as he could to the N-32, turned left and left again at the crossroads. There is no truth in the story that he attacked the American column by moving across the fields.[5] The ground between the Thirimont road and the N-23 is marshy and it would have taken much longer to have gone that way.

Sternebeck then moved down the N-23, pushing American vehicles out of the way as he did so and halted about 800m to the south near House 10. As he drove down the road he fired his tank machine guns at the ditches in which the Americans had taken cover to encourage them to surrender. Since they had no heavy weapons with which to defend themselves they soon gave themselves up. In the meantime Peiper sent a message to Mohnke at Divisional Headquarters advising him of his position and saying that the Americans were withdrawing south from Malmédy. This was the situation as he saw it. He then transferred to Diefenthal's command SPW[6] and drove through the crossroads to catch up with the Spitze which he ordered on to Ligneuville. It was to be followed by the Panther of Poetschke's Adjutant, SS Lieutenant Arndt Fischer, and then Peiper himself and the SPWs of the next SS Panzer-Grenadier company, the 11th. The time was about 1330 hours.

While Peiper and the Spitze drove on to Ligneuville, the survivors of B Battery, over ninety men, and others who had been caught up in this affair, such as the eleven men of the 32nd Armored Reconnaissance

Company, were assembled by the Germans in a field just to the south of the Bodarwé Café. Whilst this was happening three trucks from B Company 86th Engineer Battalion (HP) came up the hill from Malmédy and, after halting behind the four ambulances at the rear of B Battery, were fired on by the Germans. Five of the men in these trucks managed to get away despite the fact that one of them was wounded but the sixth, Pfc John Clymire, was captured. The last four vehicles of B Battery under the command of Lieutenant Ksidzek, having dropped off the sick man at the 44th Evacuation Hospital, also approached Baugnez at this time but they soon realised they were running into the enemy and managed to turn around and get back to Malmédy without loss.

By about 1400 hours 113 Americans had been assembled in the field south of the Café Bodarwé at the Baugnez crossroads. At about 1415 hours German soldiers of Kampfgruppe Peiper, for reasons unknown, opened fire on them. After this firing ceased German soldiers entered the field and shot any surviving Americans they could find. This episode lasted no more than fifteen minutes and was completed by about 1430 hours. Whilst it took place vehicles of the Kampfgruppe continued to drive south on the N-23. It was at this time that Dave Pergrin, aware that there had been firing in the direction of Baugnez, decided to make a reconnaissance in that direction.

Kampfgruppe Peiper consisted of some 800 vehicles of which at least 600 passed through the Baugnez crossroads. Assuming a speed of about 30 kph the Kampfgruppe would therefore have taken only half an hour to pass a single point and would have been clear of the area by not later than 1500 hours. It was at about this time, and certainly before 1600 hours, that the sixty-one Americans who were still alive in the field south of the Café, attempted their escape. Unfortunately for some of them a few Germans were still in the area and they opened fire as the escapees ran to the west and north-west. At least fifteen were killed. Three more, Cobbler, Stabulis and Vairo died later, as presumably did Thomas, whose body was never found.

Sometime between 1515 and 1615 hours Dave Pergrin, after dismounting from his vehicle at Geromont and proceeding with one of his sergeants, Bill Crickenberger, towards the Crossroads area on foot, encountered three of the American survivors. He rushed them back to his HQ in Malmédy and then sent a message at 1640 hours stating that there had been some sort of massacre of American soldiers in the vicinity of Malmédy. That message was received at HQ 1st US Army at 1650 hours.

At Appendix 5 are the names, units and other relevant details, including where the bodies were found, of the 113 men standing in the field at Baugnez when the Germans opened fire.

There have been suggestions that some of the bodies found in or near the field at Baugnez were placed there after 17th December. As will be seen from the list at Appendix 5 the only possibilities appear to be Sergeant Lindt and Pfc Wald of the 200th Field Artillery Battalion. It is true that one man who was found in the field and assumed to be a victim of the shooting was nothing to do with the incident. He was Pvt Delbert Johnson of B Company 526th Armored Infantry Battalion. He was killed in the same area during an attack towards Hedomont on 3rd January 1945.

Apart from the 113 Americans in the field at Baugnez, there were others who were involved in this clash with Peiper's Kampfgruppe and who are part of the total picture. Appendix 6 shows their names, units and what happened to them.

From the lists of Appendices 5 and 6 it will be seen that eighty-four Americans, including Cobbler, Stabulis, Thomas and Vairo died and twenty-five were wounded as a result of the meeting with Kampfgruppe Peiper. Sixty-seven of the men assembled in the field south of the Café Bodarwé died in that field or within 200m of it, forty-six managed to escape from the field though four of these, Cobbler, Stabulis, Thomas and Vairo, died later. Fifty-six men survived the whole affair, of which seven became prisoners of war. There were no German casualties.

On 14th, 15th and 16th January 1945, Major Giacento Morrone, Captain Joseph Kurcz and Captain John Snyder, all doctors at the 44th Evacuation Hospital in Malmédy, carried out autopsies on the bodies recovered from and around the field at Baugnez. The bodies were still frozen and fully clothed on arrival at the hospital. The vast majority had watches, rings, money and other valuables on them, which contradicts the statements of most of the survivors that the Germans stole everything worthwhile from them before they were placed in the field. An analysis of the reports, all of which make extremely disturbing reading, shows that forty-three of the bodies had gunshot wounds to the head, at least three suffered severe blows to the head, three had been crushed, two had received some form of first aid before death and nine still had their arms raised above their heads. It is clear that terrible and usually fatal injuries were inflicted at close range. Even the most impartial reader has to ask himself what manner of men could have inflicted such injuries on their fellow human beings?

Before turning to possible explanations for this tragedy it should be noted that before and during the American advance from Malmédy in January 1945, artillery fire from both sides hit Baugnez, including the area immediately around the Café Bodarwé. The autopsy reports on the American dead show that at least fifteen were hit by shell or mortar fragments after death. There is also evidence to show that in at least five cases eyes had been removed from their sockets – and in one case the autopsy report suggests that the man was still alive when this happened. Whilst anything is possible, it seems unlikely that even the most depraved or crazed soldier would carry out such an act and, just as happened to other dead and wounded later in this battle, crows or similar birds of prey were the more likely culprits.

There are eighty-four names on the Belgian Memorial at the Baugnez Crossroads. Some are mis-spelt; Pvt Louis Vairo's name was mistakenly deleted a few years ago – in the opinion of the author it should be put back and that of Delbert Johnson who, as already mentioned, was not connected with the 'Malmédy Massacre', removed.

The 'Malmédy Massacre' continues to provoke as much argument today as it did during the subsequent War Crimes Trial at Dachau in 1946. Most Americans take the view that it was probably a premeditated massacre, or at best, a spur of the moment shooting of defenceless men. Those Germans who were involved, or who take an interest in the affair, and various pro-German writers, naturally attempt to provide some sort of justification for the shooting.

Twenty-one American survivors of the Baugnez affair made statements to the US authorities in Malmédy on 17th December, the same day as the 'massacre' and on the 18th – long before there was any possibility of collusion or anyone putting ideas into their heads. They all told essentially the same story – after surrendering to a German armoured column and being disarmed, they were assembled in a field south of the crossroads; German soldiers then opened fire on them with machine guns and rifles. In most cases the survivors mentioned one or two pistol shots before the machine guns fired. They said that soldiers then entered the field and shot anyone who showed any signs of life. Following this the German column continued to drive past, with some of the vehicle crews taking pot-shots at the men lying in the field. All but one of the survivors insisted that no attempts to escape had been made before the shooting started and that the escape attempt came at a much later stage when they thought all the Germans had left the area.

Media interest in the 'Malmédy Massacre', particularly in later years, has led inevitably to this relatively simple story being embellished, even by some of those who were directly involved. One survivor, as recently as 1989, actually talked of seeing SS General Sepp Dietrich, the 6th Panzer Army Commander, goose-stepping past the field as the Americans stood there! Even the surviving officer, Virgil Lary, talked of 'Tiger' tanks, '88mm' guns and 'large numbers of German tanks' forcing them to surrender. Such embellishments and exaggerations inevitably played into the hands of those who wished to cast doubt on the survivors' original version of events.

Apart from some minor inconsistencies, such as Lieutenant Lary saying on 18th December that after escaping he got a lift into Malmédy in a truck but later changing the story to one of two Belgian ladies helping him to get there on foot aided by a makeshift crutch, the only real point in contention is whether or not there was any attempt to escape which might have caused the Germans to open fire. This point will be discussed later.

Peiper had allegedly left the Baugnez area before the shooting at the prisoners started, but after the war he described how he had seen three groups of Americans before he moved on to Ligneuville – those with their hands up, those lying on the ground and in the ditches pretending to be dead and a third group who, after pretending to be dead, got up and tried to run to nearby woods. He said his men had fired warning shots at the latter two groups.[7]

Most German apologists, and certainly many former members of the Leibstandarte, subscribe to the explanation given by Peiper's Adjutant, Hans Gruhle,[8] who said that there was a gap of about ten minutes between the Spitze and Command Group leaving Baugnez and the main body of the KG arriving. During this time the Americans were left to their own devices and, since they had made no attempt to march to the rear, the main body mistook them for a fresh American unit and therefore opened fire, hitting them for a second time. Quite how he could have known what happened that tragic afternoon is a mystery since he was allegedly travelling at or near the rear of the column! With the passing of time this story too has become embellished to a point where the surrendered Americans, having recovered their arms, actually opened fire on the main body of the KG. It is, at least to this author, beyond belief that supposedly intelligent people can still advance the idea that 'green' and terrified soldiers who had already surrendered, should pick up their rifles and pistols which hardened Waffen SS soldiers had left lying around, in order to engage tanks and armoured half-tracks! It is perhaps even more extraordinary that the same hypothesis has been recently propounded by an American who claims to be an historian and uses both his post WW II army rank and 'US Army Ret' in association with his name.

Nevertheless, it has to be said that Peiper's men faced a very real problem in deciding what to do with their prisoners at the Baugnez crossroads. According to all German reports and Peiper himself, he left the area in a hurry to get to Ligneuville and capture the American headquarters there. He ordered the rest of the KG to follow up as quickly as possible. But what were those at the crossroads to do with the prisoners? Armoured columns have no spare manpower to look after prisoners and neither Sandig's follow-up infantry nor the men of the 3rd Parachute Division were anywhere near Baugnez at that time! Over one hundred enemy, even if they have surrendered and been disarmed, cannot be left to their own devices. Nor could they be told to start marching into captivity, because there was a simple problem of geography. KG Peiper had penetrated American lines on a very narrow front and this meant that from the German point of view the enemy lay along the N-23 to the north-west in Malmédy, the N-32 to the north-east in Waimes and the N-23 to the south in Ligneuville (Map 9). There was simply no road along which they could order the prisoners to set off and it was more than possible that more American combat units might at any moment move south from Malmédy, only 4km away. A combination of these factors – an angry SS Obersturmbannführer in a hurry, no spare men to guard prisoners, no route to the rear available and the possibility of American combat troops arriving at any moment, must have created a nightmare scenario for the man in charge – whoever he was! It must also be remembered that, as any experienced soldier knows, there are certain circumstances when there is little option but to kill prisoners. A clear example is given later in this book, and recent D-Day reminiscences by British veterans have revealed that no prisoners were taken in the very early stages of the Normandy landings because there was simply nowhere to put them. It is therefore quite possible that the senior responsible German at the crossroads decided to take the simplest and most practical way out of his dilemma by giving an order to shoot the prisoners. It is even possible that Peiper himself gave the order before he moved on.

But then we must come back to the other possibility which is that the Germans opened fire because, after the prisoners were assembled in the field, there was an attempt to escape. It is after all legal to shoot escaping prisoners of war. And there is evidence to support this idea. In October 1945 one of the American survivors, in part of a sworn statement, counter-signed by one of the chief prosecuting officers, Lieutenant Raphael Schumacker, and witnessed by a sergeant named Frank Holtham, said:

'. . . I decided to try to get away and walked slowly northwardly, but upon reaching a little dirt road or lane decided not to cross the lane or go around it. Sergeant Stabulis, Flack and I were together on this proposition. We turned around, slowly retraced our steps. . . . The group of soldiers in front of me were standing still and I slowly walked southwardly towards the fence at the south end of the field, more or less using the men in front as concealment. I know that Sergeant Stabulis and Pfc Flack were behind me. About two-thirds of the way towards the fence there were no more men to provide concealment so when I reached this point I ran towards the fence as hard as I could, crawled through it and then turned to my right and headed for the woods west of the field as fast as I could. Machine gun fire was opened up at me but I was lucky enough to make it to the woods without getting hit and was picked up by the 30th Division a couple of days later. . . . I would like to add that as I came out from behind the crowd into the clear and headed for the south fence, two single shots were fired, which were either pistol or rifle in my opinion.'

Pfc Flack's body was found in the field with a bullet hole in the head; Sergeant Stabulis's body was found on 15th April 1945, a kilometre south of the field.

It would seem therefore that there was at least one successful escape from the field before the shooting started, in addition to five men, Bower, Conrad, Garrett, Graeff and Schmitt, who got away from the front of the B Battery convoy soon after it came under fire from the Spitze. It is also clear from various testimonies that there was some movement and jostling in the field before any of the shooting started, and certainly once the first pistol shots rang out several men attempted to push their way to the rear of the group. A number of survivors mentioned an American officer shouting 'Stand fast.'

In summary it can be said that there is little or no evidence to support the idea of a premeditated massacre – particularly in view of the facts that Peiper's KG had already sent many prisoners to the rear in the normal manner in the early stages of its advance, and that over half the Americans in the field survived both the main shooting and the administration of coup de grace shots by the Germans who entered the field. Nor is the theory that the main body of the KG mistook the men in the field for a fresh combat unit sustainable. Suggestions of a mass escape attempt also lack credibility.

So how can we explain what happened at the Baugnez crossroads on 17th December 1944? There seem to be only two reasonable possibilities – the first being that one of the Germans, possibly a tank crewman named Fleps who admitted firing the first shot and whose tank commander, Hans Siptrott, even today confirms[9] that Fleps fired one or two shots', saw the three Americans make a break from the main body as described in the sworn statement made to Lieutenant Schumacker in October 1945; he fired at them and this triggered other Germans on the road opposite the field to open fire with their rifles and machine guns. In the resulting chaos some Americans attempted to flee to the rear and the Germans continued shooting – in other words the 'massacre' started accidentally. But, even if this is true, it in no way excuses the deliberate killing of wounded and surrendered men by those Germans who entered the field after the main shooting.

The other possibility is that, faced with the problem of what to do with so many prisoners, a few of whom had already escaped, and a requirement to keep the KG moving, someone took a deliberate decision to shoot them. The sheer number of Americans in the field, and the fact that they were standing in a group, meant that many were physically shielded by the bodies of their comrades. After the main shooting it was therefore necessary to send some soldiers into the field to finish off the survivors. Those who went into the field, many of them very young and perhaps firing their weapons at a human being for the first time in their lives, lost control when faced at close quarters with dead and horribly injured men. They found themselves taking part in a frenzy of killing. But this is neither in accordance with the normally accepted 'rules of war' nor with the Geneva Convention. Such actions are unacceptable and must be condemned by any civilized society. Having said that, which 20th century army has a blameless record?

NOTES

1. These facts were obtained through interviews with, and letters from, American survivors and Germans who were present at Baugnez on 17th December 1944 and by analyses of testimonies given by survivors to officers of the Inspector General, 1st US Army immediately after the incident, and as evidence at the Dachau Trial in 1946. In some cases the interviews were with, or the letters were written to, my friend John Bauserman who made their contents available to me. Discussions were also carried out with Col David Pergrin who interviewed some of the survivors within a few hours of the shootings. Extensive research was also carried out into autopsy reports, documents showing exactly where bodies lay before they were recovered and statements made to US investigating officers by German suspects and other witnesses before the Dachau Trial. All these documents are held in the US National Archives.
2. Sternebeck to author loc. cit., 1 Oct 1985.
3. Manfred Thorn, driver of tank number 734 in 7th SS Pz Coy, to author March 1994.
4. Peiper's testimony at Dachau Trial.
5. Sternebeck to author loc. cit., 1 Oct 1985.
6. Letter from Fischer to author 29 May 1989.
7. Tiemann, *Die Leibstandarte IV/2*, pp. 63–4.
8. Ibid., pp. 65–6.
9. Manfred Thorn, driver of tank number 734 in the 7th SS Pz Coy and current acquaintance of Siptrott, to author March 1994.

CHAPTER XII

Sunday Afternoon 17th December

The Continuing Scene

Although CCB of the 9th Armored Division had moved south to St Vith from the Faymonville area at about the same time as Peiper left Lanzerath, its administrative echelons, or 'trains' as the Americans call them, remained behind temporarily in Ligneuville. These trains consisted of the service companies of the 14th Tank, 16th Field Artillery and 27th Armored Infantry Battalions.[1] The 14th Tank Battalion Service Company was located just to the north-east of Brigadier Timberlake's Headquarters in the Hôtel du Moulin, in a triangle of roads to the west of the N-23. It consisted of a transport platoon, a kitchen and the supply trucks of the Battalion HQ and four tank companies, some thirty-four 2½-ton trucks in all. Half the Battalion Maintenance Platoon had remained behind to finish repairs to an M4A3 tank dozer (a tank with a bull-dozer blade on the front) and a 105mm self-propelled assault gun with its engine out. The Service companies of the other two Battalions were in the southern half of the village, south of the Amblève river. The ranking officer was a Captain Seymour Green, the Supply Officer of the 27th Armored Infantry, and as such he was the overall Trains Commander.

At about 1330 hours an American soldier came running down the hill into Ligneuville shouting that Germans were just up the road to the north and approaching fast. He may well have been a survivor from the front of B Battery. The story that a bulldozer drove into the village to give the warning is almost certainly erroneous. It will be recalled that Timberlake and two of his officers were having lunch in the Hôtel at this time. One of the officers, a Major Kelakos, is said to have confirmed the German approach with the result that Timberlake and his small party evacuated at speed leaving their lunch. Captain Green of the 27th Infantry also carried out a recce, having told the trains to 'bug-out', but was less lucky in that he ran into Sternebeck's Spitze and was captured.

Sternebeck halted just short of the Amblève river bridge at about 1345 hours.[2] The Amblève is little more than a stream at this stage but the bridge was a substantial stone one. He sent pioneers forward to check for demolitions and they came under small arms fire. Apart from any other Americans firing at the Spitze, the main fire came from a Sergeant Lincoln Abraham manning the 50 calibre machine gun on the assault gun. He was in fact the mess sergeant. Following Sternebeck's two tanks and two SPWs into Ligneuville was Fischer's Panther. Just as he passed the Hôtel du Moulin his tank was hit in the rear by a shot from the American tank dozer which was positioned by a barn only about 100m to the north. The Panther burst into flames. A follow-up SPW was also knocked out. Next to arrive were Peiper and Diefenthal in their command SPW and realising they were highly vulnerable the driver put the SPW under cover to the left of the church. Peiper is said to have grabbed a panzerfaust and to have started to stalk the tank dozer but following closely behind him a 251/9 SPW of the 11th SS Panzer-Grenadier Company did the job for him with a shot which knocked out the dozer.

In 1989 Fischer described this action as follows:

When our advance more or less came to a halt at the crossroads I passed Peiper's order, he was in an SPW right behind me, on to Sternebeck. He was to take Ligneuville immediately, to secure the bridge which was strategically important to us and at the western edge of the village he was to wait for further instructions. I also told him that an HQ of considerable rank was possibly in the town. The other units were instructed to advance to Ligneuville without delay. We knew that the Spitze with its two tanks and few SPWs was very weak. As we had no other armoured vehicles immediately available, my Panther and behind me Colonel Peiper in his SPW followed the Spitze as fast as we could. To start off with I did not notice any fighting and therefore wanted to cross the bridge. On the bend before the bridge I was shot up from behind. My Panther went up in flames. We got out of the tank under machine gun and rifle fire coming from nearby houses. We were burning like torches as only a couple of hours before we had re-fuelled, including our jerrycans, in Büllingen. In doing so we had soaked our clothing in petrol. My driver never managed to get out and was burned to death. I believe that Colonel Peiper gave me cover by fire and managed to protect us from American fire from the nearby houses. . . . Peiper bandaged me as well as he could and handed me over to a doctor who arrived later.[3]

Fischer had been Peiper's Adjutant in Russia and, as we shall see, became his dentist after the war.

The majority of the Americans managed to get out of Ligneuville and there is no truth in the story of a serious tank battle to the south of the village. This story, which talks of the Germans losing a Panther and two armoured cars and the Americans two Shermans and an M-10 TD, originated with Peiper in a post-war interview[4] and has been repeated by many writers. The truth is that there were no US tanks in or south of Ligneuville at that time other than the one already mentioned. As the After Action Report of CCB says: 'The only vehicles available for trains protection were half-tracks. Tanks could not be spared from the front.' It is fairly easy though to see how the story arose as the number of vehicles lost on each side more or less equates with what happened around 1400 hours in the village itself. American losses were: the tank dozer, assault gun and kitchen truck and four trailers of the 14th Tank Battalion and seven unspecified vehicles of the 16th Field Artillery. At least twenty-two men including two officers of the 27th Armored Infantry were captured and they were taken into the Hôtel and other local houses. Some time later eight of them were shot by a member of the KG within 50m of the Hôtel on the other side of the road towards Malmédy.[5] The reason for this atrocity is unknown but it has been said that the Germans were in an ugly mood after some of their own dead had been buried in the village. One of the eight Americans who died was Sergeant Lincoln Abraham; sadly he is shown as Abraham Lincoln on the post-war memorial.

Peiper's column had become very disorganised by the cross-country movement after Büllingen and the various events of the day. He was also conscious of the American air threat. He decided therefore to reorganise and wait for darkness before proceeding to Stavelot. When the KG did move off, sometime around 1700 hours, Kremser's 1st SS Panzer Company took the lead. By then, Preuss's 10th Panzer-Grenadier Company Group had extricated itself from the Thirimont valley and rejoined the column, and von Westernhagen's Tigers were beginning to arrive in the village, near which they remained for the night. Being basically on a one-tank front, Peiper's column had of course churned up every road and track it had used in its advance. This had made it extremely difficult for the vehicles at the rear to follow and so the Tigers had taken various routes to reach Ligneuville, some of them coming in on the Heppenbach–Born–Kaiserbarracke road (Map 6). They had also suffered many breakdowns. According to one fitter, his company had only two combat-ready tanks by the Sunday evening.

The number of Tigers operating with Peiper has been a subject of much controversy. The 501st SS Heavy Panzer Battalion should have had forty-five Tigers. Nevertheless, because the official equipment state of the 501st dated 10th December 1944 shows only fifteen tanks, many writers have assumed that this was the number with Peiper. They have ignored the fact that tanks required to bring units up to full strength were often still in the pipeline and were being fed forward as and when they were ready. Ex members of the 501st insist that the Battalion was at full strength on the 16th December. Whilst on the subject of tank numbers it is noteworthy that by this stage of the advance, as well as suffering the loss of many Tigers due to breakdowns, Peiper had also lost twenty-five per cent of his 1st SS Panzer Battalion. Three Panthers and three Type IVs had been lost or immobilised due to mines or enemy action and eight Panthers and four Type IVs had broken down, some of which would be repaired and rejoin within a relatively short time.

Meanwhile in Malmédy Dave Pergrin knew that one company of engineers could not possibly hold the largest town in the region without substantial reinforcements in the form of infantry, artillery and some TDs. His decision to stay put and try to delay the Germans therefore took considerable courage.

Pergrin's first action was to order his own C Company at Stoumont to join him as soon as possible. In the same message to his Rear HQ at Haute Bodeux he asked for a roadblock to be set up at Stavelot covering the Amblève bridge there. He knew that the security of Stavelot was vital for the defence of Malmédy. Pergrin's message made a major impact on both his own HQ and on Colonel Wallis Anderson, his immediate superior. To Major Ed Lampp, his Operations Officer at Haute Bodeux, it meant that the 291st was to be fully committed to the defence of Malmédy in a combat role. To Anderson it meant that a German tank column was only 20km from his own HQ and, on a less personal and perhaps more important note, only 25km from HQ 1st US Army at Spa. He wasted no time in informing Hodges's staff through the Chief Engineer there, Colonel Bill Carter.

At fifty-six Anderson was much older than the average US Army Colonel in 1944 but he was also much more experienced. He was a veteran of General Black Jack Pershing's pursuit of Pancho Villa into Mexico in 1915 and he had seen service in World War I. Between the wars he served in the Pennsylvania National Guard but his full-time job was as a civil engineer on the Pennsylvania Railroad. He was a strict disciplinarian, never overgraded his officers, never drank coffee or alcohol and went to bed at 9 pm whenever he could! Inevitably he was highly respected. By the time of this battle he knew the Ardennes well and he was to play a major part in halting the advance of KG Peiper.

Captain Moyer of C Company 291st received Pergrin's message at 1530 hours, telling him to move his company to Malmédy. He was also told to send a squad to set up the road block at Stavelot. This was in fact a waste of resources since C Company 202nd Engineers was already in the town. Unfortunately both Anderson and Pergrin's S-3, Major Lampp, seem to have forgotten them. It was a rude awakening for C Company at the Château Froidcour near Stoumont and at the local railway station where they were based, to have to move. It was also a nasty shock for the de Harenne family, owners of the Château. They were told of the American move, and the reason for it, during dinner that evening. Monsieur Charles de Harenne, his wife Marcienne and one daughter with her young son, decided to stay on in the Château; but their sons Georges and Edouard and their young wives who were sisters, one with a baby, and youngest son Maurice, decided to flee west to the girls' home near Namur. They all piled into a tiny two-door, 8hp Ford Anglia car. Georges, an officer in the Belgian Lancers, had already been a prisoner of the Germans after being captured in May 1940 but had been released through ill health. Edouard at twenty six and Maurice, sixteen, were prime candidates for a labour camp in Germany. Little did they realise that the Château was to become the centre point of the fighting between Peiper and the Americans and that the woods in which they had been hunting only the day before would soon be full of soldiers locked in a life and death struggle.

Pergrin's message about a massacre near Malmédy was received at Spa at 1650 hours and no doubt helped to focus minds on the seriousness of the situation. Ten minutes later the 99th Infantry and 526th Armored Infantry Battalions and A Company 825th TD Battalion, already on stand-by, were ordered to proceed to Malmédy at once. At the same time Pergrin sent a further message to Wallis Anderson telling him that the German column had moved south from Baugnez. He had learned this from the B Battery survivors.

To the south Kampfgruppe Hansen's leading elements, the Jagd-panzers with the 1st SS Panzer-Grenadiers mounted, reached Born around 1430 hours having advanced through Valender and Amel. The 2nd SS Panzer-Grenadier Battalion was following and behind that came Fast Group Knittel which had overtaken Hansen's 3rd Battalion Group while it was making its long diversion through Lanzerath and Honsfeld.

At 1530 hours Colonel Devine ordered all remaining 14th Cavalry units to withdraw to a general line Recht–St Vith and by 1630 his own HQ was at Poteau with C, E and F Troops of the 18th Squadron and C Troop of the 32nd Squadron. Devine had it in mind to counter-attack towards Born the following morning. Half an hour later he ordered the rest of the 32nd Squadron back to Vielsalm.

During the afternoon the Command Post of CCR 7th Armored Div-ision set up in Recht. Also in the village was the Rear HQ of CCB and a company of Shermans of the 17th Tank Battalion. The rest of the Battalion under the command of Lieutenant Colonel John Wimple was just to the south-east of Recht on the St Vith road. The Germans say their Jagdpanzers and Panzer-Grenadiers arrived in Recht at about last light.[6] The Americans say it was very much later, around 0200 hours, on the Monday morning. Both sides agree that the Americans withdrew after a forty-five minute engagement, setting fire to the wooden bridge on the Poteau road as they did so to prevent the Germans following. The Germans say they went firm for the night having knocked out four or five Shermans with their Jagdpanzers. The German timings seem more plausible since it would otherwise be difficult to explain why the Jagdpanzers took twelve hours to cover the 5km between Born and Recht.

At 1730 hours the 3rd SS Panzer-Grenadier Battalion Group with its towed anti-tank guns reached Deidenberg behind Fast Group Knittel. The CO of the Battalion, SS Captain Böttcher, received orders at the time to clear the Kaiserbarracke crossroads of enemy troops at first light the following morning to open the way for Knittel. It is not clear who these American troops were, if indeed they existed at all, but it is possible they were remnants of Devine's 14th Cavalry Group.

KG Sandig was still in its assembly area and Skorzeny's KG 'X', now under the command of SS Captain von Foelkersam, was stalled just to the west of Losheim. It is not at all clear why it was not launched in the direction of Waimes and Baugnez during the Sunday afternoon. Once Peiper turned south the way was clear and the Skorzeny force could easily have penetrated to the west, bypassing Malmédy.

NOTES

1. Description of events based on AARs and letters to the author from Col Cecil Roberts of the 14th Tk Bn dated 23 June 1987, a map overlay signed by Maj Chandler, S-3 of the 14th Tk Bn, a sketch produced at the Bn Reunion on 23 Aug 1987, letter from Col Dwight Hull of the 16th FA Bn dated 3 Aug 1987 and letter from Maj Glen Strange of the 27th AI Bn dated 14 Jul 1987.
2. Sternebeck to author loc. cit., 1 Oct 1985.
3. Letter to author dated 29 May 1989.
4. MS # C-004 Joachim Peiper, *Kampfgruppe Peiper 15–26 Dec 1944*, Historical Division, European Command.
5. Letter dated 3 Feb 1987 to John Bausermann from Joseph Mass of the 27th AI Bn, who survived this shooting.
6. Tiemann, *Die Leibstandarte IV/2*, p. 76.

CHAPTER XIII
Sunday Evening 17th December

Hesitation

General Hodges had accepted General Simpson's offer of his 30th Infantry Division on the Sunday morning. This resulted in a phone call to Major General Leland Hobbs near Aachen telling him to move his Division south as soon as possible. Units received a warning order at 1140 hours and the first Regiment, the 119th, was on the move at 1625 hours. The 117th and 120th Infantry Regiments were directed on the Malmédy area and the 119th further to the west around Aywaille (Map 3).

Stavelot (Map 10) had been a hive of activity all day on the 17th. From early in the morning the major fighting components of the 7th Armored Division, Combat Commands A and B, had been transiting the town, and units fleeing to the west had been coming in on the Malmédy road. These included the 44th Evacuation Hospital and the Reinforcement Depot from Malmédy itself. Many civilians were also trying to get away from the German advance, especially young men of military age. The only units stationed in the town were C Company of the 202nd Engineer Combat Battalion, temporarily part of Colonel Anderson's 1111th Engineer Group, the 1st Army Map Store in a building in the Tannerie Courtjoie, a small repair unit at the station and a detachment of the 518th Military Police in the Café Pax. Just to the north of Stavelot on the old road to Francorchamps, was the main dump of Fuel Depot Number 3, containing nearly a million gallons of gasoline; other parts of the Depot were near Mista and Blanchimont, between Malmédy and Francorchamps, but they would be cleared by midday on the Monday. The main dump was being guarded by sixty men of 3rd Company, 5th Belgian Fusiliers, under the command of Captain Burniat[1] who had established his headquarters in the Château Malacord at the foot of the Francorchamps road.

It was dark and about 1830 hours when the squad of C Company 291st Engineers arrived with orders to set up a road block covering the main bridge in the town. Sergeant 'Chuck' Hensel[2] was in charge and with him in the squad 2½-ton truck were twelve other men; the chaotic traffic situation was such that it had taken them an hour and a half to cover the 15km from Stoumont. Major Lampp, the Battalion S-3, had sent the 291st's assistant Motor Pool officer, Lieutenant Cliff Wilson, to help Hensel site the road block and to act as a liaison officer. They found no one at the bridge, which was a very substantial stone one. It was obvious to Wilson and Hensel that if their CO and B Company were in Malmédy the approach they had to defend was the one coming from Ligneuville over the bridge into the town. They therefore crossed the bridge to the south side and drove up the hill to the southeast on the road called by the Belgians 'Vieux Château'. About a kilometre from the bridge they found the perfect spot for a road block with a sheer drop of some 100 feet to the Amblève river on the left, or north, side of the road and a twenty-foot cliff on the right (Map 11). Hensel deployed his men and by about 1930 hours he had a 'daisy-chain' of anti-tank mines laid on the road, a 30 calibre machine gun and bazooka sited and a sentry posted beyond the mines to warn any Americans who might choose to use the road that night.

At 1900 hours the 82nd Airborne Division near Reims in France received a warning order from SHAEF Headquarters to prepare to move east. The Division, together with the 101st, formed the XVIIIth Airborne Corps; it was the only strategic reserve available to Eisenhower but by this time General Hodges was so concerned about the situation that he asked the 12th Army Group Commander, Bradley, if he would press Ike to release it to him. Bradley agreed and the Airborne Corps was consequently ordered to the 1st Army area.

At a much lower level and no doubt spurred on by Pergrin's message that Peiper had moved south from Baugnez, Colonel Anderson sent for another engineer company to come to Trois Ponts. He chose the 51st Engineers at Marche and its CO, Lieutenant Colonel Harvey 'Scrappy' Fraser, a 28-year-old who had only been in command for three days, selected his C Company. Anderson was only too aware that, after moving south from Baugnez, it would be a simple, yet logical, move for Peiper to turn west at Ligneuville and so threaten Stavelot, Trois Ponts and the route to the Meuse river (Map 3). At the same time as Anderson gave his order, Pergrin ordered all his A Company's machine guns and gunners from Werbomont to Malmédy.

The Panthers of Kremser's 1st SS Panzer Company set off from Ligneuville some time after dark, around 1730 hours, at the head of Peiper's column. It seems that Peiper did not accompany them. Certainly no one claims to have seen him from late afternoon until about 2300 hours. It is likely that his Divisional Commander, Mohnke, came forward to Ligneuville during the late afternoon or early evening with a small tactical HQ and that he and Peiper spent some time discussing the situation and having a meal. Mohnke was definitely in the forward area that afternoon; Böttcher, the CO of Hansen's 3rd Battalion, subsequently confirmed that Mohnke gave him orders at Deidenberg around 1600 hours[3] and the owner of the Hôtel du Moulin, Peter Rupp, said Mohnke and Peiper were in the Hôtel on the Sunday evening. There is confirmation that the Leibstandarte Headquarters was set up in the Hôtel during the night and Gruhle established Peiper's Main HQ in the Hôtel des Ardennes in Ligneuville at the same time.

The Kampfgruppe moved at little better than walking pace towards Stavelot. This is not surprising in view of the fact that it was pitch dark, the narrow, tree-lined road was icy and had many sharp, steep corners and the Germans had no idea when or where they might run into the enemy. Consequently commanders led their vehicles on foot for much of the way and made frequent halts while scouts investigated the route ahead. The difficulties of driving a 46-ton Panther under these conditions can be easily appreciated.

Between Ligneuville and Pont the Chief of Staff of the 7th Armored Division, Colonel Church Matthews, ran into the Spitze and was killed (Map 6).[4] His driver managed to get away and reached CCB HQ in Recht around 2045 hours. The officers there were naturally alarmed to learn that a German tank column was only 5km away to their north. It seems that the Spitze missed the turning to Stavelot 3km out of Ligneuville and continued on towards Recht. When the mistake was realised a local Belgian was made to join the Spitze and show the way – a gun to his head being ample encouragement! It seems that he managed to escape, but in the hamlet of Vau Richard two more locals, Emile Glaude and Jules Califice were 'conscripted' and forced to act as guides. They travelled in two captured American jeeps which were leading the column. This story is confirmed by the then Secretary of Stavelot, Monsieur Joseph Dejardin and a well known local historian, Monsieur Serge Fontaine.

It was about 1900 hours by the time the Spitze reached Chuck Hensel's road block just beyond Vau Richard, and it so happened that Hensel decided at this very moment to put another man, Bauers, out in front with his sentry, Private Bernie Goldstein, who was about 50m beyond the daisy-chain of mines. Behind the mines Hensel had two men manning a bazooka and behind them two more with the 30 calibre machine gun. The squad truck was facing back down the hill towards Stavelot. As Hensel and Bauers approached Goldstein they heard him shout 'Halt', and this was quickly followed by machine gun fire in their general direction. The story has often been told that this was an act of incredible bravery by Goldstein who, having heard German being spoken by men on the leading vehicle, tried to halt the enemy despite being armed with only a rifle. The story is apocryphal. Hensel confirmed to the author in 1982 that Goldstein was there only to stop Americans running on to his mines. It should be obvious anyway that no sensible soldier would deliberately try to stop an enemy running on to a defensive minefield. What in fact happened was that Goldstein, having heard vehicles approaching and expecting them to be American, naturally tried to stop them. Little did he realise they were Peiper's Spitze.

To this day the men of the 291st say the lead vehicle was a Panther, with paratroopers mounted, and that Corporal Morris and Private Gadziola fired their bazooka which at least immobilised it. As we have heard, the local Belgians believe it was a captured US jeep. It does not really matter. What does matter is that Hensel's road block had achieved its purpose – it had halted KG Peiper – and the effect of this would be dramatic. Hensel tried to get forward to see what had happened to Goldstein but this proved impossible due to German small arms fire. He need not have worried though; as Hensel coasted back down the hill to the bridge with the rest of his men in the squad truck, Bernie Goldstein was at that moment 'high-tailing' it over the hill to the west – he too was on his way back to the bridge. Hensel met Lieutenant Wilson in Stavelot and after reporting what had happened, left at 2200 hours for Trois Ponts where he found his platoon commander, Lieutenant Rombaugh, with two squads of C Company at the Amblève bridge. At 2245 hours Anderson's HQ at Trois Ponts was informed that the road block south of Stavelot had been forced to withdraw due to an enemy attack.

Colonel Anderson now had a crisis on his hands. C Company of the 51st had not yet arrived in Trois Ponts and the only troops immediately available to him were Rombaugh's two squads at the Amblève bridge and the A Company squad defending his own HQ. Pergrin had the whole of his B Company and the remainder of C Company in Malmédy. Of A Company, the 1st Platoon was literally 'missing' on its way back from Grand Halleux and the other two had not yet arrived back in Werbomont from Born. He could not risk taking the squads away from the Amblève bridge. He therefore told Major Lampp at Haute Bodeux to send him one of the Werbomont platoons as soon as they got back to base.

Once again Anderson seems to have completely forgotten Chinlund's C Company of the 202nd Engineers in Stavelot. For some inexplicable reason Chinlund had received no orders at all during the day. He and his company appear to have been totally forgotten, not just by Anderson and the 1111th Group staff, but by the V Corps engineer staff, Chinlund's own CO and Pergrin's S-3 at Haute Bodeux. This was a tragedy because this full company of combat engineers had the capability of providing a basic defence of Stavelot, just as Pergrin was doing in Malmédy and, most important of all, of preparing the vital Stavelot bridge for demolition. It has to be said, though, that Chinlund made no attempt to find out what was going on despite the fact that he could see a continuous stream of traffic moving west through Stavelot from dawn to dusk and his Group HQ was only 5km down the road in Trois Ponts. As one of his Squad Leaders, John Stevenson, wrote in 1990:

> We began to notice military units moving through Stavelot, apparently to the rear. For me and my immediate circle of friends this activity caused some concern but not alarm. As the day went on it appeared to me that our Company Commander, Lt Chinlund, had not been informed about what was happening. I think he began to feel the C Company had been overlooked as orders to withdraw were being given to other units.[5]

At about 2230 hours Chinlund decided it was time to join the others and moved his company out.

While Anderson and the Americans may have had a crisis on their hands there is no doubt that Peiper and the Germans had a problem too. To them it was only natural that a major road centre like Stavelot should be defended, and Hensel's road block had merely confirmed this. Then, looking down from the heights above the town, all they could see was a blaze of lights from US vehicles transiting the town. As the commander of one of Kremser's Panthers, Zimmermann, said 'We could see the lights of vehicles and hear them. I had the impression the Amis [Americans] were withdrawing.'[6] Even so it was dark, they had never seen Stavelot before and they knew that the only way into the town was over the Amblève bridge. It was inconceivable to them that it would not be prepared for demolition and defended. There were several other major factors to be considered in deciding whether or not to attempt an advance into and through the town. First, the KG was spread out all the way back to Ligneuville and its artillery was not deployed; secondly, infantry would be needed to assault the bridge and they would have to be brought forward; and thirdly, and perhaps most importantly, everyone was tired out. Maybe the panzer-grenadiers had managed to 'cat-nap' in the back of their freezing SPWs but commanders like Peiper, Poetschke and Diefenthal, and many drivers, had not slept for over forty hours. After considering all these factors Peiper decided to delay his attack until daylight. Little did he know that the bridge was not prepared or defended and that the only combat troops in town, C Company of the 202nd Engineers, were about to move out. Peiper's tanks could have driven straight through.

In September 1945, during an interview with Major Ken Hechler of the US Army, Peiper painted a totally different version of events in Stavelot on the 17th December, in what appears to be an attempt to present himself in a much more heroic light.

He said:

At 1600 . . . we reached the area of Stavelot, which was heavily defended. We could observe heavy traffic moving from Malmédy toward Stavelot and Stavelot itself seemed clogged up completely with several hundred trucks. That night we attempted to capture Stavelot but the terrain presented great difficulties. The only approach was the main road and the ground to the left of the road fell very sharply and to the right of the road rose very sharply. There was a short curve just at the entrance to Stavelot where several Sherman tanks and anti-tank guns were zeroed in. Thereupon, we shelled Stavelot with heavy infantry howitzers and mortars, resulting in great confusion within the town and the destruction of several dumps. . . . At 1800 a counter-attack circled around a high hill 800 metres east of Stavelot and hit my column from the south . . . the counter-attack consisted entirely of infantry. After the counter-attack was repulsed, I committed more armoured infantry to attack Stavelot again. We approached the outskirts of the village but bogged down because of stubborn American resistance at the edge of Stavelot. We suffered fairly heavy losses, twenty-five to thirty casualties, from tank, anti-tank, mortar and rifle fire. Since I did not have sufficient infantry, I decided to wait for the arrival of more infantry.

This account belies nearly all the true facts – the timings are wrong, the description of the ground is inaccurate, Stavelot was not shelled or mortared that night, there were no American tanks in the town until 1600 hours the following day, there were no US infantry there either until 0345 hours on the 18th and no Americans were capable of launching counter-attacks on the 17th.

Meanwhile in Malmédy, Lieutenant Colonel Hansen with his 99th Infantry Battalion, consisting mainly of first-generation Norwegian Americans, had just arrived to reinforce Dave Pergrin, who at 2315 hours was ordered to send the 629th Equipment and 962nd Maintenance Companies west to Modave near the Meuse.

On the Leibstandarte's southern axis little of importance happened during these hours (Map 6). At about 1830 hours Colonel Devine of the 14th Cavalry, with some of his staff, set out from Poteau for St Vith in an attempt to see Major General Alan Jones of the 106th Division. They ran into part of Hansen's KG and were shot up. Devine and two of his officers survived and made their way on foot to St Vith, but Jones did not believe Devine's story that he had run into tanks on the way and relieved him of his command. Devine returned to his HQ at Poteau at about 2330 hours and handed over command to the CO of the 18th Squadron, Lieutenant Colonel Damon. The Group Executive Officer, Lieutenant Colonel Augustine Duggan, who had been with Devine in the skirmish near Recht, was still missing. In another version of this story Devine reached St Vith safely but Jones refused to see him and it was on the return journey, at about 1930 hours, that the cavalrymen were shot up. Whatever the truth, Devine was evacuated through medical channels to Bastogne in the middle of the night as a non-battle casualty. His combat career had been tragically short; he had never been popular with his officers or men and in the confusion of those first hours of battle he received no direction or support from his superiors.

As for the Germans, they were having a relatively quiet time with Hansen's Jagdpanzers and 1st and 2nd SS Panzer-Grenadier Battalions halted at Recht and the 3rd SS Panzer-Grenadier Battalion around Deidenberg preparing to secure the Kaiserbarracke crossroads at first light for Knittel's advance from Born.

Back in Germany KG Sandig finally crossed the Divisional Start Point south of Schmidtheim[7] at 2200 hours but found the route not only clogged with other vehicles and horse-drawn transport but also torn to shreds by the many tracked vehicles which had already used it. The para-military Todt organisation had been tasked with maintaining all the main routes essential to the offensive but the adverse weather conditions defeated its best efforts. Particular attention was paid to the route from Losheimergraben to Honsfeld and on to Amel but despite this Sandig's progress was to be painfully slow.

During the Sunday evening Otto Skorzeny attended a staff conference at Dietrich's 6th Panzer Army Headquarters.[8] He reported that he had been unable to launch any of his KGs and suggested they should be combined and used as a conventional unit. This was agreed and he was ordered to assemble them south of Malmédy and report to Mohnke at Ligneuville for further orders. He moved into the Rupps' chalet beside the Hôtel du Moulin during the night.

NOTES

1. Letter to author dated 5 May 1987 from Belgian Lt Col Roger Hardy, National Secretary 5th Bn Fusiliers and a member of the Bn in Dec 1944.
2. Charles (Chuck) Hensel described the events of the 'Stavelot Roadblock' to the author and Peter Crocker in 1982, on the spot where it happened.
3. Tiemann, *Die Leibstandarte IV/2*, p. 94.
4. Cole, *The Ardennes: Battle of the Bulge*, p. 289.
5. Letter to the author dated 8 Feb 1990.
6. Tiemann op. cit., pp. 81–2.
7. Ibid. op. cit., pp. 93–4.
8. Skorzeny, *Skorzeny's Special Missions* and ETHINT 12.

CHAPTER XIV

Monday 18th December

The Southern Route

According to its commander, SS Captain Otto Holst,[1] the 1st SS Jagdpanzer Company began its advance from Recht (Map 6) to the important road junction at Poteau at 0600 hours on the Monday morning, long before first light. He said he reached Poteau at 0700 hours and, although receiving some artillery fire, proceeded on towards Petit Thier, leaving a small detachment to secure the road junction. Holst claimed to have reached Petit Thier at 0800 hours, just as the 3rd SS Panzer-Grenadiers began their advance to secure the Kaiserbarracke crossroads for Fast Group Knittel. There he ordered the commander of his 1st Platoon, SS Lieutenant Piegler, to move on to Vielsalm to see if the bridge over the Salm river was intact. At 0830 Piegler apparently returned to say the bridge was down and so Holst decided to return all the way back to Recht, his job, as far as he was concerned, done. He got back at 1000 hours. In fact the bridge over the Salm was not demolished at that time and it seems unlikely that Piegler advanced as far as Vielsalm.

This account begs a number of questions: why was Holst asked to undertake this operation on his own? Surely it would have made sense for the rest of the Jagdpanzers and the 1st SS Panzer-Grenadier Battalion to have followed Holst? Why did Holst withdraw all the way back to Recht when he had secured a strategic point like Petit Thier, from where there are two routes to crossings over the Salm river, one at Vielsalm and the other at Grand Halleux? How did Holst manage to get through the Poteau road junction twice, once in daylight, when elements of four Troops of the US 14th Cavalry were positioned there preparing to advance towards Born at first light? The most logical explanation to all these questions is that there was no advance from Recht by Holst's Jagdpanzers or anyone else before first light on the Monday morning.

During the night command of the US 14th Cavalry Group had changed four times. Colonel Devine had been relieved and evacuated after handing over to Lieutenant Colonel Damon of the 18th Squadron, who had been ordered to report to HQ VIII Corps at 0100 hours. Lieutenant Colonel Ridge of the 32nd Squadron had therefore taken over, only to be relieved at 0220 hours by the missing Group Executive Officer, Lieutenant Colonel Duggan, who had suddenly reappeared from the skirmish near Recht the previous evening. Duggan immediately ordered Major J.L. Mayes, the same Mayes who had tried to retake Lanzerath on the 16th, to form a Task Force (TF) to recapture Born in the morning. Quite why he selected the poor S-3 of 32nd Squadron and not its CO is unclear. The TF consisted of most of C Troop 32nd Squadron, the last three anti-tank guns of A Company 820th TD Battalion and the remnants of C, E and F Troops of the 18th Squadron.

TF Mayes advanced from Poteau soon after first light but after 300m it ran into the Panzer-Grenadiers and Jagdpanzers of KG Hansen moving southwest from Recht. The result was the destruction of the main part of the TF. The survivors withdrew to Poteau, where they continued to resist until midday when Lieutenant Colonel Duggan ordered a withdrawal to Vielsalm. The scene around Poteau was one of chaos, with eight 8" howitzers of the 740th Field Artillery Battalion abandoned nearby. Only three armoured cars, two jeeps, one TD and a solitary Stuart light tank of the original TF managed to withdraw, carrying some of the wounded with them, although most of the men eventually managed to reach Vielsalm on foot. By midday the road to Vielsalm was wide open. Hansen's KG was well structured to exploit this opportunity and the whole route from Amel to Poteau was clear of enemy. The only impediment to Hansen's advance was an ad hoc force of stray tanks, infantry, cavalry and engineers at Petit Thier, which had been assembled there by an enterprising lieutenant of the 23rd Armored Infantry Battalion who christened it 'TF Navaho'. CCR of the 7th Armored Division came across this force as it moved to Vielsalm in the early morning and took it under command.

In view of the favourable situation it is not surprising that Hansen felt both frustration and anger when, at 1400 hours, he received inexplicable orders[2] to withdraw to Recht and secure it for the further advance of the 9th SS Panzer Division Hohenstaufen, part of the reserve II SS Panzer Corps. KG Hansen, having broken contact, was to advance via Logbiermé and Wanne to Trois Ponts in support of Peiper. This decision was illogical and wasted a golden opportunity which would not be presented again. If Hansen had been allowed to strike for Vielsalm on the Monday afternoon there is little doubt that he would have been successful, with potentially catastrophic results for the St Vith sector. The whole of the 7th Armored and 106th Infantry Divisions and CCB of the 9th Armored would have been put at risk. Fortunately for the Americans this was not to be and Hansen went firm at Poteau, Recht and Kaiserbarracke as ordered. During the afternoon CCA of the 7th Armored Division, under the command of Colonel Dwight Rosenbaum, moved to cover the Division's left flank by advancing with the 48th

Armoured Infantry Battalion and part of the 40th Tank Battalion towards Poteau. Naturally this force ran into Hansen's Jagdpanzers and Panzer-Grenadiers and by last light the Germans were holding north of the old railway cutting and CCA to its south. The Germans had no orders to attack and the Americans were not strong enough to do so.

By midday the 3rd SS Panzer-Grenadiers had cleared the Kaiserbarracke crossroads for use by Fast Group Knittel but it seems that Knittel had already decided to switch from Hansen's southern route to Peiper's. Leaving his reinforced Reconnaissance Group to follow on he hurried to catch up with the Leibstandarte's tanks.[3]

NOTES

1. Holst to author loc. cit., 2 Oct 1985.
2. Tiemann, *Die Leibstandarte IV/2*, p. 111.
3. Knittel, statement at Landsberg/Lech on 15 Mar 1948.

CHAPTER XV

Monday 18th December AM

The Defence Builds

Between midnight and dawn on the Monday major US reinforcements reached Malmédy (Map 12). Pergrin with his 180 engineers had bravely stayed in the town when everyone else had abandoned it and with their mines, demolitions, light machine guns and bazookas, for which they had precious little ammunition, the engineers had set up road blocks on all approaches. Without infantry and anti-tank guns however, they had little hope of preventing the Germans seizing the town whenever they wished. It had been fortunate that Malmédy had not been on Peiper's route and that the 12th SS Panzer Division had been unable to advance beyond Krinkelt and Rocherath (Map 7). The first infantry to arrive in Malmédy were the 'Norwegian' Americans of the 99th Infantry Battalion and they were basically complete by 0300 hours. Shortly after that the 526th Armored Infantry less two companies, and A Company of the 825th TD Battalion less a platoon, came in and deployed on the east and south sides of the town. This group was subordinated to Lieutenant Colonel Hansen, the CO of the 99th Infantry Battalion. A Company and the missing TD platoon had been diverted to Stavelot. By first light a reasonable defensive posture had been adopted.

At 1010 hours Colonel Walter Johnson, commanding the 117th Infantry Regiment of the 30th Infantry Division arrived in Malmédy. He brought with him his 3rd Battalion under the command of Lieutenant Colonel McDowell. They had been expecting to find the town in German hands and were relieved to find Pergrin and Hansen there with the situation under control. They were disgusted, though, with the scenes which met their eyes – abandoned American equipment, clothing, documents, food and even liquor everywhere they looked. McDowell's men immediately started to prepare positions on the south-east side of the town.

Just before midnight on the Sunday/Monday night seventy-five men of C Company 51st Engineer Combat Battalion under the command of Captain Sam Scheuber, arrived in Trois Ponts (Map 13).[1] This was the company Colonel Wallis Anderson had asked for that afternoon. Up to the time of their arrival the only engineers in the town had been a squad of A Company 291st Engineers guarding Anderson's HQ in the Hôtel Crismer and, as already mentioned, the two squads of Dave Pergrin's C Company under Lieutenant Rombaugh, at the Amblève river bridge.

As its name suggests there are three bridges in Trois Ponts, the Amblève and Salm river bridges in the town itself and a second Salm bridge 2km to the south on the Vielsalm road. Scheuber set up his HQ in the railway station and put his men to work preparing the two main wooden trestle bridges in Trois Ponts; thus relieving Rombaugh's two C Company squads which were sent back to the Château Froidcour in Stoumont, together with Chuck Hensel and his men who had turned up from the Stavelot road block. Scheuber also decided to put out protective road blocks using his eight bazookas, six 50 and four 30 calibre machine guns. During the night a half-track of B Company of the 526th Armored Infantry Battalion, towing a 57mm anti-tank gun, turned up in Trois Ponts. It had been on its way to Malmédy but, after becoming detached from its convoy, had taken the wrong road. Colonel Anderson immediately commandeered both half-track and gun and ordered his S-4, Captain Robert Jewett, to site the gun to cover the approach road from Stavelot. Obviously the gun needed support and Scheuber provided Lieutenant Richard Green and his platoon. About 0800 hours on the Monday morning the balance of C Company, a further sixty-five men, arrived from Marche. Scheuber was now capable of improving his defences and he put a platoon under Lieutenant Fred Nabors with two bazookas on the high ground a kilometre east of Trois Ponts astride the road coming in from Wanne. After putting a small rear guard on the Werbomont road, Scheuber ordered what little was left of C Company to occupy the buildings which over-looked the Salm river. The Trois Ponts defences were virtually complete.

It will be remembered that Lieutenant 'Blinkey' Chinlund, command-

114

ing C Company of the 202nd Engineers, had decided to quit Stavelot at about 2300 hours on the Sunday night. Colonel Anderson saw the Company driving through Trois Ponts, stopped Chinlund and at 0015 hours ordered him to return to Stavelot and 'defend the bridge' (Map 11). Squad Leader John Stevenson in his 1990 letter went on:

> We arrived at some sort of Headquarters. It was dark. It seemed that the people there were preparing to leave. As I understood it C Company received instructions to return to Stavelot to <u>defend</u> the bridge until <u>relieved</u>. I underline those words because I distinctly remember hearing them . . . we drove back to Stavelot and the various squads took up positions at the approach to the bridge. It was still dark. Sergeant Skuta told me to take some members of my squad and place anti-tank mines on the bridge surface. I and five or six members of my squad, including Bob Lehnert, John Dan and Mike Onderko carried ten to twelve mines to the opposite side of the bridge. We placed them in two rows spaced so that a vehicle could not drive on the bridge without hitting a mine. We activated the mines by pulling the pin.

Chinlund's HQ was re-established in a house some 100m back from the bridge near the Tanneries. Having placed a 50 calibre machine gun to cover the mines and squads on the eastern and northern approach roads, Chinlund was satisfied he had obeyed Anderson's orders and reported accordingly at 0100 hours. The possibility remains that he had misunderstood his orders and that Anderson in fact intended him to prepare the bridge for demolition.

During the move of the 526th Armored Infantry Battalion and A Company 825th TD Battalion to Malmédy during the Sunday/Monday night, someone at HQ 1st Army in Spa took the decision to divert part of the force to Stavelot, and orders for this to happen were received at 0025 hours whilst the group was on the move between Spa and Francorchamps. The 526th Executive Officer, Major Paul Solis, was put in charge and A Company of the 526th under Captain Charles Mitchell and the four 3" guns of the 1st Platoon, A Company of the 825th, under Lieutenant Doherty, were ordered 'to block roads south and east of Stavelot'. The Battalion S-1, Lieutenant John Pehovic, accompanied the group.

Sometime before midnight Private Bernie Goldstein of 'Stavelot Road Block' fame turned up at the Stavelot bridge where he found Lieutenant Cliff Wilson, the 291st Liaison Officer, in a jeep being driven by Private Lorenzo Liparulo. After listening to Goldstein's report of what had happened and how he had been lucky to escape, Wilson issued the extraordinary order for the two privates to drive up the hill to the old road block site to see if any Germans were there and if so what they were doing. Wilson did not accompany them. Goldstein and Liparulo drove a short distance beyond the bridge and then halted to listen. They were quietly smoking cigarettes when suddenly they were fired on by machine pistols; Goldstein was hit three times in the leg and hip and Liparulo in the chest, head and leg. Goldstein, thinking Liparulo was dead, managed to get back to the bridge for a second time. Wilson reported what had happened by radio to Colonel Anderson at 0135 hours. Poor Goldstein was looked after initially by C Company of the 202nd and then evacuated.

At 0140 hours Anderson received permission from V Corps to 'destroy bridges if required'. Fifteen minutes later he was given the very welcome news that the 291st platoon, which he had asked Pergrin's HQ for before midnight, was on its way to Stavelot from Werbomont and, much more importantly, that an armoured infantry company and TD platoon were also being sent there by HQ 1st Army. It was going to be a very tense hour-and-a-half wait, though, before any of these forces arrived. In the meantime he would have to rely on Chinlund.

Owing to road congestion and the time taken to reorganise the 526th Infantry column it was 0345 hours before Solis's Task Force (TF) arrived in Stavelot. One of Dave Pergrin's officers, Captain Lloyd Sheetz, who had been sent to HQ 1st Army earlier that evening with a written report of the alleged massacre at Baugnez, met the TF and briefed Solis that the engineer road block had been fired on and forced to withdraw, most units had fled but the situation was now quiet and the town in American hands. Sheetz said that no enemy had been seen and the 291st outpost had probably been fired on by German paratroopers or a recce patrol.

For Major Paul Solis and his subordinate commanders, Mitchell and Doherty, Stavelot presented an enormous problem.[2] They had never seen the town before, it was pitch dark and they had no maps of the place. The officers proceeded on foot to Chinlund's HQ which they took over as TF HQ and he briefed them on the geography of the town including details of the main bridge and another foot bridge just to its west. Despite the darkness Solis knew he had to act and he ordered Captain Mitchell, commanding the armoured infantry company, to place two platoons along the river to cover the bridge itself, and to keep the third platoon in reserve with his three 57mm infantry anti-tank guns. Doherty's four 3" TDs were also to remain in reserve in the market square. Mitchell's Company was a very large one with 250 men, all carried in half-tracks. It was armed with ten 50 calibre machine guns and had an anti-tank platoon of three 57mm guns commanded by 2nd Lieutenant Rogers. He and his men were, however, 'green' soldiers who had never seen action.

While Solis was trying to organise some sort of defence of Stavelot, Captain James Gamble commanding A Company of the 291st arrived in the town from Werbomont with Lieutenant Arch Taylor and his 3rd Platoon. This was the reserve force asked for earlier in the night by Colonel Anderson. Learning that a 291st soldier was missing, presumed dead, south of the bridge, Captain Gamble bravely crossed and rescued Liparulo who in fact was still just alive. Sadly he died of his wounds the following day. Then, finding not only Chinlund's engineer company in the town but even armoured infantry and TDs, Gamble decided his presence was no longer necessary and he withdrew his small force to Trois Ponts where he reported to Anderson who sent him on to the 291st HQ at Haute Bodeux.

And so at 0600 hours on the Monday morning the Americans had established primitive defences in front of Peiper's Kampfgruppe and to its north, at Malmédy, Stavelot and Trois Ponts. One of their problems, however, was that, apart from the engineers, no one else had seen the places they were defending in daylight; also, few had ever been in action before.

NOTES

1. The description of events at Trois Ponts is based on AARs, *Holding the Line* by Ken Hechler and *Die Leibstandarte IV/2* by Ralf Tiemann.
2. Charles Mitchell and other veterans of A/526th AI Bn described events in Stavelot to the author on 21 May 1991 during a return visit to the town. Similarly, the author accompanied a group of LAH veterans when they re-visited Stavelot on 1 Oct 1985 and again on 6–7 Jun 1991.

CHAPTER XVI

Monday 18th December AM

The Thrust for the Meuse

Despite their tiredness the Germans spent the rest of the Sunday night preparing for their first-light attack on Stavelot. Peiper, in his temporary HQ in a gabled house at the west end of Vau Richard, could see from his map that even after he had cleared a way through the town he still faced the problem of crossing the Amblève and Salm bridges in Trois Ponts (Map 13). He therefore made a two-phase plan designed to put his KG on the Werbomont road to the west of Trois Ponts by midday. Phase I required Diefenthal's panzer-grenadiers to seize the hill to the south of the Stavelot bridge, around the small suburb of Stokeu, before first light (Map 10). The bridge itself would have to be checked for demolitions and made safe for his tanks to cross. If it was defended this would involve seizing the bridge so that the pioneers could do their work. Artillery and mortars would have to be deployed to support both the attack on the bridge and the battle to clear a way through Stavelot.

Once the bridge was secured, Phase II would see tanks of the 1st SS Panzer Battalion, led by Kremser's 1st Company, drive over it as rapidly as possible and continue on to the west without pausing. The panzer-grenadiers would clear the buildings on either side of the route through the town for the rest of the column but it was not their job to secure Stavelot – that was for follow-up troops. At the same time as the Panthers of the 1st and 2nd SS Panzer Companies crossed the bridge, roughly 0800 hours, the 6th and 7th Type IV SS Panzer Companies, together with Sievers's 3rd SS Pioneer Company and at least a platoon of paratroopers, would advance from Vau Richard via Butai, Hinoumont, Wanne and Aisomont, with the aim of securing Trois Ponts from the east and, in particular, the Salm river bridge in the town.

By about 0400 hours Diefenthal's panzer-grenadiers had secured Stokeu and the hill leading up from the bridge to the site of Hensel's old road block, on the rue du Vieux Château (Map 11). It was his men, of course, who had shot up Goldstein and Liparulo; Hensel's mines had been cleared and the necessary mortar and artillery support deployed. The next step was to secure the bridge, and in this the Germans would be unexpectedly helped by the Americans.

Sometime after 0400 hours Solis's CO in Malmédy, Lieutenant Colonel Irwin, called on the radio and ordered him to establish road blocks around Stavelot as quickly as possible. Shortly afterwards Colonel Anderson called him with instructions to relieve the engineers in the town as soon as he could. Although Solis complained that no detailed reconnaissance was possible until daylight, he knew he had to take further action. He therefore instructed Captain Mitchell to deploy a road block of a squad of infantry and one 57mm anti-tank gun at the foot of the Francorchamps road in the town at the junction with the Haute Levée. The TF had come into Stavelot on this road and had seen the huge fuel dump on the east side of the road to the north of the town. Solis knew he had to give it some additional protection. He then ordered Mitchell to put a strong force at the site of Hensel's old road block and support it with further troops south of the river. Lieutenant Jack Doherty would provide two of his TDs for this force.

Even after talking to ex-members of A Company and the TD Platoon, and studying the relevant After Action Reports, it is still impossible to be certain about what happened next or the precise organisation of the American force which crossed to the south side of the bridge. It is however, reasonably certain that at about 0530 hours Captain Mitchell ordered his 2nd Platoon, under Lieutenant Harry Willyard, with four of its five half-tracks, one having broken down on its way to Stavelot[1], to cross the bridge and drive up to the site of Hensel's road block; two 3" guns of A Company 825th TD Battalion, commanded by Sergeants Whaley and Armstrong, were also told to cross but Lieutenant Doherty, the 1st Platoon commander, did not go with them. Coordination between the two groups seems to have been non-existent since none of the 825th survivors remember anything about the armoured infantry-men being south of the bridge and in 1994 Captain Mitchell wrote. 'I was not aware that any other units may have been sent across the bridge'.[2] Some veterans say that only two of Willyard's half-tracks crossed the river, but why he would leave half his platoon behind is unclear. At the same time the 3rd Platoon, under 2nd Lieutenant James Evans, less the squad at the foot of the Francorchamps road, was told to establish itself in the area directly south-east of the bridge. The 1st Platoon of 2nd Lieutenant Charles Beardslee, with its fifty-six men, two 50 and five 30 calibre machine guns and five bazookas, was to remain on the north bank of the river covering the bridge. John Stevenson of the 202nd Engineers wrote in 1990:

> I was standing by Sergeant Skuta at the approach to the bridge when two half-tracks drove up. The half-tracks were followed by other vehicles. One man in a half-track appeared to be in charge. He was probably an officer. He said "get your mines off the bridge; we're taking over." He acted, we thought, quite cocky.[3]

At just about 0600 hours Willyard's 2nd Platoon, having crossed the bridge, ran into Diefenthal's panzer-grenadiers on the rue du Vieux Château and was shot up; so were the half-tracks towing the two TDs which at the time were only about 70m beyond the bridge. The 3rd Platoon ran into similar trouble on the Stokeu hill. Willyard managed to lead most of his 2nd Platoon and one of his half-tracks back across the bridge and on up to the town square. The half-tracks towing the TDs tried to turn round but this proved impossible. The vehicles and guns were lost and six men killed, including Sergeant Armstrong. One wounded man, Calvanese,[4] managed to take cover in a house on the hill and the following day was smuggled back to safety across the bridge by the Belgian occupants. 2nd Lieutenant Evans of the 3rd Platoon was killed, as was Sergeant Ellery in charge of a machine gun squad just south of the bridge. 2nd Lieutenant James Wheelwright took over com-mand and re-established the 3rd Platoon on the north bank of the Amblève.

As the Americans withdrew, obviously in some disorder, the Ger-mans followed up with their 11th SS Panzer-Grenadier Company. They managed to cross the bridge but came under heavy fire from Mitchell's men on the north bank. Heinz Tomhardt, commanding the 11th SS Company, was wounded and one of the platoon commanders, Horn, killed. The Germans could not hold the bridge and withdrew to the south bank, but not before the 9th SS Pioneers had checked for demolitions and found the bridge clear.

The time was now after 0700 hours and it was beginning to get light. Mitchell (or was it Solis?) decided this was the moment to deploy his two spare 57mm anti-tank guns just 30m to the north of the bridge where they could cover it. By now C Company of the 202nd Engineers had withdrawn to the town square. John Stevenson wrote:

> We felt we had been relieved of our duty to defend the bridge. Sergeant Skuta told us to go up to the schoolhouse where a kitchen had been set up and eat breakfast. Just as we got there flares went up on the far side of the bridge and guns began to fire from over there. We immediately ran towards the town square.

SS Senior Sergeant Rayer of the 11th SS Company described the bridge battle as follows:

> 11th Company was given the order to take the bridge . . . 1st and 2nd Platoons only were available; due to mechanical problems the rest of the company was further back. Only Wilfer's section of my platoon was available. The bridge was taken but could not be held. The company established itself on one side of the bridge and was in a very difficult position. Enemy tanks continued to move and we expected a counter-attack. We were fired on from all sides but couldn't do much about it. We had quite considerable losses including Tomhardt, Horn and several others. On Diefenthal's order I took over the company. At first light our tanks came to us. As soon as they arrived we continued on.[5]

At 0800 hours, as Peiper's mortars and artillery opened fire on Stavelot, Kremser's Panthers began a rapid descent of the rue du Vieux Château. Zimmerman in the lead tank described it thus:

> Colonel Peiper himself detailed off my tank to lead the attack through Stavelot which was to happen at first light. The whole crew was given a very precise briefing: 'immediately after the bend there's an anti-tank gun [this was one of the American TDs] – you'd better go in fifth gear. There's one of our officers lying in the middle of the bridge. Don't know if he's dead or wounded. The bridge is secure. Watch out for that officer.' Slowly it got light. We ran our engines to warm them. Drivers: 'go!' We met no resistance. The anti-tank gun was standing there – we rammed it out of the way. On to the bridge! No officer. No sooner were we over the bridge than we were hit. Gunner 'open fire!' The 75mm fired but didn't hit. Our gun was pointing

crazily in the sky after the hit. Driver 'accelerate!' We drove over the trail of the anti-tank gun. It broke and ended up on the driver's hatch. Great fire from all sides. Gradually it decreased and we were through.[6]

Zimmermann had been hit by, and had eventually run over, one of Mitchell's 57mm guns, commanded by a Sergeant Smith, just to the north of the bridge. It is not clear whether the second gun, covering Smith's and located by the Café Colinet, was abandoned or managed to withdraw.

The sight of the Panthers driving fast towards them was too much for the American infantrymen of the 1st and 3rd Platoons covering the north bank of the Amblève river and, not surprisingly, they withdrew. Part of the 3rd Platoon was cut off for a time in the Tanneries but most managed to get back to the town square. In view of the tank threat Lieutenant Doherty now deployed his two remaining TDs – one, under Sergeant Celentano, to a position some 300m from the market square on the Malmédy road where it could fire at tanks coming down the hill towards the bridge, and the other, commanded by Sergeant Hauser, to cover the main route from the bridge to the square, the rue du Châtelet. Rather than present easy targets the tanks consequently diverted left up the very narrow rue Haut Rivage and then turned left again up the rue Neuve and so out towards Trois Ponts. This outflanking manoeuvre and the fact that panzer-grenadiers were advancing towards Hauser's TD through the flanking buildings caused him to 'spike' his gun with a phosphorus grenade and withdraw with the rest of the American infantry.

Meanwhile the other TD under Sergeant Celentano had brought the rue du Vieux Château under sustained fire. Several of the houses were set on fire and at least one Panther knocked out. Kremser, the commander of the 1st SS Panzer Company was wounded during this battle and another Panther was immobilised by a hit on its road wheels. Its commander, SS 2nd Lieutenant Hans Hennecke, took over Kremser's Panther and the 1st Company. The Americans claimed to have knocked out four German tanks during this battle, but just as this was an exaggeration so was the account of SS Senior Sergeant Rayer of the 11th SS Panzer-Grenadier Company when he claimed that American tanks were moving around on the north bank of the river whereas in fact there were no US tanks with the Solis TF at all.

In the middle of this struggle for Stavelot a battery of American 50 calibre, trailer-mounted, anti-aircraft machine guns drove into the town on the Malmédy road (Map 10). It was D Battery of the 203rd AAA Battalion, part of the 7th Armored Division trying to get through to St Vith. The guns deployed temporarily and opened fire across the river. Despite pleas from Solis and/or Mitchell to stay, their commander decided that fifteen minutes was enough and that this was no place for him and his men. He led his Battery away to the north.

By 1000 hours this stage of the battle for Stavelot was over and the Americans had abandoned the town to Peiper's column. Mitchell's 1st and 2nd Platoons withdrew with the one remaining TD of Doherty's 1st Platoon to Malmédy, which they reached at midday. The C Company engineers went out to the north. Bill Doyle, who in 1944 was commanding their 3rd Platoon on the north edge of Stavelot, wrote in 1990 'I did not know the unit was leaving – some one brought a message over from 2nd Platoon that the outfit had "bugged-out".'[7] John Stevenson wrote:

> We ran to the railway tracks behind the town where we found two others from our squad . . . the four of us kept moving, cautiously, in the direction the buzz bombs were flying. We spent the night in the woods. In the morning we found a fuel dump which was being evacuated. We helped a soldier load a truck and climbed aboard. He drove to a town where we found the rest of our Company.[8]

Major Solis, Captain Mitchell and Lieutenant Wheelwright, with the remaining twenty-seven men of his 3rd Platoon, and the squad and 57mm gun from the bottom of the Francorchamps road, withdrew towards Fuel Depot Number 3. When they reached the Ferme Bonaparte, 3km north of Stavelot Solis ordered them to halt. Fearing that the SS tanks would follow up in an effort to capture the fuel they so desperately needed, he then told the Belgian guards and American GIs to set fire to the petrol to form a barrier at the southern edge of the fuel dump. This they did after a certain amount of trouble actually trying to ignite it. The story of Peiper's tanks being met and repelled by a wall of fire has been told many times and portrayed vividly in the Hollywood film *Battle of the Bulge*. It never happened! None of Peiper's tanks or men went anywhere near the fuel dump or even up the Francorchamps road.[9] Peiper was far more interested in securing the Trois Ponts bridges and had no intention of risking a time-consuming diversion to the north, even for much needed fuel.

A Company of the 526th Armored Infantry had three killed, fifteen wounded and twenty men missing in this battle. Doherty's TD Platoon lost three of its four guns and had six killed and two men wounded, while D Battery of the 203rd AAA Battalion had five men wounded. Chinlund's engineers lost only equipment.

There are two interesting footnotes to this episode. First, in May 1991 Captain Mitchell told the author, during a veterans' visit to Stavelot, that he never saw Major Solis during the actions in the town – the first time he saw him after receiving the order to re-establish the road block south of the river was at about 1100 hours at the road block covering the fuel dump. Secondly, it would seem that the decision to put troops across the Amblève before first light led directly to the collapse of the American defence. In view of the fact that stone and brick buildings lined the north bank of the Amblève, and in the light of subsequent events, it is clear that a company of 250 infantrymen, armed with twenty heavy machine guns and eighteen bazookas, supported by four 3" TDs, three 57mm anti-tank guns and a company of engineers equipped with mines, explosives and further bazookas and light machine guns, should have been able to hold the Germans south of the river. Moreover it was a tragedy that no attempt was made to prepare the Stavelot bridge for demolition before Peiper attacked. If Major Solis had taken the basic precaution of checking that this had been done as soon as he arrived in Stavelot, the events of 18th December might have turned out very differently and many lives, both American and Belgian, might have been saved.

The sounds of Peiper's main attack on Stavelot could be clearly heard by the defenders of Trois Ponts. Anderson was reasonably confident that the town could be held, particularly since both main bridges were now prepared for demolition. He had already sent a squad of A Company's 1st Platoon to guard the lower Salm bridge 2km south of Trois Ponts, but at 0830 hours he decided it was time to reinforce the small force and to have the bridge prepared. The rest of the A Company Platoon under Lieutenant 'Bucky' Walters was ordered there with instructions to blow it if any Germans appeared on the east bank.

Just before the N-23 enters Trois Ponts from Stavelot it passes under two very substantial railway viaducts (Map 13); there is then a T-junction, with the left turn going into Trois Ponts and the right turn going due north towards La Gleize. Peiper's planned route was to turn left at the junction, cross the Amblève river after 200m and then turn right over the Salm bridge and so out on the Werbomont road. Covering this route, the Americans had established an elaborate road block. On the west side of the viaducts Captain Sam Scheuber had positioned a 2½-ton truck with a 50 calibre machine gun mounted on its cab manned by Staff Sergeant Fred Salatino and Corporal Jacob Young. On the east side of the viaducts, on the bend just forward of the Lifrange Hôtel (now the Auberge du Vieux Moulin), the 57mm anti-tank which Colonel Anderson had commandeered during the night was sited facing east with its crew of four armoured infantrymen and Lieutenant Richard Green of 3rd Platoon, C Company 51st Engineers immediately behind it. The half-track used to tow the gun was backed into a driveway on the opposite side of the N-23 with its driver and Captain Robert Jewett, Anderson's S-4. Six more 526th infantrymen and some members of Green's Platoon were in a ditch to the rear of the 57mm. Two hundred metres to the east of the gun Green had posted three men in a jeep and 50m beyond them, out of sight of the anti-tank gun, were two more infantrymen with a daisy chain of mines. The idea was that the daisy chain would be pulled across the road if German tanks appeared, the men would then dash back to the jeep, which in turn would quickly drive back to warn the crew of the 57mm.

At 1000 hours Colonel Anderson ordered his HQ to pack up for an emergency withdrawal and sent his S-3, Major Webb, to brief HQ 1st Army on the current situation. At 1105 hours Anderson sent his HQ staff to join Pergrin's HQ at Haute Bodeux and at about this time Peiper's Panthers left Stavelot for Trois Ponts. As they drew level with a small bridge across the Amblève at a place called Petit Spai, about 700m east of the 57mm anti-tank gun, Corporal Frazier and Private Beiker pulled their daisy chain of mines across the road and ran back to the jeep, which drove quickly back to Green's position and reported the German advance. The commander of the lead Panther and of the 3rd Platoon in Kremser's 1st SS Panzer Company, SS Senior Sergeant Strelow, calmly got out of his tank and removed the mines before continuing.[10] As his Panther approached the bend in front of the 57mm, a Panther to his rear spotted the American anti-tank gun and fired several rounds in its direction. After returning a few rounds the 57mm was knocked out and all four members of its crew killed. They were Lillard McCollum, Donald Hollenbeck, Dallas Buchannan and James Higgins.[11] Captain Jewett said afterwards that he saw eight German tanks approaching and he and Green felt they had no chance of stopping them. At this time, about 1145 hours, they heard a loud explosion to their rear as the Amblève bridge was blown on Anderson's order. They knew that their job was basically done and that they were now cut off from the rest of C Company in Trois Ponts. They took the very reasonable decision to withdraw to the north in the half-track and 2½-ton truck. Green and his men got back to Trois Ponts at 1500 hours by coming in from the west and Jewett and the surviving members of the 526th Infantry rejoined the 1111th Engineer Group HQ at Modave forty-eight hours later.

Peiper's problem now was to get his tanks through the twin railway viaducts, which he did not realise had been abandoned. Panzer-Grenadiers were deployed to work their way along the river bank and clear the viaducts, which they did of course without opposition. At about 1230 hours Peiper and Diefenthal came forward to the viaducts to assess the situation. Peiper said later 'We were standing below the railway bridge and received rather severe fire from the bridge further down.'[12] They knew the Amblève crossing had gone and so had no alternative but to turn north to La Gleize and then hope to rejoin the N-23 further west beyond Haute Bodeux (Map 14).

But what of Peiper's other thrust on Trois Ponts by his Type IV tank companies and their accompanying pioneers and paratroopers? They had set off at 0800 hours from Vau Richard using a Belgian, Fernand

Hopa, as a guide – his body was found later near Butai. At about 1200 hours the leading three Type IVs reached Lieutenant Fred Nabors's 2nd Platoon of C Company 51st Engineers at a place called Noupré on the high ground about one kilometre due east of Trois Ponts (Map 13). Nabors had two bazookas, one of which was sited covering directly up the Aisomont road and the other in a flanking position also covering the road. The flanking bazooka let the first Type IV tank reach anti-tank mines laid on the road and then fired at the second tank. Unfortunately it missed and for some reason the head-on bazooka failed to fire. The tanks then opened fire on the Americans, putting them to flight. They made their escape through the thick pine forest and eventually took up new positions on the south flank of C Company in Trois Ponts. Shortly after this, at about 1300 hours, Anderson ordered the Salm river bridge in the town blown. Although the mines at the Noupré position were soon cleared there was now no way for the 6th and 7th SS Panzer Companies to get through Trois Ponts. Colonel Anderson's and Sam Scheuber's defence had been successful in more or less the way they had planned it. KG Peiper was not going to get through Trois Ponts that day. In fact there was another reason why the Type IV tank companies could not advance further – they were out of fuel.[13] Although the range of the tanks was roughly 200km, this was reduced to about 100km at the most in the conditions under which they had been operating. From their assembly area near Blankenheimerdorf to Aisomont is about 100km and they had averaged only 2km per hour. Despite the top-up in Büllingen their tanks were now dry. When the bad news was relayed to Peiper he ordered them to rejoin the main column by returning through Stavelot as soon as a petrol resupply reached them.

At 1155 hours, after ordering the Amblève bridge blown, Anderson told his own HQ and that of the 291st Engineers at Haute Bodeux to withdraw to Modave. At the same time he sent his Motor Pool Officer, Captain Lundberg, in person to warn HQ 1st Army at Spa that they were in great danger. At 1210 hours he sent one more vital message to Pergrin's S-3, Major Lampp, at Haute Bodeux. He was to provide troops to prepare the bridge over the Lienne river at Neufmoulin (Map 14). It was to be blown on Anderson's order or if German tanks approached. Having himself observed nineteen Panthers pass through the viaducts at Trois Ponts and turn north, Anderson was in no doubt that Peiper was heading for this bridge.

NOTES

1. Rick Cauterucio, a member of 2nd Platoon, to author loc. cit., May 1991.
2. Article by Charles Mitchell in *The Pekan*, magazine of the 526th AI Bn, dated Jun 1994.

3. Letter to author dated 8 Feb 1990.
4. Calvanese to author loc. cit., 1989.
5. Rayer, statement at Dachau 26 Apr 1947.
6. Tiemann, *Die Leibstandarte IV/2*, pp. 81–2.
7. Letter to author dated 16 Jan 1990.
8. Letter to author dated 8 Feb 1990.
9. Sgt Ed Keoghan of the 291st Engrs was in position on the Francorchamps road above Stavelot from approximately 1000 hours on 18th Dec until the arrival of the 117th Infantry at about 1300 hours; he confirmed that no Germans approached the fuel dump – Holt Giles, *The Damned Engineers*, p. 233; also Hans Hennecke and other LAH veterans to author loc. cit., 7 Jun 1991.
10. Strelow's citation signed by Poetschke, Peiper, Mohnke and Priess.
11. Various reports that Strelow's tank was "crippled/exploded/immobilized" are certainly inaccurate since the Panther was, in fact, knocked out 9 km to the west in an air-attack later in the day (see photograph 17).
12. Peiper's testimony at Dachau Trial.
13. Sternebeck to author *loc. cit.*, 1 Oct 1985.

CHAPTER XVII

Monday 18th December PM

Casting the Net

Monday afternoon saw a major strengthening of the Malmédy defences (Map 12). At 1300 hours the Command Post of Colonel Branner Purdue's 120th Infantry Regiment, part of the 30th Infantry Division, was established in Bevercé, 2km north of the town. At this stage the plan was for the Regiment to act as a reserve. Accordingly one battalion was deployed at Bevercé, one to the east of Malmédy at Chodes and the other to the west on the Malmédy–Stavelot road.

Recall that during the morning the 3rd Battalion of the 117th Regiment (3/117) had already taken up positions on the south-east side of Malmédy. Now another battalion of that Regiment, the 2nd under Major Ammon (2/117), arrived and set up to the west of the town between Burninville and Masta. It reported knocking out three German tanks within ninety minutes of arrival. Over the next few days it continued to report enemy forces massing opposite its positions and various other enemy actions. It is difficult, indeed impossible, to identify who these German forces were or where they came from, and it seems more likely that this Battalion, knowing its brother battalions were heavily engaged and not wishing to be left out of the action, invented some opposition for itself. There were certainly no German tanks anywhere near it on the Monday afternoon.

The remaining battalion of the 117th Infantry, the 1st commanded by Lieutenant Colonel Robert Frankland (1/117), had arrived in the Malmédy area at about 0800 hours that morning. But when at 1030 hours news arrived through an unknown officer of A Company of the 526th Armoured Infantry that his unit had been forced to withdraw from Stavelot, Frankland was ordered to recapture the town without delay (Map 10). The Battalion moved via Francorchamps and arrived about 1300 hours in the area of the fuel dump where Major Solis was in position with 3rd Platoon, A Company of the 526th. It was impossible to drive further due to the burning petrol which, far from forming a barrier for Peiper's tanks, was now preventing Frankland's Battalion advancing rapidly on Stavelot. There was nothing to do but de-truck the Battalion and advance on foot. Frankland ordered the fire put out and the 526th Platoon to move to a position above Stavelot where it could cover the advance of his Battalion. He had been given the assault gun and mortar platoons of the 526th Armored Infantry for support and these were deployed for the same purpose. Keeping C Company in reserve, Frankland then ordered his A Company, under the command of Captain John Kent, with the 2nd Machine Gun Platoon of Lieutenant Frank Warnock under command, to advance on the west flank and Captain Spiker's B Company, with the 1st Machine Gun Platoon of Lieutenant Graeser, on the east. This advance began at about 1330 hours.

The third Regiment of the 30th Infantry Division was the 119th commanded by Colonel Edwin Sutherland. It had moved via Eupen, Verviers and Theux and was planning to deploy its 1st and 3rd Battalions in the Stoumont area and the 2nd Battalion further to the west in Werbomont (Map 3). It was hoped they would all be in position by last light. In support of Sutherland's Regiment were the 197th Field Artillery Battalion and A Company of the 823rd TD Battalion. The other two 105mm artillery battalions and the 155mm battalion of the Division were supporting the 117th and 120th Regiments.

Major General Jim Gavin, temporarily commanding the XVIIIth Airborne Corps, had given orders for his own 82nd Airborne Division to move to Bastogne starting early on Monday 18th December. Having done so, he set out for General Hodges 1st Army Headquarters at Spa which he reached at 0900 hours on the Monday morning. He found the place in a state of chaos with rear elements of the HQ pulling out rapidly. After urgent discussions with Hodges it was agreed that one of the two available airborne divisions should be diverted to confront the German armoured column which was, at that moment, attacking Stavelot. Gavin issued the necessary orders to direct the 82nd to an assembly area around Werbomont. He asked for it to be given tank, TD and artillery support and for the assembly area to be protected. Since his Division was being moved in open-topped 2½-ton trucks and 10-ton trucks and trailers, without any heavy weapon support, it was extremely vulnerable and would remain so until it could deploy and be reinforced. Accordingly, Major Hal McCown's 2nd Battalion of the 119th Infantry (2/119) was ordered to move to the Werbomont area as quickly as possible to provide cover for the concentration of the 82nd Airborne Division.

Gavin himself arrived in Werbomont mid afternoon and, driving east to the Lienne river at Neufmoulin (Map 14) found, at about 1600 hours, a squad of 2nd Platoon, A Company of the 291st Engineers, under Staff Sergeant Pigg and their Platoon commander Lieutenant Edelstein, busily preparing the bridge there for demolition. This was the party requested by Colonel Anderson when he saw Peiper's tanks turn north at Trois Ponts. Gavin knew from his map that there were two other bridges across the Lienne further to the north (Map 15) but Edelstein, after explaining that he did not have enough explosive for more than one bridge, assured the general that those to the north were incapable of supporting the weight of tanks. Gavin drove away reassured.

Major Robert Yates had been the Commanding Officer of the 51st Engineer Combat Battalion for a short period in 1943 but this 6'3" Texan was a flamboyant character who was not unknown for minor misdemeanours and on 18th December 1944 he was the Battalion Executive Officer. At 1330 hours he arrived in Trois Ponts for the daily liaison meeting at the 1111th Group HQ, totally unaware that he was walking into a battle situation. He was therefore a little surprised to be told by Colonel Anderson that he was to take charge at Trois Ponts and that he, Anderson, would be leaving for HQ 1st Army shortly. Yates, however, was just the man for the job. He and Captain Sam Scheuber set to work at once to reorganise the defence of the town now that both main bridges were blown (Map 13). Observation posts were set up on the railway embankment, mines laid east of the viaducts and to the north on the N-33 and the men organised into two basic groups. The defenders would be all to the west of the Salm river, with one group under Lieutenant Green in the north part of the town and the second group in the south and angled back to the west.

It will be remembered that during the morning Lieutenant 'Bucky' Walters had been ordered to reinforce his squad of A Company 291st Engineers at the other Salm bridge to the south of Trois Ponts and prepare it for demolition. Having ensured the charges were properly laid Walters reurned to Trois Ponts, leaving Sergeant Jean Miller with orders to blow if Germans tried to cross. On his return Walters and his two remaining squads and the 291st squad commanded by Sergeant Hinkel, which was guarding Anderson's Command Post, were placed under Major Yates's command. They were to act as an infantry reserve.

The 291st report of events at the southern bridge on the Monday afternoon says that Sergeant Miller and his squad were aware of the tanks of the 6th and 7th SS Panzer Companies at the top of the hill above the bridge but, knowing the northern Salm bridge was blown, they were not too concerned – any approach would have to be from Aisomont or Wanne to Spineu and then north up the N-28 on the east bank of the Salm. For enemy foot soldiers, however, there was no problem and Miller's men were not surprised when they saw Germans come directly down the hill and approach the bridge. Miller let the Germans remove the defensive mines before he touched off the charge. There seems little doubt that the Germans were men from the 3rd SS Pioneer Company who had accompanied the Type IV tanks in their thrust to Trois Ponts. Suggestions that this demolition took place twenty-four hours later can be discounted.

The decision for the American engineers to stay in Trois Ponts made military sense but required guts. A simple look at the map revealed that Peiper's tanks moving north from the town would inevitably turn west and then be behind any force left in Trois Ponts (Map 14).

CHAPTER XVIII

Monday 18th PM to Tuesday 19th December Dawn

Recoil

At about the time the Kampfgruppe's tanks turned north from Trois Ponts, Gustav Knittel left his Reconnaissance Battalion Group on the Hansen route and moved to catch up with Peiper. He gave orders for his men to follow him via Kaiserbarracke, Pont and Stavelot (Map 6). At this time the commander of the 2nd SS Panzer Reconnaissance Company, SS Lieutenant Manfred Coblenz, was south of the Kaiserbarracke crossroads protecting the junction from any possible American advance on that flank. He was therefore the last to arrive in Stavelot where, at about 1330 hours, he found the rest of the Fast Group halted south of the river with orders for him to bring it forward when he arrived. By this time a considerable proportion of Peiper's Kampfgruppe had passed through Stavelot, including twenty-five Panthers and at least seven Tigers. Diefenthal's Panzer-Grenadier Battalion with Koch's six 150mm heavy infantry guns and Rumpf's 9th SS Panzer Pioneers were also through. At least fourteen flak vehicles of Major Wolf's Battalion had crossed the Amblève but the 10th SS Panzer Anti-Aircraft Company had lost two of its vehicles and had both its commander, Vögler, and his second in command wounded during an air attack by seven P-47s in the Buchholz/Honsfeld area. Still left to cross the river was the whole of Kalischko's 1st SS Panzer Artillery Battalion, the bulk of the Tigers, all the KG support elements and of course the two Type IV tank companies near Wanne with their associated pioneers and paratroopers.

Coblenz had been a member of the Leibstandarte since 1939 and was an experienced soldier; he took no chances and dismounted his Company before leading them across the bridge to clear the way for the vehicles of the Battalion Group. In 1986, during a visit to Stavelot with the author, Coblenz insisted that he and his men were fired on by Belgian civilians. No one was hit and the whole of his 2nd Company, Knittel's HQ, three Puma armoured cars and some schwimmwagens of the 3rd Company, parts of the 4th Company including the three 150mms of the Infantry Gun Platoon, and five of the six 105mm guns of Butschek's 5th SS Panzer Artillery Battery[1] got through Stavelot at this time.

Meanwhile Peiper's tanks had followed the flooded water meadows of the Amblève, past the dead arm of the river at Coo (Map 14) and then, after passing under the blown railway viaduct, they turned west up the hill to La Gleize which they entered at about 1330 hours. In the village the 1st SS Panzer Company, led by SS 2nd Lieutenant Hans Hennecke,[2] turned sharp left off the N-33 on to the minor road leading to Cheneux and eventually back to Peiper's planned route, the N-23 from Trois Ponts to Werbomont. There was no opposition in La Gleize though three Belgians fell victim to machine gun fire as the tanks sprayed the houses in a search for possible American positions. After passing beneath the spires of the Château Froidcour, Hennecke's lead Panther emerged from the trees to overlook the Cheneux bridge. Peiper said later 'We saw some persons rushing around the bridge and since we had to expect that this bridge too would be blown, the Spitze stopped and opened fire.'[3] The Cheneux bridge was not in fact prepared and the persons near the bridge were Belgians, four women and a man. One of the women was killed outright by the machine gun fire, one died later from her wounds and another and the man were wounded. In 1991 Hennecke insisted that he had seen US soldiers at the bridge and in 1993 the author learned from a well known local historian, Monsieur Gérard Grégoire, that the Belgian man had unwisely been wearing an American GI's top coat. Even so, in good visibility and at a range of only 300m, it is difficult to understand how such a mistake could have been made.

Shortly after Hennecke's Panthers crossed the bridge and started their slow climb into Cheneux, the leading elements of the KG were struck by US fighter bombers. Two F-6 aircraft (adapted Mustangs) from the 67th Tactical Reconnaissance Group, piloted by Captain Richard Cassady and 2nd Lieutenant Abraham Jaffe called in the P-47s. This was the first of a series of attacks that afternoon by a total of thirty-four P-47 Thunderbolts and two Royal Air Force (RAF) Typhoons. The P-47s, flying from airfields at Asch and Chievres, could each carry two 1,000lb and one 500lb bombs and mounted eight 50 calibre machine guns. The RAF Typhoons, from 247 Squadron based at Eindhoven, mounted tank busting rockets and were just two of a total of fifty-two RAF aircraft which flew armed reconnaissance flights on the 18th December in the Malmédy/St Vith areas.

A Belgian report speaks of two separate attacks on the front of Peiper's column, the first occurring when the Spitze was near the Cheneux bridge at about 1400 hours and the second, an hour later, when it was near the next village to the west, Rahier. These, and other strikes reported by both American and German ground troops, equate well with US and British air force records. The first attack would seem to have been made by four P-47s of the 386th Squadron[4] which reported bombing a tank and strafing in the Stavelot area between 1335 and 1500 hours. Peiper said he lost a total of five to seven vehicles from his column and the History of the Leibstandarte talks of three Panthers and five SPWs being hit. Certainly one Panther was immobilized between the Cheneux bridge and the village. Belgian reports also speak of forty SS wounded being taken to local farms, the Gillet mill near Cheneux and to the nearby Château de la Vaulx Renard. The second attack mentioned by the Belgians, when the Spitze was near Rahier, was almost certainly made by four Thunderbolts of the 390th Squadron between 1445 and 1505 hours.

The heaviest attacks on the KG started at 1440 hours and affected the whole length of the column as far back as Lodomé (Map 10). At 1416 hours the 1/117 Infantry, from its position on the hill directly north of Stavelot, said it could see 'hundreds' of enemy vehicles south of the river. This resulted in a firm request for an air strike by the Regimental Commander at 1435 hours. Sorties began at 1440 hours and went on until 1610 hours. They were flown by twelve P-47s, in groups of four aircraft each, from the 386th and 387th Squadrons and the four aircraft from the 390th Squadron already mentioned which attacked the head of the column near Rahier. Another major attack by fourteen aircraft of the 396th Squadron began at the same time and ended at 1530 hours. The Typhoons were operating in the Stavelot area between 1445 and 1515 hours.[5] Most sorties reported attacks against tanks, half-tracks,

131

armour generally and motor transport but not all the strikes hit the Germans. Four P-47s of 387th Squadron 'bombed motor transport' 2km north of Stavelot and the RAF Typhoons, as well as claiming one tank probably destroyed and one damaged in Stavelot, claimed to have struck half-tracks to the north of the town. The strikes to the north of Stavelot were almost certainly against the 1st and 2nd Battalions of the 117th Infantry; indeed, at 1545 hours the 2nd Battalion reported its positions had been hit by two friendly aircraft. German anti-aircraft fire was very effective. US air force reports show that one P-47 was shot down and eight others damaged. SS Sergeant Karl Wortmann, commanding one of the KG's Wirbelwinds, said that after the attack Peiper personally congratulated his flak gunners.

During the air attacks Peiper himself took cover in an old concrete bunker just to the west of the Cheneux bridge. It was as well he did for it was virtually opposite the Dumont farm, which received a direct hit. It was in this bunker and during the air strike that Knittel eventually met up with Peiper.[6] Also during the afternoon the KG's radio officer, Krause, arrived with his vehicles[7] and Peiper was able to communicate once more with his Divisional Headquarters.

The critical delay in the advance of the KG caused by the air strikes was one of three important factors which were to have serious consequences for Peiper. The delay, the timely arrival of Frankland's 1/117 Infantry in Stavelot and the failure of German follow-up units to secure Peiper's lifeline meant that vital elements of the KG, including resupply vehicles and the whole of the 1st SS Panzer Artillery Battalion, would never cross the Amblève.

By 1500 hours A and B Companies of the 1/117, advancing into Stavelot, reached the approximate line of the rue Neuve, market square and avenue Ferdinand Nicolay (Map 11). Five minutes later an observer from the 118th Field Artillery Battalion, the guns of which were now deployed to the north-west of Malmédy, reported the 1/117 being attacked by ten tanks and infantry. At 1520 hours the 1/117 itself reported twelve German tanks in Stavelot. These reports were correct. Remember that the 6th and 7th SS Panzer Companies near Wanne to the east of Trois Ponts had run out of fuel. By draining fuel tanks they had managed to produce enough petrol for five Type IVs of the 6th Company and one of the 7th to try to rejoin the KG as instructed through Stavelot. These included the tank of the commander of the 6th Company, SS Lieutenant Benno Junker, and the tank of the commander of the 7th Company, SS Captain Oskar Klingelhöfer. Leaving the truck-mounted pioneers of the 3rd SS Pioneer Company with the remaining Type IVs under the command of Sternebeck, SS Lieutenant Sievers accompanied the six Type IVs with his two SPW-mounted 1st and 2nd SS Pioneer Platoons. At roughly the same time Tigers of the 1st Company of the 501st, led by SS Lieutenant Jurgen Wessel, started to cross the Amblève bridge.[8] None of these troops were trying to attack the 1/117 in Stavelot – they were merely trying to catch up with Peiper.

Whereas the Type IVs and Pioneer SPWs succeeded, the Tigers were less successful. After Wessel and two others had crossed, a third Tiger commanded by SS Senior Sergeant Brandt was damaged during the air attack when it was just short of the bridge, blocking the way for the following tanks. Meanwhile Wessel himself had got into trouble in the very narrow rue Haut Rivage, where he claimed to have received two hits 'on the nose' from an anti-tank weapon causing him to run backwards and become embedded in a house. Photographs of the Tiger taken immediately after the battle, however, show no visible damage and it seems unlikely that a frontal shot from a bazooka would have stopped a Tiger. It could well have been driver error. Anyway, Wessel changed to the Tiger behind him and drove, via the even narrower Hottonruy, on towards Trois Ponts. Brandt's Tiger, damaged near the bridge, eventually managed to cross but needed track repair, so it and another Tiger, commanded by SS senior Sergeant Werner Wendt, remained in Stavelot overnight with their paratrooper escorts.

It is hardly surprising that, whilst the air strikes were going on and the bridge area was busy with German tanks and SPWs, A and B Companies of the 1/117 held their positions in the northern part of the town. Between dusk and 1800 hours Frankland's Battalion was reinforced by five Shermans of B Company 743rd Tank Battalion and three M-10s of C Company 823rd TD Battalion, one M-10 having got stuck in the mud 2km north of Stavelot. Two of the Shermans retired to the rear for maintenance while the other three moved to the region of the market square. As darkness fell the 1/117 claimed it was holding the northern half of Stavelot but still having trouble with German tanks. These were almost certainly the two Tigers which had remained in the town north of the river and a Panther of the 1st Company which had broken down in the same area.

Staff Sergeant Pigg and his squad of A Company 291st Engineers arrived at the Neufmoulin bridge over the Lienne river at about 1500 hours (Map 15). They met a stream of refugees from Trois Ponts and other local villages who told them German tanks were in Trois Ponts. Anderson's choice of which bridge to prepare for demolition had proved to be the correct one. The stone bridge at Cheneux would have taken far longer than the wooden trestle structure at Neufmoulin and any engineer squad coming from Werbomont would not have had time to reach it and do the job before Peiper's tanks got there.

Anderson's 1111th Engineer Group HQ and Pergrin's 291st Engineer HQ crossed the bridge before 1600 hours and Pigg's Platoon commander, Edelstein, dropped off as they did so. Remember that Major

General Jim Gavin visited the site as well that afternoon and went away reasonably satisfied. By 1600 hours the 180-foot timber trestle bridge was prepared for demolition. A double circuit was used to connect 2500lbs of TNT on the bridge piers to the detonator which was placed in an old sentry box some 50m back from the bridge. Corporal Chapin was responsible for firing the charges. The squad truck, which was far from reliable mechanically, was positioned at the bottom of the hill just to the west of the bridge with its engine running. The driver, Kovacs, was instructed to start driving if the bridge was blown and everyone would run and try to jump on board! Lieutenant Edelstein then decided he should do something about the approach roads on the west bank of the Lienne, so he sent Sergeant Billington and two men with some mines to the south and Corporal Bossert and Private Rondenell to the north. Both groups had orders to pull their daisy chains of mines across the road if German vehicles appeared so that the firing party would have time to blow the bridge. Whilst two soldiers were sent out on the road to the east of the Lienne to act as sentries, the remaining engineers remained at the west end of the bridge with a 30 calibre machine gun.

The air attack on the KG near the village of Rahier ended at 1505 hours and, after clearing the disabled Panther and other destroyed vehicles out of the way, Peiper was able to continue his advance some time after 1530 hours. The column rejoined the N-23 3km west of the village at about 1615 hours. As the lead Panther started down the N-23 towards Neufmoulin the jeep carrying Captain Lundberg and his driver Private Snow, returning from Spa to rejoin Anderson's HQ, crashed into it.[9] One of the Americans died instantly; at the Dachau Trials in 1946 SS Sergeant Zwigart was sentenced to death for shooting the other one in cold blood beside the road, a charge he strongly denied.

It was still daylight and provided there was no trouble at the Lienne bridge, Peiper expected to reach Werbomont shortly after last light. It has often been said that from Werbomont the ground becomes much more open and suitable for tanks and that it would have been a comparatively simple matter for Peiper to drive through to the Meuse that night. Whilst it is true that the country is more open to the west of Werbomont, this argument ignores the fact that the largest obstacle on Peiper's route still lay across his path – the Ourthe river (Map 1). He would have known that by this time the chances of finding a bridge over it were extremely remote. Lying as it does in the bottom of a deep, heavily forested valley, the Ourthe would be a major problem for an armoured force, even today with modern obstacle-crossing equipment.

It was about 1645 hours when the leading Panther rounded the bend 100m from the Lienne river bridge. The two sentries, Privates Lufsey and Sansbury, had taken cover in the woods when they saw the tanks coming and eventually made their way to Trois Ponts and joined up with the engineers there. The Americans say the lead tank fired its main armament without effect and that Corporal Chapin, following Edelstein's gesticulations, then blew the bridge. Despite machine gun fire from the German tanks, those engineers who were able ran and jumped aboard Kovacs' truck as it ground its way slowly up the hill and away on the road to Werbomont. The demolition had been successful and no vehicle could cross the Lienne at Neufmoulin. The departure of the squad truck meant of course that the bridge protection parties to the north and south, Sergeant Billington, Corporal Bossert, Rondenell and two others, were left without transport to get back to Werbomont. All except Rondenell were lucky and not a little surprised when Major General Gavin turned up on his way back from Bastogne, where he had issued orders to the temporary commander of the 101st Airborne Division, Brigadier General McAuliffe of 'Nuts' fame, and gave them a lift. Private Rondenell remained hidden in the woods a few hundred metres north of the bridge site, complete with his daisy chain of mines. Lieutenant Edelstein also missed Kovac's truck and took twenty-four hours to catch up with his Company.

As Pigg and the few remaining members of the A Company Platoon drove west they came across American troops in position near Oufni, 2km from the bridge. They were G Company of Major Hal McCown's 2/119 with three 57mm anti-tank guns of the 119th Infantry Regiment's Anti-Tank Platoon and four M-10s of Lieutenant Art Cunningham's 2nd Platoon, A Company 823rd TD Battalion, all sent there to cover the concentration of Gavin's 82nd Airborne Division. The group was backed up by the Regimental 105mm Cannon Company.

Looking at the Lienne river today it is difficult to understand how Peiper's tanks could have failed to wade across and continue their advance. It is normally a slow, shallow stream which can be easily walked across in many places, especially close to the bridge site. It should be appreciated, however, that in December 1944 the Lienne, like all the rivers in the Ardennes, was in full flood. It is also tree lined, with water meadows on both banks. Even so there is evidence to suggest that Peiper ordered his leading elements to attempt a crossing between the bridge site and Neucy and that not surprisingly they failed. But still he did not give up. The 10th and 11th SS Panzer-Grenadier Companies were ordered to move north and try the bridges at Les Forges and Moulin Rahier. It was dark by the time they crossed the wooden trestles, which were strong enough for their SPWs but incapable of taking tanks – as Edelstein had told General Gavin. The 11th SS Panzer-Grenadier Company crossed the nearest bridge at Les Forges and as it drove south along the far bank of the river, Private Rondenell emerged from the woods and quickly pulled his daisy chain of mines across the road. One of the SPWs hit a mine and was immobilised. Rondenell took over four days to find his way back to Modave where he rejoined his company. He was later awarded the Bronze Star for this action.

The Germans, having cleared the mines and the disabled SPW, drove on south; on reaching the Neufmoulin bridge site, they missed the turning to the right on to the N-23 and followed the river as far as Trou de Bra. It was only then that they realised they were lost, and turned back. Meanwhile Preuss's 10th SS Company had crossed at Moulin Rahier, 4km north of Neufmoulin. It moved via Chevron and Habiemont before running headlong into the 119th Infantry group at Oufni. Not surprisingly four SPWs and fifteen men were lost to the three 57mm anti-tank guns and four M-10s. One panzer-grenadier was captured and for the first time the Americans were able to identify positively the 1st SS Panzer Division.

The sharp engagement at Oufni is a classic example of how various after action reports can differ in their descriptions of the same incident. It is certain that the Germans lost four SPWs and at least fifteen men. However, Georg Preuss said later that his company was decimated by the time it withdrew back across the Lienne. He may of course have meant that it was decimated in relation to its start state on the 16th December and not by the action at Oufni. The After Action Report of the 119th Infantry Regiment, although saying that a defensive line was occupied east of Werbomont, makes no mention at all of the action at Oufni, and this in spite of the fact that, according to casualty reports, it suffered five men killed, thirty wounded and had ten more missing in action. The *Combat History* of the Regiment says the German column consisted of six SPWs loaded with infantry and six Tigers; it claims four SPWs were destroyed and fifteen enemy killed, whereupon the Tigers and two surviving SPWs 'turned round hurriedly and withdrew to the first defilade from which they sent 88mm shells screaming in the general direction from which the surprise American attack had come'. No German tanks of any sort, least of all Tigers, had of course been able to cross the Lienne. General Gavin in his book *On to Berlin* provides yet another version of what happened and gives the credit for stopping the Germans to a bazooka man and infantry small arms fire. He claims to have seen 'five knocked out German armoured vehicles, including armoured cars and self-propelled guns, with several German dead lying along the road' at the site the next morning!

Having heard radio reports from his panzer-grenadiers about events west of the Lienne and the state of the two bridges over it, Peiper realised he had no real chance of continuing on the N-23 to Werbomont. He therefore recalled the 10th and 11th Companies and ordered the whole column to turn round and withdraw behind the Amblève at Cheneux. He had decided to advance on the following morning along the N-33 through Stoumont[10] – this would give him the chance of joining

Route C via Remouchamps or Lorcé, or of rejoining route D further west (Maps 3 & 14). The withdrawal began at about 2100 hours. By then at least four Tigers had caught up and were near Neufmoulin but they were desperately short of fuel, to a point where they had to drain tanks and tow each other back.[11] The Germans continued to hold the Neufmoulin area till after 2230 hours but by midnight they had gone. The Belgians in Rahier reported 125 armoured vehicles moving east through the village during the night, including thirty tanks. On their way through Cheneux Peiper ordered Major Wolf to remain there with his flak vehicles and form a bridgehead west of the Amblève for possible use by follow-up forces when they arrived. Fuel was now becoming a critical problem and although Peiper still intended to advance west with as many tanks as possible, the surviving Panthers of the 1st SS Panzer Company, which had led all the way from Ligneuville, were forced to remain in La Gleize on their return. And so began the German occupation of La Gleize, where the locals had danced at a 'Liberation Ball' in the Echo des Campagnes café only the evening before, and which within a week would be almost totally destroyed.

Following their withdrawal from Neufmoulin, the units which were earmarked to attack Stoumont on the Tuesday morning formed up in the woods surrounding the Château Froidcour (Map 16). The area is known as the St Anne's woods, after the small chapel dedicated to St Anne which lies within the forest. There are reports that the Germans lit fires and sat around them singing! Peiper set up his HQ in the estate farm just to the east of the Château and it was there that his personal staff officer, SS Captain Gerhard Neuske, who had been acting as a Liaison Officer to the Leibstandarte HQ,[12] joined Gruhle, Krause and the other members of the KG HQ. Neuske brought bad news – Sandig had only just crossed the Siegfried Line, Hansen had been ordered to go firm at Recht and, worst of all, Stavelot had not been secured and the KG's lines of communication were therefore incomplete. When Knittel reported, at about the same time, that two-thirds of his Fast Group had reached La Gleize,[13] Peiper ordered him to give his men some rest and then, at first light, to go back and reopen the route through Stavelot from the west.

In 1986 Coblenz told the author[14] that the Fast Group had been delayed reaching La Gleize, first of all by the air strikes, and then by a huge crater in the road near the Petit Spai bridge caused by an American air force bomb. This was at a point where the cliff and railway embankment on the north side of the road came closest to the Amblève river and the crater therefore formed a major barrier to vehicles (Map 13). It is possible that the explosion had been enhanced by the bomb hitting the unexploded mines used in the engineer road block earlier that morning. Coblenz again dismounted his company and they worked with picks and shovels till nearly 2300 hours to level off the crater. A schwimmwagen from the 3rd SS Recce Company of the Battalion arrived while they were doing this and reported that the Company had suffered casualties as it had passed through Stavelot. When they eventually reached La Gleize the whole Group of over 500 men were told to sort themselves out and get some rest. Knittel established his own main HQ, together with three Puma armoured cars, at the Moulin Maréchal, a kilometre due east of the village on the N-33.

There was one part of Knittel's Fast Group which Peiper badly needed for his own use – the 5th SS Artillery Battery. He therefore ordered Butschek to set up the five guns in Cheneux and to the west of the Château de la Vaulx Renard, where they could support the first-light attack on Stoumont and, if necessary, Wolf's troops in Cheneux.

La Gleize was a busy place during the night – as well as Knittel's men and the tanks of the 1st SS Panzer Company, the six Type IVs from Wanne arrived together with the two SPW Platoons of the 3rd SS Panzer Pioneer Company and some paratroopers. By dawn five Tigers had taken up positions in the village and one more was on the N-33, a kilometre to the east of the village and just above Knittel's main HQ – it was immobilised but still operable. The last tank to arrive was Hennecke's Panther: the driver, Bahrnes, had managed to get it going again and had driven on, without a vehicle commander, to catch up with the KG. This gave Peiper a total tank strength of six Tigers, nineteen Panthers and six Type IVs. Four more Tigers were north of the Amblève but they were to see action with Knittel rather than Peiper. At least twenty-seven Tigers, nine Panthers and twenty-two Type IVs remained south of the river and Peiper would never see them – they had either broken down or been delayed due to fuel shortages.

The Americans were also busy during these hours of darkness. A platoon of Shermans from C Company 743rd Tank Battalion joined the force from the 119th Infantry which had halted Preuss's Panzer-Grenadiers at Oufni and at 2100 hours the other two Battalions of Colonel Sutherland's Regiment moved in to confront Peiper's KG. Regimental HQ was established in Stoumont station, which lies 4km west of the village itself down by the Amblève river, together with 1/119, commanded by Lieutenant Colonel Herlong (Map 14). 3/119 under Lieutenant Colonel Fitzgerald, supported by two platoons of A Company 823rd TD Battalion, arrived in Stoumont village at 2100 hours (Map 16). Sutherland promised Fitzgerald he would send him two Sherman platoons from C Company 743rd Tank Battalion as soon as they arrived.

In 1984 the acting commander of L Company 3/119, Lieutenant David Knox, quoted from a diary he kept at the time:[15]

I went forward to get the order. Here is the story I got from Colonel Fitzgerald. There was definite tank activity to our front. He estimated that there were about thirty tanks. He said he was going forward on a little recce. I got the rest of the information from Captain Stewart. The other two rifle companies were going to set up in the main part of the town. Our company would organise on the little knoll on the left. This part of the town was called Roua. I went back and moved the company up to our area. It was dark by then and must have been at least 2200 hours. We set up without much trouble. The (three 57mm) anti-tank weapons set up in our area also. I went back to Battalion to tell them our situation and to see if they had any more information. Major Rogerson was sitting in the corner. He had the story that the tanks we could hear moving around were stuck down near the river. [Author: The Amblève river, flowing through a deep ravine, separates Stoumont and Cheneux. The sounds were Peiper's tanks returning from Neufmoulin.] No one seemed to be concerned about the situation. Captain Del Bene, the S-3, said 'If they try to come after us in the morning, we'll sure give them hell.' I gave my situation and went back. On the way Sergeant Kirby found the coloured truck drivers and told them where to put the vehicles. There was no question about the tank activity. There seemed to be plenty of it. I could hear the Germans hollering at each other. I spent the rest of the night getting anti-tank mines put out and answering the telephone.

Fitzgerald's Battalion HQ set up in Stoumont's Boys' School in the middle of the village. David Knox was not quite correct about the other two companies being in the main part of the village. I Company was at the east end on the north side of the road and nearest to the enemy, and K Company under Lieutenant Kane, with the eight 3" TDs of A Company 823rd TD Battalion, was south and west of the N-33.

A surprising but highly significant addition to the whole American defensive arc running from Werbomont round to Stavelot came at 1330 hours on the Monday afternoon when the 110th and 143rd Anti-Aircraft Artillery (AAA) Battalions were given the mission of anti-mechanised defence. Before first light on Tuesday the 19th the 143rd Battalion HQ was in Werbomont with B Battery in position astride the N-23, D Battery was in depth at Aywaille and two 90mm guns of C Battery had joined Fitzgerald's 3/119 in Stoumont. Unfortunately one came off the road near the village and was immobilised but the other was put in place near the large church, covering the N-33. The 110th had two guns some kilometres north of Stoumont on the road to La Reid and two more south of Spa on the road to La Gleize covering another large fuel dump. The other guns of the two Battalions were deployed outside our area of direct interest.

Another major reinforcement during the night was the arrival of the 82nd Airborne Division in Werbomont. After being redirected from Bastogne, Colonel Reuben Tucker's 504th Parachute Infantry Regiment closed on Werbomont by 0315 hours. The freezing journey had taken thirteen hours. The 505th Regiment, 703rd TD Battalion and 376th and 456th Parachute Field Artillery Battalions all arrived in the same area before first light, as did the Corps Commander, Major General Matthew Ridgway, the 505th's Colonel Ekman and one of his battalion commanders who had all been back in England when the offensive started.

It is again interesting to speculate on the fate of this famous Division if Peiper had not been delayed in the various stages in his advance – the twelve hours before the paratroopers had cleared the way for his tanks on the Saturday, the wasted opportunity at Stavelot on the Sunday/Monday night, the demolition of the bridges at Trois Ponts on the Monday morning, the air attacks on the Monday afternoon and the timely blowing of the Neufmoulin bridge. Without any one of these delays or happenings it is likely that Peiper's tanks would have hit Gavin's men at their most vulnerable – undeployed, unprepared, on ground they had never seen and without tank support.

Back in Trois Ponts and in a much smaller dimension, Major Bull Yates with Captain Sam Scheuber's C Company engineers were doing their best to give the impression that they were much stronger than they really were. They were helped by a 105mm M-7 howitzer which had tipped into the Salm river when crossing the bridge in the centre of the town. The engineers had blown it up in case the Germans captured it and the consequent explosions of its ammunition went on for most of the night giving the impression of artillery support. Six 2½-ton trucks were driven out to the west without lights and then returned with headlights blazing to give the impression of reinforcements arriving and snow chains were fitted to the tyres of a four-ton truck in the hope that the enemy would think the defence had tanks in support. It is highly unlikely that Germans were aware of any of these imaginative measures since the only ones around were those driving as quickly as they possibly could through the viaducts and then turning north to catch up with Peiper, but it did show considerable initiative on the part of Yates and the engineers.

Further east in Stavelot Frankland's 1/117 Infantry consolidated their positions in the town during the evening and Lieutenants Murray of A Company and Foster of B Company directed the three Shermans of B Company 743rd to cover the entrances of the rues Haute and Chaumont leading out of the market square on its north side (Map 11). The 113th Field Artillery Battalion was now deployed at Ster, near Francorchamps, and its 155mm guns joined the 105s of the 118th Battalion in firing interdiction missions throughout the night on the area of the bridge and the roads running north from it. Between 2030 and 2100 hours the B Company Shermans claimed two SPWs and a jeep-type vehicle disabled, plus six Germans killed from both tank and small arms fire; and at 2135 hours the American infantry claimed three US half-tracks and three US jeeps full of enemy destroyed. It seems likely that these vehicles and men were from Knittel's Battalion – the statement that the vehicles were American is probably an After Action Report error. A photograph taken immediately after the battle clearly shows a knocked-out 251/9 SPW from Knittel's 4th SS (Heavy) Recce Company in the town square.

Whilst on the subject of claims a word has to be said about those made by C Company 823rd TD Battalion during this period. The Battalion After Action Report speaks of German attacks being launched 'west and east of Stavelot' during the Monday afternoon (Map 10). It claims the three M-10s of the 1st Platoon destroyed a Panther and SPW, while the 2nd Platoon, 3–4km to the east of the town near Masta, 'destroyed two Panthers and one SPW with one additional Panther being listed as possible, and probably destroyed a total of eight to ten additional tanks all believed to be Tigers.' In the first place there were no German attacks east or west of Stavelot that afternoon. Secondly, according to their own unit report, the M-10s remained on the high ground to the north of the town until after dark. If this is true they would have been firing at ranges of over a kilometre at fleeting targets passing through the town. It is therefore difficult to accept the first claim. A 1/117 Infantry report confirms that neither the tanks nor TDs came into the town until after dark. With regard to the claims made for the 2nd Platoon it has to be said that from the positions given in the unit report, the nearest German tanks would have been on the Vau Richard/Stavelot road – a minimum range of 1,800 metres. It seems highly unlikely that the platoon could have hit, let alone destroyed, any tank at this range.

In Malmédy it was a quiet night for the Americans; by 2100 hours B Company 823rd TD Battalion had reinforced the garrison and been placed under the command of Colonel Purdue's 120th Infantry Regiment.

It was also a quiet time for KG Hansen at Recht on the Leibstandarte's southern route. KG Sandig had finally reached Büllingen and was preparing to advance to Stavelot at first light.

NOTES

1. Knittel, statement at Landsberg/Lech 15 Mar 1948.
2. Hennecke to author loc. cit., 8 Jun 1991.
3. Peiper's testimony at Dachau Trial.
4. See Chapter IX note 14.

5. 247 (Typhoon) Sqn RAF – Records for 18th Dec 1944, held in PRO Kew, London.
6. Knittel, statement at Landsberg/Lech 15 Mar 1948.
7. Peiper's testimony at Dachau Trial.
8. Wessel, statement in Hannover 2 Jan 1984 and letter from Wendt dated 22 Sep 1991.
9. Zwigart, extrajudicial statement before Dachau Trial.
10. ETHINT 10.
11. Wortmann to author loc. cit., 8 Jun 1991.
12. Neuske, statement in Munich 31 Jan 1948.
13. Peiper's testimony at Dachau Trial and Knittel's statement at Landsberg/Lech on 15 Mar 1948.
14. Coblenz to author loc. cit., 22 Jun 1986.
15. Letter from Knox to author dated 2 Oct 1984.

CHAPTER XIX

Tuesday 19th December

Stoumont – The Last Strike

At 0700 hours on Tuesday morning, as promised by Colonel Sutherland, Lieutenant Walter Macht arrived in Stoumont with ten Shermans of the 1st and 2nd Platoons, C Company 743rd Tank Battalion (Map 16). The other Sherman Platoon was with Major McCown's 2/119 covering the 82nd Airborne Division's concentration area at Werbomont. Macht deployed a platoon of five Shermans with I Company at the east end of the village and the other platoon of four with Lieutenant David Knox's L Company at Roua on the north flank. His own tank remained near Lieutenant Colonel Roy Fitzgerald's Battalion HQ in the Boys' School in the centre of Stoumont. Over one hundred civilians had taken refuge in the crypt of the church; recall that there was a 90mm anti-aircraft gun just to the east of the church, under the command of Lieutenant McGuire, three 57mm anti-tank guns with L Company in Roua and eight 3" TDs of Captain Bruce Crissinger's A Company 823rd TD Battalion with K Company, covering the south-eastern approaches to the village. Mines had been laid and although the 197th Field Artillery Battalion was still in the process of deploying into a gun area at Nonceveux, 8km away, these considerable forces, deployed as they were on ground favouring the defence, should have been able to hold Stoumont without too much difficulty. Seen from the German angle, the N-33 leaves the St Anne's woods next to the Gatekeeper's Lodge of the Château Froidcour and runs west for 800m before bending right round a slight hill and then almost at once enters Stoumont. On the left there was a small orchard where the gendarmerie now stands and then a house known as the Robinson House, which still looks as it did in 1944. Again looking west from the Lodge, the ground to the left of the road slopes very steeply down to the cliffs above the Amblève river and it is impossible to deploy vehicles on this flank for the first 500m. On the right of the road there is a gently sloping hill which hides the village until the very last moment. It is covered with fields, criss-crossed by barbed-wire cattle fences.

The Germans' greatest ally on the Tuesday morning was fog, which shrouded the whole Amblève valley and its surrounding hills, reducing visibility to a maximum of 50m.

Peiper made a very simple plan which entailed Panthers of 2nd SS Panzer Company driving straight down the N-33 into Stoumont while panzer-grenadiers of the 9th SS Company, pioneers of the 9th SS Pioneer Company and paratroopers hooked round to the south of the village on foot. SS Lieutenant Christ's tanks had orders to deploy off to the right of the road if they ran into serious opposition. The 11th SS Panzer-Grenadier Company remained in its SPWs on the N-33 together with five Panthers of Christ's Company as a reserve to be deployed if needed.[1] The fog affected both sides but hindered Peiper only in that his meagre artillery was masked. This blindness had a much more serious effect on the Americans because their tanks and TDs could not see to bring accurate fire to bear on their attackers. Although the After Action Report of the 743rd Tanks talks of 'about forty tanks' attacking Stoumont, Peiper used only seven Panthers and one or two Type IVs. The 823rd TD Report says their guns were refused permission to fire flares when they first heard enemy tanks approaching but it is difficult to see how this could have helped in fog. The reality was that in the reduced visibility the panzer-grenadiers, pioneers and paratroopers got amongst the TDs and overran them before they could fire a shot – it seems they were abandoned by K Company. At the same time, about 0830 hours or shortly afterwards, the Panthers drove as fast as possible down the N-33 and this proved too much for I Company and the Sherman platoon – they pulled out and by 0910 hours I Company was back at the church. McGuires's 90mm gun knocked out the leading Panther at a range of less than 100m but not, according to Captain Crissinger, before it had run over his most northerly TD. A second Panther was damaged but could still move, and while Christ and another followed up on the road, three more Panthers manoeuvred round to the right flank. By 1000 hours the battle was over – Macht's Shermans, which surprisingly had suffered no losses, carried out some of the infantry while others fled to the woods north of the village; many were captured. Colonel Sutherland at Stoumont station (Map 14) knew his 3rd Battalion group was in trouble and despatched C Company of

1/119 to help stem the tide; as the Company reached Targnon it ran into the men of 3/119 retreating and knew it was too late – it moved back with them. Lieutenant McGuire's 90mm gun had to be abandoned but not before the crew removed the sight. David Knox's diary recalls L Company's experience that morning:

Just before daylight I checked the men in position and changed some of them. Then four tanks arrived in our defense area which made us feel much better. About 0830 tanks or half-tracks began to cover over the rise to our front. The tankers with us wasted no time with them. Two were knocked out and no more were trying to come over. [These two tanks were almost certainly those hit by the 90mm.] We realized, however, that there were probably plenty behind. We knew this because they kept throwing direct fire rounds into our buildings. At the same time we could hear a hell of a fight going on to our right, in the area defended by Companies I and K. About this time Lt Parramore called me on the sound-powered phone and told me that these two companies were getting pushed back. That wasn't good because our flank would soon be very vulnerable. I immediately checked with battalion. They told me that there had been some trouble but that everything would be OK. I could hear the other company commanders on the radio occasionally. Discussion was held on use of Powell's stuff, which meant artillery. The answer seemed to be that it would be available if we could hold out an hour. The [81mm] mortars were set up and could fire. Lt Conway, the mortar observer, arrived at our CP about this time. It was now about 0900. Lt Parramore called me again and told me that Companies I and K were being pushed back again or still and that I had better find out what was expected of us. That was a mighty good idea and one that had been occupying my mind no little bit. I called on the radio, 'Hullo Thorn 3, Hullo Thorn 3, we are concerned about the situation on the right, can you tell me what is going on?' Here is Colonel Fitzgerald's answer that I will always remember, 'I too am concerned – the situation is grave. You will continue to hold.' So I told Lt Parramore we would have to hold. I didn't like it any better than Parramore did but he had just a little more realistic picture of the whole thing because he could see men practically running to the rear. I kept close to the radio. The Germans had by this time set up a machine gun or a tank just behind the rise to our front 250 yards and were firing down the street just outside our CP. About that time I heard Lt Kane, the company commander of Company K, call up very excitedly. I knew he was being over-run by plenty of tanks from his flank and rear. Our orders were to hold. It wasn't good. About this time the tanks with us started to pull out. Now it was bad – very bad. I wasted no time in getting hold of the radio. I said, 'What do you mean hold and you take the tanks away. What do you mean?' The answer, 'Continue to cover the withdrawal of the battalion.' Lots of things went through my mind in a hurry. It sounded like an order to sacrifice Company L to save what they could of the other units. I asked, 'Give me clarification. It is useless without the aid of tanks. How long do you expect us to hold?' Then I got the answer I wanted, 'I will have to leave that to your judgement,' Colonel Fitzgerald said. My mind was made up. We had better get out in a hurry. Lt Parramore had told me too much about the situation on the right to make the answer anything else. It didn't take us long.[2]

US losses in the battle were heavy – 3/119 had 290 casualties, of which two were killed, twenty wounded and the rest were prisoners; it also lost its three 57mm anti-tank guns. C Battery 143rd AAA lost both its 90mm guns; A Company 823rd TD Battalion lost all eight TDs, six half-tracks and had nine men wounded and sixteen missing. Lieutenant Francis Sweeney, commanding the 1st Sherman Platoon, was wounded in the head and Lieutenant Clyde Thornell of the 2nd Platoon slightly wounded in the back by shrapnel. The tanks and the TDs blamed the infantry for withdrawing and leaving them exposed in poor visibility and Lieutenant Springfield of A Company 823rd claimed to have been the last American out of Stoumont. There were the usual exaggerated claims of German tanks and SPWs destroyed. The 1st Sherman Platoon claimed two tanks, one SPW and many infantry; the 2nd Platoon with L Company put in for three tanks, two SPWs and many infantry and even the TDs claimed one Tiger destroyed. In fact it had been an easy victory for Peiper's men – one Panther lost and one damaged and there had been no requirement to deploy the 11th SS Panzer-Grenadiers. It is not surprising that Leibstandarte cameramen were able to film laughing panzer-grenadiers and paratroopers congratulating each other and drinking beer that morning outside the Café Constant Grégoire in the main street and Diefenthal watching, with obvious satisfaction, as American officers led their men in surrender behind the church. In the same sequence a Type IV tank is shown moving round the southern edge of the village – it is almost certainly one of those mentioned by Knox which over-ran Lieutenant Kane's K Company 'from his flank and rear'. There have been suggestions that some scenes in this film were staged for the cameramen after the fighting; whilst this may have been true on 18th December on Hansen's southern route, it is inconceivable that Peiper would have wasted time or fuel at the Stoumont stage of his advance.

Peiper himself drove forward in a schwimmwagen as soon as Stoumont was captured. He set up in the first house on the left as one enters the village, the Robinson house, and there he discussed the battle and continuing situation with Poetschke, von Westernhagen, Diefenthal and some of his essential staff officers.[3] Peiper took a personal interest in the US 90mm gun abandoned nearby – he had hoped to make use of it but, although it was in full working order, the sight was gone and there was no ammunition.

With the Americans in retreat Peiper's natural instinct was to follow up quickly. His over-riding problem now, however, was lack of fuel. He had used relatively little ammunition but unless he could obtain more petrol he could go no further in any strength. He decided to send out two reconnaissances to the north – one from Stoumont on the road to La Reid and the other from La Gleize towards Spa. He also ordered his Type IV tanks back to La Gleize, with instructions for SS Captain Klingelhöfer of the 7th SS Panzer Company to return to Stavelot, find his Company and bring it forward. In order to provide some infantry support for his tanks in La Gleize, the 9th SS Pioneers were sent back there whilst the 3rd SS Pioneers, paratroopers and most of his panzer-grenadiers were told to take up defensive positions in Stoumont. American prisoners were taken back to the Château Froidcour and locked in the attics, whilst all wounded were cared for in the cellars.

With fuel now at a critical level seven Panthers of Christ's 2nd Company, including one already damaged, at least one and probably two Wirbelwinds and the 11th SS Panzer-Grenadier Company, made ready to make one last probe to the west. Peiper[4] ordered them to clear the scattered mines left by the Americans as they withdrew and to advance, at about midday, to and beyond Stoumont station (Map 14). There has been much speculation about Peiper's intentions at this time; the American Official History by Hugh Cole, for example, says:

> The advance through Stoumont offered a last opportunity, for mid-way between Targnon and Stoumont station lay an easy approach to the river, a bridge as yet untouched, and a passable road rising from the valley to join the highway leading west through Werbomont, the road from which Peiper's force had been deflected.

This supposition totally ignores the fact that, having crossed the Targnon bridge over the Amblève, it was still necessary to cross the Lienne river in order to move west (Map 15). Not only were the Lienne bridges incapable of taking tanks but, as anyone who visits the area will see, it is impossible, even today, for a column of heavy vehicles to climb out of the Lienne valley except by the route to Oufni which Preuss's 10th Company had already taken. It is noteworthy that Map VIII in Cole's Official History is incorrectly drawn and does not show the need to cross the Lienne. The supposition also ignores the fact that Peiper already knew that strong American forces were in position to the east

146

of Werbomont and that there was therefore no point in trying to advance on that part of Route D again. No, Peiper's real intentions were very simple – he was moving towards Route C at Aywaille which could be reached either via Remouchamps or Lorcé; from there he could follow it through Esneux or switch back to Route D at Tinlot. His eyes were still set firmly on the Meuse (Map 3).

Despite the rout of the Americans in Stoumont, Peiper's small force still faced major opposition in its advance to the west. By 1200 hours 1/119 had taken up a very strong position, just west of the Zabompré Ferme, in the narrow valley to the west of Stoumont station where the N-33, railway line and Amblève river all run side by side (Map 15). Its frontage, covering the road which the Germans had to clear, was only 200m wide and the American right flank rested on the river. The only slight problem was on the left flank – here the ground was heavily forested and rose sharply from the road. By 1210 hours the remnants of 3/119, less L Company which had retreated to the north, and Lieutenant Macht's ten Shermans had fallen back through the six hair-pin bends which separate Stoumont from its station. While the infantry withdrew behind their sister Battalion, the Shermans took up position with the 1/119. Further reinforcements arrived at 1230 hours in the form of the remaining Platoon of four TDs from A Company 823rd and two more Shermans from the 3rd Platoon of C Company 743rd Tank Battalion – the other three needed maintenance. These TDs and Shermans had been with 2/119 all night defending Werbomont, but at first light they were ordered to join 1/119. 2/119 itself was ordered into Divisional reserve to the east of Remouchamps at 1530 hours.

Other significant additions to the American defences were a 90mm anti-aircraft gun of the 143rd AAA Battalion at Stoumont station and another 90mm with an M-51, both of the 110th AAA Battalion, positioned just to the west of the Zabompré Ferme. When Lieutenant McGuire had reported earlier that morning that one of his guns was immobilised in the mud at Stoumont, Lieutenant Leon Kent, commanding C Battery 143rd AAA Battalion, attempted to replace it with another 90mm; however, it did not have time to deploy before Stoumont was lost and it eventually set up at the station.

A further very important player was about to enter the action on the American side – it was the 740th Tank Battalion commanded by Lieutenant Colonel George Rubel. There was only one problem – it had no tanks! It had recently arrived in Europe and on Monday 18th December was sitting at Neufchâteau waiting for instructions to draw tanks. At 1245 hours orders were received from the Assistant Armoured Officer at 1st Army to send one company to the Ordnance Vehicle Depot at Sprimont, near Aywaille, where it was to draw any combat vehicles it could use and then to deploy into delaying positions at Remouchamps

(Map 3). Rubel moved at 1400 hours and C Company, in trucks, followed him at 1510. On arrival at Sprimont Rubel learned that German armour was less than twelve miles away. He was horrified to find that out of twenty-five tanks in the Depot only fifteen could be made operable by cannibalisation and even then they would be short of many essentials including radios and full combat loads of ammunition. This was not the fault of the Ordnance Depot – its job was to repair and recondition tanks which had become unserviceable in combat. After working all night and up to midday on Tuesday, C Company under Captain Berry had four-teen Shermans, five duplex drive tanks and an M-36 ready and in pos-ition at Remouchamps. Rubel decided, on his own initiative, to order the rest of his Battalion forward; they arrived at Sprimont during the Tuesday morning and continued to draw whatever vehicles could be made to work including M-5s, M-7s and even M-8s.

During the morning the S-2 of the 119th Infantry, on his way back to Stoumont station from HQ 30th Infantry Division, found Captain Berry with his odd looking Company near Remouchamps. He explained that his Regiment was in trouble and pleaded with Rubel and Berry to come to its aid. Rubel said he had orders to stay where he was and any change would have to be made by higher authority.

It was about midday when the seven Panthers of SS Lieutenant Christ began their cautious advance down the hill from Stoumont (Map 14). They knew that several Shermans and infantry armed with bazookas had withdrawn in front of them and that if they ran into this type of enemy on the steep, twisting road with its six hair-pins, they had no chance at all of being able to deploy. In most other armies infantry would have led this advance on foot but this was not the way of the Waffen SS and Peiper. To their surprise and relief the Germans reached the hamlet of Targnon without trouble at about 1240 hours, but as the leading vehicles emerged from the cover of the buildings they came under fire from the guns of the 197th and 400th Field Artillery Battalions. They withdrew for a short time but were again ordered on. But then, as the leading Panther rounded the bend some 200m east of Stoumont station, it was knocked out by the 90mm of C Battery 143rd AAA Bat-talion. The Unit After Action Report goes on to claim a second German tank knocked out and the road consequently blocked. Certainly the lead Panther of SS Sergeant Roepeter was knocked out just short of the station and a second Panther of SS Sergeant-major Knappich was so badly damaged (it had already been hit in the attack on Stoumont) that it was forced to withdraw all the way back to La Gleize.[5] The isolated US 90mm was destroyed by its own crew after they came under machine gun fire from their right flank.

The American position on the N-33 was incredibly strong. Covering the 300m wide valley there were twelve Shermans, four TDs, the remaining 90mm and M-51 and a complete battalion of infantry, with two field artillery battalions in direct support. Nonetheless, after some inevitable delay and despite the losses already suffered, the remaining five Panthers, followed by the 11th Panzer-Grenadiers in their SPWs, continued their advance beyond the station. As they rounded the bend just by the turning to the Zabompré Ferme, the first two Panthers were knocked out and the third was immobilised,[6] either by being hit or getting stuck as it deployed to the left of the road by the railway tracks. It is unclear exactly who or what knocked out the Panthers but they obviously ran into a classic tank ambush; a letter written by Captain Bud Strand who commanded D Company of 1/119 during the battle gives a clue:

> Around 3 pm on 19th December we could hear German tanks ahead of us coming down the road towards our position . . . we were dug in on the curve in the road with our tank supports and waited. When the Panther tanks came round the curve in sight of us our tanks cut loose at them and . . . the shells hit the cobblestone road and ricocheted up under the belly of the tanks where their armour was thin and exploded the tanks. These young inexperienced tankers of ours fired four shells and knocked out three Panther tanks.

The Germans claim they never had time to return fire before they were hit. Artillery certainly struck the whole German column, causing some fifty to seventy casualties, mainly to the panzer-grenadiers in their open-topped vehicles. It was a hopeless situation and SS Major Poetschke gave the very necessary order to withdraw. There are reports that Peiper himself was in the vicinity of the station at the time and approved the order. The acting commmander of the 11th SS Panzer-Grenadier Company, SS Senior Sergenat Rayer, described the action at the station as follows:

> Our leading tank was knocked out by an anti-tank gun by the station. I was ordered to take the station on foot. We did this after light resistance. We took two prisoners . . . we were ordered to take out enemy tanks and anti-tank guns on the right of the road. We failed in close combat and only extracted with great difficulty and losses.[7]

The story of the battle at Stoumont station has been complicated by George Rubel's version in his book *Daredevil Tankers*. He says that at 1400 hours, the time the leading Panther was knocked out just short of the station, Major General Hobbs, commanding the 30th Infantry Division, arrived at his position at Remouchamps and told him that General Hodges had authorised the attachment of the 740th Tank Battalion to his Division. He in turn was attaching it to Sutherland's 119th Regiment and Rubel was to move out at once in support. He goes on to say that

Captain Berry's C Company moved immediately and he followed to report personally to Colonel Sutherland. On the way they encountered Macht's Shermans withdrawing to the west saying they were low on fuel and ammunition and that the infantrymen were also moving back. The 743rd After Action Report says their tanks were relieved at approximately 1600 hours; the infantry were presumably men of Fitzgerald's 3/119. According to Cole's official history and Rubel's account, Berry's tanks arrived in the area of the Zabompré Ferme at 1530 hours. It was foggy down by the Amblève and there was a slow drizzle – visibility was reduced to less than four hundred metres. Rubel's account goes on:

> We advised Lt Col Herlong, Battalion Commander 1/119, that we were coming in to help – that we would commence our attack at 1600 hours and asked him to attack abreast of us as we came into his position. Lt Powers spearheaded the attack. He had gone scarcely eight hundred yards when he saw a Panther tank about 150 yards ahead at a curve in the road. His first shot hit the gun mantlet, ricocheted downward, killed the enemy driver and bow-gunner and set the tank on fire. Powers kept moving and about 100 yards further on came upon a second tank. He fired one round which hit the Panther's front slope plate and richocheted off. His gun jammed and he signalled Lt Loopey (then Sgt Loopey) to move in quickly with his TD. Loopey's first round with his 90mm gun set the tank on fire, but he put in two or three more shots for good measure. By this time Lt Powers had cleared his gun and had resumed his advance. About 150 yards further on he came upon the third Panther. His first shot blew the muzzle brake off the Panther's gun and two more shots set the tank on fire.

How can this quite different claim by Rubel for the destruction of the three leading Panthers be reconciled with the other reports? The main consideration must be that of timings. It is clear from all the reports, and German survivors, that the action by the station took place at about 1400 hours. It is also clear from the 119th Infantry reports that the main clash at the Zabompré Ferme occurred at about 1500 hours and was complete by 1600 hours. This is confirmed by the 743rd Report. It must be remembered that, after the loss of the Panthers, the 11th Company Panzer-Grenadiers attempted for some time to clear a way forward on the right flank.It is also clear from Rubel's own report and the official History that Berry's tanks did not begin their advance from the Zabompré Ferme area until 1600 hours when visibility was even further reduced – after the battle there was over! Nevertheless, it would be unfair to accuse George Rubel of dishonesty even if he, like so many others on both sides, was prone to exaggeration. No, he and Berry were telling the truth when they claimed the Panthers. What they did not realise was that the German tanks were already 'dead' when Powers and Loopey fired on them. This is an easy mistake in the heat of any battle and would be even more likely in fog, drizzling rain and the dusk of a winter evening.

With Peiper's advance elements only 8km south of Spa it is hardly surprising that during the morning General Hobbs was being bombarded with demands by 1st Army that he should defend the road running due north from Stoumont to La Reid, which was 4km to the west of Spa. The trouble was that Hobbs had no troops left who were anywhere near the right place. His only reserve was 2/119 and that was still at Werbomont. Accordingly he asked Sutherland to get the remnants of Fitzgerald's 3/119 to reorganise and move round to join David Knox's L Company which had withdrawn to the woods north of Stoumont. Its eighty or so men had taken up a position near Monthouet, 2km north of Stoumont, where it joined a 90mm gun of A Battery 110th AAA Battalion under the command of Captain Silverman and a TD, two Shermans and some armoured cars cobbled together by HQ 1st Army. A further seventy men of 3/119 joined the force later in the afternoon under Captain Stewart, who had been put in command of what was left of the Battalion when Fitzgerald was relieved. It will be remembered that Peiper had ordered a reconnaissance towards La Reid during the late morning. At about 1400 hours the German party moved to within 500m of the American group but made no attempt to advance further. The only other activity in the vicinity of Stoumont that afternoon was artillery fire from the four 90mm guns of C Battery 110th AAA Battalion at 1510 hours directed against German armour in the village. The Commanding Officer of the 110th AAA, Lieutenant Colonel Curren, directed this fire himself from a light aircraft, causing the tanks to take cover. No hits were claimed. The tanks were the four remaining Panthers of Christ's 2nd SS Panzer Company which had positioned themselves there following the capture of Stoumont.

At 1520 hours General Hodges, now back at Chaudfontaine, reorganised his forces. He gave Major General Matt Ridgway's XVIII Airborne Corps the following formations: its own 82nd Airborne Division, the 119th Infantry Regiment with its attached 740th Tank Battalion, to be known as the 119th Regimental Combat Team (119 RCT), and a new and vital formation, CCB of the 3rd Armored Division. Major General Hobbs' 30th Infantry Division would also be transferred from Gerow's V Corps to Ridgway before dawn on Wednesday. Hodges' orders were simple – destroy all German forces north of the Amblève river and prevent crossings of the Salm river in and to the south of Trois Ponts. The Corps staffs were to have a busy night preparing the necessary plans and orders.

The addition of Brigadier General Truman Boudinot's CCB of the 3rd

Armored Division to Ridgway's Corps gave him real striking power. It comprised two reinforced battalions of the 33rd Armored Regiment and included four Sherman companies, two Stuart light tank companies, a battalion of armoured infantry, reconnaissance, mortar, assault gun and engineer platoons, and the 391st Armored Field Artillery Battalion. Before the German offensive started CCB was resting in the Stolberg/ Mausbach area, not far from Aachen. At 0900 hours on the Tuesday, as Peiper was attacking Stoumont, the Combat Command was put at three hours' notice to move and detached to V Corps. At 1315 hours it was ordered to concentrate in the Theux area as soon as possible and by 2300 hours the 1st Battalion Group of the 33rd Armored Regiment was at La Reid and the 2nd Battalion Group just west of Spa.

The following is a summary of Peiper's overall situation at midnight on the Tuesday/Wednesday night (Map 16). His main HQ was in the Froidcour farm; in the Château itself basic medical facilities had been set up in the extensive cellars; however, since there was no electricity the dining room table had to be used for operations during daylight hours so that the doctors could see what they were doing. American prisoners were held in the attics. Monsieur and Madame de Harenne, a daughter with her four children and some twenty servants, estate workers and refugees were made to stay in the cellars for their own safety and in some cases to take food and drink to the prisoners and wounded.

Poetschke was in command of the Stoumont sector with his HQ in the Château lodge; he had under command five Panthers of the 2nd Company, the majority of Diefenthal's 3rd SS Panzer-Grenadier Battalion, one or two flak-wagons of the 10th SS Panzer Anti-Aircraft Company and the SPW element of the 3rd SS Panzer Pioneer Company. Major Wolf with his Luftwaffe Flak was at Cheneux (Map 14); he had been reinforced by what was left of the 11th SS Panzer-Grenadier Company at 2300 hours after it had withdrawn from Stoumont station. Back in the area of La Gleize under von Westernhagen's command were six Tigers, at least six Panthers, six Type IVs and the 9th SS Pioneers. The majority of the civilians had left the village – some to Borgoumont, most to La Venne (Map 18).

The 1st SS Panzer Division had reached its high-water mark just beyond Stoumont station in the late afternoon of Tuesday 19th December. It was to advance no further. Meanwhile, what of the other spearhead divisions of Hitler's great offensive? Where had they got to by midnight on the Tuesday/Wednesday night?

The Leibstandarte's running mate, the 12th SS Panzer Division Hitlerjugend, had by now been transferred to the II SS Panzer Corps in an attempt to break into the American defences on the 'North Shoulder' (Map 7) and open up Route C to the west. It had been extracted from the messy battle for the twin villages of Krinkelt and Rocherath and had already failed in its first attempt to strike north-west from Büllingen and capture Dom Bütgenbach. Just after midnight on the Tuesday night the Americans gave up the twin villages and pulled back to Elsenborn – the North Shoulder was now firm.

The 9th SS Panzer Division Hohenstaufen had replaced the 12th SS Panzer Division in I SS Panzer Corps. Recall that it had started to relieve KG Hansen at Recht at midday on Tuesday and it was now planning to move against Grand Halleux and Vielsalm whilst masking the US 7th Armored Divison at Poteau (Map 6).

Further to the south, in the German 5th Panzer Army area, the American 422nd and 423rd Infantry Regiments of the 106th Division had surrendered on the Schnee Eifel, but St Vith was still holding out in a salient occupied by two infantry regiments, CCB 9th Armored Division and the whole of the 7th Armored Division. This salient was blocking General Hasso von Manteuffel's LXVI Corps. Further south still LVIII Panzer Corps was in the Houffalize area and although the XLVII Panzer Corps had failed to take Bastogne, it had outflanked the town on the north side and would soon do so on the south (Map 1).

Four days after the start of the offensive, German forces were nowhere near, let alone over, the Meuse; but despite all his problems Peiper, as planned, had made the best progress. He had covered over 100km in 72 hours. Forty-six years later, using the very latest technology and equipment, it took the British 1st Armoured Division only two hours less to cover the same distance in the 1991 Gulf War.

NOTES

1. Tiemann, *Die Leibstandarte IV/2*, p. 103, Hofmann to author loc. cit., Jun 1991; statement by Rayer at Dachau 26 Apr 1947.
2. Letter to author dated 2 Oct 1984.
3. Neuske, statement at Munich 31 Jan 1948 and Peiper's testimony at Dachau Trial.
4. Peiper's testimony at Dachau Trial.
5. Hofmann to author loc. cit., 8 Jun 1991.
6. Statements by veterans of 2nd SS Pz Coy in 1991.
7. Rayer, statement at Dachau 26 Apr 1947.

CHAPTER XX

Tuesday 19th December

West of the Amblève

Jim Gavin's 82nd Airborne Division was complete in the Werbomont area by 1000 hours on Tuesday. The actions of the 325th Glider Infantry Regiment and the 508th Parachute Infantry Regiment need not concern us, but the 504th and 505th Parachute Infantry Regiments, which were to advance on Cheneux and Trois Ponts respectively, are very much part of our story (Map 14). Not surprisingly it took some time to sort things out after the long, bone-chilling journey from France! Corporal George Graves of HQ 504th Regiment described his journey and arrival in Belgium as follows:

I was in a 2½ ton truck instead of the vans which had been filled with about fifty men who had to stand. Our serial, the first, pulled out of the gate of Camp Sissonne at 1017 (on Monday) for destination unknown. We were packed into the truck like sardines in a can. It was cold and damp; I had a bad headache and felt generally miserable . . . we all agreed that this was the shortest notice we had ever been given for a mission and that the situation must be pretty bad to throw us in helter skelter. . . . We passed through Bucy, Montcornet, Rozoy, Liart, Charleyville–Messières, Flize, Sedan, Bouillon, Libramont heading due north-east. . . . The coming of night relieved us somewhat from the fear of being bombed. It was bitterly cold now and I dozed off to sleep. At 3 am (Tuesday) after our truck had become lost amid the confusion on the roads and the pitch black of the night, we arrived at our destination which we found to be the little Belgian village of Werbomont. . . . We took over a farmhouse for a CP. The former GI occupants we learned from the Belgian owner had taken off in great haste for the rear at 5 pm the previous afternoon. Such was their hurry that they left behind a large pot of coffee, a full case of 10-1 rations, bread and even uneaten pork chops. . . . We were all sweating out dawn as the big trailer trucks were all jammed up together in the town, making a prime target for the Luftwaffe. . . . We had no anti-tank support except our 57mm pea shooters. . . . After daylight it was very foggy for which we were most thankful. . . . The congestion of the trucks was breaking up as they moved off to

154

the west out of harm's way. Two of our 80th AA 57mm guns were being emplaced about fifty yards from the CP. The battalions were digging in frantically. . . . I had not slept any for 33 hours and was exhausted so about 3 pm I unrolled my pack and lay down on the floor to get some sleep. At 1730 Capt Hauptfleisch (the S-1) shook me and told me to get up and be ready to move out immediately. . . . The Regiment was going to try to seize the town of Rahier about 8 miles north-east of Werbomont. It was not clear whether the enemy held the town or not. The 1st and 2nd Battalions were to move at 1800 with HQ Company following the 2nd Battalion which would be in the lead.[1]

At 1900 hours on the Tuesday night the 1st and 2nd Battalions of the 504th Regiment crossed the Lienne river at Les Forges, leaving the 3rd Battalion in reserve at Chevron (Map 15). The plan in fact was for the 1st and 2nd Battalions to go firm in the area of Meuville and Rahier. Once this was complete 3/504 was to advance to Froidville. The orders issued to Colonel Reuben Tucker, commanding the 504th, were to be prepared to repel any attacks coming from the east. Little did the Americans realise that Peiper's thrust for the Meuse was permanently stalled owing to lack of fuel.

Corporal Graves described the night advance:

The night was pitch black as we formed silently on the road outside the CP. A heavy fog had descended and the air was damp and chilly. Captain Hauptfleisch, Griffin and myself were at the head of the company column which was single file on either side of the road. It was 1930 when the last of the 2nd battalion passed us and we fell in behind their column for what my vivid imagination let me believe might be our last march. We set off at a pretty fast pace and despite the dampness of the night, I was soon sweating. The country was hilly and heavily wooded. It was on this march that I saw my first flying bomb; suddenly I saw a series of flashes streaking across the sky with terrific speed. Some seconds later I heard a peculiar chug, chug which sounded like two or three large diesel trucks going up a steep grade. The thing travelled so fast it was out of sight before we even heard it. Some of the boys who had seen and heard them in London told me what it was. After the first one passed, I heard many more but they were hidden in the clouds. After marching about two miles we began to hear the rumble of artillery, the first I had heard since coming to Werbomont. It was landing to the north of us, not too far away [Stoumont]. . . . We were directly behind Company D in the order of march. When the company turned off the main dirt road we naturally followed them. This led us down a narrow cow lane. We wallowed for about 15 minutes, knee deep in mud before the company in front of us stopped. Lt Col Harrison (1st Bn CO) who was behind our company came running down the line raising hell. . . . We had to turn our column inside out, causing a lot of confusion, swearing and apprehension. . . . As it was I thought Col Harrison was going to burst a blood vessel. We finally got turned round and back on the main road again, our boots weighted down with four inches of mud. . . . We arrived at the little village of Rahier at about midnight. There was a great deal of firing of all types to the north and east of us. A moon had come out so it was possible to see the houses of the village. Not a living thing outside ourselves stirred, not a sliver of light shone anywhere. The deathlike calmness in the village itself was eerie to say the least.

On the German side the only activity west of the Amblève on the Tuesday night was when the badly depleted 11th SS Panzer-Grenadiers arrived in Cheneux[2] and put out a screen of machine gun squads to the west of the village, specifically near the Rahier culvert, just over halfway to the village (Map 14).

The 505th Parachute Infantry Regiment, under the command of Colonel Ekman, moved forward from Werbomont at midday and had battalions in Haute and Basse Bodeux by last light. It planned to move on to the Salm river line, including Trois Ponts, by first light.

In Trois Ponts itself Tuesday was a relatively quiet day for Major 'Bull' Yates, Sam Scheuber's C Company 51st Engineers and 'Bucky' Walters and the three 291st squads. It is surprising there are no reports of Knittel's SS Reconnaissance Battalion returning from La Gleize around midday and moving east through the railway viaducts for its attack on Stavelot from the west. The only C Company report of significance was the arrival of three M-8 assault guns and fifteen men of the 85th Reconnaissance Squadron, part of the 82nd Airborne Division, in Trois Ponts from Basse Bodeux at 2000 hours. They were ordered by Yates to set up to the west of the town.

NOTES

1. Graves, *Blood and Snow – the Ardennes*.
2. Rayer, statement at Dachau 2 Apr 1947.

CHAPTER XXI

Tuesday 19th December

Malmédy and La Gleize

Tuesday saw a major reorganisation in the Malmédy sector (Map 12) with the 120th Infantry Regiment assuming full responsibility for all defensive measures. Attached to Colonel Branner Purdue's Regiment were the 30th Division's Reconnaissance Troop, Lieutenant Colonel Harold Hansen's 99th Infantry Battalion (Separate), HQ and B Company 526th Armored Infantry Battalion with A Company 825th TD Battalion less Doherty's Platoon attached, two-thirds of Dave Pergrin's 291st Engineers and the HQ and B Company of the 823rd TD Battalion. The Shermans of A Company of 743rd Tank Battalion were withdrawn at 1000 hours and 2/120 was in Divisional reserve at Bevercé, to the north-east of the town; nevertheless, there were a lot of troops available to defend Malmédy.

Lieutenant Colonel Ellis Williamson's 1/120 Infantry, supported by 1st Platoon, B Company 823rd TD Battalion and 3rd Platoon, A Company 825th TD Battalion, on the eastern flank of the town, had already made contact with the 1st Infantry Division at Waimes and had sent out patrols to the south-east – no enemy were found. It had also taken over Pergrin's old road block position on the N-32 a kilometre north of Geromont. Lieutenant Colonel Peter Ward's 3/120 was holding the south-west sector, but Pergrin retained responsibility for the demolitions on the Warche river bridge at the west end of Malmédy, the large railway viaduct on the Stavelot road and the three railway underpasses. The convenient railway embankment which runs roughly east to west on the southern side of the town was manned by I and L Companies 3/120, B Company and a machine gun platoon from HQ Company of the 526th Infantry, two TDs of 2nd Platoon, A Company 825th TD Battalion and B Company of the 99th Infantry. The remainder of the 99th were in reserve near Bevercé. Dave Pergrin's engineers, now relieved of responsibility for five of their original road blocks, put out more mines, while his machine gunners thickened up the infantry on the railway embankment. During the afternoon K Company 3/120 established a strong position on both sides of the timber trestle bridge over the Warche river at the western end of the town. It seems that the other two TDs of 2nd Platoon, A Company 825th were located by a house on the south side of the bridge.

The four M-10s of 2nd Platoon B Company 823rd TD Battalion were held as a mobile reserve behind the railway embankment. Two 90mm, one 40mm and two quadruple 50 calibre anti-aircraft guns, under the command of Lieutenant Robert Wilson of the 110th AAA Battalion, also joined the defences and were placed on the high ground to the north of the town in a position where they could dominate the southern approaches.

With 3/117 now relieved of its commitment in Malmédy, Major General Hobbs ordered Colonel Walter Johnson to use it to attack La Gleize (Map 18). A Company of the 743rd Tank Battalion, from Malmédy, was placed under command and ordered to link up with 3/117 in the Francorchamps area before the advance down the Roanne valley. 1/117 was already fully involved in the defence of Stavelot and 2/117 was holding the high ground between there and Malmédy; so in order to be better positioned to control his Regiment, Colonel Johnson moved his HQ to Francorchamps, alongside Hobbs's Divisional HQ in the Hôtel des Bruyères. It was operational by 1545 hours.

The Shermans of A Company joined 3/117 at 1400 hours in Ruy; the 2nd and 3rd Platoons under Lieutenants Jenkins and Couri then accompanied the infantrymen of K Company to Cour, via Andrimont, where they were established by last light. The Company Commander and 1st Platoon of Lieutenant Mattison moved with L Company down to Roanne where they observed several German tanks at the edge of woods near La Gleize. There were of course six Tigers and at least four Panthers in the area of the village at this time and they were joined by five Type IVs and two more Panthers before dark. The Americans said an infantry 57mm anti-tank gun, together with three Shermans, disabled a Panther but three other German tanks were out of range. One of their own Shermans burst into flames after being hit by what they claim was an 88mm round fired at a range of 2000 yards; three of the crew were killed. It seems likely that this round was fired either by a Tiger from the northern part of La Gleize known as Hassoumont, or possibly, if it was not 'dead', by the Tiger which had broken down on the hill leading into the village from the east. I Company 3/117 was in Ruy by last light.

In the village of La Gleize SS Lieutenant Rolf Reiser, who had been posted to Peiper's KG after the offensive started, caught up at about midday. He had reached Stavelot the previous evening in a motorcycle and side car and had managed to get through the town on foot between parts of Knittel's Battalion and the Tigers. After resting he spent the morning walking to La Gleize. In the afternoon he met Poetschke near the Château Froidcour and was immediately appointed Adjutant. Poetschke had already lost his first Adjutant, Fischer, when his Panther had been hit in Ligneuville and his replacement, Kramm, had been wounded in one of the air attacks. Reiser says they met Peiper and that he was present when the decision was made to send out reconnaissances for fuel. As we have heard, the one sent north from Stoumont on the La Reid road did not get very far but the patrol from La Gleize advanced through Cour towards Spa. It comprised four vehicles, probably all SPWs although the Americans talk about an armoured car and a light tank. The Germans were on the right track because further up this road, beyond the turning to Andrimont and south of Spa, was Fuel Depot Number 2, containing over two million gallons of petrol! It was protected by two 90mm guns and three M-51s from D Battery 110th AAA Battalion under the command of the Battery Commander, Captain Reiver. The German patrol ran into the American road block near the Andrimont turning at 1615 hours and after a short engagement withdrew. The Americans claim to have killed several enemy and damaged the light tank and one half-track, for the loss of one man killed and another wounded. If the timing given for this action is correct the Germans were lucky to be able to withdraw without running into the Shermans and K Company 3/117 advancing to Cour from Ruy. This was the second time Peiper's force had come within a few kilometres of enough fuel for both SS Panzer Corps!

It will be remembered that Klingelhöfer had been ordered to go back to Stavelot and try to bring his 7th SS Panzer Company forward to join the KG. After some rest he set off in his Type IV tank sometime in the late afternoon; near Coo, halfway to Trois Ponts, he ran into a Divisional liaison officer sent forward by Mohnke with an air force radio intended to improve communications with the KG. This officer, who had crossed the Amblève at Petit Spai, warned Klingelhofer that the Americans were holding Stavelot and that the 6th and 7th SS Panzer Companies were unlikely to get through. Klingelhofer turned back and joined Knittel's Main HQ at the Moulin Maréchal where three Puma armoured cars, an anti-aircraft platoon and a Tiger commanded by SS 2nd Lieutenant Handtusch, were already deployed – the Tiger cleverly concealed in a barn.[1] This group, which became known as 'Blocking Group Mill', was responsible for protecting the rear of the KG, specifically the N-33 approach from Trois Ponts. A strong US patrol from the direction of Roanne surprised it late in the day but was easily beaten off by machine gun fire from a Puma. Belgian reports say the 3/117 Infantry captain leading this patrol was killed; however, a forward outpost of L Company 3/117 was established at the Isidore Fontaine farm a kilometre south of Roanne, only 600m from the German force at the Moulin Maréchal.

Five Type IVs of the 6th SS Panzer Company took up their final positions in the La Gleize area late on Tuesday. At 0240 hours on Wednesday L Company 3/117 at Roanne reported hearing two enemy tanks moving out towards Borgoumont, 2km north-east of La Gleize – two Type IVs and a Tiger were certainly found in the area known as Les

Tscheous, halfway between the two villages, after the battle. It is also probable that at about this time the six 150mm guns of Koch's 13th SS Infantry Heavy Gun Company deployed in the Pré de Froidcour, an orchard just south of the church in La Gleize.

During the Tuesday/Wednesday night 2/120 Infantry, the Divisional reserve, moved from Bevercé, north-east of Malmédy to Ruy and was joined by Lieutenant Macht's C Company of the 743rd Tank Battalion after its battles at Stoumont. Lieutenant Disbrow, commanding the 3rd Platoon, was killed during the move when his tank overturned and three of its Shermans were still missing due to maintenance problems in the Remouchamps area.

NOTE

1. Tiemann, *Die Leibstandarte IV/2*, p. 124.

CHAPTER XXII

Tuesday 19th December

Stavelot

SS Major General Mohnke's primary concern on the Tuesday morning was to resupply and reinforce Kampfgruppe Peiper. KG Sandig was expected to arrive in the Stavelot area by late morning; until it did he was short of the infantry necessary to seize the Stavelot bridge and clear a way through the town (Map 10). Radio communications with Peiper were not good but Mohnke was probably aware that Knittel's Reconnaissance Battalion had been ordered to attack Stavelot from the west and re-establish the link with the rest of the Leibstandarte. Mohnke was also short of artillery. He had the 1st SS Panzer Artillery Battalion, which should have been with Peiper but had been unable to get through Stavelot, deployed around La Bergerie and Beaumont; but the 3rd SS Panzer Artillery Battalion of SS Captain Guss, with its two 150mm batteries and one 100mm Kanon battery, had not yet arrived. It was moving behind KG Sandig and was unlikely to be within range until late in the day at best.

Mohnke had already directed Hansen, after relief by the 9th SS Panzer Division at Recht, to mask Trois Ponts and move north to join Peiper. The American defenders in Stavelot were under the command of Lieu-

1 Jochen Peiper, Commander 1st SS Panzer Regiment and KG Peiper, wearing swords to his Knight's Cross awarded for his part in the Ardennes offensive.

2 Hitler, accompanied by Sepp Dietrich and an unknown officer, inspecting "Die Leibstandarte" in Lichterfelde Kaserne, Berlin, December 1935.

3 Himmler with Peiper at Mauthausen Concentration Camp 1941.

4 Himmler inspecting the LAH, accompanied by Dietrich and Peiper, sometime after the conquest of France.

5 Sepp Dietrich (on right), Commander 6th Panzer Army, shaking hands with Wilhelm Mohnke, appointed Commander 1st SS Panzer Division on 31st August 1944.

6 Chateau de Froidcour, Stoumont, before the war - occupied by both Peiper's men and the Americans during the fighting.

7 Dave Pergrin, Commanding Officer 291st Engineer Combat Battalion.

8 Wallis Anderson, Commander 1111th Engineer Combat Group.

9 Max Hansen, Commander 1st SS Panzer-Grenadier Regiment and KG Hansen.

10 Rudolf Sandig, Commander 2nd SS Panzer-Grenadier Regiment and KG Sandig.

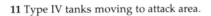

11 Type IV tanks moving to attack area.

12 Tiger II number 222, commanded by
Oberscharführer Kurt Sova, with paratroopers of
9th Parachute Regiment mounted, at
Kaiserbarracke Crossroads 18th December 1944.

13 US dead in Honsfeld 17th December 1944.

14 Werner Sternebeck, commander of
Peiper's 'Spitze' 16th-17th December 1944.

15 Waffen-SS dead in Market Place, Stavelot. Note Sherman in background.

16 Tiger II number 105, commanded by Jurgen Wessel, immobilized in rue Haut Rivage, Stavelot, 18th December 1944.

17 Panther number 131, commanded by Oberscharführer Strelow, immobilized in an air attack 18th December 1944. Note Cheneux bridge in background.

18 Gustav Knittel, Commander 1st SS Panzer Reconnaissance Battalion and Fast Group Knittel.

19 Jupp Diefenthal, Commanding Officer, 3rd SS Panzer-Grenadier Battalion, 2nd SS Panzer Grenadier Regiment – part of KG Peiper.

20 Top: Otto Holst's Jagdpanzer IV/70 in the Amblève river after collapsing the Petit Spai bridge, 21st December 1944.

21 Bottom left: Hal McCown, Commanding Officer 2/119 Infantry – Peiper's prisoner 21st-24th December 1944.

22 Below: David Knox, Officer Commanding L Company 3/119 Infantry.

23 A Sherman of C Coy 740th Tank Battalion knocked out at the La Venne crossroads on the morning of 23rd December 1944.

24 Jim Gavin, Commanding General 82nd Airborne Division.

25 George Rubel, Commanding Officer 740th Tank Battalion.

26 Jochen Peiper in April 1944, newly promoted to Obersturmbannführer and wearing Oakleaves to his Knight's Cross.

27 Peiper shortly before the Ardennes offensive.

28 Panther number 002 abandoned in La Gleize after the battle. The number would indicate it was a command tank of Peiper's KG HQ.

29 Werner Poetschke, Commanding Officer 1st SS Panzer Battalion.

30 Otto Skorzeny, Commander 150th Panzer Brigade.

31 Tiger II number 204 near the Petit Spai bridge after the battle, January 1945.

32 Panther number 221, commanded by Hauptscharführer Knappisch, in La Gleize after the battle. It was damaged during the attack on Stoumont.

33 US engineers of the 291st uncovering bodies at the Baugnez crossroads, mid January 1945.

34 Victims of The 'Malmédy Massacre', showing body tags and the Café Bodarwé in the background.

...eiper branded as a war criminal at Schwabisch-Hall.

36 Ursula Dietrich followed by Sigurd Peiper arriving at the Dachau Trial, 1946.

37 Some of those accused at Dachau 16th May 1946: Dietrich (11), Kraemer (33), Priess (45), Peiper (42), Coblenz (9), Fischer (13), Gruhle (19) and Hennecke (23).

38 Jochen Peiper in the early 1970s after retirement to Traves in France.

tenant Colonel Frankland. As well as his own 1/117 he had the four M-10 TDs of 1st Platoon C Company 823rd TD Battalion, 3rd Platoon B Company 743rd Tank Battalion, the 3rd Platoon A Company and Mortar and Assault Gun Platoons of the 526th Armored Infantry, and 1st Platoon A Company 105th Combat Engineer Battalion. The Divisional artillery, consisting of the three 105mm battalions and one 155mm battalion, was within range and able to provide fire support.

Early on the Tuesday morning the two Tigers[1] and single Panther which had remained overnight in Stavelot with their paratrooper escorts moved off to try to catch up with Peiper, taking with them the crew of SS Lieutenant Jurgen Wessel's immobilised Tiger. The Tigers reported to Knittel's Main HQ at the Moulin Maréchal and were immediately commandeered for use in his attack on Stavelot from the west. Having lost his five 105mm guns to Peiper, Knittel was determined to grab some heavy support.

The first German attempt to force a way through Stavelot seems to have occurred some time after first light when Frankland's 1/117 Infantry reported five tanks approaching the bridge. They were from the 6th and 7th SS Panzer Companies at Wanne and were supported by a company's worth of paratroopers and 3rd SS Panzer Pioneers. They were soon seen off by the Americans who, by 1000 hours, had closed to the river. A Company and machine gunners from D Company were to the west of the bridge, with a platoon in the Tanneries and B Company to the east of it with a platoon in the Hôtel de Ville alongside more D Company machine gunners. The four M-10s moved to cover the river and southern approaches at the same time. The Shermans of 3rd Platoon deployed on the west side of the town with A Company and the 1st Sherman Platoon of B Company, which was with 2/117 in the Masta area for most of the day, moved in later but not in time to engage the enemy.

Colonel Johnson's orders to Frankland at 1100 hours were simple – blow the bridge as soon as you can. This was easier said than done with German tanks sitting on the other side! There was another report of five schwimmwagens attempting to cross the Amblève at about 1030 hours but they were all destroyed – they would have been from SS Lieutenant Leidreiter's 3rd SS Reconnaissance Company, not all of which had got through the day before, although Leidreiter himself had accompanied Knittel to La Gleize.

On the Francorchamps road above Stavelot frantic attempts to evacuate the huge fuel dump were finally completed at 1300 hours – at least now if the Germans did succeed in breaking through they would be denied the petrol they so desperately needed.

A second, and much larger, attack came at 1307 hours when 1/117 reported a column of ten enemy tanks approaching the town. These were a mixture of Tigers and Type IVs, supported by paratroopers, pioneers and men of Knittel's Reconnaissance Battalion. Once again they had little chance of crossing the single bridge in broad daylight against infantry in buildings, TDs under 100m away, and observed artillery fire. The attack finally came to an end when a Tiger was hit and blocked the southern approach to the bridge. This hit was almost certainly from an M-10 of C Company 823rd TD Battalion. A graphic description of this action is provided by Captain Tom Raney of the 823rd's Reconnaissance Platoon who witnessed it together with Lieutenant McInnis, commander of the M-10s:

> Mac and I were in an observation post on the 2nd floor of a building. From a window to our front we could see the Amblève river and the bridge leading into Stavelot from the south about 150 yards from us. To our left was a window through which we could look down on one of Mac's M-10s, commanded I believe, by Sgt Ray Dudley. He was covering the bridge and the road leading to it from the south-east. This road, which descended a long hill into the Amblève valley at an angle to our location, was lined with buildings except for the last 100 yards or so before the bridge. . . . We saw the long tube of the Tiger's 88mm gun emerge from behind the last building. The M-10 gunner must have been tracking the tank with his telescopic sight, for as the Tiger cleared the building, the M-10 fired one round of armour piercing shot which penetrated the armour on the right side above the track, about 14 inches under the turret and four to five feet to the rear of the front glacis plate. The Tiger stopped in its tracks. . . . Surprisingly the tank did not burn.

Lieutenant Frank Warnock, of D Company 1/117, also had a grandstand view of this, or a very similar action, from a building overlooking the bridge:

> A Mark V or VI (a big tank with a muzzle brake on its gun) was on the south end of the bridge facing a US M-10 on the north end; the two were less than 100 yards apart. The M-10 fired two or three rounds which were seen to ricochet off the glacis plate and turret of the German tank. The enemy tank suddenly backed off and moved out of sight.[2]

Members of Warnock's platoon, machine gunners, told him they thought an M-10 round jammed the German tank's turret so that the gun could not be aimed. All told, the M-10s of C Company 823rd TD Battalion claimed a total of five Tigers, a 75mm SPW and two jeep type vehicles during the fighting on Tuesday. Whilst these claims are probably exaggerated it has to be said that the German tanks did not press their attacks on the Stavelot bridge that afternoon.

Attempts by the US 105th engineers to get on to the bridge and blow it during the afternoon failed in the face of intense German small arms and machine gun fire.

There have been suggestions that the infantry accompanying the main tank attack were panzer-grenadiers from KG Sandig. This is not so. US defences along the North Shoulder had forced Sandig to take an extremely difficult route via Heppenbach, Amel, Montenau and Ligneu-ville[3] – a route congested in its early stages by 9th SS Panzer Division moving to relieve Hansen at Recht (Map 6). The difficulties of this route can hardly be overstated since the road surfaces had been totally destroyed by the many tracked vehicles using them. In extreme cases tanks were moving through mud which came up to their turret rings! Sandig's leading truck-mounted 1st Battalion, commanded by SS Major Karl Richter, halted at Vau Richard at 1200 hours and the 2nd Battalion of SS Captain Herbert Schnelle reached Lodomé at the same time. Mohnke came forward from the Leibstandarte HQ, which it will be recalled had been established in Ligneuville the previous evening, at 1300 hours and ordered Sandig to attack Stavelot as soon as possible.[4] He further ordered all available Type IVs, Tigers and the remnants of Fast Group Knittel to support this attack. Mohnke knew that Knittel's main group was already attacking the town from the west and appreci-ated the need to attack the Americans from both directions simul-taneously.

At 1500 hours Richter's 2nd SS Panzer-Grenadier Company, under the command of SS 2nd Lieutenant Friedrich Pfeifer,[5] advanced on the bridge which had been damaged at about this time by very accurate shelling from C Battery of 110th AAA Battalion. It claimed that one salvo scored a direct hit on the bridge ramp. Pfeifer had joined the Leibstandarte from the 3rd SS Totenkopf Division in Lübbecke as recently as the previous September and, after a short spell as Adjutant to Rudolf Sandig, had been posted to the 2nd SS Panzer-Grenadier Company. Owing to the illness of the Company Commander, Jenke, he found himself in command for the offensive. In 1967 he described the attack in a letter to a friend:

Shortly before Stavelot I gave orders to dismount from the vehicles because the artillery fire became too heavy and I preferred to go through the town in the infantry manner . . . civilians had evacuated the area south of the river and it was also free of enemy troops. We arrived during the afternoon and I suspected a trap; my suspicion was confirmed because we found two dead comrades and an aban-doned Tiger immediately in front of the bridge from which some bricks were still falling. When I returned from my reconnaissance of the bridge Colonel Sandig appeared suddenly on a motor-cycle. He said things were going too slowly. I told him I needed fire support from the heavy weapons (mortars and 75mms) of the 4th Company; however, it had been delayed and I had to risk the attack with my 1st and 3rd Platoons whilst my 2nd and 4th provided fire support. When half of us had reached the north side of the bridge we were shot to pieces. With two squads we stormed across the little square on the north side into the first houses. The heaviest fire we received was from a big building marked with the Red Cross sign. [Author: the building described by Pfeifer was the former abbey. In 1944 two wings of it were a Hospice, orphanage and hospital, but the occupants had taken shelter in the cellars.]

Meanwhile, on the western flank, Stavelot was under attack by Gustav Knittel's main force. It had rested in La Gleize until mid-morning and then moved to the area of the Trois Ponts railway viaducts where it dismounted and organised for its assault. The three 150mm infantry heavy guns of the 4th Company were set up near the Petit Spai bridge to give fire support, as was the 120mm mortar platoon. During the morning a few resupply vehicles from Peiper's supply companies managed to use this bridge, but the quantities they carried forward were of no real significance.

The attack from the west started at about 1500 hours, with SS Lieutenant Manfred Coblenz[6] leading his 2nd SS Recce Company on the axis of the railway line and N-23, and with SS Lieutenant Heinz Goltz and his HQ Company held in reserve. This HQ Company consisted of bicycle, signals and pioneer platoons. The anti-aircraft platoon had remained with the Main HQ at the Moulin Maréchal. Coblenz complained later that Knittel denied him the use of his SPWs, insisting the attack be made on foot; he further complained that he lacked heavy support and, although two Tigers moved with Knittel behind his Company, they never fired a shot! These Tigers were the ones which had been in Stavelot during the night and were commanded by SS senior Sergeants Wendt and Brandt. There were in fact two additional Tigers in the area about halfway between Stavelot and Trois Ponts but neither Coblenz nor Wendt mentions them in his reminiscences, despite the fact that they are easily identifiable in photographs taken after the battle – one belonged to von Westernhagen's Adjutant, SS Lieutenant Kalinowski.

Coblenz's plan was to advance with two platoons abreast and, once he reached the western houses of the town, to swing left via the railway station and take the bridge from the north. He claimed to have been fired on by Belgians from the western houses although to this day this is strongly denied by the Belgians, who say all the weapons of their resistance forces had been handed over after the liberation by American forces on 12th September. Stavelot had been a significant centre for the local resistance during the occupation.

As Coblenz's men moved forward from the area of the Farm Antoine, about 2km west of Stavelot, they came under extremely heavy artillery fire and suffered many casualties. Despite this they managed to get to the western edge of the town by about 1800 hours but then ran into 2nd Platoon, A Company 1/117 in the area of the Château Rochettes, where Captain Kent had his CP. The five Shermans of the 743rd Tank Battalion were also on this flank. A stalemate developed with neither side being able to dislodge the other. Werner Wendt,[7] commanding one of the supporting Tigers, said he was unable to help because the entrance to Stavelot was heavily mined. He therefore took up a defensive position near the Farm Antoine where Knittel[8] established his Tactical HQ in a cellar. Brandt's Tiger meanwhile took up a position 100m west of the Petit Spai bridge covering the unit's rear against the Americans in Trois Ponts.

In an attempt to counter the American artillery fire which had hit Coblenz's men so badly, Knittel ordered Goltz to move round the north side of Stavelot and clear the hamlet of Parfondruy.[9] Although the American 105mm guns were much further back, the assault guns and mortars of the 526th Armored Infantry were indeed deployed to the north of Stavelot, but unknown to Knittel, well to the north-east of Parfondruy. Goltz had no difficulty in seizing the hamlet which was held by only a section of A Company, and then moving on to Renardmont where he was checked by Frankland's C Company in a reserve position. 1/117 reported an attack from their rear at 1720 hours but said it was brought under control by the use of artillery. Some time after this Goltz was ordered to reinforce Coblenz with his SS Pioneer Platoon[10] of about sixty men commanded by SS 2nd Lieutenant Dröge and later in the evening Coblenz tried, unsuccessfully, to infiltrate A Company's lines.

At 1930 hours, under the cover of an intense artillery barrage, Captain Rice, Lieutenant Cofer, Sergeant McKeon and Sergeant Richardson's squad of A Company 105th Engineers managed to carry 1,400 lbs of TNT on to the north span of the Stavelot bridge and blow it, creating a twenty-five foot gap – this despite the presence of the 2nd SS Panzer-Grenadiers in adjacent houses! Pfeifer claimed the bridge went at 2200 hours – whatever the truth, the way through Stavelot was finally blocked. Artillery had played a big part in the battle – the 118th Field Artillery Battalion alone reported firing over 3,000 rounds into a 1,000-yard square in Stavelot on this one day. By 2200 hours the rest of Sandig's 1st Battalion and the whole of Schnelle's 2nd Battalion were ready for a night attack on the bridge but, knowing it was blown, Sandig ordered Schnelle to attempt a crossing to the east,[11] near the Challes footbridge. This proved impossible due to the steepness of the ground, flooded water meadows and the double arm of the river. Around midnight Schnelle was told to find a crossing to the west and reinforce Knittel. Sandig's idea was to take the town from the west and thus enable pioneers to repair the bridge without direct interference.

And so ended the second day in the terrible battle of Stavelot. Seventy-five civilians, most of them old and infirm, had taken refuge in the cellars of the old abbey and another hundred were sheltering in the dairy factory south of the river.[12] But at the Legaye house, just beyond the Perron sawmill where Lieutenant Colbeck's 1st Platoon, B Company 291st Engineers had cut wood only three days before, two men, eleven women and ten children already lay dead, butchered in cold blood (Map 11). At least sixty-five other civilians died at the hands of the Leibstandarte on this horrific day – nearly half of them women and children and all of them in areas occupied or fought over by Knittel's men. Once again the *furor Germanicus* had been visited on the people of Belgium.

NOTES

1. Letter from Wendt dated 22 Sep 1991.
2. Letter to author from Warnock dated 16 Aug 1989.
3. Tiemann, *Die Leibstandarte IV/2*, p. 108.
4. Sandig to author loc. cit., 2 Oct 1985.
5. Pfeifer to author loc. cit., 2 Oct 1985.
6. Coblenz described his actions in Stavelot to the author during a visit to the town on 22 Jun 1986.
7. Letter from Wendt dated 22 Sep 1991.
8. Knittel, statement at Landsberg/Lech 15 Mar 1948.
9. Ibid.
10. Ibid.
11. Sandig to author loc. cit., 2 Oct 1985.
12. Joseph Dejardin, Secretary for Social Services for Territory of Stavelot 1941 – 84 to author loc. cit., Nov 1994.

CHAPTER XXIII

Wednesday 20th December

Stoumont

At 2200 hours on Tuesday night the 2nd Battalion 33rd Armored Regiment (reinforced), commanded by Lieutenant Colonel Bill Lovelady,[1] arrived in its assembly area near Spa and went into bivouac. The other main element of CCB 3rd Armored Division, the 1st Battalion (reinforced), under Major Kenneth McGeorge, arrived at La Reid an hour later and did the same. Early on Wednesday morning CCB was attached to the 30th Infantry Division which itself was transferred from V to XVIII Airborne Corps later in the day. It is not clear precisely when this happened but units in 30th Division were not informed until 1330 hours.

At 0400 hours Colonel John Welborn, the acting Commander of CCB, split McGeorge's Battalion into two Task Forces (TFs) – he left McGeorge to command one and gave the other to Captain John Jordan. This latter force, to be known as Task Force Jordan, consisted of two Stuart light tank platoons from A Company 33rd Armored, F (Sherman) Company of the 33rd Armored, and F Armored Infantry Company and the Mortar and Assault Guns Platoons of the 36th Armored Infantry Battalion.

Major General Matt Ridgway's orders for dealing with KG Peiper north of the Amblève river in Stoumont and La Gleize (Map 14) were received by Colonels Welborn and Sutherland by 0800 hours. They were simple – the 119th Regimental Combat Team (119 RCT) under Sutherland and Task Force Jordan (TFJ) were to secure the north bank of the Amblève river from inclusive Stoumont to inclusive La Gleize. The first phase of this operation would be the capture of Stoumont and although both 119 RCT and TFJ were given it as their initial objective no overall commander was appointed!

Standing high above the Amblève, with cliffs down to the river on its south and west sides and rising, forested ground to its north, Stoumont dominates the Amblève valley to the west.

To reach it the Americans had to advance through the six hairpin bends of the N-33 and then capture a fortress-like structure, known as the St Edouard Preventorium, which stands at the west end of the village above the main road (Map 16). It was a home and school run by Catholic nuns for some two hundred deprived and needy children. These terrified women and children, and some priests, had taken shelter in the cellars[2] and had been there since before Peiper's attack the previous day. They were joined by some fifty people from the church crypt on the Tuesday evening.

Peiper, as well as deploying panzer-grenadiers to delay the American advance, had established a strong defensive position in the village under Werner Poetschke's command. Five Panthers covered all approaches from the west and north, including of course the main N-33 and the minor road to the north-west leading to Monthouet and La Reid.[3] It will be remembered that a small German force, probably pioneers, had set up on this road the previous afternoon. The 3rd SS Panzer Pioneers were in the Preventorium and north-west part of the village, including Roua, the 9th SS Panzer-Grenadiers and 12th (Heavy) SS Panzer-

167

Grenadier Company with its heavy mortars and anti-tank weapons were in the main and western parts of Stoumont and Preuss's much weakened 10th Company was in reserve near the Château Froidcour.[4] Recall that the 11th Company had been sent to Cheneux. In accordance with normal practice the Germans had scattered mines as they withdrew from the station the previous evening.

At about first light, TFJ from La Reid and Sutherland's 119 RCT from the Zabompré Ferme area, set off in drizzling rain on their advance to Stoumont. Captain Jordan knew that he was secure as far as the hamlet of Monthouet where the remnants of 3/119 and the scratch 1st Army defence force were in position under the command of Captain Carleton Stewart. In the case of 119 RCT, Colonel Sutherland had no idea when or where he might encounter the Germans.

Sutherland led with the Shermans of Captain Berry's C Company 740th Tank Battalion, followed by B Company of Herlong's 1/119 Infantry. The four M-10s of 2nd Platoon, A Company 823rd TD Battalion were under command.

George Rubel described the advance as follows:

Our plan for the 20th was to attack at daybreak, seize Targnon quickly and continue rapidly to seize the town of Stoumont. The tank part of the job was to spearhead the attack and as soon as the village of Targnon was captured, to place two or more tank platoons on its high ground to support the attack on Stoumont. We asked the Divisional artillery to fire on Targnon 'on call' only. They were also to fire several short preparations on Stoumont during the course of the previous night and to keep interdiction fire covering the road from Stoumont to La Gleize. . . . The attack jumped off on the morning of the 20th as planned and Targnon was taken by noon. Lt Tompkin's (then Staff Sergeant) tank hit a minefield about 1000 yards east of Targnon which blew both tracks off. One enemy halftrack, one Panther and one enemy-held Sherman were engaged and destroyed during the day. The attack proceeded slowly from Targnon and by dark had failed to reach Stoumont by about 500 yards. Stoumont, like Targnon, was situated on top of a hill and afforded a perfect field of fire for the enemy. During the afternoon the enemy launched three heavy, fanatical, counter-attacks which drove our infantry back several hundred yards, but each time they were driven back, they quickly regained the ground.[5]

According to the 119th Infantry the RCT had crossed five minor minefields by the time it reached a position just short of Stoumont at 1720 hours and had been supported by artillery during the whole of its advance.

In the meantime TFJ reached the Monthouet position at about 1100 hours. At midday, and a little further on, the leading Sherman went up on a mine. German pioneers in the nearby ramshackle Comperé farm withdrew but at 1315 hours Jordan's tanks were again held up by some sort of road block by the hairpin bend above Stoumont, in the area known as La Rochette. It was a totally unsuitable place for tanks to try to get forward, with a sheer drop on the right of the road and steep, thick woods on the left. The only way forward was on the road and this led inevitably to the loss of the leading tank as it rounded the bend, probably to tank fire. It was impossible to deploy vehicles off the road and, after some fierce close range fighting in the vicinity of the Prevot farm, Jordan withdrew his force back to Monthouet. He would advance no further on Wednesday.

Some time after dark C Company 1/119 managed to get into the Preventorium and at about 2000 hours, after vicious hand to hand and room to room fighting, captured it from Sievers's 3rd SS Panzer Pioneers. Despite the crash of grenades and constant chatter of machine guns, the terrified civilians in the cellars survived without casualties – both sides appear to have respected their safety. The loss of this vital building was not something which Poetschke could tolerate if he wished to hold on to the village, and at about 2300 hours he ordered a violent counter-attack from the high ground at the back of the Preventorium. It swept the Americans out of the building – thirty-four GIs were captured. By midnight the Germans had re-established their defences but the Americans were only a few hundred metres away with Herlong's B Company on the north side of the road and A Company to the south.

George Rubel gives an account of these events:

The key to the capture of Stoumont was a chateau [the Preventorium] about 300 yards north-west of the village and about 200 yards north of the road along which our tanks were forced to attack. This building changed hands at least three times during the day and night of the 20th. At about 2100 [2300] hours Jerry retook all but one room of it. This room was held by infantrymen of the 1st Battalion who had decided to fight it out there. The fact that we had men in the building, and our line was within 200 yards of it, precluded bringing Division artillery fire on it. We managed to hold our ground during the night and started planning for the next day's attack.[6]

Speaking of his own Battalion's situation on the Wednesday, Rubel goes on:

During the day the Service Company had cleared the knocked out Jerry tanks off the road [at the Zabompré Ferme] and had evacuated our own tank that had been hit by the mines. The assault guns had gone into position. Division artillery had attached them to the cannon company of the 119th Infantry. D Company had gone into position in reserve along the Amblève river near Remouchamps. B Company, less 2nd Platoon which had been attached to C Company, was still drawing equipment at Sprimont. The Battalion forward CP remained with the 119th Regimental CP at Lorcé.[7]

Captain Berry's Company was therefore very strong with five platoons.

The absence of a single American commander in the Stoumont area had not helped the day's events. To rectify this situation General Hobbs appointed his Deputy to take command of both forces and at 2200 hours Brigadier General Harrison arrived and set up TF Harrison. He was a much respected officer in the 30th Division, having won a Distinguished Service Cross for his outstanding leadership during 'Operation Cobra' in the Normandy breakout. Hobbs also gave him one of the Divisional reserve units, McCown's 2/119, which during Wednesday had moved from east of Werbomont to a new location near Lorcé.

NOTES

1. Letter from Lovelady to author dated 1 May 1989.
2. Henlet, *The Tragedy of St Edouard's*.
3. Described by LAH veterans in 1991.
4. Peiper's testimony at Dachau Trial.
5. Rubel, *Daredevil Tankers*, chapter IX.
6. Ibid.
7. Ibid.

CHAPTER XXIV

Wednesday 20th December

Cheneux

By 0440 hours on Wednesday morning the 1st and 2nd Battalions of Colonel Reuben Tucker's 504th Parachute Infantry Regiment were digging in around Rahier and the 3rd Battalion had moved forward to Froidville (Map 15). Corporal Graves of the Regimental HQ takes up the story:

After looking around the village without much success and banging on locked doors, I got the village schoolmaster out of bed. He let us into his house which was attached to the village school . . . the village dance hall was big enough to take in all the miscellaneous CP sections and the message center. . . . The battalions had all reached the area and were engaged in digging in around the town for an expected attack in the morning. The situation was still pretty obscure even to the battalion commanders. Lt Col Harrison was pacing the floor worrying about the non-arrival of the 1st Battalion's four 57mm anti-tank guns which was the only defense the battalion had against the German armoured columns known to be very close by. Colonel Willems [CO 2/504] had set out from Werbomont . . . in a captured German half-track we had picked up the previous day; it had not shown up [this was a SPW 251/9 mounting a 75mm gun and had been lost by the 10th SS Panzer-Grenadier Company on the Monday in its encounter to the west of the Neufmoulin bridge; it was manned by a scratch crew from C Battery 80th AAA Battalion]. . . . The schoolmaster told us that fifty German tanks had been in the town the day before but had turned round and gone north after making a reconnaissance of the area. This made us all sweat. . . . I sat up in the kitchen listening to the Colonels weighing the gravity of the situation. Everyone thought that come the dawn, the Germans would blast the town to pieces. The 'Big Picture' of both the friendly and enemy situation was almost a complete blank. The 57mm guns had finally arrived which made everyone breathe a lot easier. At 7 am I went down to the CP to do some interpreting as the Colonel wanted to get the town completely evacuated of civilians to get them out of harm's way. I found the house attached to the dance hall crowded with children, old men and women. It was hard to tell them that they must leave, quickly. One old lady about eighty started to cry. I helped them carry some trunks full of clothes and china down into the cellar. . . . They grabbed a few scraps of food and some blankets and left on foot going down the road to Werbomont. It was a heart-rending sight to see an old couple hobbling along, leaning on each other.[1]

The Americans had no idea of where or how strong the Germans were in the Cheneux area. In fact Major Wolf had fourteen Luftwaffe flak guns in the village and the battered remnants of the 11th SS Panzer-Grenadier Company which had arrived there during the night after its battle at Stoumont station and the Zabompré Ferme. In and to the east of Cheneux were the five 105mm guns of Butschek's 5th Battery. During the morning the 6th SS Panzer-Grenadier Company of SS Captain Schnelle's 2nd Battalion, part of Sandig's 2nd Regiment, arrived to reinforce the garrison.[2] The Battalion had crossed the Petit Spai bridge, to the east of Trois Ponts, just before first light and moved on foot to La Gleize, where SS Captain Schenk's Company was ordered on to Cheneux.

Major General Ridgway's orders to Jim Gavin were simple – eliminate all German forces west of the Amblève and Salm rivers to as far south as Vielsalm (Map 14). In accordance with Gavin's plan, at about midday on the 20th, Colonel Tucker gave orders to Lieutenant Colonel William Harrison for 1/504 to secure the hamlet of Brume, on the high ground above Trois Ponts, with one company, and to use the rest of his Battalion to take Cheneux. Harrison chose A Company for the Brume task and ordered B and C Companies to advance on Cheneux at 1300 hours.

Corporal Graves:

Captain Hauptfleisch wanted the S-1 section to have a place apart from the rest of the CP so we took over a farmhouse on the outskirts on the road to Cheneux. . . . The 2nd Battalion was dug in across the road from the house in a large sloping field. . . . At about 1300 hours the 1st Battalion passed by the house on the road going toward Cheneux. . . . The boys were in very high spirits and I heard one man shout out 'Four more shopping days to Christmas, pass it back.'. . . . Lt Madruga who had just come back from hospital in England the day before we pulled out for Belgium after being wounded in Holland, stopped off at the CP to joke with us and said he was still full of good old IPA [English beer] which was a hell of a way to go into battle.[3]

B Company 1/504, commanded by Captain Helgeson, led the advance towards Cheneux with platoons on each side of the road. It ran into a small group of Germans with a machine gun 500m east of Rahier by a culvert over a small stream. The advance continued after one enemy had been killed and one captured. A thousand metres further on the Americans ran into the forward line of the main German position (Map 17). It was centred round the two westerly houses of Cheneux belonging to the Boutet and Gaspard families. The 1/504 Unit Diary records:

With 3rd Platoon on the left of the road and 2nd Platoon on the right, the Company continued the advance handicapped by ground haze which limited visibility to 200/300 yards and heavy machine gun fire from the outskirts of the town. 1st Platoon was ordered by Captain Helgeson to turn the enemy's right flank. The captured enemy half-track was put between the attacking platoons, thus enabling the return of fire against the machine guns and 20mms. After receiving heavy fire however, the half-track moved back. 1st Platoon advanced 200 yards past the other platoons' base of fire where it was pinned down by a 20mm and two MG-42s with a squad of riflemen 100 yards from the enemy forward lines. Contact was lost with Battalion and C Company's mortars were falling on the rear of the Company [another report says enemy mortar fire killed six men and knocked out the B Company radio]. The position then held by B Company was a table top criss-crossed by barbed wire fences. Ground haze made the adjustment of artillery difficult. At 1700 hours Captain Helgeson ordered the Company to withdraw 200 yards to the edge of the woods. An orderly withdrawal was made, one platoon at a time and the Company reorganised and set up a perimeter defence at the wood's edge. At 1845 hours Captain Helgeson gave the CO the situation.

This report was passed on to the Regimental Commander, Colonel Tucker, who at once ordered Harrison to launch a night attack and capture the village. H hour was set for 1930 hours and Harrison attacked with B Company on the right of the road and C Company on the left; two M-36 TDs of B Company 703rd TD Battalion were to be in support between them and the attack was to be preceded by a ten minute artillery barrage. The companies were formed into four assault waves, 50 yards in depth from each other.

For unknown reasons the artillery did not fire and when the paratroopers of B and C Companies advanced at 1930 hours, the two TDs did not accompany them. B Company attacked over ground sloping gently to the right and then dropping very steeply to the l'Abreuvoir stream. Its attack frontage was therefore limited to about 100m and it had four barbed wire cattle fences to cross. C Company had flat ground, no cover at all and numerous cattle fences between them and the village. Not surprisingly both companies took appalling casualties from the German flak wagons and machine guns. American reports speak of very heavy mortar fire as well. By 2200 hours the assault companies had advanced only 400m and were held up by at least one 20mm two hundred metres to their front in a reverse slope position in the village.

Despite committing his HQ Company machine gun platoon and losing five of its eight guns, Harrison could not get his men into the main part of Cheneux. It is reported that in desperation he personally ordered the leading M-36 forward and after it knocked out the guilty 20mm with two rounds, the depleted Parachute companies took possession of the high ground at the western end of Cheneux – west of the Gespard house – or as the US Official History describes it: 'this slight toehold'. It was 2300 hours. The SS men still held the main part of the village around the church where most of the villagers had taken refuge. The 1st Battalion had suffered 225 casualties; B Company had no officers and only eighteen men left and C Company was down to three officers and twenty-eight men. HQ Company had suffered four killed and thirty wounded. Rather than admit that it had been an ill-conceived attack, launched without coordinated artillery support and without any help from the two other battalions which stood idle all that day and night, even General Gavin exaggerated the size of the opposition. He claimed later that the two companies of the 1/504 had attacked the well-organized defences of the 2nd SS Panzer-Grenadier Regiment, surrounded by barbed wire and heavily reinforced by mobile flak guns, mortars, machine guns and assault artillery!

Paratrooper Curtis Adiot of B Company 1/504 described this experience 'live' to Robert Barr, a BBC War Correspondent, at the end of this first phase of the battle:

They opened fire on us and we all had to split and just get in the best way we could. One officer out of our Baker Company had two squads and we went way to the right flank to outflank this 20mm flak wagon which had the companies all pinned down in the open fields; we got around and the officer was knocked out, so a bazooka man, he was not a bazooka man but he grabbed a bazooka and myself led the twelve or fourteen men on around; he knocked out two half-tracks and got another one – got a hit on another one, I don't know whether it was knocked out or not, and at the same time we had approximately a platoon or maybe a company, you couldn't tell, of Jerries at this heavy strongpoint. There we lost quite a few men wounded and we had to pull back and get some more men from the Company and bypass the strongpoint and get men on in below it.

Robert Barr: How has that helped today's fighting?

Adiot: Well if the 20mms hadn't have got out of there, there wouldn't have been enough of us left I expect to do any fighting.

It would seem from this that the troublesome 20mm may have withdrawn and not been knocked out by the M-36.

Corporal Graves relates his experience that night:

I was awakened by the noise from a terrific battle. . . . We figured the 1st Battalion must have run into something very rough. Tracers were flying all over the field across the road from the house where the 2nd Battalion was dug in. Heavy artillery was crunching in below us. All hell was breaking loose; to top it all the air was full of the fateful chug, chug of robots overhead in great numbers. . . . I was lying open-eyed, listening to the bursting crack of 20mm shells around the house with a great deal of apprehension, when Lt Madruga whom I had just talked with earlier in the day burst into the house bleeding badly from two wounds. He said they had to have more ambulances up in the 1st Battalion area in a hurry. A few moments later, Captain Duncan (Bn S-3) an old soldier who had seen a lot of fighting as a company commander and was not one to be easily excited in the heat of a battle, came in saying the 1st Battalion was being cut to ribbons.[4]

At 2300 hours the Regimental Commander came forward and Harrison told him he could advance no further without reinforcement. Tucker promised him a company from 3/504 but they both knew it would take several hours to arrive.

NOTES

1. Graves, *Blood and Snow – the Ardennes*.
2. Tiemann, *Die Leibstandarte IV/2*, p. 116 and Peiper's testimony at Dachau Trial.
3. Graves op. cit.
4. Ibid.

CHAPTER XXV

Wednesday 20th December

Trois Ponts

Late on Tuesday 19th December, Major General Jim Gavin ordered Colonel William Ekman's 505th Parachute Infantry to close up to the Salm river. Lieutenant Colonel Vandervoort's 2nd Battalion was given the task of seizing and holding Trois Ponts itself, the 3rd Battalion was directed on the Rochelinval area (Map 14), 5km to the south and the 1st Battalion to the south of that.

By 1300 hours on Wednesday the Regimental HQ of the 505th and 2/505 were complete in Trois Ponts (Map 13); the HQ moved later to Dairomont. The paratroopers were amazed to find 'Bull' Yates, with Sam Scheuber and his engineers already established in the town. While Yates concentrated his men in the area to the north of the Salm bridge, Vandervoort took over the area south of it with his F Company. D Company was sent down to cover the area by the lower Salm bridge site and E Company was initially held in reserve. Mortars were set up and the 456th Parachute Field Artillery Battalion deployed its guns in support.

The next step was for a platoon of the 307th Airborne Engineer Battalion to repair the Salm bridge in the town centre. Then, during the afternoon, Lieutenant Meddaugh's E Company and a 57mm anti-tank gun commanded by Lieutenant Wurtlich, crossed the river and advanced to the high ground on the Aisomont road. Vandervoort[1] has

175

blamed this ill-conceived decision to put a whole company, rather than a small outpost, across the river on the Assistant Divisional Commander of the 82nd Airborne Division, Brigadier General Ira Swift. Whether this is true, or whether he ordered this move himself, will never be known, but it offered E Company and the gun as hostages to fortune. As the *History of the 505th Parachute Infantry Regiment* put it: 'All were agreed that they could have held the Salm river line until hell froze over because, for defense, it may well have been the best position the Regiment held during the whole war. The river itself was a perfect barrier against enemy armor.'

The E Company paratroopers took up a position near Noupré, the same area where Sam Scheuber's platoon of engineers had run into trouble with Peiper's Type IV tanks on the Monday. Meddaugh deployed six bazooka teams on the north side of the road, Lieutenant Walas's 2nd Platoon astride the road, Lieutenant Bailey's 1st Platoon to the south of it and kept Lieutenant Jensen's 3rd Platoon in reserve. The 57mm was in support at a bend in the road.

It will be remembered that Max Hansen's KG, after being relieved by the 9th SS Panzer Division at Recht on Tuesday, was to advance to the Wanne area via Logbiermé (Map 6). It began its advance through the appallingly difficult Bois de Reuland at last light and reached Logbiermé during the Wednesday morning. The move to Wanne continued and reconnaissance parties pushed out from Wanne and Aisomont after last light. E Company 2/505 reported hearing vehicle movement at 2000 hours and at 2030 two SPWs hit Meddaugh's position – the first was immobilized on mines and the second knocked out by a bazooka. Vandervoort says this incident occurred at 0300 hours on the Thursday morning. Certainly at 2000 hours C Company 51st Engineers reported intensified enemy artillery fire in Trois Ponts resulting in two men being killed and one wounded.

Hansen's KG continued to concentrate during the night and would be complete by first light Thursday. He knew from his reconnaissance parties that the Americans were on his side of the Salm and he determined to do something about them. The scene was set for an American disaster.

NOTE

1. Vandervoort, *Trois Ponts*, p. 2.

CHAPTER XXVI

Wednesday 20th December

La Gleize

On Wednesday morning General Hobbs decided to use McGeorge's armoured Task Force (TFM) against La Gleize with the 3/117 Infantry in support (Map 18). Accordingly K Company and the two 743rd Sherman platoons remained at Cour to support McGeorge on that route, the 1st Sherman Platoon of A Company remained at Roanne with L Company and I Company 3/117 stayed in Ruy. Hobbs kept the whole of C Company 743rd Tank Battalion with the 2/120 Infantry at Ruy as his Divisional reserve.

It was fortuitous for Peiper that Sandig's 2nd SS Panzer-Grenadier Battalion, after crossing the Amblève at Petit Spai, arrived in La Gleize around mid-morning. The 6th Company was sent on to reinforce Cheneux but the rest of the Battalion took up positions on the eastern approaches to the village. Diefenthal's weakened 11th Company was already in Cheneux and the rest of his much reduced 3rd SS Panzer-Grenadier Battalion in Stoumont. There was therefore an urgent need for more infantry to support the tanks and 9th SS Pioneers in La Gleize. The latter had laid mines on the Borgoumont road but Peiper was very conscious of the vulnerable north-east approach from Francorchamps.

Recall that Major McGeorge's 1st Battalion (reinforced) of the 33rd Armored Regiment split into two TFs at 0400 hours on the Wednesday morning. Captain Jordan took one part and McGeorge was left with I (Sherman) Company and the Assault Gun Platoon of the 33rd Armored, the 2nd Infantry Platoon of D Company and the Mortar Platoon of the 36th Armored Infantry Battalion and an engineer squad of D Company 23rd Engineer Battalion. TFM moved off from La Reid at roughly the same time as TFJ, first light, and joined up with K Company 3/117 and the two Sherman platoons at Cour at 1022 hours. This latter group then advanced in thick fog to the hamlet of Borgoumont, 2km north-east of La Gleize, which it reached at 1130 hours.

By far the most powerful element of CCB was Lieutenant Colonel Bill Lovelady's 2nd Battalion (reinforced) of the 33rd Armored Regiment. It consisted of two Sherman companies, a Stuart light tank company, an armoured infantry company, reconnaissance and engineer platoons, four 75mm assault guns and a battery of armoured field artillery. Lovelady's task, as set by the Corps Commander, was to move from the Spa area where he had bivouacked on the Tuesday night, through Ruy and Roanne, and to clear any German forces on the east bank of the Amblève down to Trois Ponts, and then on the north bank as far as Stavelot where he was to make contact with Frankland's 1/117 Infantry. The problem was that these very clear orders were not transmitted to Lovelady. He did not even know his TF was part of XVIII Airborne Corps. In a letter to the author in 1989 Lovelady said:

> General Boudinot, CCB Commanding General, was in Paris when we received orders to leave Germany, Stolberg. Colonel Welborn was in charge and moved CCB and attached elements to Verviers where we would get maps from 1st Army and further orders. Colonel Welborn met with McGeorge, Jordan and me at a cafe there. The maps had not arrived and he told me to spend the night near Spa. The next morning I was to 'take off' on my assigned route and keep going until I ran into Germans and then contact him. We were also supposed to be attached to 30 Infantry Division and would contact them somewhere round Stavelot. Colonel Welborn directed the attacks of Jordan and McGeorge and, being a senior commander I suppose, left me on my own.

Since no proper maps were available Lovelady used a civilian road map – not that it mattered much as there was really only one way he could go; to Ruy, Roanne, the N-33 and then, after the Trois Ponts railway viaducts, on the N-23. It was a wholly unsuitable route in that he would be forced to advance, like Peiper, on a one-vehicle front and would be open to ambush the whole way with the river on one side and steep, forested hills on the other. Welborn's last words to Lovelady were 'Give 'em hell, Bill!'

TFL moved south from Spa at first light, through the Bois de Geronstère and then, 2km north of Cour, turned south-east and took the very steep, narrow and twisting road through Andrimont to Ruy. From there it moved down the Roanne valley road, past the 3/117 position at the Fontaine farm, to join the N-33 to Trois Ponts. It was foggy and the tanks moved slowly. The road from Roanne to the junction with the N-33 passes only 600m from the Moulin Maréchal where Handtusch's Tiger, Klingelhöfer's Type IV and the three Pumas were blocking the Trois Ponts approach; but the mill is below the level of the Roanne road and is obscured by trees. There is a story on the German side that Handtusch declined to engage the American column on its way south, fearing it was too strong. This may well be true – on the other hand it could be that TFL slipped by in the poor visibility. Either way Handtusch has been blamed – the fact that Klingelhöfer was the ranking officer seems to have been forgotten. Whether 'Blocking Group Mill' could have prevented or seriously delayed TFL's move down the N-33 must of course remain an open question, but there can be no doubt that the insertion of a powerful armoured TF between La Gleize and Trois Ponts was to prove disastrous for Peiper.

Lieutenant Hope's E (Sherman) Company was in the lead when, sometime after midday, TFL ran into a small enemy column of two towed 75mm anti-tank guns and a single truck at the N-33 road junction. Not surprisingly these were knocked out and a number of Germans killed. After reporting this contact Lovelady was ordered to continue towards Stavelot. Shortly after this, near Coo railway station, the leading Shermans encountered a much larger German column containing three SPWs, one schwimmwagen, two towed anti-tank guns, one towed 150mm gun, one Hummel 150mm self-propelled gun [the only one in the 1st SS Panzer Division!], five ammunition trucks, two unspecified trucks and an indeterminate number of infantry. These also were all destroyed or captured. Both these German columns were part of Sandig's 2nd SS Panzer-Grenadier Battalion group which had crossed at Petit Spai earlier that morning. Recall that its 6th Company had reinforced the German garrison in Cheneux while other panzer-grenadiers had been held in La Gleize. It can well be asked how and why part of Sandig's KG could cross the Amblève and reach La Gleize without opposition, but not a much needed resupply column? The explanation can only be inefficiency, a breakdown of communications and/or confusion at Divisional level.

It was late afternoon as Hope's Shermans approached the Trois Ponts viaducts.

In the meantime TF McGeorge began a wary advance from Borgoumont, still in thick fog, at 1400 hours; after a few hundred metres, in the area of Les Tscheous where L Company 3/117 had reported the sound of enemy tanks the night before, it lost a Sherman to direct fire. A further few hundred metres on, at 1440 hours, TFM ran into a strong enemy road block just beyond the culvert where the Nabonruy stream runs under the road. The Americans say it consisted of a tank, anti-tank gun, some self-propelled guns and dismounted machine guns and could not be bypassed due to the difficult terrain. This was true for vehicles but certainly not for infantry on their feet; it reveals the clear reluctance on the part of the Americans to stray far from roads and tracks.

In 1951 Doctor Bastin, whose house was located at Les Tscheous, published an account of this incident in an article called 'Borgoumont and the von Rundstedt Offensive':

Around two o'clock the Americans who have decided to enter La Gleize get going. I have been invited to join the column so I can show the soldiers the unevenness of the ground; lanes, brooks and mainly nests of machine guns. There are twenty-five tanks, 200 men and about a dozen FI [members of the Resistance] from Spa commanded by Decerf, alias Mickey. They are the young men who walk in front of the first tank along the fences. After an hour we are approaching the village; one can distinguish already the villa Closset a few metres away in the thick fog; we lie on the ground and the lead tank fires a shell into the front of the house. I feel it advisable to go back about ten metres, level with the second tank. We soon get up and start walking again. Then another stop . . . a machine gun is firing in the fog; a soldier is hit in the knee . . . the dead leaves flutter over our heads; two feet away from my shoulder the earth is disturbed by bullets, just like a mole. I have had enough. . . . I'm not going any further . . . but as far as I can see everyone has had enough and then the 'We go back' order is passed round.

An explosion in front of the tank I am lying near. . . . I do not understand at first that it is a mine; the Sherman is hardly shaken and moves forward straightaway. While I am moving back towards the Nabonruy, the lead tank, which is also backing, causes a second mine to explode – the rubber tracks are burning – the men open the hatch, not too worried about getting out . . . the tank catches fire and explodes.

TFM, supported by K Company 3/117, then took up positions between the stream and Les Tscheous, but not before losing a further Sherman, commanded by Lieutenant Wanamaker, which exploded after being hit by tank fire during a short lifting of the fog. The whole crew was killed. At 2020 hours according to the CCB After Action Report, but 1800 hours according to the Belgians, the American infantry advanced again under the cover of darkness. A member of 2nd Platoon, D Company 36th Armored Infantry Battalion, Robert Kauffman, described his experiences that night in an unpublished article called 'The Red and White Path – One Soldier's Odyssey':

Our squad had been ordered that night to cross a narrow bridge and then leave the roadway, ascend partway up a hill and then follow a course that would parallel the road. As we made our way up the hill, all that we could hear was the snipping of the wire cutter as our squad leader made his way through several cattle fences that obstructed our path. We reached a point perhaps fifty yards from the road and then began a movement parallel with the roadway, crossing a brook that flowed off the hill and then proceeding a few more yards. In the quietness of the night, we heard the unmistakable sound of the bolt of a machine gun being pulled back into the load position. Everyone hit the ground and froze. Then everything ripped loose. The machine gun, which was no more than a very few yards from the forward man in the squad, opened fire. Fortunately for us, the gun must have been set to fire on that narrow bridge that we had just crossed [the Nabonruy stream culvert]. Had it not been for his discipline in firing into his preassigned target and had he merely turned the gun a few degrees to the left, the gunner would have without question made casualties of us all. No sooner had the machine gun opened up, than the night was alive with heavy rifle fire and the unmistakable sound of exploding hand grenades all around us. We had walked into a perfect trap. To make the scene complete, there was the pop of flare guns, followed by the eerie light of the flares and the swishing sound as they burned and illuminated the area. We had moved into an L shaped German position, with the machine gun at the end of the short leg of the L. Then from one end of the enemy position to the other, there rang out a chorus of shouts and curses and demands to surrender in German and halting English like counterpoint to the deadly serenade of machine gun and rifle fire and exploding grenades, played under a canopy of descending flares. Our squad was lying on the ground head to toe, each of us trying frantically to crawl bodily into our steel helmets to escape the blistering torrent of fire. It was then that the order to pull back was breathlessly and hoarsely whispered along the line. The prospect of getting out of there seemed at the moment to be just about nil. One of our men became so disoriented that he crawled in the wrong direction and was captured. The rest of us squirmed to a 180 degree turn and tried to make our way back. I was immediately faced with the prospect of crossing the small brook which had a cattle fence passing right over it. The lower strand of wire was too high to get over because of the firing and too low to get under but the man behind me became impatient with my efforts and solved my dilemma by placing his foot firmly on my posterior and literally catapulted me across the brook and through the wire. As I crawled on my stomach I passed several motionless forms of men whom I presumed to be dead. After some distance of crawling on my stomach I was able at least to get on my hands and knees and then after some distance more, being beneath the trajectory of fire, I was able to stand up. The machine gun was still pouring fire on to the bridge that we had crossed earlier, so using it was out of the question. It was therefore necessary to wade through the stream that the bridge passed over. . . . In spite of all that happened that night, it was always the sound of the shouts, the jeering and the cursing in German, the voice of the enemy, that made the deepest and the most searing impression on my memory.

Not all the American attackers were able to withdraw. The Germans launched a quick counter-attack and by 2030 hours had cut off part of

K Company and TFM in the part of La Gleize known as Hassoumont; only an advance by the Shermans supported by more infantry enabled the Americans to get out.

At 1940 hours General Hobbs placed TFM under Brigadier General Harrison's command and, at 2145 hours, he in turn put K Company under McGeorge, who by 2115 hours had withdrawn into Borgoumont where the 2nd and 3rd Sherman Platoons, A Company 743rd were already established. They had taken no part in the day's actions. After their bloody experiences of Wednesday afternoon and evening it was time for the Americans to re-think their tactics for the capture of La Gleize.

CHAPTER XXVII

Wednesday 20th December

Stavelot

At 0300 hours on Wednesday morning Mohnke cancelled Sandig's order to Schnelle for his 2nd SS Panzer-Grenadier Battalion to reinforce Knittel;[1] instead it was ordered to move to La Gleize and reinforce Peiper. The Battalion, after marching by way of Hinoumont, Wanne and Aisomont (Maps 6 & 10) managed to cross the small bridge at Petit Spai and Schnelle's leading elements were in La Gleize at 1000 hours. It will be remembered that the 6th Company moved on to Cheneux to bolster Major Wolf's defences west of the Amblève.

Recall also that Pfeifer's 2nd SS Panzer-Grenadier Company, part of Sandig's 1st Battalion, had secured a foothold on the north side of the Stavelot bridge on Tuesday evening (Map 11). In his letter of 1967 Pfeifer said:

> We maintained our position on the other river bank for about eighteen hours but only had one MG left and no more ammunition. We had no contact anymore with the other bank. When dawn came we began our retreat across the Amblève, downstream from the bridge under heavy fire. I recollect the undertaking cost twenty-three men their lives. If the 4th Company had been on the spot and we had had reasonable fire support it might have looked different, but he (Sandig) had been too impatient.

After a difficult withdrawal, with his men having to swim back Pfeifer took up a position opposite the Tanneries, downstream from the bridge. With B Company of Frankland's 1/117 Infantry covering the site, the four M-10s of C Company 823rd TD Battalion and two Sherman platoons of B Company 743rd Tank Battalion in the town, plus plentiful artillery support, there was little hope of Karl Richter's 1st SS Panzer-Grenadier Battalion ever recrossing the river anywhere near the old stone bridge.

Another version of events in the vicinity of the bridge on Wednesday morning is given in *Curlew History – The Story of the First Battalion, 117th Infantry, 30th Division* by William J. Lyman:

> The first attack that day came early in the morning from across the river in the vicinity of the bridge. Droves of brave but foolish SS infantrymen, apparently 'hopped up' with drugs, attempted to assault the First Platoons of A and B by swimming the Amblève. As might be expected, the exposed Germans proved ideal targets and were literally slaughtered.

The Story of the 30th Infantry Division – Work Horse of the Western Front has yet another version:

> At 4 am on the 20th the enemy began wading the icy river opposite Company A of the 117th Infantry in the south-west part of Stavelot. The Americans responded with flares and gun fire. Sergeant William Pierce swam the river, doused a house with gasoline and set it ablaze. Bridge construction material was brought down to the far shore of the stream. American riflemen, machine gunners, artillery and mortars slaughtered this attempt, although a small birdgehead was established for about an hour in the first row of houses, under the cover of direct tank fire from across the river.

It is interesting to see how the latter report marries up with certain aspects of Pfeifer's version even though there is a twelve-hour difference in the timing of the German attack and a seventeen-hour difference in the time the Germans spent on the north side of the river! Perhaps most interesting of all is the fact that the official log of the 117th Infantry has only three relevant entries for the morning of 20th December: '0350: S-3 to all Bns. All report no activity. 0830: S-3 checked with A Co CO and was told 2 tanks and Inf are in lower end of town which [and?] they are going to get them out.' The only reference to enemy bridging on the same day is at 1330 hours: '1st Bn reports Germans bringing up heavy logs on S bank of river at (7195–0080) evidently for bridging river at this point.' The grid reference given is near the site of the old stone bridge but it is now clear that no serious attempts were ever made to construct a bridge in this area.

During the early hours of Wednesday morning F Company 2/120

Infantry in Malmédy was ordered to move to Cheneu, just to the north-east of Stavelot, and be prepared to support Frankland's 1/117 in the town if required. It arrived at 0700 hours. At about 0830 hours Coblenz, from positions in the Château Lambert and the houses on the western edge of the town, launched a new attack. His plan[2] was to swing to the north of the main road and again try to approach the bridge from the direction of the railway station. His 2nd SS Reconnaissance Company of four platoons, two commanded by sergeants and two by 2nd lieutenants, had been reinforced by the sixty pioneers of SS 2nd Lieutenant Dröge; the Tigers of Wendt and Brandt were in support. Coblenz advanced with SS 2nd Lieutenant Siebert's 2nd Platoon on the right of the road and this was soon threatening the Château Rochettes where A Company 1/117 had its CP. The full fury of the German attack fell on A Company and the machine guns of Frank Warnock's D Company Platoon; Sherman tanks of B Company 743rd were in support but do not seem to have played a significant part in the battle. The 743rd After Action Report makes no mention of any losses but the 117th Infantry Report says one Sherman was lost. In the same way, and just as surprisingly, the 823rd TD Battalion Report has no combat entries for 20th December although its M-10 Platoon was supporting Frankland's Battalion until the afternoon, when it was withdrawn.

Whatever the tanks and TDs were doing that morning, the American infantrymen were having a difficult time and by mid morning they had been forced back a few hundred metres to the level of the railway station. Captain Kent was forced to deploy his reserve platoon and artillery was called down by Lieutenant Foote on the positions his Platoon had vacated. Meanwhile Goltz and the HQ Company of Knittel's SS Reconnaissance Battalion were threatening the town from the north-west and Frankland was forced to use his reserve C Company to keep them out. At 1142 hours he reported the German attack being slowed down, mainly by artillery and he asked for an air strike. He was told none could be flown before 1300 hours. Shortly after this, however, Coblenz's attack petered out – although the Americans did not realise it, his men were exhausted and his force not strong enough to advance further. The Tigers, which Coblenz said played little part in the battle, withdrew to their original positions near the Antoine farm and Petit Spai bridge. At 1255 hours Frankland heard that the Shermans were pulling out 'for maintenance' – his angry complaint was answered when Colonel Johnson ordered the tanks to leave sufficient of their numbers forward at any one time to ensure proper support.

The Wednesday afternoon was relatively quiet in Stavelot except for the exchange of artillery fire. The major activity appears to have occurred in front of 2/117 to the south of Masta. Major Ammon's Battalion reported German troops to its south who appeared to have crossed the Warche river west of Bellevaux and then advanced west into the Burteaumont forest and along the Amblève towards Challes. It is not clear where these Germans came from but they may well have been some of Otto Skorzeny's men based in the Ligneuville area. In any case 2/117 claimed to have pushed them back and early that evening to have used A Company 105th Engineers to blow the Challes footbridge.

The most important event of the Wednesday afternoon was the entry of TF Lovelady into the battle of Stavelot (Map 13). Recall that just before last light Lieutenant Hope's lead Sherman was turning through the double Trois Ponts railway viaducts, unaware that just to the east of them Knittel had Brandt's Tiger on the north side of the river and two 75mm anti-tank guns of SS Lieutenant Erich Waegner's 4th Company on the south bank facing west. The Shermans were nose to tail and within minutes the first four were destroyed and Lieutenant Hope killed. TFL found itself in a highly vulnerable situation – it was strung out on a single road with the river on its right flank and steep, forested hills on its left. Deployment off the road was impossible. In the darkness and fog Major Stallings, Lovelady's Executive Officer, took command of the forward part of the TF which consisted of the reduced E (Sherman) Company now under the command of Lieutenant Cliff Elliott and Lieutenant McCord's E Armored Infantry Company, less a platoon which was back at Coo with Captain Edmark's D (Sherman) Company. B (Stuart) Company under Lieutenant Shipman, and Lieutenant Gray's Reconnaissance Platoon, were at the Roanne valley junction and Lovelady's CP was at Moulin de Ruy (Map 18). Neither Bill Lovelady nor Major Stallings had any idea that paratroopers of the 82nd Airborne Division and the engineers of the 51st and 291st were across the river from them in Trois Ponts.

By early evening A Company 1/117 had managed to reoccupy its old positions on the western side of Stavelot but Coblenz's men were holding the houses around the Basse Voie bridge and the Château Lambert and Goltz's Company was firm in the western hamlets of Parfondruy and Renardmont (Map 10).

NOTES

1. Sandig to author loc. cit., 2 Oct 1985.
2. Knittel, statement at Landsberg/Lech 15 Mar 1948 and Coblenz to author loc. cit., 22 Jun 1986.

CHAPTER XXVIII

Wednesday 20th December

Malmédy

The 30th Division's task in Malmédy was relatively simple (Map 12). It was not required to eject any Germans from anywhere, only to prevent them advancing north of the railway line which runs roughly west to east to the south of the town, and from crossing the Warche river at the west end of Malmédy. Colonel Branner Purdue's 120th Infantry, already reinforced, was also required to keep contact with the 1st Infantry Division on its left flank at Waimes.

There was no fighting in the Malmédy sector on the Wednesday. In the latter part of the day Skorzeny's 150 Panzer Brigade,[1] consisting of KGs X and Y, assembled in the Ligneuville area for action against the town the following day. Unbelievably, Lieutenant Wolf's KG Z had still been unable to reach the attack area and was seen as a potential reserve. KG X was under the command of SS Captain von Foelkersam; it was equipped with one Sherman and five camouflaged Panthers and comprised two infantry companies of about one hundred and twenty men each and a heavy company with two panzer-grenadier, two heavy mortar and two anti-tank platoons and also pioneer and signal platoons. KG Y, under Captain Scherff, had the same organisation but StuGs (armoured assault guns) instead of tanks. The detailed organisation of these KGs is shown at Appendix 1.

I SS Panzer Corps's instructions to Skorzeny were simple – on Thursday he was to advance on Malmédy and open up both Route C for 12th SS Panzer Division and the N-23 to Stavelot so that Peiper's lifeline could be re-established.

German intelligence on Malmédy was sketchy; it was based on one of Skorzeny's own commando patrols[2] which had got into the town on the Sunday and found only Pergrin's few engineers. They had no idea that since then it had been strongly reinforced.

Skorzeny was given no artillery support and he aimed to achieve his mission by the use of surprise. Both KGs were to attack in the dark, KG X from due south and KG Y down the N-32 from the Baugnez crossroads. KG X was targeted, not on the town, but on the Warche river bridge and the vital road junction south of Burninville.

Unfortunately for Skorzeny one of his men was captured near Malmédy on the Wednesday afternoon and revealed, under interrogation, that the town was to be attacked at 0330 hours on Thursday morning. Before midnight all American units were warned.

NOTES

1. Skorzeny, *Skorzeny's Special Missions*.
2. ETHINT 12.

CHAPTER XXIX

Thursday 21st December

All Fronts

In the Froidcour farm, in the centre of what became known to the Germans as 'The Cauldron', farmer Masson was allowed to milk his cows, under guard, early on the Thursday morning. The milk was needed for the wounded and dying of both sides in the Château.

For Peiper, in his makeshift Command Post in Masson's farmhouse, the ultimate military nightmare was coming true – he was facing an enemy on three fronts (Map 14), he had hardly enough fuel for his tanks even to adjust their fire positions, his five 105mm artillery guns and six 150mm infantry guns were nearly out of ammunition and he was burdened with both prisoners and wounded. To the west the American 119 RCT with the tanks of Jordan and George Rubel was about to attack Stoumont for a second time; across the river in Cheneux paratroopers were already in the outskirts of the village and behind him in La Gleize, TF McGeorge was redeploying for another attack. Peiper knew that Stavelot was in American hands and that tanks were blocking the N-33 north of Trois Ponts. He had been told that Hansen's KG had arrived at Wanne but he had no idea if and when it might be able to break through and resupply him with manpower, fuel and ammunition. He had no choice but to fight on in the hope that relief would soon arrive.

Ten kilometres away in the relative comfort of the Hôtel des Bruyères in Francorchamps, General Leland Hobbs was not without his problems. He was nowhere near achieving his mission of clearing the Germans from north of the Amblève and west of the Warche rivers between Stoumont and Stavelot. It was clearly time for a new plan. He had already tasked Brigadier General Harrison with recapturing Stoumont and La Gleize. This freed Johnson's 3/117, less K Company, for other tasks. Harrison had considerable forces under his command to achieve his aim – Sutherland's 119th Infantry Regiment, Rubel's 740th Tank Battalion and Task Forces McGeorge and Jordan. Hobbs now ordered Colonel Walter Johnson of the 117th Infantry to clear the Germans from the large, heavily wooded area between La Gleize and Stavelot, including the hamlets of Ster, Renardmont and Parfondruy. Johnson already had two of his Battalions, the 1st and 2nd, holding Stavelot itself and the ground between there and Malmédy. With only his weakened 3rd Battalion available he clearly needed more infantry and Hobbs gave him E and F Companies of the 120th Infantry. Since Task Force Lovelady was now located, indeed trapped, in Johnson's area of operations, it too was put under his command.

Major General Jim Gavin was much nearer to achieving his task. Colonel Ekman's 505th Parachute Infantry Regiment had already closed up to the Salm and secured Trois Ponts; it only remained for Tucker's 504th Regiment to complete the job by clearing the Germans out of Cheneux – even so, Gavin's men would be very stretched to cover the whole river line from Cheneux to Grand Halleux.

The balance of forces on Thursday morning was therefore heavily weighted against the Germans. Peiper could only muster the equivalent of two tank companies, about thirty tanks, no more than six infantry and pioneer companies, some twenty anti-aircraft vehicles and eleven artillery pieces for which there was virtually no ammunition! Knittel had four tanks, the equivalent of about two infantry companies and only three guns which were out of ammunition. The Americans, excluding their force in Malmédy, had an order of battle of fourteen tank companies, forty-seven infantry companies, two TD companies and an astonishing thirty-six artillery batteries with more than ample ammunition. It had become a very one-sided contest and there seemed little Mohnke, Hansen and Sandig could do to assist their old comrades other than support them with the Leibstandarte artillery which was now deployed on the high ground south of the Amblève. Nevertheless, they would continue to try to achieve a breakthrough.

CHAPTER XXX

Thursday 21st to Friday 22nd December

Stoumont

At 0330 hours on Thursday morning Brigadier General Harrison placed TF Jordan under the command of the new CO of the reinforced 3/119 Infantry, Lieutenant Colonel Bision, and issued orders for the capture of Stoumont (Map 16). 1/119 with Rubel's 740th Tanks was to attack from the north-west, seize the Preventorium and exploit into the village; 3/119 with Jordan's TF under command was to attack from the north through Roua and then advance to the eastern end of the village; Major Hal McCown's 2/119 was to make a wide enveloping movement through the northern forest known as the Bois de Bassenge and cut the N-33 between Stoumont and La Gleize, just to the north of the Château Froidcour. The timing of this attack is unclear – a clue is given in Lieutenant David Knox's letter to the author dated October 1984:

An attack order was finally issued at 0530 hours. We moved out [from Monthouet] at 0630. It was very foggy. Company L was naturally one of the lead companies in this affair because we had more men left than any other unit. By about 0800 we were in position above the town. It was so foggy that we couldn't see over 25 feet. It was about 500 yards down to the town. We were in the edge of the woods. The jump-off time was changed. It was finally set for 1245 hours.

What delayed the start of the attack? George Rubel describes a pre-dawn attack by the Americans but this is not mentioned by anyone else and certainly not by Colonel Sutherland under whose command Rubel was operating. The 119th Infantry Report says the Germans counter-attacked 119 RCT at 0500 hours and after knocking out three American tanks, the attack ended at 0730 hours. It seems fairly clear therefore that the Germans launched another counter-attack[1] before dawn and Rubel, in retrospect, wrongly described this as an American attack. He wrote:

The attack was resumed at 0400 hours. It moved forward about 100 yards when an AT gun knocked out the lead tank. Lt Oglensky, who was riding the tank, found that his gun had been rendered useless and fearing that Jerry was about to begin a tank attack he placed his own tank crosswise in the road to form a road block. As he was doing

189

this another shot hit his tank. He ordered his crew to get out and go to the rear, while he took over the tank immediately in the rear. He had hardly got aboard when an enemy panzerfaust hit the tank and the machine started to burn. He and his crew dismounted and almost at the same instant two more tanks were hit by panzerfausts. That left four tanks in the road – three of them on fire . . . the heat was so intense that it was impossible to get close enough to fasten a towing cable.

It is noteworthy that Rubel goes on:

During the day the enemy made *several more fanatical counter-attacks* [author's italics] but the infantry stood their ground on each attack. Casualties were running high. We had lost five tanks and the infantry battalion nearly 200 men. The chateau (Preventorium) was a source of great trouble to us. It had to be taken before we could take Stoumont.[2]

Rubel was certainly right about the infantry casualties – 1/119 had lost five platoon commanders and B and C Companies were down to about sixty men each.

The rescheduled American attack was to begin at 1245 hours but before this could happen the knocked-out Shermans had to be removed from the main road. The action taken to overcome this problem is described by Rubel:

Before the attack could be resumed however, the four tanks that had been knocked out near the chateau [Preventorium] had to be removed. We decided to lay a smoke screen and under cover of it send the recovery vehicle forward, attach a line, and tow the tanks off the road. Lt Oglensky's tank, which had not burned, was believed to be in running condition, and T/5 James E. Flowers volunteered to drive it off the road. It stuck out like a sore thumb and any movement toward it brought down all kinds of fire. Flowers somehow made it, entered through the escape hatch and drove it back into our lines. In the meantime, Captain Walter Williams and his Battalion maintenance section with their recovery vehicles had moved the three burned out tanks.[3]

The 119th Infantry Report says its 1st Battalion and accompanying tanks attacked at 1245 hours but was held after only 200 yards by withering machine gun and small arms fire. It goes on that at 1545 hours the Battalion Group was ordered to withdraw to its start positions. Monsieur Serge Fontaine, the local Belgian historian, suggests however, that before they were forced to retreat the GIs managed to get into the Preventorium again and release their comrades cut off in the single room. A harrowing account of what it was like in the cellars of the

Preventorium during the fighting is provided by the Abbé Hanlet in his book *The Tragedy of Saint Edouard's.*

The American tanks fire point blank and incessantly into our walls which collapse over our heads. The grenades fall with a crash on the paving stones of the big hall and each time we are shaken. Somewhere near the kitchen a shell pierces the floor and brings down the cellar ceiling. Around the air vents of our underground hiding place bullets are raining and hit like hail stones during a storm. Every moment the house is shaken by shells . . . the crowd of 250 people regroup towards the centre around the nuns and away from the air vents . . . they pile on top of one another . . . one lies on the floor making oneself as small as possible; one would like to crawl into the ground so as not to be crushed by the house collapsing on our heads. One prays and begs with such fervour but it is impossible to say Mass and so instead one gives a general absolution. Suddenly, with dreadful noise, a shell has burst through the vault of our cellar, filling the dark underground room with smoke, acrid with dust and powder. People scream, howl and beg – 'Help! We're civilians!' In this tragic situation a priest rushes up the stairs to the kitchen to beg the fighters for a truce to evacuate the people but a German, seeing a figure in the darkness behind him, empties his revolver on the foolhardy messenger who, by a miracle, manages to get back to the cellar.

David Knox describes the accompanying attack by 3/119 and TFJ from the north:

The artillery barrage started and we took off with it. No one showed any interest in going, but they knew it had to be done. It was so foggy that one of our men found himself ten yards from a German MG before he knew it. Collins was a hero here; he had knocked one position out with his Browning automatic rifle when it stuck. He grabbed the Jerry gun, turned it around and knocked the other crew out. It was too foggy though, the attack just wasn't working. I told Captain Stewart that contact was lost on our right. There was nothing left to do but pull back. The first plan was to go back in again – immediately. Everyone had been pushed about as far as he could be. Nerves were being broken on men whom one would have thought would never weaken. Finally we got word to hold up for the night. We organised with the light tanks and dug in.[4]

In amplification of this account the 119th Report says that at 1330 hours five German tanks were encountered in front of K Company 3/119 and that at 1512 hours the Battalion was ordered to withdraw to the woods and dig in for the night. Serge Fontaine confirms the number of tanks and credits a K Company bazooka man with knocking out one of them.

The CCB 3rd Armored Division Report gives very little detail of TFJ's attack, merely stating that the TF sighted six enemy tanks in Stoumont and by 1400 hours was within 200 yards of its objective. In fact, just as on the previous day, Jordan never got beyond the bend in the road at La Rochette. After 300 yards he ran into tank fire and at 1515 hours, like the others, he was ordered to pull back to Monthouet, leaving an outpost to his front.

The most successful part of the day from the American point of view was the advance by McCown's 2/119 Infantry. They swung north and east behind the 3rd Battalion at Monthouet and by H hour at 1245 hours were 1,000 yards north-east of Stoumont and ready to attack. At 1405 hours they reached the road above the Château Froidcour, just by the St Anne's chapel, where they set up a road block of felled trees backed by mines.[5] The Battalion, after advancing a few hundred yards towards the Château Froidcour, then ran into Georg Preuss's weak but determined 10th SS Panzer-Grenadier Company. Major McCown was captured and the Battalion forced back. Major Nathaniel Laney, the Executive Officer, took over and at 1512 hours the Battalion was ordered to withdraw and fall in to the right of 3/119 at Monthouet. This withdrawal was completed by 1700 hours. McCown later wrote: 'On the afternoon of 21 Dec at about 1600, I, my radio operator and orderly were captured by a German patrol. I was taken back to the main HQ at La Gleize, passing through several areas where fire fights were going on between my men and the surrounded Germans.'[6]

It had not been a good day for the Americans – Herlong's 1/119 had suffered twenty-two men killed, ninety-four wounded and eighty-one missing in the fighting. At 1600 hours Brigadier General Harrison reported: 'The real picture is that two of these battalions (the 1st and 3rd) are in pretty bad shape. . . . We can stop them alright, [but] . . . I don't think the troops we have now, without some improvement, can take the thing [Stoumont].'

The only 'improvement' readily available was air power and so Harrison planned an extensive use of this and artillery for the following day.

In the meantime, according to George Rubel, Captain Berry's C Company was busy:

That night Captain Berry crawled through the enemy lines and made a circle of the chateau [Preventorium] to find out if there was any possibility of getting tanks up off the road to attack it from the northwest. He found a place where he thought he could build a corduroy road to lead from the main highway (N-33) up over the embankment to this building. Upon his return to friendly troops he asked for volunteers to help build the road. At about midnight he got four tanks up there and personally directed their fire by running from one tank to another. Before morning he had knocked out two enemy tanks, had captured the chateau and had rescued 22 infantrymen who were trapped there. This feat cleared the way for the capture of Stoumont which we then planned to take early on the morning of the 22nd.[7]

The claim that four tank crews captured the St Edouard's Preventorium and released the trapped infantrymen where a company of infantrymen had already failed is hardly credible and Serge Fontaine's version of events the more likely. It is another sad example of exaggerated claims detracting from what were clearly brave deeds; without wishing to belittle the obvious bravery of Captain Berry and his men, it has to be pointed out that by the time these actions were supposed to be taking place there were in fact very few Germans left in Stoumont.

Soon after last light Peiper had withdrawn all but a few snipers and machine gunners whose task was to deceive the Americans into thinking there had been no withdrawal. As a result of increasing American pressure, intense artillery fire and a critical shortage of tank main armament ammunition, as well as fuel, Poetschke had already, by midday Thursday, made contingency plans to withdraw to the area of the Château Froidcour and St Anne's woods. Tanks were now restricted to firing only if they could be fairly certain of a first-round 'kill'.

Two things caused Peiper to evacuate the village shortly after last light.[8] The first was the vulnerability of his northern flank, as shown by McCown's Battalion cutting the N-33, and the second was a radio message from Mohnke telling him that Hansen's men were crossing the Amblève with orders to advance via Coo to La Gleize (Map 14). These factors, coupled with the impending loss of Cheneux, brought Peiper to the inevitable conclusion that it was time to concentrate his whole force in the more easily defended hill-top village of La Gleize, where he already had a firm base. He moved there himself at 1600 hours after giving orders for the withdrawal to begin soon after last light.

The hardest decision for Peiper was what to do with his wounded. It is a matter of principle in most armies that as far as possible wounded are not left to fall into enemy hands, but the Leibstandarte took this principle further than most. After their experiences in Russia where they had seen their wounded often killed or mutilated, the LAH had gone to the extreme of even shooting their most badly wounded men rather than let them fall into Soviet hands. As we shall see, even in this battle against Americans, Peiper tried to negotiate a deal for the return of his wounded once the immediate fighting had ceased. On this Thursday evening, though, he decided to take only his walking wounded and his unwounded American prisoners back to La Gleize. Some eighty badly wounded Germans and a few Americans were left at Froidcour in the care of a terrified German medical NCO and two American medics; one of the Americans, Everitt Smith, later described how Peiper personally explained the difficult situation to him.

According to Belgians who were in the Château over this period the scene there was quite horrific. There was no electricity, so operations and amputations were carried out on the dining room table or at night by the light of candles brought from the chapel; since no medical units had crossed the Amblève, the unit doctors had to operate without anaesthetics and with saws and scissors normally used by the gamekeeper for cutting up deer and wild boar; severed limbs were lying in the garages and gardens together with mutilated bodies, some with their eyes pecked out by chickens and birds; the stench of death was all-pervading and the cries of the wounded heartrending – a member of the de Harenne family described how three truck-loads of dead were removed from the Château when the battle was over.

The Germans, who it is said behaved correctly during their time in the Château, ordered the de Harennes, their servants and the other refugees in the cellars to sew Red Crosses on bed sheets for display on the roofs but this did not prevent some seventeen missiles, all American, penetrating the building and removing the top of one of the turrets. Even so the Château escaped severe damage and no one inside the building is known to have been hurt.

Peiper's men avoided the N-33 on their move back to La Gleize and used the lower road which passes the Masson farm before joining the road from Cheneux to La Gleize. The Americans did not detect the withdrawal – the Belgians, in their cellars, did! Serge Fontaine's description gives an impression of what it was like:

A strange calm follows the dreadful storm of the two previous days and the few shots during the night. From the church, where the disordered confusion of living on top of one another is driving people out of their minds, people rush outside and make for their homes – famished, exhausted, with cattle to feed and houses to check, there are many reasons for the rush. They cross quickly through the ruins, jumping over twisted metal and tanks which are strewn across the roads. The rush home or towards what is left of them, is carried out under the indifferent gaze of SS men prostrate behind their machine guns. The Robinson house cellars empty as well . . . at St Edouards a fixed idea haunts everyone – to leave, to leave as soon as possible! Walls no longer offer the safety that is wanted; after taking Holy Communion for the last time, while others parcel together a few belongings, some go up to the ground floor; the building appears deserted – no more Germans! Leaving the children to wait, Mother Superior, another nun and a gardener, carrying high a makeshift white flag, walk through the ruined village on their way to the Château Froidcour to ask for help.[9]

194

It was 0900 hours on Friday morning as Mother Superior began her dangerous journey and it was at this moment that the American artillery barrage opened up! Poor visibility had again prevented any air support but Brigadier General Harrison was determined to contain his casualty rate by a lavish use of firepower. Serge Fontaine describes its effects with simple clarity:

> An exceptional artillery barrage catches everyone unawares, far from their shelters; the nuns run to the Robinson cellars. A shower of steel and fire descends on the unhappy village with a deafening roar and causes more damage now than in all the other days put together. This highly destructive fire is concentrated to start with on St Edouard's and then it spreads out and the line of explosions advances like a steam roller through the village. As there are no more SS in the Preventorium a wounded American soldier climbs on to the terrace with a white sheet but the fire forces him back into the cellar – he leaves the sheet for the observers to see and soon they order the fire to lift further into the village. Some scouts risk an entry into the building and discover 250 civilians inside, all in tears and begging to be allowed out of this place of terror. While the destruction continues the evacuation begins. Walking over rubble, metal and corpses they cross the muddy fields helped by the GIs who carry children and support the weaker people. The evacuation is painful, almost in line with the machine gun fire and from time to time everyone has to crouch down when a German shell explodes too near or an American one drops short. The sick and aged are taken away immediately in jeeps while the rest of the long procession gets to Targnon on foot where four big lorries wait to take them to Lorcé.[10] (Map 14)

The bombardment lasted continuously until 1400 hours. By then, of the one hundred and fifty houses in the village, one hundred were uninhabitable, thirty-five completely destroyed and five burned. Fontaine continues: 'Advancing with the Shermans the infantry take over the village without shooting. The German snipers who are able, leave their posts and retreat via Froidcour, avoiding any fight.'[11] A witness in Monceau, across the valley to the south, described how he saw two lines of soldiers, German and American, moving at the same time to the east but hidden from each other by the curvature of the hill.

TF Jordan and 3/119 Infantry began their advance at 1320 hours; they met no resistance and by 1410 hours had taken Roua, where the infantry remained whilst TFJ moved to the high ground at the east end of Stoumont on the north side of the N-33.

1/119 and Rubel's tanks moved at 1418 hours and after again meeting no resistance were firm around the ruined church at 1445 hours. 2/119 moved through them and took over Froidcour by 1700 hours. Much against their wishes Monsieur and Madame de Harenne and their unfortunate companions were forced to evacuate their home after only a few minutes to collect what possessions they could carry and move to Lorcé. The HQs of 119 RCT and George Rubel set up in their place. Sadly, when the de Harennes eventually returned to their formerly beautiful home in May 1945, they found the household silver and other valuables had been stolen and the gardens wrecked by tanks and other vehicles.

According to some Belgian sources one Tiger, eighteen Panthers, one Type IV, three tracked anti-aircraft vehicles, one anti-tank gun and ten other German vehicles were found abandoned or destroyed between the Zabompré Ferme and the St Anne's chapel. This count is probably exaggerated.

Four civilians from Stoumont died as a result of the German offensive.

NOTES

1. At the Dachau Trial Peiper said he counter-attacked in Stoumont in the night 20th–21st.
2. Rubel, *Daredevil Tankers*, chapter IX.
3. Ibid.
4. Letter from Knox to author dated 2 Oct 1984.
5. Peiper's testimony at Dachau Trial.
6. *Annexe I to Part C of Intelligence Notes No 43 dated 6 Jan 1945*, HQ US Forces, European Theater.
7. Rubel op. cit.
8. Peiper's testimony at Dachau Trial.
9. Article in *Publicité Idéale* by Serge Fontaine 1970.
10. Ibid.
11. Ibid.

CHAPTER XXXI

Thursday 21st December

Cheneux

Shortly before midnight on Wednesday/Thursday night G Company of the 3rd Battalion, 504th Parachute Infantry Regiment was ordered to reinforce the exhausted 1st Battalion clinging desperately to the western extremities of Cheneux (Map 17). Exactly how one further company was meant to improve the situation in Cheneux and why the rest of the 3rd

Battalion or the whole of the 2nd Battalion were not used remains a mystery!

G Company arrived in Cheneux at about 0300 hours on the Thursday morning and was immediately launched into a night attack which failed at a cost of one killed and twenty-five wounded. It was then placed in a position at the rear of the depleted 1st Battalion to create an all-round perimeter defence.

At 0745 hours after, according to the Americans, a half-hour artillery barrage, the Germans counter-attacked out of the main part of Cheneux to retake the western high ground. They were repulsed with heavy losses.

At 0845 hours the rest of Lieutenant Colonel Julian Cook's 3rd Battalion was ordered to move through the Bois de Rahier and seize the hamlet of Monceau, just to the south of Cheneux. Companies H and I reached the area south of Monceau at 1530 hours after a difficult advance. H Company occupied the hamlet and was immediately pinned down by 20mm fire from Cheneux. During the six hours it took 3/504 to reach Monceau, Cheneux itself was relatively quiet. According to some Belgian sources both sides used the period to collect their wounded and dead. Suggestions of a semi-official truce however, seem hardly credible. Many of the civilians who had taken refuge in the small village school were moved by the Germans into the church. With women and children at one end and men at the other they feared a massacre. They were made to lie down facing the altar for their better protection – not surprisingly Father Durieux used the opportunity to give a general absolution!

Corporal Graves takes up the story on the American side:

At 1130 Lt Voss, Webb and myself left the CP for the 1st Bn CP to try and get some estimate of the casualties and find out what disposition could be made of the dead if any. After walking about a mile up steep, heavily wooded, hills we came to a road junction where five German vehicles had been knocked out. [Almost certainly flak-wagons by the Boutet House.] The surrounding area was the worst example of what happens when a great number of men are killed and wounded that I ever saw. Broken rifles, loose ammunition, countless helmets, bloody GI clothes and bandages, all sorts of miscellaneous equipment, belts of machine gun ammo and mortar shells, were strewn around the bald hilltop and ditches alongside the road – not to mention the dead. The living, glassy eyed and expressionless, were hugging their holes scraped out of the banks bordering the road. The overall scene was so sickening that it made you want to shout out to God and ask him why all this was necessary.

In order to get to the little farm house which was the 1st Bn CP, a fire swept road had to be crossed. We hugged the side of the bank until we reached the shelter of a knocked out German half-track. Lt Voss made a dash for it across the road. Bullets began to zing around the end of the half-track, making Webb and myself look at each other and ask ourselves what the hell we were doing there. We finally got up the nerve to rush across the road to the house. Our worst fears as to what was taking place were confirmed. The staff was in sort of dazed condition. They told us in an offhand manner that the house was being fired at from three directions. They all seemed so tired that they gave the impression of not giving much of a damn whether they lived another half-hour or not. Conditions in the 1st Battalion were bad. The only reports we could expect would be rough estimates. Company B had lost all eight of its officers and the 1st Sergeant. A Staff Sergeant was commanding the remnants of the Company which they thought was about 30 men. Company C had lost 5 officers and about 55 men wounded, a rough estimate of 15 killed. HQ 1st Bn had had 2 officers killed, 2 or 3 enlisted men killed and about 30 wounded. Company G which had come up to reinforce them had had its 1st Sergeant killed and some 25 men wounded. In reality no one knew exactly who was killed and who was alive. Colonel Harrison, already the holder of the DSC and Silver Star, sat propped up against a hay stack in the barn, looking at the floor and absent mindedly fingering a straw. He said the assault across the top of the hill crossed with many barbed wire fences was far worse than any nightmare he had ever imagined as a solid sheet of 20mm flak and MG fire raked the assault waves from three sides. That morning they had beaten off one strong counter-attack and they were wondering if they had the strength to beat off any more. Some houses in the town were occupied but the whole town was not yet cleared. We took a rough estimate at what was thought to be the remaining strength of each company and left for our S-1 CP. On the way back I looked at some of the bodies in the ditches to see if I knew any of them – the same boys who were laughingly shouting 'Four more shopping days until Christmas' only the afternoon before. I didn't recognise any personally but I could recognise what they must have gone through.[1]

At 1700 hours both the German and American commanders gave orders – Peiper for a withdrawal back to La Gleize and Tucker for 1/504 and G Company 3/504 to clear Cheneux and H and I Companies 3/504 to advance north-east from Monceau. The attack was timed for 1750 hours – after dark. H and I Companies reached the high ground over-looking the Amblève river near the Château de la Vaulx Renard and claim to have come under 20mm and tank fire. It was further claimed that when the paratroopers tried to cross the Vaulx Renard bridge they were prevented by machine gun fire from the right bank.

In Cheneux itself there was some minor skirmishing but most of the Germans had left by the time G Company and two TDs reached the main part of the village by the church at about 1830 hours. The last remaining machine gun officer of 1/504 was killed in this final action. By 2300 hours the Americans were holding the river line between the Cheneux and Vaulx Renard bridges – 3km to their south-east, A Company 1/504 was occupying Brume and then there was another gap of 1.5km to 2/505 in Trois Ponts. It was a very extended front but one which the Germans were incapable of exploiting.

Fourteen German flak wagons, five 105mm guns, two 75mm anti-tank guns, six SPWs and four trucks were found in Cheneux – they were all out of petrol. German casualties are unknown except for a medical orderly and fourteen severely wounded men captured. Some American survivors talk of 'piles' of German bodies and the Belgians mention a figure of two hundred but this is unconfirmed.

A final word from Corporal Graves about the 1st Battalion as it withdrew the next morning:

> The shattered remnants of the 1st Bn came straggling listlessly down the road, a terrible contrast to the happy battalion which had only two days before gone up the same road wisecracking and full of fight. They were bearded, red eyed, covered with mud from head to foot, and staring blank-facedly straight to the front. No one spoke. What few officers were there in the small column were indistinguishable from the men except for the markings on their helmets. They carried their rifles any way that seemed comfortable, some in Daniel Boone fashion. They had written a page in history which few would ever know about. Already there was talk of a Presidential Citation to record for posterity what was plainly written on their faces in Rahier that morning. To millions of Americans at home the name Cheneux was meaningless. In the swirling holocaust of fire and fury which had descended on the peaceful valley of the Amblève river in Belgium, it might not even be mentioned in the newspapers, such was the confusion of places, units and deeds being churned around in the Witch's Brew which was the present battle of the Ardennes.[2]

Six civilians from Cheneux died as a result of the German offensive and the village was shattered – the survivors were evacuated to Lorcé.

NOTES

1. Graves, *Blood and Snow – the Ardennes*.
2. Ibid.

CHAPTER XXXII

Thursday 21st December

Trois Ponts

On Thursday morning Max Hansen ordered his 1st SS Panzer-Grenadier Battalion and the 1st Company of Jagdpanzers to cross the Amblève at Petit Spai while his 2nd Battalion closed up to the Salm river south of Trois Ponts[1] (Map 13). At the same time SS Captain Böttcher was told to evict the Americans from their positions east of the Salm river, using his 3rd Battalion and the 2nd SS Anti-Tank Company of SS Lieutenant Giesicke with its ten Jagdpanzers.

Böttcher attacked Lieutenant Bill Meddaugh's E Company 2/505 Airborne shortly after first light. The Americans say four 'tanks' hit Lieutenant Walas's 2nd Platoon, straddling the Aisomont road, head on. Infantry then began to outflank the Company's positions through the woods on its southern flank. Despite accurate supporting fire from the 456th Parachute Field Artillery Battalion and the 81mm mortars of Lieutenant John Cooper's Platoon, Walas's men were overrun, and despite the commitment of the reserve platoon, the American position became untenable. At 1330 hours F Company was ordered across the river either to stabilise the situation or help to extract E Company. At 1550 hours the order was given for E Company to withdraw, covered by F Company.

Some time after the war Lieutenant Colonel Benjamin Vandervoort wrote a flamboyant account of the day's events. In it he says he could see, from his mortar observation post on the west side of the river, 'the road clogged with Tiger and Panther tanks, Panzer-Grenadiers (in vehicles and afoot), self-propelled artillery and mobile flak towers.'[2] He goes on to blame General Swift for not allowing him to withdraw E Company even after he knew it was in serious trouble. This, he says, forced him to commit F Company. Eventually, according to Vandervoort, the General ordered him to get his men back:

I then jumped into my jeep and took off for the E Company position. As we passed the 57mm AT gun, the crew were getting ready to move back into the town. We arrived at the Company CP at the same time that a combined infantry and tank assault was culminating its attack on the Company's foxholes. Four or more tanks, with infantry, were closing across the open area to the right front and spraying the edge of the woods with machine gun and cannon fire. . . . I ran to Meddaugh and told him to get his men into town, to constitute the battalion reserve, and TO DO IT NOW! Bill passed the word to his Company to withdraw. They began moving back through the woods accompanied by a hailstorm of bullets pruning bark and leaves from trees. . . . Meanwhile Corporal Russell, my driver/radio op, had whipped the jeep around. . . . I jumped back in and we started down to Trois Ponts – urged by swarms of 9mm slugs from Schmeisser machine pistols. Halfway down the road we passed the 57mm AT gun jackknifed into a ditch and abandoned by its crew. . . .[3] When they (the troopers) reached the edge of the bluff they jumped down the sheer cliff, picked themselves up and ran the 100 yard gauntlet across the two roads, railroad bed and river under the cover of friendly protective fire delivered by our troops on the other side of the river . . . a number of the troopers injured their backs and limbs – sprains and breaks – leaping down the cliffs but no one was left behind. Other members of the Company would grab the injured and drag them along.[4]

Major 'Bull' Yates and Sam Scheuber's C Company 51st Engineers knew that the paratroopers were in trouble as early as 1100 hours and at 1500 hours Scheuber ordered Lieutenant Milgram and six enlisted men to prepare the Salm bridge for demolition.

The withdrawal of the 2/505th paratroopers soon became a rout with, as Vandervoort had described, men jumping from the cliffs above the railway lines in order to get away. By 1630 hours both companies were west of the Salm and, according to the 51st Engineers, the bridge was blown at 1700 hours. The 505th claim their B Company 307th Engineers blew it at 1820 hours but, inevitably, there are a number of discrepancies between the airborne and engineer reports. The earlier time seems more logical. Casualties for F Company are not quoted but E Company lost thirty-five killed and wounded during this fighting.

In the middle of the battle, at about 1500 hours, Yates received an order from Colonel Anderson's 1111th Engineer Group HQ to withdraw his force to Modave – he sent a classic reply saying he could not do so since he was covering the withdrawal of the 82nd Airborne Division! Yates, Scheuber and Walters eventually left Trois Ponts with their valiant engineers at 1930 hours, but not, as will be seen, before Yates had played another important role in relation to events at the Petit Spai bridge. He would be awarded the Bronze Star for his actions at Trois Ponts, and Scheuber and Milgram the Silver Star.

Although the 51st Engineers make no mention of it, a 505th report talks of up to a company's worth of SS men wading the river at a place called Ristonvennes after the withdrawal and managing to get into some of the western houses near the Salm bridge before being mopped up by D Company. 'Bucky' Walters of the 291st Engineers also talks of two platoons of SS infantrymen being cut down by his men as they tried to cross the Salm bridge before it was blown. Vandervoort has a slightly different version:

> It was an opportune time for the Germans to start pushing into the town. . . . E Company was in momentary disarray. F Company was still on the other side of the Salm [he does not say how or when it came back]. D Company was downstream holding off another attempted crossing. Battalion Headquarters, HQ Company, and those damned engineers, were all that stood in the way of a major breakthrough. Troopers and engineers, dug in along the river bank and in the houses, fought back with their 30 and 50 calibre machine guns. We blew the highway bridge over the Salm as soon as the last E Company trooper cleared the area. More German infantry opened fire along the bluff. The Germans and Americans engaged in rapid-fire machine gun and rifle fire exchanges at ranges from 150 to 300 yards. The Germans began hosing the streets of Trois Ponts with their automatic weapons but the exposed rim of the cliff was no place to duel with dug-in defenders. The paratroopers settled down to some old fashioned sharp shooting and spilled a lot of blood on the bluff.[5]

Vandervoort then goes on to describe a Tiger, 'with white skull and cross bones of the SS insignia' clearly visible, appearing on the cliff and taking his men under direct fire until it was forced to withdraw after being hit by a phosphorus bomb from one of the Battalion mortars. Although Vandervoort exaggerates when he describes his enemy as 'an exceptionally well-equipped Panzer Kampfgruppe of great size' and E Company facing 'the better part of a Panzer Division', it has to be remembered that those who fought at places other than Bastogne have always been irritated by the prominence given to that place and the 101st Airborne Division by most historians and film makers. Vandervoort ends his short article: 'That December day was not a highly publicized action like Bastogne. But in a way, pound for pound, little E Co did more.'[6] In fairness it also has to be pointed out that there were indeed at least three to four Panthers and about eight Type IV tanks from KG Peiper west of Wanne at the time of this fighting, although there are no other reports of them taking part in any action on 21st December.

American pride was hurt at Trois Ponts but at the end of the day the west bank of the Salm was secure and that was all that really mattered. No Germans would be able to cross the river in Trois Ponts to support Peiper, although their dominating position on the eastern hills would make life extremely uncomfortable for the Americans in the town below until they abandoned it on Christmas Eve. The only other consolation for Mohnke and Hansen was that no Americans would cross to their side of the river whilst they were responsible for the Trois Ponts front.

NOTES

1. Tiemann, *Die Leibstandarte IV/2*, p. 126.
2. Vandervoort, *Trois Ponts*, p. 6.
3. This statement is at variance with a report by a member of the 112th Infantry Regiment, Clarence Blakeslee, who took part in an attack in this area on 6th Jan 1945. In his book *A Personal Account of WWII by Draftee #36887149* he states: 'On a curve where it could control the road, was an American anti-tank gun with three soldiers sprawled dead over the gun.'
4. Vandervoort, *Trois Ponts*, pp. 7–9.
5. Ibid., pp. 9–10.
6. Ibid., p. 11.

CHAPTER XXXIII

Thursday 21st December

La Gleize

By Thursday morning only about fifty Belgians remained in La Gleize[1] – amongst them the parish priest Abbé Louis Blockiau, Mme Maria Grégoire, the Georges family, Alfred Kreutz and Armand Baltus. Those who had not fled to Borgoumont and La Venne were sheltering in the cellars of the Ecuries de la Reine, the Georges farm and with families like Alphonse Maréchal, Julia Delvenne and Joseph Dewez where there were twenty-two in one room. The village was rapidly becoming an armed camp. Tank crews had dug in their vehicles to protect their vulnerable tracks and as Schnelle's 2nd SS Panzer-Grenadiers arrived they took up positions with the 9th SS Pioneers to support the armour.

Extraordinary efforts had already been made to get fuel through to Peiper's beleagured Kampfgruppe; there are even reports of attempts to float half-full jerry-cans down the Amblève river; although feasible this seems far-fetched. Certainly one former SS man told the author[2] that he and others were made to hand carry two half-full jerry-cans from Petit Spai to La Gleize – half-full because they were not strong enough to carry full ones! He had been an ammunition handler in Knittel's 150mm infantry gun platoon and when they had run out of ammunition on Wednesday he had become a fuel carrier. After reaching La Gleize he was made a stretcher bearer and sent to the Château Froid-cour to help out there.

The structure of Peiper's defence was already beginning to take shape (Map 18). The village of La Gleize lies on a 'saddle' of land running about 1,000 metres in roughly a north–south direction; Peiper had set up strongpoints at the four corners of this saddle – in a clockwise direction they were: Les Montis and Hassoumont in the north and the Weri-mont farm and the Dinheid hill feature in the south. As more tanks and troops became available they took their places on the 'saddle' between these points – from La Coulée at the southern end to the Café Renard-Jehenson at the northern. Koch's six 150mm infantry guns and the many, now unwanted, SPWs were parked in an orchard below the church known as the Pré de Froidcour.

The American artillery bombardment which would eventually destroy the village started on Wednesday; over one hundred guns and thirty-six mortars would be used. It continued all day Thursday, adding to the misery of the rain and drizzle which soaked everyone and everything and severely reduced visibility.

Soon after first light on Thursday TF McGeorge advanced once more from Borgoumont, supported by K Company 3/117 and the 2nd and 3rd Sherman Platoons of A Company 743rd Tank Battalion. I and L Companies of 3/117 had moved off from the Roanne valley on their new mission of clearing the Bois de la Borzeu between Roanne and Stavelot (Map 19). As McGeorge's tanks approached Hassoumont they were halted by Rumpf's 9th SS Panzer Pioneers, backed by four Type IV tanks, a Tiger and a Panther. A second attempt, at about 1330 hours, failed when the Shermans, attempting a left flanking movement, were engaged by Handtusch's Tiger, Klingelhöfer's Type IV and the Pumas at the Moulin Maréchal. In the late afternoon McGeorge decided to try from a new direction; he left K Company, the 2nd Platoon of D Company 36th Armored Infantry and the 2nd Sherman Platoon at Borgoumont, and began a move to the east which would place his tanks in a position to advance the following day, using the axis of the N-33 Trois Points–La Gleize road. The 3rd Sherman Platoon of A Company went with him by mistake. Fortunately for McGeorge, 'Blocking Group Mill' had gone before he completed his move. It withdrew after dark from the Moulin Maréchal to the Werimont farm in La Gleize in accordance with Peiper's decision to concentrate what was left of his KG in the village.[3]

Peiper arrived in La Gleize at about 1600 hours and established his own quarters in the cellar of Mme Boulanger's house. The KG Command

Post was set up in the cellars of Father Blockhiau's presbytery and the Hôtel de Ville and school. Diefenthal's medical officer, Dr Dittmann, organised a crude aid post in one of the cellars. The American prisoners were held in the church and various other cellars in the village. Between last light and midnight the defenders of Stoumont, Cheneux and the Moulin Maréchal completed their withdrawals and the small hilltop village was turned into a veritable fortress.

The exact layout of the La Gleize defence force is of course impossible to ascertain but its essential elements are clear. North of the village in the areas known as Les Montis and Hassoumont there were, as already mentioned, the 9th SS Pioneers with four 6th SS Panzer Company Type IVs, a 3rd Company Tiger and a Panther. At the north end of the village itself, centred around the Ecuries de la Reine and crossroads, were two Panthers of the 1st and 2nd SS Panzer Companies and at least one flak-wagon. Close to the homes of Mme Boulanger and Maria Georges near the southern crossroads were two Tigers and a Panther. A further 2nd Company Panther, outside the Boulanger's garage on the N-33, guarded the eastern approach into the village. Five more Panthers were clustered around the Hôtel de Ville and the church. The two strongpoints south of the village were located on the high ground known as the Dinheid at the south-west corner, where a Panther and single 6th Company Type IV covered the western approaches from Stoumont and Cheneux, and at the Werimont farm at the south-east corner. This farm dominated the N-33 and the Roanne valley. The 2nd Company Tiger of SS Lieutenant Dollinger and two Panthers already located there were joined by SS 2nd Lieutenant Handtusch's Tiger, SS Captain Klingelhöfer's Type IV, three Pumas and at least two flak-wagons from the Moulin Maréchal. Located with all these tanks were the panzergrenadiers of Diefenthal and Schnelle. Peiper's total strength was now less than 1,500 men.

NOTES

1. The final dispositions of Peiper's forces and the civilians left in La Gleize and its immediate environs were ascertained from numerous sources, especially Gérard Grégoire and Serge Fontaine. A number of LAH veterans including Hans Hennecke, Heinz Hofmann, Karl Wortmann and Rolf Reiser were also helpful. Photographs showing German equipment abandoned in the village provided vital additional evidence.
2. During a *Pied Peiper* Battlefield Tour 16 Sep 1989.
3. Peiper's testimony in Dachau Trial.

CHAPTER XXXIV

Thursday 21st to Monday 25th December

Malmédy

When Otto Skorzeny's men advanced down the hill from the Baugnez crossroads at 0300 hours on the Thursday morning, Lieutenant Colonel Ellis Williamson's 1st Battalion of the 120th Infantry and the four TDs of 3rd Platoon, A Company 825th TD Battalion were ready for them. It will be recalled that Captain Scherff's KG Y comprised two infantry companies, a strong HQ Company with heavy mortars, and five StuGs camouflaged to look like Shermans. The fact that this attack was launched nearly four hours before the attack by KG X on the south-west side of Malmédy (Map 12) may indicate that it was seen by Skorzeny as more of a decoy than a serious attempt to capture the town. By attacking that much earlier he probably hoped to draw US reserves to the eastern approach.

The leading infantry company of KG Y hit B Company 1/120 Infantry near the railway crossing on the N-32. Captain Murray Pulver, the Company Commander, described what happened in his book *Longest Year*:

Company B was given a position on the main road leading south to St Vith . . . we quickly set up a road block at a small settlement called Mon Bijou . . . at 3 am an American half-track came down the road followed by a column of tanks and other vehicles. The half-track hit a mine and lost its front wheels . . . when the half-track was disabled a group of German soldiers moved forward and one yelled 'Hey! We're American soldiers – don't shoot!' But they didn't fool those two great soldiers. Sergeant Denaro let loose with his Browning automatic rifle and Sergeant Henderson fired and knocked out a TD following the half-track. Very soon the whole of 1st Platoon were engaged. The road was narrow with a high bank on the right and a gully on the other side making it impossible for the German tanks to advance. Barbed wire prevented foot soldiers circling us to get the mines off the road. . . . Very soon we began receiving heavy mortar and machine gun fire. . . . I think every gun in the 230th Artillery fired in our support . . . things remained pretty hot until daylight. We could hear the tanks moving around but our artillery was giving them hell. Soon the tanks backed off, turned round and retreated. . . . We lost two men killed and had four wounded.

This was one of the first occasions when American artillery used a new and highly secret 'Pozit' fuse. This caused a shell to burst above, rather than on contact with, the ground, thus showering fragments over a much wider area. This had a devastating effect on the attacking German infantry and Scherff's KG, having also lost two StuGs, was stopped dead in its tracks. One of the StuGs had been abandoned practically intact after a high explosive round had caused minor damage at the rear.[1]

Skorzeny's main attack came at 0650 hours, not 0400 hours as some reports say, against the American right flank. It will be remembered that the main Malmédy defence line was the railway embankment which still runs roughly west to east on the south side of the town. B Company of the 99th Infantry Battalion (Separate), with two TDs of 2nd Platoon, A Company 825th TD Battalion, was responsible for the rue de Falize railway underpass. B Company 526th Armored Infantry had its 2nd and 3rd Platoons with the other two TDs of 2nd Platoon, A Company 825th covering the other two underpasses, whilst its 1st Platoon with two company 57mm anti-tank guns was sited at the main railway viaduct over the N-23 road leading into Malmédy from the west. I and L Companies of Lieutenant Colonel Greer's 3/120 were located in the western part of the town, well inside the railway embankment and they do not seem to have been involved to any extent in the day's fighting. K Company on the other hand, with a machine gun platoon of M Company and the four towed TDs of 1st Platoon, B Company 823rd TD Battalion, sited as they were in the area of the Warche river bridge and the vital road junction just to its west, would bear the brunt of the German attack.

A large paper factory still stands just to the east of the bridge, as does a two storey single house on the opposite side of the road. The HQ of 1st Platoon, B Company 823rd TD Battalion was located in the house with two of its TDs nearby; the other two TDs were north of the river. South of the paper mill was a large open area, now much built over, stretching some 600m before the ground rises quite steeply – this area had been heavily mined and sown with trip flares by Dave Pergrin's 291st Engineers, some of whom were still manning machine gun posts on the railway embankment. Four M-10 TDs of the 2nd Platoon, B Company 823rd TD Battalion were in reserve in a central position behind the railway embankment. In addition to the 230th Field Artillery Battalion, five other artillery battalions were capable of firing in support of the Malmédy defences and it will be recalled that two 90mm, one 40mm and two quadruple 50 calibre anti-aircraft guns of the 110th AAA

Battalion were deployed on the north side of Malmédy. In reserve, in the area of Bevercé, were 2/120, the rest of Harold Hansen's 99th Infantry and B Company, less one platoon, of Rubel's 740th Tank Battalion which had now arrived as part of General Hobbs's Divisional reserve.

Despite all these forces there were two serious defects in the Malmédy defences. In the first place the Americans had not appreciated that the road junction just to the west of the Warche river bridge was more important to the Germans than the town itself. Its capture would open up the N-32 to Francorchamps, I SS Panzer Corps's Route C, and the N-23 to Stavelot. This misappreciation had led to insufficient forces being positioned at the Warche bridge/road junction complex, and this weakness was further exacerbated by the boundary between the 117th and the 120th Regiments being drawn too near the vital road junction – as Cole's *Official History* puts it: 'It must be said that the responsibilities of the two sister regiments at the vaguely defined inter-regimental boundary were none too explicit.'

The other incredible weakness was that neither the Warche bridge nor the large railway viaduct on the N-23 could be blown because the detonators had been removed. The man who had been in charge of both these demolitions was Master Sergeant Ralph McCarthy, the construction chief of Dave Pergrin's 291st Engineers. It had always been the intention of Colonel Carter, the 1st Army Chief Engineer, to withdraw Pergrin's Battalion from Malmédy as soon as it could be relieved by the 30th Division's engineers; but Hobbs had argued for it to remain under his command and he had won the day. In preparation for their expected withdrawal McCarthy's men had handed over responsibility for the demolitions to the infantry and for safety reasons the detonators had been removed!

As soon as the warning was received that the Germans were likely to attack, McCarthy was woken up and told to find his men and get back to the demolitions. Since they were dispersed round the town McCarthy woke the first three men he could find and drove them out to the paper factory where he dropped them off, telling them that the detonator for the bridge demolition was 'on the windowsill of that paper mill'. The three men were T/5 Consiglio and Privates Mitchell and Spires. McCarthy then returned to the railway viaduct. As Consiglio and his comrades moved towards the paper factory the entire area was illuminated by flares set off by the attacking infantry and tanks of von Foelkersam's KG X; this was followed by tank fire. The engineers took cover in the lone house opposite the factory.

One part of KG X followed the rue de Falize towards the railway underpass where the leading Panther 'brewed up' on a mine. The 99th Infantry After Action Report says the attacking column consisted of three US jeeps, one half-track, an American M-8, a Tiger and two Shermans. The 825th TD Report speaks of a jeep, half-track and Tiger being knocked out. In fact there was only one Sherman in the whole of Skorzeny's force and the so-called Tiger was of course a Panther. For some two hours the accompanying infantry tried to breach the American defences at the railway embankment but B Company 99th Infantry and the TDs of the 825th held firm and, helped by proximity-fuzed artillery fire, the Germans were repulsed with, according to the 99th Infantry, one hundred killed. The 825th TD section claimed to have captured two jeeps and an M8 in working order and rather magnanimously added in their Report: 'Company B, 99th Inf Bn also engaged the enemy at this point.' They admitted the loss of one of their TDs and to suffering four casualties.

As soon as flares illuminated the area in front of the paper mill the main group of KG X headed straight for the Warche bridge. The fact that it could not be blown was a tragedy for the defenders. The History of the 120th Infantry Regiment says two 3rd Battalion outposts were overrun before the enemy reached the area of the paper factory. The lone house, where the engineers had taken cover, became the centre of severe fighting. The TDs sited there took the attacking tanks under fire but the house was soon surrounded by German infantry and it was not long before the 823rd crews abandoned their TDs. They managed to remove or destroy the firing pins and sights on all four guns before most of them took refuge in the house along with Pergrin's three engineers and some members of K Company – thirty-three men in all. By 0830 hours one of the Panthers had crossed the bridge to the north side whilst others covered it from near the house.

When it began to dawn on the Americans that the Germans were focusing on the road junction and the boundary between the two Regiments rather than the town, a crisis of confidence began to set in. At 0840 hours G Company 2/117th Infantry, on K Company's right, was on full alert and a section of 3rd Platoon, C Company 823rd TD Battalion operating with it, was moved to face the threat. A single gun of this section claimed to have destroyed a Tiger, a Sherman, a German manned M-10 and two more Panthers or Tigers! One can only marvel at the imagination of its crew – two days later Master Sergeant McCarthy of the 291st was told to check the whole area north of the Warche river for abandoned German vehicles – he found none!

Rumour then began to take over – at 1030 hours an unconfirmed report said there were Germans in Meiz, a kilometre north-west of the road junction. This was untrue but certainly by midday the Germans had driven two K Company platoons some distance to the north of the bridge/road junction area and had written down the third platoon. Survivors took shelter in the paper factory and one of them Private First Class Francis Currey, was to be awarded a Medal of Honor for his gallantry during this action. Lieutenant Kenneth Nelson, commanding the Machine Gun Platoon with K Company, was to be awarded a posthumous Distinguished Service Cross for his part in the fighting and his Platoon sergeant, John Van Der Kamp, the same medal. The situation was now considered serious enough to move the reserve 2nd Battalion of the 120th to the area of Burninville, north of the threatened road junction and to deploy two 90mm AAA battalions as far back as Francorchamps.

It is not clear how many, if indeed any, more Panthers crossed the river but by early afternoon the situation had begun to stabilise. KG X was simply not strong enough to break through. Two Panthers had been disabled near the bridge, one by Francis Currey,[2] and the paper mill was holding firm. American artillery fired 3,000 rounds during this battle. Amazingly, the lone house too remained in American hands – this despite the fact that, believing it to be in German hands, the Americans took it under fire at about 1000 hours with both artillery and machine guns from the railway embankment.

T/5 Consiglio of the 291st Engineers and a K Company corporal eventually got out of the house in the early afternoon and managed to get back to the main US position behind the railway embankment; there they reported that the house was still in US hands and that only twelve men remained alive out of the original thirty-three. In view of the fact that tanks and infantry were fighting around the house for several hours, it is remarkable that anyone survived there at all; but this report, and similar statements that entire TD crews were killed or wounded, are not supported by the actual casualty returns. The 30th Division return for 21st December shows B Company 823rd TD Battalion had one man wounded and six missing; the 1st Platoon lost all four TDs, although two were later recovered, two half-tracks, four jeeps and a 1½-ton truck with trailer; 3/120 Infantry suffered seven men killed and five wounded. The 291st Engineers had Mitchell killed and Spires wounded at the lone house and another man, Holbrook, killed by mortar fire. The 526th Armored Infantry counted four men wounded.

Pergrin's men had seen more than their fair share of the fighting – T/5 John Noland was awarded a Silver Star for pulling a daisy chain of mines across the road by the Falize underpass and Corporal Issac McDonald a Bronze Star for doing the same thing at another position.

For Otto Skorzeny, observing the action on the high ground to the south, it was obvious that by mid afternoon his attack had failed at considerable cost. His tanks had barely managed to cross the bridge and none of his force had breached the railway embankment. Von Foelkersam, who had personally led his men in the battle around the paper factory, came limping back on the arm of a medical officer, wounded in his bottom. By 1525 hours the Germans were clear of the road junction, bridge and paper factory area; at 1600 hours two M-10s of 2nd Platoon, B Company 823rd, led by Lieutenant Rohatsch, moved through the Falize underpass and, quoting the After Action Report:

> . . . fired on two German tanks concealed in buildings south of their positions. After first knocking off a corner of a building to expose the tank hiding behind it three rounds of AP sent the tank up in flames. Another tank in the vicinity was also destroyed but it is believed that this tank might have been previously damaged by friendly artillery.

The tank mentioned behind the building was a disguised Panther later found beside the café at La Falize. The Operational Research Section of the 2nd Tactical Air Force visited the Malmédy area in early 1945.[3] It found '4 Panthers all disguised as Shermans by the addition of thin sheet metal superstructures. One of these had been destroyed by the crew and the others by American artillery'.

At the end of the day the American defences had held and, despite all the problems, Malmédy and the important road junction were safe from the Germans. The 150th Panzer Brigade had lost 150 men killed, wounded or missing.[4] Skorzeny himself was wounded in the face by artillery shrapnel as he neared his old HQ in Ligneuville that evening. Mohnke's Chief of Staff, SS Major Ziemssen, was also wounded and SS Major Ralf Tiemann on a visit from 6th Panzer Army to obtain direct information on Peiper's progress, was ordered to take over.[5]

The following day, Friday the 22nd, Dave Pergrin was ordered, rather belatedly, to demolish the Warche river bridge, the massive railway viaduct and the rue de Falize underpass. It ensured that Malmédy became a fortress on its southern and western flanks, but it proved to be a waste of time and explosives. There would be no more enemy attacks on Malmédy. Any further death and destruction to be wreaked on the town, its people and its defenders, would come from the Americans rather than the Germans.

Perhaps due to the mass evacuation of the town by all but Dave Pergrin and his brave engineers on the 16th and 17th December, there was a general misconception throughout 1st US Army that Malmédy had fallen to the Germans. The fact that the better part of two Regiments of the 30th Division, two independent battalions and numerous sub units had moved into or through the town was virtually unknown in the chaos of the American withdrawal. Even the *Stars and Stripes* newspaper, published for the American forces in Europe, described Malmédy as being occupied by the enemy, as did the Belgian national newspaper *La Libre Belgique* and the Belgian Radio Nationale on the 18th. But, even allowing for some confusion over the status of Malmédy, there can be no excuse for the bombing of the town on 23rd December at 1526 hours by six US B-26 Marauders of the IXth Bombardment Division's 322nd Bombardment Group, part of the IXth US Air Force.[6] The flight, led by Major C. F. Watson, dropped eighty-six 500 lb bombs on the town, in what the pilots described as 'unlimited ceiling and visibility'.

Malmédy lies 33 miles from the intended target, Zulpich. The pilots admitted that they had failed to find their primary target and reported that they had bombed Lammersum, six miles further on. Five of them reported 'excellent' results. This is not surprising since much civilian property was damaged and many people killed and injured; the 120th Regiment had three killed, four wounded and three men missing. After this raid a 1st US Army spokesman announced that as the Germans had entered Malmédy the town had been bombed. Peter Lawless of the British *Daily Telegraph* newspaper interrupted to tell him that he had just returned from the town, there were no Germans there and they had bombed their own troops.

The following day, Christmas Eve, at 1400 hours in perfect visibility and with the snow-covered Malmédy valley looking like a Christmas card, eighteen B-24 heavy bombers of the VIIIth US Air Force struck again, causing massive damage.[7] The main square and town centre were levelled and many other parts of the town devastated by bombs and fires. The 120th Regiment casualty return for the day shows ninety-eight killed, wounded and missing, although some of these casualties occurred in the three companies of the Regiment which by then were involved in the fighting around Stavelot. The 291st Engineers, who did sterling work with their heavy plant and skilled manpower, had one man killed and Captain Conlin, whose B Company had been in Malmédy since before the offensive started, was badly injured. No evidence to explain this bombing has been found in air force reports and the unit responsible remains unknown.

On Christmas Day at about 1600 hours there was a third and final raid. Four Marauders of the 387th Bombardment Group,[8] led by a pilot of unknown rank, named Anderson, dropped sixty-four general purpose bombs on the town, despite ground to air recognition panels which had by then been displayed on many buildings. The intended target was St Vith, twelve miles to the south, and aircraft to ground visibility was three to four miles!

The Malmédy town memorial names 178 civilians killed during the three air raids; many more were injured. Although the IXth Bombardment Division acknowledged the mistakes made on the 23rd and 25th, the IXth Air Force did not. The only official reference ever made to these tragic raids was when General Carl Spaatz mentioned an alleged mis-bombing of Malmédy during an Allied Air Commanders' Conference on 4th January 1945. In post war years various excuses for these attacks have been offered in mitigation; the real reason why they happened is very simple and was known to those responsible within a few hours – human error.

NOTES

1. 2nd Tactical Air Force Operational Research Section Report No.19 dated 9 Jun 1945.
2. Currey to author 12 Sep 1994.
3. 2nd Tactical Air Force Operational Research Section Report No.19 dated 9 Jun 1945.
4. ETHINT 12.
5. Tiemann, *Die Leibstandarte IV/2*, p. 131.
6. *Malmédy, Belgium, Mistaken Bombing 23 and 25 Dec 1944*, prepared by Royce L. Thompson, European Section, OCMH. 5 Jun 1952.
7. Ibid.
8. Ibid.

CHAPTER XXXV

Thursday 21st to Monday 25th December

Stavelot

Recall that, while Max Hansen's Jagdpanzers and 3rd SS Panzer-Grenadier Battalion were chasing the two companies of the 505th Airborne off the Wanne heights east of Trois Ponts, his 1st SS Battalion and another company of Jagdpanzers had been ordered to cross the Amblève at Petit Spai. Mohnke's plan was for this group to reinforce the depleted Fast Group Knittel on the north bank and then for the combined force to seize Stavelot from the west (Map 10). At the same time Sandig was ordered to attack the town from the south with his one remaining panzer-grenadier battalion. When Sandig complained that he had no chance of success Mohnke threatened to have him shot if he did not comply with the order![1] Accordingly, early on Thursday morning, SS Major Karl Richter's 1st SS Panzer-Grenadier Battalion prepared to wade and swim the Amblève river. The eighteen 150mm and six 210mm werfers (mortars) of SS Major Klaus Besch opened up as part of the supporting fire plan but were ineffective, their rounds being described by Friedrich Pfeifer[2] of the 2nd SS Panzer-Grenadier Company as landing 'above and beyond the town'. At the last minute the attack was cancelled – Mohnke had relented, knowing full well that his men had no chance against the well established Americen defences. The log of the 117th Infantry does, however, have an entry for 0930 hours saying the enemy was 'swimming across the river toward our B Company . . . all swimmers have been killed so far.' There is no reference to this on the German side and from this time on there were certainly no more attempts to cross the Amblève in Stavelot.

In the meantime the leading elements of Hansen's 1st SS Panzer-Grenadier Battalion, commanded by SS Major Emil Karst, had crossed the small bridge at Petit Spai and climbed the 200m cliff north of the Stavelot to Trois Ponts railway line. As soon as the leading infantry were across Hansen ordered the twenty-five ton Jagdpanzer IVs of the 1st SS Anti-Tank Company to follow over the bridge. Why neither Mohnke nor Hansen thought of using the twenty plus Type IV tanks of the 6th and 7th SS Panzer Companies sitting at Wanne is one of the most puzzling aspects of this operation. They had been refuelled and sitting idle for the past forty-eight hours, yet Sternebeck told the author in 1985 that he had been without orders the whole time he was in that area. Maybe the fact that both company commanders, Junker and Klingelhöfer, were forward with Peiper accounts for the extraordinary inactivity of this potentially powerful force. It is all the more surprising when one recalls that Mohnke's Divisional Headquarters was located in the same area.

Much against his better judgement the commander of the 1st Jagdpanzer IV Company, SS Captain Otto Holst,[3] gave the order for his driver to cross the Petit Spai bridge – it collapsed and Holst and his crew were lucky to escape the raging waters of the Amblève. The rest of the day would see desperate attempts by panzer pioneers to bridge the river. Their first attempt was swept away by the strong current and second destroyed by American artillery fire which had zeroed in on the site and caused appalling casualties to the pioneers and others who were ordered to help with the bridging. Not altogether surprisingly, it was Major 'Bull' Yates, personally leading a reconnaissance patrol from Trois Ponts, who spotted the bridging attempts at Petit Spai and passed the information to the artillery. Again the Americans were using Pozit fuses with dramatic effects.

The American plan for clearing the Germans north of the river on Thursday involved both Bill Lovelady's Task Force and Lieutenant Colonel McDowell's 3/117 Infantry, less K Company which was with TF McGeorge on the La Gleize front. It will be remembered that TFL was strung out in the Amblève valley, from Moulin de Ruy to the railway viaducts at Trois Ponts, behind which Major Stallings with E (Sherman) Company and two platoons of E Armored Infantry Company had taken refuge the previous evening. Since it was impossible to advance through the viaducts against the Tiger and Knittel's anti-tank weapons guarding that approach, or easily to extract this force from their difficult position, Lovelady ordered the nine Shermans of Lieutenant Richard Edmark's

D Company, with an artillery forward observer named Charlie Corbin and an attached armoured infantry platoon, to move from the area of Petit Coo, via Biester, up on to the high ground to the east and then towards Stavelot through the hamlet of Parfondruy. To support this thrust I and L Companies of 3/117 were to advance from Roanne, through the Borzeu forest, on to the hamlets of Renardmont and Ster respectively. Jump-off time was planned for 0830 hours.

By 0950 hours I Company was 2km short of Renardmont and L Company was on the high ground a kilometre short of Ster. At 1140 hours I Company still had a 1,000 metres to go, L Company was in Ster, which was free of enemy, and the Shermans had reached a position 1,500 metres south-west of Ster. Shortly after this I Company reported it was engaged in a firefight near Renardmont and at 1230 hours Edmark's tanks were 500m short of Parfondruy. They reached the hamlet an hour later and ran into Knittel's men and artillery and mortar fire. The Villa l'Epilogue was a particular German stronghold. The German artillery was deployed just south of the river in the vicinity of Wanne and Aisomont and could almost see the American tanks from its gun positions.[4]

At 1432 hours Colonel Johnson of the 117th Infantry ordered Edmark to assist I company in its efforts to clear Renardmont, which was being defended by Goltz's men, and then move towards the western houses of Stavelot where Coblenz's reinforced 2nd SS Reconnaissance Company was holding out against Frankland's 1/117 Infantry. At 1450 hours Johnson cancelled this order and told Edmark to get on towards Stavelot. At 1600 hours Edmark reported he was advancing from Parfondruy on Stavelot but receiving fire from Renardmont. Twelve minutes later the advance on Stavelot was halted and Edmark told to finish clearing up Parfondruy and then, if possible, to help I Company in Renardmont.

The battle was now getting very confused. At 1635 hours some Shermans of B Company 743rd Tank Battalion, operating with 1/117, opened fire by mistake on some of Edmark's Shermans from near the railway track east of Parfondruy. This was apparently due to four of D Company's tanks getting on the 'wrong road' and driving towards C Company 1/117's positions. Anyone who visits this area, even today when the roads are much improved, will soon appreciate how difficult it must have been to find a way through the maze of small roads which crisscrossed the area – even without an enemy. The four D Company tanks, commanded by Lieutenant Kessel, managed to reach the C Company lines without being hit and were then attached to Frankland's 1st Battalion.

This already very confused situation was even further complicated by the arrival in the late afternoon of Karst's 1st SS Panzer-Grenadiers at the farm Masures, only a few hundred metres from L Company at Ster. By 1800 hours Goltz had been forced out of Renardmont; he arrived after dark at Knittel's Command Post at the Farm Antoine on the N-23 with only half a dozen men; Kalatschni, the only other officer in his Company, had been killed. Coblenz's men were still holding on in the houses to the south and west of Stavelot station where they had been under attack all day by Frankland's 1/117. In 1946 Coblenz described some of the fighting:

> I was in the first house on the left side of the street [By the Basse Voie bridge]. The Americans employed a reinforced combat patrol at this house. They were able to work to about 30 metres but because I had a better position I repulsed them after a heavy fire fight and with hand grenades. The enemy disengaged himself . . . the artillery fire continued with short interruptions until the evening. The general situation was very critical. . . . I couldn't personally intervene on the righthand side of the street . . . the slightest movements were put under heavy machine gun and mortar fire, above all the sharpshooters were the most dangerous . . . on account of the preceding attack and the identification of loud tank noises from the neighbourhood of Stavelot railway station. . . . I could count on the main attack the following day.[5]

Some time after dark Coblenz went back to Knittel's Command Post in the farm Antoine[6] and complained that it was pointless remaining where he was, losing men all the time, unless he could be reinforced: his plea fell on deaf ears. On his way back:

> I passed 2nd Lieutenant Siebert, my 3rd Platoon commander, who reported he had repulsed the enemy after heavy fighting and that he had also had to shoot some US prisoners. He did not state the exact number. I asked him why he had to shoot prisoners. He explained that his platoon consisted of only nine men and he could not spare anyone to guard prisoners. Siebert said; 'The skirt was everywhere too short; on the left they were raising hell and because of further enemy movements I could not afford to do without a single man. I had no one to guard the prisoners.'[7]

One of Siebert's men, Erich Makamul, added further details in 1948:

> In the afternoon we had a severe attack supported by tanks from the front and from the right hand side of our platoon and through a forest ravine from infantry. The enemy succeeded in carrying forward this attack up to about 50–80 m of our positions. He was, however, repulsed . . . as in our platoon there were only a few men and as we had neither slept nor eaten for several days, but always had to be on guard, we were totally exhausted. One man, as a consequence of overexhaustion, suffered a nervous breakdown. In the evening of this 21st we had to dig out two or three men of a machine gun crew of

our platoon who had been wounded and buried through tank shells in the first house on the right hand side of the street, in the direction of the lumber-yard, opposite the railway station . . . they had to take cover in the basement of the building. All the men of the machine gun crew . . . were wounded or buried. From the voices in the adjoining basement they could tell that it was full with civilians. Probably all women and children . . . after each detonation they could hear the cries and moans of the civilians.[8]

Gustav Knittel made a statement about the fighting, also in 1948:

The clear orders by the Division and comradeship with KG Peiper forced me to hold my hopeless position in this incomplete bridgehead with extremely weak forces vis-a-vis a superior tank enemy both in front of me and to my rear. . . . On 21st the situation of the elements of my Battalion employed in the bridgehead became even more desperate . . . there was not a single man in reserve.[9]

During the Thursday night Karst's 1st Panzer-Grenadiers engaged the Americans in fierce fighting in and around Parfondruy, particularly around the area of the Chapel St Lucie. The dividing line between the combatants lay in a rough half circle from Ster, through Renardmont and Parfondruy, to the houses between the station and Basse Voie bridge near the N-23.

During the Thursday/Friday night pioneers of SS Major Richard Scheler's 1st SS Panzer Pioneer Battalion managed to construct an infantry bridge across the Amblève at Petit Spai. With the Trois Ponts front deadlocked and neither side really capable of forcing a crossing, Hansen was told to leave a minimum force there and use the new bridge for the rest of his 3rd SS Panzer-Grenadier Battalion which was to break through to Peiper. Mohnke had finally accepted that he was not going to capture Stavelot – Knittel's SS Reconnaissance Battalion had been reduced to little more than a small company and Karst's 1st SS Panzer-Grenadier Battalion, operating with it on the west side of Stavelot, had few of its heavy weapons north of the river. Hansen was therefore ordered to use both his 1st and 3rd Battalions for a final desperate attempt to get through to Peiper.

Friday morning, which dawned misty with sleet showers, saw both sides preparing to attack – the Americans by using Edmark's force of Shermans and armoured infantry, together with the infantry of the 1st and 3rd Battalions of the 117th, to capture Parfondruy and the western houses of Stavelot, and the Germans by attacking north-west from Ster with Karst's Battalion and through Biester and Coo with Böttcher's 3rd SS Panzer-Grenadiers.

Soon after first light the Americans launched their attack against

Coblenz's men in the western houses of Stavelot using Shermans and infantry. After severe fighting most of the Germans were killed or captured but a few survivors managed to hold on to their positions in the Château Lambert which controlled the Stavelot to Trois Ponts road. Dröge, the Pioneer Platoon commander, was captured and most of his men killed. A Company of 1/117 reported at 1330 hours: 'Having to knock down houses to clear area of Stavelot we are fighting for.' SS Senior Sergeant Werner Wendt[10] in his Tiger was ordered by Knittel to support Coblenz's beleaguered men but after being hit on the turret ring he ended up back at Petit Spai with his radio operator dead and a broken gearbox – the tank could no longer be driven but its gun was operable. Coblenz,[11] after being wounded in the leg, was captured with eighteen of his men quite early on in the battle – at about 0900 hours; he was taken to Frankland's Command Post in the farm La Bricoque north of Stavelot for a fairly tough interrogation.

An entry in the 117th Infantry log timed at 1020 hours says: 'Colonel Johnson reports atrocity slaying of civilians in Renardmont to G-5. States many were shot in their beds. Requests photographer be sent to take pictures of evidence.' According to the After Action Report of CCB a Lieutenant Luten of Lovelady's HQ saw the bodies of three old men, a woman, six children and a baby whom he considered had been murdered in Parfondruy.

Bill Lovelady's Battalion surgeon, A. Eaton Roberts, wrote of these matters in his book *Five Stars to Victory* in 1949:

> When D Company with infantry liberated the tiny village [Parfondruy] they found only a few living civilians, huddled in the dark corners of cellars, too terrified, too overcome by grief, to move or welcome American troops with their usual hearty greetings. For, strewn about the houses were the corpses of whole families from babies to parents and grandparents. . . . Compassion for the victims and burning hate for the foe welled up simultaneously in the hearts of the soldiers who witnessed these gruesome scenes. . . . With doubled efforts, Task Force Lovelady suddenly became a wild beast, stampeding enemy positions with increased ruthlessness and ferocity.

Such anger and hate can sometimes lead men to commit the very crimes which have given rise to that anger – in 1989 Lovelady wrote to the author:

> On 23rd December a messenger from 30th Inf Div contacted me and requested that I send prisoners back for interrogation. Gen Hobbs wanted to identify German units. I sent two back – the escort returned in about 30 minutes and reported the prisoners had jumped out of the jeep and they had had to shoot them. I repeated this operation

since the General was applying pressure and the escort came back with the same story. It then occurred to me that this was the way wars were supposed to be fought – everybody killing everybody – our group had seen too many atrocities. . . . I could never get any further information from my escorts as to the true story.

Coblenz and his men could expect, and certainly received, little sympathy from their captors. He was sentenced to life imprisonment at the 1946 Dachau War Crime Trials but released in 1951. SS Lieutenant Heinz Goltz who, at the age of twenty-three, had commanded Knittel's Headquarters or Staff Company was sentenced by the Belgians, in July 1948, to fifteen years imprisonment for atrocities in the Stavelot area. Knittel, the overall commander in the area, disclaimed any responsibility – in a 1948 statement he said:

> I myself did not participate in the attack and was not present in any of the positions of the 2nd Company and the same applies to the Staff Company in Ster. . . . I did not know anything about retaliatory action of any kind or about losses among the citizens except for the actual combat.[12]

Coblenz certainly agreed with Knittel's statement that he took no part in the attack – he told the author that Knittel never left his Command Post in the Farm Antoine during the whole period of the fighting in and around Stavelot!

The intended advance by Karst's 1st SS Panzer-Grenadiers was a total failure – Karst himself was killed by shrapnel before it even started. SS Captain Herbert Rink took command but the Americans were much too strong and the Battalion ended the day blocked on a line from the Point de Vue de Ster to a point south of Ster itself, where Kessel's Shermans were helping out L Company 3/117. I Company 3/117 was in blocking positions in Renardmont and Parfondruy, also supported by D Company Shermans.

During Friday morning SS Captain Karl Böttcher left his 10th SS Panzer-Grenadier Company to protect the high ground directly east of Trois Ponts and, as ordered, led the rest of his 3rd SS Battalion over the infantry bridge at Petit Spai. He then scaled the steep cliffs on the north bank and advanced through the Coreu forest to the high ground, with his 11th Company on the left flank and 12th Company on the right. They reached the summit before 1600 hours and then swept down through Biester capturing Lovelady's Aid Station at Petit Coo, which was protected by a few Stuart light tanks of Lieutenant Shipman's B Company and the Battalion Reconnaissance Platoon. The Stuarts withdrew behind the Coo railway bridge[13] and most of the Reconnaissance Platoon, including its commander Lieutenant Gray, was taken prisoner.

This bold and aggressive action split TFL into three parts, caused panic in the forward element under Major Stallings, where there was even talk of surrender, and consternation in Lieutenant Edmark's D Company group which was now also cut off from the rest of the Task Force. Both sides were now in crisis, for although the 3rd SS Panzer-Grenadier Battalion had achieved a lot, it had been at great cost – its commander, Böttcher, had been wounded and many men killed. The Belgians reported more than 160 corpses being picked up in the fields around Biester. Faced with these losses and with the 1st SS Battalion stalled around the Masures farm and Ster, it was clear to Hansen that he was not going to advance any further towards La Gleize. Peiper received a message from Mohnke at 1700 hours telling him that the relief efforts had failed.[14] The Headquarters of the 1st SS Panzer Division (LAH) had by this time moved into the Château at Wanne.

At 1935 hours General Hobbs placed 2/120 Infantry under the command of Colonel Johnson's 117th Infantry Regiment and he in turn gave its E Company to Lovelady. Böttcher's 3rd SS Panzer-Grenadiers were now under the command of SS Lieutenant Haft who had been sent over from his 10th Company south of the river. By midnight both sides were exhausted, not least by the incessant artillery bombardments to which they were being subjected. As well as the twenty-four werfers, twenty-two 150mm, four 100mm and twenty-four 105mm guns available to the Germans in this sector, the Americans had twenty-four 75mm, ninety 105mm and forty 155mm guns in range. To this must be added the large number of mortars possessed by each side.

With Haft's men still at Petit Coo and Biester and Rink's 1st SS Panzer-Grenadiers concentrated around the Point de Vue de Ster, General Hobbs's orders to clear the area north of the river required resolute action. Colonel Johnson hoped to provide this on the Saturday by using the Stuart tanks of Lovelady's B Company and E Company 2/120, with a machine gun platoon from H Company, to push south on the axis of the N-33 and link up with the Stallings group near the Trois Ponts viaducts. At the same time Stalling's E Company Shermans and Lieutenant McCord's armoured infantry were required to attack north up the N-33 and crush any German forces between the two US elements. In the centre, L Company 3/117 was to withdraw from Ster, swing west through the woods and then sweep south through the Point de Vue de Ster to the railway line where it would turn east. I Company 3/117 would replace L Company in Ster with one of its platoons, whilst the others would remain in Renardmont and Parfondruy. The D Company Shermans of Lieutenant Edmark would remain in Ster and Parfondruy. 1/117 was required to push strong combat patrols west down the axis of the N-23. To ensure that Lovelady's right flank was secure the 105th engineers were told to blow the Amblève bridge at the Coo cascade.

Jump-off time was set for 0830 hours; with a favourable weather forecast it was hoped that air attacks would at last be able to interdict the German artillery.

The American advance on Saturday morning did not go well. It took until 1115 hours for TFL's Stuarts, with major help from E Company 2/120, to recapture the Aid Station at Petit Coo. Staff Sergeant Paul Bolden of E Company won a Medal of Honor for his bravery in the actions in the village. Then, whilst the Stuart tanks remained on the N-33, the infantry moved east on to the high ground between Petit Coo and Ster. At 1440 hours they were still over a kilometre from the river in the wooded area to the west of the farm Masures and under heavy fire. Five minutes later L Company 3/117 reported it was near the farm Masures but had enemy between it and the I Company platoon in Ster village. It had already sent a message saying 'Necessary to kill all enemy as they won't give up easily!' At 1535 hours Colonel Johnson told Lovelady that F Company 2/120 was on its way to support E Company on its eastern flank but, whilst he was to retain command of all the tanks, the commanding officer of 2/120 (to be known as CO Task Force 'Hickory') would command the infantry. Lovelady was to move his tanks 'up with the infantry'. By 1600 hours Biester had finally been cleared of Germans – the 12th SS Panzer-Grenadier Company had lost its second commander, SS 2/Lieutenant Dick, and had almost ceased to exist, and SS Lieutenant Frank Hasse, the commander of the 11th Company and holder of the Knight's Cross, was dead. CO TF Hickory was ordered to link up with L Company 3/117 and 'button up for the night'. Half an hour later L Company was placed under his command. Then, in the mist and failing light of the day, the situation began to degenerate into chaos with E Company coming under suspicion for firing on L Company and it was 1900 hours before things were sorted out.

At this time the remnants of the 1st and 3rd SS Panzer-Grenadier Battalions were still holding the area known as the Six Moines in the Coreu forest; and the few remaining members of the 1st SS Reconnaissance Battalion had withdrawn to the area of Knittel's Command Post at the Farm Antoine on the N-23, where there were still four Tigers – those of von Westernhagen's Adjutant, SS Lieutenant Kalinowski, SS Senior Sergeants Wendt and Brandt and one other whose commander remains unknown. To the east of the farm Frankland's 1/117 had finally captured the Château Lambert.

Bill Lovelady, CO TF Hickory and Lieutenant Colonel Duncan, commanding the 743rd Tank Battalion of the 30th Division, were called in for a conference with Johnson at 1955 hours. He told them that the Germans had to be cleared from the north bank of the Amblève and, whilst G Company 2/120 was to be made available for the following day's operation, TFL was to be withdrawn and replaced by Shermans of the 743rd Tank Battalion. This was not going to be easy though, because Lovelady's command was still split into three parts – Edmark's D Company had remained with I Company 3/117 and the After Action Report of CCB 3rd Armored Division describes what had happened to the Stallings group:

> At 0900 hours an attack and attempt was made to break through and regain contact with the main body but strong infantry resistance and mortar fire was encountered and the attempt unsuccessful. During the day this force lost two light tanks but took three prisoners and killed many enemy infantrymen.

In fact 1st Army's order for the 30th Infantry to release CCB 3rd Armored had met with strong opposition from General Hobbs during the Saturday evening; he insisted that its retention was essential if he was to finish off the Germans north of the river, particularly in La Gleize. In the end the Corps Commander, Matt Ridgway, supported Hobbs and CCB stayed with his Division for a further day.

The American plan for Sunday 24th December was little changed from the previous day but involved more infantry. From a line running due east from Petit Coo to the farm Les Masures, E and F Companies 2/120, with L Company 3/117 under command, were to attack due south to the Stavelot/Trois Ponts railway line; at the same time G Company 2/120, starting from I Company 3/117's firm base in Parfondruy, was to drive south-west, and 1/117 was to advance south of the railway line towards the farm Antoine. None of Edmark's Shermans, nor those of the 743rd, appear to have advanced with the infantry although they presumably gave fire support.

The advance started disastrously when G Company was hit by both German and American artillery firing short, causing heavy casualties. Companies E, F and L seemed to fare little better against strong German resistance; by dusk they were dug in less than half way to their objective. The only real tank activity of the day was the final breakthrough to the Stallings group south of Petit Coo. It was described in the After Action Report: 'After a stiff fight this was accomplished . . . our losses were relatively light.' The link-up was completed at 1100 hours and by 2300 hours that night TF Lovelady had been relieved of its commitment to the 30th Infantry Division. In terms of actual combat it had achieved little; but most significantly, its mere physical presence between Stavelot and La Gleize had ensured the eventual destruction of KG Peiper.

Incredibly, by last light on Sunday the few survivors of Knittel's SS Reconnaissance Battalion and two of the four Tigers were still in control of an area north of the river at Petit Spai and the survivors of Hansen's two Battalions were in firm control on the high ground south of the old bridge site and on the hills known as 'Les Sept Montagnes'. Hansen had lost over five hundred men and Knittel sixty killed, two hundred wounded and twenty missing.[15]

That evening Knittel told his last few men and the crews of the Tigers to withdraw before first light on Christmas Day. Most crossed the river at about 0400 hours by using the remains of the infantry bridge; SS Senior Sergeant Brandt was killed by a shell before he could do so but his tank managed to wade back across the Amblève and Wendt and his driver got back after putting explosive charges in the gun barrel and engine compartment of their tank.[16] When the Operational Research Section of the 2nd Tactical Air Force[17] visited the area near the Antoine farm in early 1945 it found 'a Royal Tiger facing east; there were no visible signs of damage . . . the fighting compartment had been burnt out.' At the Petit Spai bridge site it found:

> . . . another Royal Tiger facing east but its gun was pointing west. The rear half of the turret was smashed and the roof over the driver's and hull gunner's compartment was stove in. . . . The complete absence of human remains suggests that the crew baled out . . . the destruction of this tank was seen by an officer of the 740 Tank Bn . . . he said it was hit by a bomb dropped from a P-38 on 25th December 1944.

By Christmas morning TF Harrison had secured La Gleize and was available for action in the Stavelot area. Brigadier General Harrison had under his command the 119th Infantry, the 740th Tank Battalion less B Company, the 120th Infantry still with L Company 3/117 under command, and A Company 823rd TD Battalion. General Hobbs orderd him to 'Attack east 25 Dec 44 . . . seize Obj "A" [the high ground south of Ster and north of the railway line], reduce enemy resistance N of L'Amblève river and make contact with 117th Inf.' The 117th Infantry with the 743rd Tank Battalion was ordered to 'Continue defence of present positions and support attack of TF Harrison by fire.' Advancing at 0900 hours on Christmas day TF Harrison experienced no resistance and as its men looked down from the railway line on to the Amblève river they saw the Germans had gone. The battle of Stavelot and its environs was over at last. It had cost the Americans sixty-five killed and one hundred and seventy-four wounded; a further sixty-three men were missing. One hundred and forty-two Belgians had died and seven more would soon die as a result of injuries received during the fighting[18].

NOTES

1. Sandig to author loc. cit., 2 Oct 1985.
2. Pfeifer to author loc. cit., 2 Oct 1985.
3. Holst to author loc. cit., 2 Oct 1985.

4. A German artillery observer, Siebert, and his American equivalent, Charlie Corbin, both described their respective positions to the author during separate visits to Stavelot in the late 1980s.
5. Coblenz, statement at Schwabisch Hall 15 Apr 1946.
6. Coblenz to author loc. cit., 22 Jun 1986.
7. Coblenz op. cit., 15 Apr 1946.
8. Makamul, statement at Freiburg 31 Aug 1948.
9. Knittel, statement at Landsberg/Lech 15 Mar 1948.
10. Letter from Wendt dated 22 Sep 1991.
11. Coblenz to author loc. cit., 22 Jun 1986.
12. Knittel, statement at Landsberg/Lech 15 Mar 1948.
13. Aurio Pierro of B/33rd Armd to author loc. cit., 11 Sep 1994.
14. Peiper's testimony at Dachau Trial.
15. Knittel, statement at Landsberg/Lech 15 Mar 1948.
16. Letter from Wendt dated 22 Sep 1991.
17. 2nd Tactical Air Force Operational Research Section Report No.19 dated 9 Jun 1945.
18. Exact names provided to author in Apr 1994 by Joseph Dejardin, Secretary for Social Services for the Territory of Stavelot, 1941–1984.

CHAPTER XXXVI

Friday 22nd to Sunday 24th December

La Gleize

Apart from American artillery fire, the western approaches to La Gleize were quiet all day on Friday (Map 18). Task Force Harrison was fully occupied, first of all bombarding, and then securing Stoumont, the Château Froidcour and the area of the St Anne's woods. The only reported activity was down by the old railway station of La Gleize, 500m south-east of Froidcour, which Sutherland's 119th Infantry occupied by the evening.

It was a very different story on the eastern side. During the early hours of the day members of Peiper's Kampfgruppe, probably Rumpf's 9th SS Panzer Pioneers and some of Schnelle's Panzer-Grenadiers, moved north-east from Hassoumont and occupied the houses in the area of Les Tscheous. Doctor Bastin, returning to his village just after dawn to get food and other things for the evacuees in Borgoumont, found himself arrested and locked in his cellar. At 1245 hours tanks of the 743rd Tank Battalion at Roanne reported seeing enemy infantry moving towards Borgoumont and at 1310 hours there was a further report of three hundred enemy infantry and four tanks moving from the area of the Nabonruy stream towards Les Tscheous. Whilst the

224

numbers of infantry are certainly exaggerated, Serge Fontaine confirms in his writings[1] that a column of German tanks, led by a captured Sherman, moved to Les Tscheous on the Friday morning:

> The column of panzers, preceded by a Sherman, is sighted from Roanne before it enters 'Tscheous' and brings on itself some violent artillery fire. The Sherman explodes under the weight of shells right in the middle of the road . . . the other crews attempt to clear the way with cables but with no success as the artillery has a firm hold on its prey; the track of one of the panzers breaks opposite the 'Tscheous' hotel and the tank slides back on the bank unrolling its thick steel ribbon. Little by little they draw back, losing a third tank two hundred metres from the bridge (Nabonruy) and they get back to Hassoumont at 1500 hours, kept in check by the dense rain of shells of all calibres.

The tanks were a Tiger of the 3rd Company and two Type IVs of Junker's 6th SS Panzer Company; the log of the 117th Infantry confirms that at 1420 hours artillery was requested to deal with a Tiger in the area of Les Tscheous. Quite why Peiper wanted to push such a powerful force out on the Borgoumont road at this late stage is unclear. Maybe he felt that this was his most vulnerable flank and he felt hemmed in in Hassoumont? Whatever the reason it cost him dear – the intense artillery fire forced his infantry to withdraw back to Hassoumont and he lost all the tanks!

American artillery fire was now beginning to be the most decisive factor in the battle of La Gleize. In order to understand its scale it should be noted that, in the six days of fighting in the three general areas described, the 30th Division artillery alone fired 57,275 rounds. The once picturesque village was being reduced to rubble and survival was only possible by taking refuge in the tanks themselves, or even better in the strong stone cellars of the local houses. Fortunately for the defenders the Americans always stopped their bombardments just as their tanks and infantry began their attacks and this allowed the Germans to man their battle positions in time to resist the assaults. For the remaining civilians it was a nightmare – Serge Fontaine describes what it was like for those who had taken shelter in the church:

> Two GIs and some Germans have built a fire for warmth using furniture as firewood. The whole time debris is falling from the walls and arches around them . . . a shell tears open the wall behind the choir, another demolishes the corner walls above the crypt and undermines the supports of the church tower. The smell of powder burns their throats as they huddle against one another near the choir stalls . . . more wounded are brought in . . . in the morning the arch crumbles

under a large explosion and the little group is showered by debris
. . . this is enough, one must leave this dangerous place before it
collapses entirely. Swiftly, through a gaping hole behind the choir,
the people get out and walk along the road to Cheneux, sucking on
the frozen grass to quench their thirst and their burning throats . . .
going to ground many times along the sloping hedges . . . they at
last reach the US lines somewhere below St Anne's [Chapel].[2]

It will be recalled that late on Thursday McGeorge had left his infantry
in Borgoumont and moved his I Company Shermans to an area just to
the south-west of Roanne. From there he planned to advance, on the
Friday, west through the area known as the Minières. Unfortunately
for his men this approach was dominated by the two Tigers, two Panthers and single Type IV at the Werimont farm and by the other German
tanks at Hassoumont.

Preceded by a thirty-minute intense artillery bombardment McGeorge
began his advance at 1400 hours. His Shermans managed to reach the
first major bend in the road, just below the village, by 1515 hours but
then everything went wrong. The two leading tanks ran on to mines
and the two rear ones were immobilised by tank fire. The rest of the
US column was then subjected to heavy fire from a variety of weapons.
The Task Force fell back in disarray to the line of the Roannay stream;
it had achieved more than it realised – both Tigers at the Werimont farm
had been put out of action, almost certainly by artillery fire (that of SS
Lieutenant Dollinger, number 213, stands in La Gleize to this day).
Any elation which Peiper might have felt in defeating this attack soon
evaporated with the news, at 1700 hours, that Hansen's attempts
to break through to him had failed. After discussions with von
Westernhagen, Poetschke and Diefenthal, Peiper sent a message to
Mohnke at the Château Wanne demanding permission to break out.

At about 2000 hours on Friday night three JU 52 transport aircraft
attempted a parachute drop[3] of desperately needed fuel and other essential supplies to the KG – only ten per cent fell within Peiper's very
limited defensive perimeter and in the first clear and moonlit night for
ages his men had to watch with dismay as the rest fell behind US lines.
The clear night also brought with it the dreaded prospect of US air
strikes in the morning.

Brigadier General Harrison's orders to Colonel Sutherland's 119 RCT
for Saturday were to advance from a Line of Departure running roughly
north-west to south-east through the Château Froidcour, seize La Gleize
and effect a junction with TF McGeorge. The 504th Parachute Infantry
was not involved and would hold its current positions south of the river.
To achieve his mission Harrison planned to lead with two battle groups
and keep one in reserve. 3/119, with TF Jordan attached and with two

self-propelled and two towed TDs from A Company 823rd TD Battalion, was to advance on the axis of the N-33, the light tanks taking a flanking route through the forest to the north. 1/119, with the Shermans of Captain Berry's C Company 740th Tanks and two self-propelled TDs, was to follow the axis of the Cheneux to La Gleize road, south of the N-33. Each Battalion group was to have a platoon of B Company 105th Engineers in support. 2/119, less F Company, was to be in Regimental reserve and follow 1,000 yards behind the advance on the N-33. F Company, with the Stuart tanks of D Company 740th, was to remain in defence in Roua and Stoumont. The 119th Cannon Company was to join the 197th Field Artillery Battalion in providing fire support.

On the east side of La Gleize McGeorge's tanks were to attack again using the same axis as the previous day, whilst his infantry element advanced from Borgoumont.

There were by now a number of superfluous commanders under General Hobbs. Brigadier General Truman Boudinot had returned to reassume command of CCB but found TFM and TFJ under Harrison's command and Lovelady under Colonel Johnson of the 117th Infantry; Colonel Sutherland of the 119th was under Harrison and George Rubel's tank companies were all with someone else as were Lieutenant Duncan's 743rd companies. George Rubel was not a man to remain idle for long, and on the Thursday he had organised for his personal use a self-propelled 155mm gun! The following story from his book sounds a bit far-fetched but is corroborated to some extent by Serge Fontaine:

I had the 155mm SP gun set up near the castle [Froidcour] and had Lt Merritt place his 105mm assault guns on the rise of ground extending south of the castle. The 155mm SP showed up like a steeple on a church and I was sure that the enemy would knock it down before it had fired five rounds. To take all possible precautions, I had the artillery plaster the town – then the 105mm assault guns opened up. With all this fire Jerry did not dare stick his head up and while it was going on I opened fire with the 155mm SP over open sights. I stood on top of a wall directly above the gun and called range and deflection to the crew. The crew, by the way, had been augmented by using my radio operators, cooks and jeep driver as cannoneers. We fired 192 rounds during the afternoon.

It has to be said, however, that from Froidcour it was only possible to see the area of the church and Hôtel de Ville; the rest of the village was obscured by trees.

Despite their overwhelming superiority, particularly in artillery, none of the American actions on Saturday was successful. McGeorge started at 0900 hours with a mainly infantry advance from Borgoumont by K Company 3/117 and men of D Company 36th Armored Infantry, sup-

ported by 2nd Platoon of A Company 743rd Tanks. I Company's Shermans were to advance up the N-33 a little later. The infantry advanced
very slowly, or as Serge Fontaine describes it 'foot by foot'. He goes on:

> They get to the area of Les Tscheous by the early hours of the after-
> noon – Doctor Bastin is freed from his cellar at 1400 hours. They at
> last succeed, house by house, to oust the SS . . . the Shermans of the
> 743rd get bolder and are pushing forward towards the village when
> a flank attack from the German panzers puts everything back into
> question again; this counter-attack brings the enemy back near the
> 'Tscheous' hotel but the GIs will not give it up again . . . the surround-
> ing meadows, strewn with corpses tell a lot about the intensity of the
> fighting.[4]

McGeorge detached a section of Shermans from I Company to try to help
out his infantry at Tscheous but they were unable to get into effective fire
positions without themselves coming under fire from the German tanks
at Hassoumont. The rest of the I Company Shermans managed to get
quite close to the Werimont farm position but by 1530 hours they too
were pinned down by tank fire from their flank.

Things went no better on the western side of La Gleize. As Rubel put
it in his book:

> We resumed the attack at daybreak on the 23rd but it soon fizzled
> out and no gain was made. The enemy was covering our attack with
> all types of fire. Most of it came from La Gleize but the thing that
> stopped us was the flanking fire from the high ground north-west of
> the town. This fire had caused a lot of casualties.

The area referred to was Les Montis and Hassoumont. The After Action
Report of CCB is depressingly short in its description of what happened
to TFJ:

> At 1007 hours F Company of TF Jordan's Force [the armoured infantry
> company] encountered a minefield covered by one 20mm gun on the
> road from Stoumont to La Gleize but by 1115 the engineers had the
> road cleared. Again at 1330 his Force was held up on the road by
> enemy tanks.

The 119th Infantry Report gives a little more detail:

> The 3rd Battalion [with TFJ] attacked at 0830 and advanced to (the
> east edge of St Anne's woods) where the right company was held up
> by an enemy road block. One tank was knocked out by enemy tank
> fire. At 1310 the road block was cleared and the Battalion advanced
> approximately 150 yards, where it was held up by automatic, 20mm
> and direct fire weapons in and around La Gleize. Contact with a Task
> Force of CCB was made at [Nabonruy stream] at 1320.

According to Serge Fontaine, Jordan lost two tanks, the second in the minefield.

Lieutenant David Knox gives a personal account of what it was like in an infantry company – L Company 3/119:

> The next morning [Saturday] we took off for La Gleize. It had been a very cold night. Frost was on the ground. The three rifle companies were to approach the town over three different roads or routes. According to the map it looked good – phase lines to check in on and all sorts of big plans. We started on the way. By noon we realised that we were on about the only road there was and also that the road we were on didn't seem to be on the map. It was very confusing. There was no route into town. Over on the other side of the next draw we could see a red parachute that had been used to drop supplies to the German troops. There was supposed to be an air show that afternoon, but something happened and it didn't come off. This was the first good day since the breakthrough. The planes were probably used on more important objectives. Night came and we ground-hogged for the night. The order came down that all troops would have gas masks by midnight. The Germans must be really making this thing 'all out'. . . . That whole night was spent in trying to get artillery lifted that was falling very near our third platoon. Everything was being dropped in La Gleize that night. Everything. As I shivered I thought, 'Tomorrow is Christmas Eve.'[5]

Knox's Company had been given the extremely difficult task of advancing through the thick woods to the north of the N-33.

The attack by the southern group is also described in the 119th Report:

> The 1st Battalion [with Berry's Shermans] attacked east at 0830 and advanced to the [La Venne] crossroads before meeting any resistance. At this point an enemy minefield covered by anti-tank fire was encountered. One tank burned and another disabled by the anti-tank fire before it was knocked out by our tanks. The minefield was removed and the Battalion advanced approximately 300 yards, where it was held up by automatic and direct fire weapons on the high ground in and south of La Gleize. The remainder of the day was spent in reconnaissance and directing artillery fire on enemy positions.

The Panther and single Type IV on the Dinheid feature on the southwest side of the village completely dominated that flank and had given Berry's Company all the trouble. Peiper had indeed sited his tanks well!

A fascinating account of his personal experiences on the Saturday was given in a letter written by Captain Bruce Crissinger, the commander of A Company 823rd TD Battalion, in June 1992:

> By the morning of 23rd December Stoumont had been retaken. . . .

Colonel Herlong [CO 1/119] told me that enemy tank fire had knocked out 3 supporting Shermans and told me to see what I could do about it. Lt Cunningham and I walked to the right of the wooded front and then down a macadam road toward La Gleize, under a railway overpass with a dead German by the roadside and a few hundred yards farther to a hill top. From the bank on the left side of the road an infantry soldier spoke to us. He said his position was the OP and that a machine gun had been firing out in front. In my former artillery training OP meant Observation Post while in infantry lingo it meant outpost. Nothing more was between him and the enemy. We continued downhill for 1 or 2 hundred yards when we were fired on by a machine gun. Probably a submachine gun but not a fast firing burp gun. The bullets were so close that they cracked like Chinese firecrackers. We hit the roadside ditch with Cunningham facing toward the front and me the other way. Another burst brought dirt down the bank by my face. From the time we jumped into the ditch I didn't see Cunningham again until we met much later in the States. So what I tell you now was his account told probably 1½ years later. Cunningham jumped up, turned around and hit the ditch again. Another burst hit him in the arm. He said 'that one got me' and then shortly thereafter 'I'm going on out'. I stayed where I was and listened to our 105s going over and hoping they would hit that machine gun.

In about half an hour I heard footsteps on the road. Someone kicked me on the foot; I turned over and there were two German soldiers looking at me. One carried a sub machine gun and the other a rifle. They wore either tanker or paratrooper helmets. [They were paratroopers who had joined the KG at Lanzerath.] They took everything I had of value, broke the M-1 (rifle) I was carrying and we took off down a bank to the right of the road to a railroad track, picked up some tank ammunition that had been dropped by plane and then climbed a steep bank to a grove of evergreens. There was a large bunker in the grove covered with poles and dirt and containing several Germans including some officers. I jammed myself in with them while the American artillery pounded the grove. They were not a happy group. I was turned over to a rather small thin soldier with a hare lip and carrying a sub machine gun. He took me back through various manned positions, machine gun etc. As we came up a lane into La Gleize a Mark IV came toward us and the tank commander swiveled his periscope in order to get a good look at me. I was turned over to an interrogation officer who was originally from Chicago and spoke perfect English. He had a shrapnel hole in his helmet. He was not happy either. From there I was taken to a house and sent downstairs into a basement. An SS soldier with a Spandau sub machine gun sat on the top step of the stairs down to the cellar. There were 30 to 40

American soldiers in the cellar including 4 A Co men. Sometime much later, maybe 9 or 10 o'clock at night, we heard fire crackling overhead in the house above us, compliments of the American artillery, possibly white phosphorus. We were ordered out by the guards. There was no panic. Everyone went out in a good and orderly manner. The scene in the street beside the house was chaotic. The town was on fire. 30 to 40 GIs huddled together, American artillery shelling the town and a very wild SS soldier waving a Spandau sub machine gun from side to side and yelling 'Officer, Officer.' Since he spoke with a heavy accent it took me some moments to realise he meant me. When I was recognised I was taken to Lt Col Joachem Peiper's CP. It was in a cellar that was entered from an outside cellarway. I think there was a blanket for a door. I went through and for some reason recognised who was in charge and snapped probably the best salute I have ever given. There were 4 or 5 other German officers. Peiper was wearing a type of coverall and no helmet. A very good looking man who spoke slow, good but not perfect English. Shortly thereafter Major Hal McCown was brought in. He gave me a quick and very surprised handshake.

It will be recalled that McCown, the ex-commanding officer of 2/119, had been captured two days before near Froidcour. He had been briefly interrogated by Peiper himself but after failing to give any information McCown was sent away to a cellar where he was interrogated again in a manner he had been taught to expect when under training in the States. In his statement of 6th January 1945 McCown says:

I was placed in a chair, apart from the other occupants of the cellar, where the light of a small electric bulb would fall mainly upon my face, leaving the rest of the room in semi-darkness. One of the NCOs drew his Luger, examined the clip, reloaded the weapon and laid it on the table in front of him. . . . The only distracting feature to an otherwise perfect setting as far as they were concerned, was the frequent crashing of an American artillery concentration, sometimes quite uncomfortably close. The next thirty minutes was spent in an attempt to extract from me the information I had refused to give to the commander earlier that afternoon [Thursday]. I was surprised to see that as my failure to respond to their threatenings continued they grew no angrier but instead seemed to lose interest in the procedure. Finally I was taken to another cellar where a warrant officer searched me thoroughly, taking my flashlight and knife but leaving me my wrist watch, ring, a little food I was carrying and my personal papers. I was conducted to a very small cellar which contained four other American officers, all lieutenants of my own Regiment.[6]

McCown gives many interesting insights into the state of Peiper's Kampfgruppe at this time:

During the entire time I was in this town I gathered all the information I could from other captives as well as German officers and men (who talked to a surprising degree) about the strength, dispositions and condition of the Germans in that area. . . . An amazing fact to me was the youth of the members of this organisation – the bulk of the enlisted men were either 18 or 19, recently recruited, but from my observations thoroughly trained. There was a good sprinkling of both privates and NCOs from the years of Russian fighting. The officers for the most part were veterans but were also very young . . . captains and lieutenants ran from 19 to 27 years of age. The morale was high throughout the entire period I was with them despite the extremely trying conditions. The discipline was very good. . . . The physical condition of all personnel was good, except for a lack of proper food, which was apparent more strongly just before I escaped from the unit. The equipment was good and complete with the exception of some reconditioned half-tracks among the motorised equipment. All the men wore practically new boots and had adequate clothing. Some men wore parts of American uniforms, mainly the knit cap, gloves, sweaters, overshoes and one or two overcoats. I saw no one however, in American uniforms or in civilian clothes. The relationship between the officers and men, particularly the commanding officer, Col Peiper, was closer and more friendly than I would have expected. On several occasions Col Peiper visited his wounded, and many times, as we were climbing the steep hills (during the breakout from La Gleize) I saw him speak a couple of cheering words and give a slap of encouragement on the back of heavily loaded men.

Later on during the night on 21st December [Thursday] at approx 2300 I was again taken to the cellar HQ of Col Peiper. I found him in a very much different mood from his former cold, impersonal attitude. He and I talked together from 2300 until 0500 the next morning – our subject being mainly his defence of Naziism and why Germany was fighting. I have met few men who impressed me in as short a space of time as did this officer. He was approx 5ft 8inches in height, 140 lbs in weight, long dark hair combed straight back, well shaped features, with remarkable facial resemblance to the actor, Ray Milland. . . . He was completely confident of Germany's ability to whip the Allies. He spoke of Himmler's new reserve army quite at length saying that it contained so many new divisions, both armored and otherwise, that our G-2s would wonder where they all came from. He did his best to find out from me the success V-1 and V-2 were having and told me that more secret weapons like those would be unloosed. He said a new submarine campaign was also opening up and they had been told that there had been considerable tonnage sunk in the English Channel just recently by the new underwater attack. The German Air Force, he said, would now come forth with many new types and which, although inferior in number to the allies, would be superior in quality and would suffice their needs to cover the breakthrough in Belgium and Holland and later to the French coast.

Concerning treatment of prisoners by the SS, I can state that at no time were the prisoners of this organisation mistreated. Food was scarce, but it was nearly as good as that used by the Germans themselves. The American prisoners were always given cellar space to protect them from the exceedingly heavy American artillery barrages. . . . The men were considerably overcrowded and were allowing the guards to bully them a little. I organised the entire group of some 130 into sections, appointed a First Sergeant and laid down a few rules concerning rotation sleeping, urinating, equality and distribution of food and got the German Warrant Officer in charge of prisoners settled upon a fairer method of giving water to prisoners and providing ventilation.

I was taken back the morning of 22 December (Friday) and again placed in the small cellar with the other four American officers. All that day American artillery pounded the town incessantly, even the guard detachment, consisting of five Germans, came down into our cellar, heavily overcrowding the tiny room. In the afternoon a 105 shell made a direct hit on the wall of our cellar, throwing the German sitting beside me half-way across the room. A hole approx 2½ft in diameter was knocked in the wall. Lt Henley and Lt Youmans of my Regiment helped pull the German out from under the rubble and got him on the floor of the undamaged part of the cellar. Within a few minutes another shell landed a few feet outside the hole in the cellar wall and shrapnel and stone flew through the room. Lt Henley was killed instantly and three Germans were wounded. One of the Germans died within about 30 minutes. We administered first aid as well as we could. For several hours, while the shelling continued without appreciable let-up, the dead and wounded, together with those who were unhurt, were cramped close together in the unharmed half of the small cellar. Late in the afternoon parties of American enlisted men came to the cellar and removed the dead and wounded; the litter bearers told me that German casualties had been heavy throughout the town.

At 1400 hours on Saturday Peiper received permission to break out. His request to do so had been passed by Mohnke to Priess at HQ I SS Panzer Corps with a recommendation that the request be approved. Priess passed it on to 6th Panzer Army where permission was denied. Priess then delegated responsibility to Mohnke who, knowing the situation was hopeless, gave permission. The story that Peiper was ordered to bring out all his wounded, vehicles and weapons is nonsense – it was clearly out of the question.

Peiper immediately held a conference with his senior commanders.[7] He was apparently very calm. There was only one possible escape route and that was to the south, over the Amblève, south again and then east to join the rest of the Division. One of Skorzeny's commando officers, a naval lieutenant thought to be named Schulz or Schmidt, who had ended up with the Kampfgruppe, was ordered to find a way over the Amblève as soon as possible. It was agreed that all lightly wounded men would accompany the march-out column and as many weapons as possible would be taken. All others would be rendered useless, but vehicles including tanks were not to be blown up or immobilized except during US artillery fire for fear of warning the Americans that a withdrawal was planned. Some of the less seriously wounded being left behind were given the job of sabotaging as many tanks as possible after the main body had left. The badly wounded were to be left behind in the care of SS Lieutenant Doctor Willi Dittmann. The plan was for all who were to leave La Gleize to parade in the village square, opposite the church, at 0200 hours on Sunday. The password was to be 'Frohe Weihnachten'.

The Commando naval officer with two men returned to say that both the railway viaduct at La Venne, 1,500m south of the village, and the wooden bridge beneath it were intact. Between the viaduct and the railway tunnel just to the east of it, the American airborne had established a small guard post in a railway workers' hut – otherwise the way out was clear. The Commando group was told to eliminate the guards just before the planned crossing which was due to take place at about 0300 hours on the Sunday morning – Christmas Eve.

It will be remembered that care of wounded was a major concern within the Leibstandarte. In an attempt to solve this problem Peiper sent for Major Hal McCown again during the late afternoon. McCown told what happened in his 1945 statement:

He (Peiper) told me that he had received orders from the commanding general to give up his position and withdraw to the east to the nearest German troops. He said he knew it would be impossible to save any of his vehicles – that it would have to be a foot withdrawal. His immediate concern was what to do with the American prisoners, of which he had nearly 150, as well as his own wounded. He dictated to me a plan of exchange whereby he would leave all American prisoners under the command of the senior PW, a captain, to be turned over to the American commander as the Americans entered the town the next day. He said that his wounded would also be left in the cellars of La Gleize and that he would leave a German medical officer in charge of them. He had previously left a considerable number of wounded in the Château at Stoumont which had already been captured by Americans. In exchange for the American prisoners, all German wounded would then be turned over to the 1st SS Panzer Division wherever they might be when the wounded were assembled. I would then be released back to the American lines as I would be the only prisoner retained during the foot movement of the Germans east from La Gleize. I told Col Peiper that I could not give him any assurance that the exchange would be carried out as it was a matter for higher headquarters. He said that he fully understood.[8]

The American captain mentioned by Peiper was of course Bruce Crissinger who takes up the story in his 1992 letter:

Peiper's force was surrounded and out of fuel. They were going to slip through the American lines later that night, taking Major McCown with them as a hostage. I was to lead an ambulance convoy under a Flag of Truce loaded with the German wounded now in the cellars of La Gleize through into the German lines. When this had been accomplished McCown would be released. Peiper wrote a note explaining the plan which I later gave to Col Sutherland. He ignored it rightfully.

Despite McCown's remarks about German morale, not all Peiper's men wished to continue the fight. According to SS Captain Gerd Neuske,[9] Peiper's personal staff officer, one man who was caught removing his SS collar runes was reported by SS Lieutenant Rumpf as a potential deserter. He was shot against the church wall on Peiper's orders.

Between 0200 and 0300 on Sunday morning approximately eight hundred men, heavily loaded with weapons, walked out of La Gleize. Three hundred wounded remained behind. They were the last survivors of the once proud and powerful Kampfgruppe Peiper.

Early on Sunday the Americans advanced again on the shattered village – they had no idea that it was virtually undefended. According to the 119th Infantry's Report their 3rd Battalion, with TF Jordan, attacked at 0730 hours. By 0845 hours the leading elements and supporting tanks were moving into the north edge of La Gleize, stiff resistance being encountered on the hill just to the north of the village (Les Montis and Hassoumont). George Rubel says that a flanking attack was made from the north to capture the high ground on that flank. He describes it in his usual flamboyant way:

They were to crawl silently until within 10 yards of the enemy position, then were to open up with everything they had and close with the bayonet. The instant they started shooting we would open with tank, machine gun and mortar fire from our front and artillery would throw in everything they had on the town and escape routes to the south. The artillery would lift on signal; the infantry would halt 200 yards from town and Captain Berry with C Company would charge in. I was to use direct fire with the 155mm SP and was to keep it 100 yards in front of Captain Berry's lead tank. . . . The attack went perfectly and exactly as planned.[10]

David Knox saw it differently:

We took off the next morning at about 0630. The 117th was coming in from the other side of town. What was left of Hitler's best was supposed to be pretty well cut off. K and L [Companies] entered town at just about the same time. There was no fighting to do. We were soon to find out why. There were better than 200 men in town – all badly wounded. The Germans couldn't take care of their casualties. A German medical officer met us just after we entered town. He was trying to tell Lt Kane something about showing us where his wounded were. No one was too receptive.[11]

The 1st Battalion of the 119th Infantry, with Berry's Shermans, attacked at 0745 hours and by 0945 hours were 500 yards south of the village where they found the two abandoned German tanks on the Dinheid feature. They met no resistance. By 1010 hours the leading elements had reached the church. Captain 'Bud' Strand of D Company 1/119 told what he saw that day:

On the morning of Dec 24th at around 6.00 am we noticed the German equipment being blown up and set on fire, and within 30 seconds a sea of fire shone all around. We again pushed into La Gleize and got resistance from the church area, and later found a fanatic band of SS troops were holed up and giving us trouble. We directed fire into the church and knocked them out but virtually destroyed the church . . . we had no other choice . . . we captured over 100 German SS troops and released 170 of our own American GIs who had been captured earlier, plus many wounded soldiers that we found in the church. But also with sadness that through the heavy artillery fire on La Gleize, we killed many of our own GIs who were prisoners at that time.

On the east side of La Gleize TF McGeorge with K Company 3/117 reached the centre of the village by 1000 hours. There were some reports of Americans opening fire on one another but not to the extent of causing casualties.

David Knox went on to say:

One hundred fifty men and four officers of the Battalion were back with us. . . . It was a great take that we captured in that town . . . 28 tanks and 70 half-tracks. That was a real haul. Lots of it had been knocked out by our artillery . . . and the rest the Germans had destroyed themselves. The Germans began to come out on the streets. These Hitler boys were sad looking sights. Heads bandaged and hands, legs, chests and backs were badly wounded. Here was proof that our artillery was wicked stuff. I would judge that all of them were between 18 and 24.

'Bud' Strand continued:

Our Battalion Commander in looking over the German soldiers saw many of them wearing brand new GI boots and wool trousers and here our own soldiers had on boots that had soles worn through and worn out trousers. He marched the German soldiers into the town square and made them in the snow and bitter cold take off their trousers and boots. We then handed them back to our own GIs who needed them. I can still see the young arrogant German SS troops cry like babies over this as they stood barefoot in the snow and some without trousers.

On this latter point Captain Bruce Crissinger added in his 1992 letter:

I was surprised at the venom showed by the GIs toward the few walking wounded still left in the town. Anyone wearing any American equipment including shoes had to remove it. Several were walking barefoot on a very cold morning. I learned later their anger was due to the news of the Malmédy Massacre. I am glad I did not know that while a prisoner.

Reports of exactly how much German equipment was left in La Gleize on Christmas Eve vary wildly. The highest estimates for tanks come from the 119th Infantry and 743rd Tank Battalion with a figure of thirty-nine. A more realistic figure, supported by Monsieur Gérard Grégoire whose parents lived in the village and who returned there himself on 9th January 1945, is twenty-five – six Tiger IIs, thirteen Panthers and six Type IVs. At least two had been driven into German minefields by the sabotage teams. In addition there was a minimum of forty-six SPWs, six 150mm infantry guns, three Pumas, four 20mm flak weapons, four 120mm mortars and twelve other vehicles.

The 30th Infantry Division's battle with the Leibstandarte was over – it had cost 'Old Hickory' 487 casualties, of which 97 had been killed, out of an average total strength of 13,400 and a 'bayonet' strength of less than 5,000. A further 472 were listed as missing, although most of these were prisoners and at least 170 were released on Christmas Eve when La Gleize was recaptured. Casualty figures for CCB of the 3rd Armored Division and the 740th Tank Battalion are unknown but relatively insignificant, even though it is possible to account for twenty-three of their tanks being knocked out or immobilized.

Thirteen civilians from La Gleize died as a result of the German offensive.

There are two interesting anecdotes about La Gleize. Seventeen days before the German offensive the US 1st Army 'Monuments, Fine Arts and Archives Specialist Officer', Captain Walter Hancock,[12] visited the church and made a note of the gracefully carved, 14th Century statue, known as the Virgin of La Gleize. Following the battle in which the church was virtually destroyed, he visited again with permission from the Bishop to remove the statue to the Seminary in Liège for safekeeping. He found it undamaged but in a highly vulnerable situation. Most of the villagers had yet to return but neither Hancock nor the Bishop had reckoned on the few who were still there. To his surprise they strongly resisted his attempts to remove 'their' Virgin! After visiting the church to assess the situation the only thing to which they would agree was that she should be placed in the strong cellar of Monsieur Arthur Georges which, as they pointed out, had resisted all German and American attempts to destroy it! Hancock later recorded their visit to see the statue:

> Someone had a key to the door so instead of taking a short cut through a huge gap in the wall we made a conventional entrance, scrambling across heaps of wreckage and pews tossed in all directions, and stumbling over bits of uniforms, German and American, and broken weapons – the whole mass sifted through with snow.

Amongst those present were the Abbé Louis Blockiau, Monsieur Arthur Georges, the stone mason whose name is not recorded and a Monsieur Marcel Geenen, a farmer and the keeper of the destroyed La Fermette inn. Thanks to them the Virgin of La Gleize never left her village and was returned to the church in 1951 when it had been rebuilt.

The inn keeper's wife, Jenny Geenen, was the far seeing person who decided that La Gleize should keep at least one major memento of the battle. When she saw an American armoured recovery team removing Dollinger's Tiger II, number 213, from the Werimont farm she offered them a bottle of cognac for it – they accepted! It is the only remaining Tiger II in Europe which was actually involved in combat. Today it still menacingly covers the eastern approaches to the village, just as it did fifty years ago. Across the road in the church, the Virgin of La Gleize stands with her hands upraised in a gesture of supplication.

NOTES

1. Fontaine, article in *Publicité Idéale*, 1970.
2. Ibid.
3. Tiemann, *Die Leibstandarte IV/2*, p. 136.

4. Fontaine op. cit.
5. Letter to author dated 2 Oct 1984.
6. *Annexe I to Part C of Intelligence Notes No 43 dated 6 Jan 1945*, HQ US Forces, European Theater.
7. Tiemann op. cit., pp. 144–6.
8. *Annexe I to Part C of Intelligence Notes No 43 dated 6 Jan 1945*, HQ US Forces, European Theater.
9. Neuske, statement at Munich 31 Jan 1948.
10. Rubel, *Daredevil Tankers*, chapter IX.
11. Letter to author dated 2 Oct 1984.
12. Letter to author 13 Mar 1986.

CHAPTER XXXVII

Sunday 24th to Monday 25th December 1944

The Long March

When Peiper led his men out of La Gleize on Christmas Eve, they were hungry, exhausted through lack of sleep and the stress of battle, and mentally drained by the knowledge that they had failed in their mission. They knew they had to penetrate the surrounding American lines and that any route their commander chose would lead them through extremely difficult country with a minimum of two river crossings. It would inevitably be a supreme test of stamina, determination and leadership. What they did not know was that, by an extraordinary quirk of fate, the Americans in the area they were planning to cross would also be moving out – right across their path!

Due to a serious penetration by the German 2nd Panzer Division south of Werbomont towards Manhay, Major General Matthew Ridgway, Commander XVIII Airborne Corps, had decided to shorten his lines and pull the 82nd Airborne Division back to a new and more defensible position running roughly from Trois Ponts to Manhay (Map 1). At 0130 hours on Christmas Eve, just as Peiper was about to begin his march out of La Gleize, Ridgway gave orders for this withdrawal to begin.

Much has been written about this operation and, in post war years, Field Marshal Montgomery has been blamed by numerous American commentators for risking serious damage to US morale by ordering the withdrawal. Although many other legitimate criticisms can be levelled at Monty for his behaviour and actions during the Ardennes offensive, this is an unjust and inaccurate charge. Major General Jim Gavin made clear in his book *On to Berlin*:

Obviously, in the situation confronting the XVIII Corps, a withdrawal was very much in order. It shortened the section allocated to the 82nd by about 50 per cent, thus enabling us to do much better on the defensive. The new defensive position was far superior in terms of fields of fire and cover for the defenders than the old position. Finally, we would be in a much better position to launch a counter-attack when the moment for that came, and we knew it was inevitable.

And with regard to any adverse effect on morale, the *History of the 505th Airborne Regiment* has the following comment:

Most 505ers (excepting the staffs) didn't know what it was all about and merely presumed that it was another move to another position, just like a thousand and one they had made before. . . . The 1st and 2nd Battalions made the move without incident for the most part, but the 3rd Battalion's route happened to coincide with that Colonel Peiper was using to withdraw his Kampfgruppe. In the inevitable collision several violent clashes ensued. When Colonel Ekman learned of it he asked General Gavin whether he should stop the withdrawal and destroy this enemy group or continue as planned. General Gavin deemed it more important to get the new defensive line formed as soon as possible because the Division was now getting extreme pressure on its southern side (from 2nd Panzer Division), so he told Ekman to bypass the Germans if feasible.

By means of three quite separate eye-witness accounts from men who took part in this march, it is possible to build up a very clear picture of what happened. The accounts are those of Major Hal McCown[1] of the American 119th Infantry Regiment, SS Sergeant Karl Wortmann[2] of the 10th SS Panzer Anti-Aircraft Company and Monsieur Yvan Hakin,[3] a Belgian who was forced to act as a guide for the Germans. Their statements are corroborated by other American and German reports.

Peiper knew that Hansen's men were holding the Coo and Biester area on the Saturday morning; whether he knew they had been forced to withdraw south into the Bois de Coreu that afternoon is unclear, but in any case they were still the nearest German forces to him and that was presumably why he made the bridge over the Amblève at the Coo cascade his first objective (Map 19). He planned to reach it by crossing the two footbridges over the dead arm of the river, just to the west of Grand Coo. The railway viaduct between La Gleize and Coo would have been a much shorter and easier objective but Peiper, having passed under it on the 18th, knew it had been blown – a major span had in fact been destroyed by the Germans during their earlier retreat on 9th September. What he did not know was that the Coo cascade bridge had also been blown by the Americans.

Some time after 0200 hours the German column set out from La Gleize on its way up the path known as La Coulée, which led south on to the Dinheid feature and then joined the track down to La Venne (Map 18). It was a very clear and bitterly cold night. There was snow on the ground. At La Venne, Yvan Hakin and Ernest Gason were chosen as guides from amongst the Belgians sheltering in Albert Legros's cellar. At the last minute Laurant Gason took his son's place. Yvan Hakin told the author that he was made to carry a panzerfaust and Gason forced to carry ammunition. In the middle of the column came Peiper's HQ with McGown and two guards. McCown puts his position further forward:

> Col Peiper and I moved immediately behind the point, the remainder of his depleted Regiment following in single file. . . . We crossed the L'Amblève river near La Gleize on a small highway bridge immediately underneath the railroad bridge and moved generally south climbing higher and higher on the ridge line. At 0500 we heard the first tank blow up and inside of thirty minutes the entire area formally occupied by Col Peiper's command was a sea of fiercely burning vehicles, the work of the small detachment he had left behind to complete the destruction of all of his equipment.

Karl Wortmann put the time an hour later which accords with other American reports; he recalled thinking it was his sixth Christmas at war! Officers were spread throughout the column and Peiper allowed frequent pauses for the men to rest. He himself moved from group to group offering encouragement. At the front of the column was a reconnaissance element, or Spitze, charged with checking that the way ahead was free of enemy. McCown: 'No food was available at any time after we left La Gleize; the only subsistence I received was four small pieces of dried biscuit and two swallows of cognac which one of the junior officers gave me.'

On reaching the heights of Mont St Victor, Peiper could see that the bridge by the cascade on the Amblève was blown and that he would be unable to cross the river in that area. Serge Fontaine gives the following description:

> Day is breaking when the first marchers emerge at the top of the steep slope and Peiper, disorientated for a while by all the surrounding hillocks, makes a quick check with his guides and map and compass. . . . He looks for a way to safety in the valley at his feet. He watches with disappointment as the torrential Amblève drags down into the spray of the cascade the last blocks of the blown up bridge.

Thwarted in his intention of crossing the Amblève, Peiper was forced

241

to look for another escape route by climbing further up Mont St Victor (Map 14). McCown: 'Col Peiper, his staff and myself with my two guards spent all day of the 24th reconnoitering for a route to rejoin other German forces.' By now US spotter aircraft were looking for the escaping Germans and Peiper decided to lie up in the deep gully known as the Trou des Mouchettes for the hours of daylight. As darkness began to fall the column moved off again past the Calvary de la Croisette, past Brume and then down the steep slopes of the Bois de Troibaileu towards the hamlet of Henri Moulin on the Trois Ponts to Basse Bodeux main N-23 road. McCown:

> At 1700, just before dark, the column started moving again on the selected route; we pushed down into a valley in single column with a heavily armed point out ahead. The noise made by the entire 800-man group was so little that I believe we could have passed within 200 yards of an outpost without detection. As the point neared the base of the hill I could hear quite clearly an American voice call out 'Halt! Who is there?' The challenge was repeated three times, then the American sentry fired three shots. A moment later the order came along the column to turn around and move back up the hill. The entire column was half-way back up the hillside in a very few minutes. A German passed by me limping. He was undoubtedly leading the point as he had just received a bullet through the leg. The Colonel spoke briefly to him but would not permit the medics to put on a dressing; he fell in the column and continued moving on without first aid.

Wortmann talked about a sharp twenty-minute clash which resulted in some Germans being wounded, but the Belgian version of events agrees that only one German was wounded, in the knee, and says that the vanguard did not return fire in order to maintain the secrecy of the withdrawal. In the confusion caused by this incident Hakin and Gason managed to escape and return to La Venne. McCown:

> The point moved along the side of the hill for a distance of a half mile, then again turned down into the valley, this time passed undetected through the valley and the paved road which ran along the base. The entire 800 men were closed into the trees on the other side of the valley in an amazingly short period of time. Several American vehicles 'chopped' the column.

Jim Gavin added more detail:

> Earlier in the night a jeep driver had reported that as he was driving in the vicinity of Basse Bodeux he encountered troops wearing full field equipment walking in the woods towards the east. They hit the

ground and took cover and acted very evasive as his jeep neared them.

After crossing the Baleur stream the German column moved over the N-23 in small groups in the region of the Delvenne farm. Karl Wortmann put the time of crossing later, at about 2200 hours. He said they then climbed the hill past Mont de Fosse and on to the heights of Bergeval where they once again ran into American troops. The column then split into two groups in order to negotiate the battle lines which separated the American paratroopers and Hansen's panzer-grenadiers. McCown again:

> I could tell then that Col Peiper was basing his direction of movement on the explosion of American artillery fire as the probable location of his friendly forces. His information as to the present front lines of both sides was as meagre as my own as he had no radio and no other outside contact. He continuously consulted his map, indicating that he was quite thoroughly lost. We continued moving from that time on continuously up and down the rugged hills, crossing small streams, pushing through thick undergrowth and staying off and away from roads and villages. At around 2200 Col Peiper, his Executive and his S-3 disappeared from the forward command group. I and my two guards were placed in charge of the regimental surgeon whose familiar Red Cross bundle on his back made it easy for me to walk behind.

The 'surgeon' was SS Captain Doctor Neumeier, the medical officer of Poetschke's 1st SS Panzer Battalion. McCown:

> I tried in vain to find out where Col Peiper went; one friendly enlisted man of Col Peiper's headquarters told me that Col Peiper was very tired, and I believe that he and a few selected members of his staff must have holed up in some isolated house for food and rest, to be sent for from the main body after they had located friendly forces. The change of command of the unit also wrought a change in method of handling the men. A young captain in charge of the leading company operated very close to me and my knowledge of Latin as well as the German I had picked up enabled me to understand to some degree practically every order he issued. I heard him tell my guards to shoot me if I showed the slightest intention of escaping, particularly when we neared Americans. Whereas Col Peiper had given a rest break every hour or so, there were no breaks given under the new command from that time until I escaped. The country we were now passing through was the most rugged we had yet encountered. All the officers were continuously exhorting the men to greater effort and to laugh at weakness. I was not carrying anything except my canteen,

which was empty, but I know from my own physical reaction how tired the men with heavy weapon loads must have been. I heard repeated again and again the warning that if any man fell behind the tail of the column he would be shot. I saw some men crawling on hands and knees. I saw others who were wounded but who were being supported by comrades up the steep slopes; there were fully two dozen wounded in the column, the majority of whom were going along quite well by themselves. There was one captain [author: although a lieutenant this was probably Benno Junker, the commander of the 6th SS Panzer Company] who was rather severely wounded, the colonel had told me, who moved along supported by another officer and a medical NCO and was still with the unit the last I saw of him. We approached very close to where artillery fire was landing and the point pushed into American lines three times and turned back. I believe the Germans had several killed in these attempts.

Serge Fontaine indicates that this action probably happened at a place known as St Jacques, 500m south-west of Bergeval on the road to Fosse. McCown:

Finally the commander decided to swing over the bridge and come down in the next valley and try to reach their lines. I was firmly convinced by this time that they did not know where they were on the map as there were continuous arguments from among the junior officers as they held their conferences. At around midnight the condition of the men was such that a halt would have to be given and warmth and food provided. I heard the captain say that he would attempt to locate a small village where the unit could hole up for the rest of the night. At approximately 0100 I believe I heard word come back that a small town was to the front which would suffice.

The 'small town' was Bergeval. According to Serge Fontaine[4] the Germans burst into the farm of Arthur Deroanne in Bergeval and forced him to guide them through Fosseuheid to Rochelinval. McCown continues:

At this time I was not forward near the point, my guards held me back near the position which was occupied by the covering force between the village and the west, that is to say, towards the American rear. The outpost had already moved into position before firing broke out not very far from where I was standing. My guards and I hit the ground, tracer bullets flashed all around us, and we could hear the machine gun bullets cutting the trees very close over us. The American unit which I later found out was a company, drove forward again to clear what it obviously thought was a stray patrol, this time using mortar fire as well.

This was Captain McPheeter's I Company 3/505; the *History of the Operations of the 505th Parachute Infantry Regiment* gives more details of the American withdrawal:

> Most units were able to do so [withdraw], but some of the 3rd Battalion, and I Company in particular, had to fight its way through. The main body of the company was able to get through without serious casualties, but the one platoon left at the river [Salm] as a rear guard was especially hard hit and lost over half its men before it could extricate itself.

McCown:

> The mortar fire fell all around on the German position. I do not know if my guards were injured or not; shrapnel cut the trees all around us. The American machine gun and rifle fire was very superior to that of the covering force. I could hear commands being shouted in both German and English with the latter predominating. There was considerable movement around me in the darkness. I lay still for some time waiting for one of my guards to give me a command. After some time I arose cautiously and began to move at right angles from the direction of the American attack watching carefully to my rear to see if anyone was covering or following me. After moving approximately 100 yards I turned and moved directly toward the direction from which the American attack had come. I can remember that I whistled some American tune but I have forgotten which one it was. I had not gone over 200 yards before I was challenged by an American outpost of the 82nd Airborne Division.

Gavin:

> Several hours before daylight one of the platoons on the Salm river, just north of Grand Halleux, was attacked from the rear by a German force of great strength – approximately 800 men. A heavy fight ensued. A number of Germans were killed and wounded, as well as a number of troopers of the Division. Among those rescued at this time was an American major of the US 30th Division.

The Salm river was in full flood and presented a serious final obstacle to the exhausted members of the Kampfgruppe. According to Wortmann they crossed using small fords and with the tallest soldiers standing up to their chests in the raging waters to assist the smaller and weaker members. The freezing temperatures meant that men standing in the river had to be replaced after less than a minute.

On Christmas Day the 770 survivors of Kampfgruppe Peiper reached the sanctuary of Wanne. Only thirty men had been lost on the way. They had covered roughly 20km in almost exactly thirty-six hours – half a kilometre an hour! The incredible survival rate of Peiper's officers had been maintained – as far as the author can establish, every officer under Peiper's command who crossed to the north bank of the Amblève survived to reach Wanne.

NOTES

1. *Annexe I to Part C of Intelligence Notes No 43 dated 6 Jan 1945*, HQ US Forces, European Theater.
2. Tiemann, *Die Leibstandarte IV/2*, pp. 150–4.
3. Hakin to author and Crocker in early 1980s.
4. Fontaine, *Trois Ponts Décembre 1944 Quand les Ponts Volaient en Eclats*, Nov 1992.

CHAPTER XXXVIII

25th December 1944 to 8th May 1945

Götterdämmerung

Major Hal McCown last saw Peiper as a serving member of the Waffen SS at about 2200 hours on Christmas Eve 1944. He was not to see him again until he appeared as a witness for the defence in the trial of Peiper and seventy-three others at Dachau in 1946. Recall that McCown said Peiper had left the column of La Gleize survivors in company with his 'Executive and S-3'. These two officers were almost certainly SS Captains Gerd Neuske and Hans Gruhle. Peiper was apparently very tired. Later, he and his companions must have followed the column and, after reaching Wanne on Christmas Day, he set up his own Headquarters at Petit Thier, 7km to the south-east (Map 6).

On 27th December the 1st SS Panzer Division was replaced on the Amblève and Salm river front by parts of the 18th and 62nd Volks-Grenadier Divisions[1] and ordered to the Lutrebois area near Bastogne to help seize that town and assist in the drive westwards. Hitler had by now changed the emphasis of his offensive from Dietrich's 6th Panzer Army – which had clearly failed to achieve its objective – to von Manteuffel's 5th.

Despite the heavy losses already incurred in over a week's fighting, the Leibstandarte still had plenty of combat potential. In order to get an accurate idea of its tank strength however, it is necessary to look carefully at the number of tanks definitely destroyed or abandoned and to delete from the casualty list any which, although damaged, may have been later repaired. The German recovery rate for damaged equipment was extremely high. The following tank casualties can be confirmed from photographs taken after the fighting:

Tiger IIs: two in Stavelot, four between Stavelot and Trois Ponts and six in or near La Gleize – total twelve.

Panthers: one in Ligneuville, one in Stavelot, one near Cheneux, three near Stoumont station, three in Stoumont and thirteen in La Gleize – total twenty-two.

Type IVs: one at Büllingen, six in La Gleize and one at Wanne – total eight.

There were undoubtedly others but these cannot be confirmed. This means that when the Division began its move south on 27th December to join in the fighting near Bastogne, it could have had a theoretical tank strength of sixteen Panthers and twenty-six Type IVs, plus thirty-three Tigers of the Corps 501st SS Heavy Panzer Battalion. The Leibstandarte history gives no firm tank figures but Manfred Thorn, a Type IV driver in the 7th SS Panzer Company, says his Company had only ten tanks. It would seem reasonable to assume therefore that the Division had a fighting strength of about fifteen Panthers and fifteen Type IVs – roughly two companies.

When the Leibstandarte entered battle on 30th December it was organised, according to Ralf Tiemann's official History,[2] into two Kampfgruppes – one, commanded by Werner Poetschke, consisting of all the Panthers and Type IVs and a scratch panzer-grenadier force made up from Hansen's 2nd SS Panzer-Grenadier Battalion and Sandig's 1st; and a second, mainly infantry, group commanded by Max Hansen, comprising the remainder of his own SS Panzer-Grenadiers, a reconnaissance platoon from Knittel's Battalion, a company of panzer pioneers and Karl Rettlinger's 1st SS Panzer Anti-Tank Battalion. The residue of the 1st SS Panzer Artillery Regiment was still under the command of SS Lieutenant Colonel Franz Steineck. There is no mention of von Westernhagen's 501st SS Heavy Panzer Battalion (Tiger IIs) but this is not surprising since it was a Corps, not Divisional, unit. According to Peiper thirteen Tiger IIs were operational in early January, with fourteen more under repair; but since he commanded neither the Tigers nor what was left of his own Regiment at this time these figures are unconfirmed. There is, however, no doubt that the 501st fought, and suffered casualties, in the Bastogne area during the period under discussion.

Peiper took no part in the battles around Bastogne and it is most significant that between 26th December 1944 and 6th February 1945, when a press release mentions him receiving 'Swords' to his Knight's Cross from Hitler on 4th February, there is no mention of Peiper anywhere, by anyone on the German side. Allegations were made at the

Dachau War Crimes trial that he gave an order to shoot a stray and exhausted American GI at Petit Thier on 10th January 1945 in the presence of SS Major Doctor Sickel and Hein von Westernhagen; however, this precise date stems only from Peiper's own confession and does not equate with the fact that by then the whole of the 1st SS Panzer Division had been fighting in the Bastogne area for two weeks. The soldier, Wichmann, who allegedly carried out the order to shoot the GI, testified that the incident happened 'near the end of 1944 or the beginning of 1945'. Mohnke would hardly have left behind his Panzer Regimental Commander, senior medical officer and the Commanding Officer of his Tiger Battalion when he moved off to fight at Bastogne and it is unlikely that Peiper would have remained at Petit Thier after his Division moved south. It is reasonable to assume therefore that he left there by 28th December at the latest.

Peiper does not appear again as an active commander until 14th February when, as a Standartenführer (SS Colonel), he turns up commanding the 'Panzer-Gruppe' of the Leibstandarte in Hungary.[3] Suggestions that Peiper was on the Leibstandarte Divisional staff between the end of December and mid-February are hardly credible since his name appears on no staff list and all senior appointments are shown being filled by other officers. Nor is it really credible that a leader of his known ability and experience would willingly leave his men to fight without him at Bastogne. On 30th January 1945, SS Major Doctor Kurt Sickel signed a document which still exists, showing that Peiper had suffered a 'commotio cerebri' in 1945, ie, during January 1945. Commotio cerebri is a medical term for concussion or, in bad cases, mental breakdown. It is the, unsubstantiated, view of the author that as a result of the strain of command between 16th and 24th December and particularly the trauma of the march out from La Gleize on the 24th and 25th, Peiper suffered a mental, and perhaps even physical, breakdown at the end of December. It seems likely that he was evacuated to Germany for convalescence during the missing period.

Whatever the truth about Peiper, the battered remnants of the Division fought, without success, in the Bastogne area until 12th January when they began their withdrawal to an area west of Köln.[4] Once more the Leibstandarte had been shattered beyond recognition and once more it would be rebuilt. By 15th February it had a new Commander, SS Major General Otto Kumm and was ready to play its part in Operation 'South Wind' in Hungary, an operation designed to break through the Russian armies to the Danube in the vicinity of Gran. Mohnke had returned to command the Führer's Chancellery Guard in Berlin. In the one month between Bastogne and Hungary the Leibstandarte was reinforced to a strength of over 19,000 men! Nevertheless it was a hundred officers and one thousand NCOs short, although overstrength in total numbers. And once more the 'boys' were together: in Peiper's Panzer-Gruppe SS Major Poetschke was commanding the twenty-five Panthers and twenty-one Type IVs of the 1st SS Panzer Battalion; SS Lieutenant Colonel von Westernhagen was commanding nineteen Tiger IIs; SS Major Diefenthal was still in command of his 3rd SS (Armoured) Panzer-Grenadier Battalion; and SS Captain Kalischko was commanding part of the Divisional Artillery Regiment. The Infanterie-Gruppe was commanded by SS Colonel Max Hansen and comprised the 1st and 2nd SS Panzer-Grenadier Regiments (less Diefenthal's Battalion), part of the Artillery Regiment, two batteries of Flak and SS Captain Holst's Jagdpanzer Company.[5]

The fighting in Hungary was as severe as ever and by 25th February Peiper's command had been reduced to four Tigers, eleven Panthers and twelve Type IV tanks.[6] The Panzer-Grenadiers had again suffered appalling casualties.

From 25th February to 13th March the Leibstandarte took part in yet another desperate operation known as the Plattensee Offensive. It failed when the expected frozen terrain turned into a sea of mud. Hitler refused all requests to halt the attack but it mattered little for on 15th March the Russians launched their final assault into Austria and Germany. In danger of being cut off Dietrich's 6th Panzer Army withdrew south-west along the shore of Lake Balaton. When Hitler heard of the withdrawal he flew into a rage and a message was sent to Dietrich's Headquarters which read: 'The Führer believes that the troops have not fought as the situation demanded and orders that the SS Divisions Adolf Hitler, Das Reich, Totenkopf and Hohenstaufen be stripped of their armbands.' Such was Dietrich's reward for nearly six years fighting and thousands of casualties. He was deeply shocked and refused to pass on the order, but it was soon common knowledge throughout the eastern front. For men like Peiper and the others in the front line divisions of the Waffen SS, the order was probably of little consequence. They had ceased long ago to concern themselves with madmen like Hitler, Himmler and Goebbels; as early as July 1944, after the attempt on the Führer's life, an officer in the Leibstandarte had written;

> Even without the attempted murder it was bad enough that we were being commanded from Rastenberg or from the Obersalzberg . . . our lack of understanding and inner rejection of everything we heard from 'up there' or 'back home' led us to accept only one last 'Heimat', one final homeland – that was our unit.[7]

The final battles were not being fought for Hitler or his 'thousand year Reich' – they were being fought to keep the Bolshevik hordes out of the Vaterland!

By the beginning of April the Leibstandarte, which had been tasked with covering the final withdrawal of Dietrich's 6th Panzer Army, was fighting near Wiener Neustadt, 40km south of Vienna. On 12th April the 2nd SS Panzer Battalion, which for a long time had been without tanks and acting as a reinforcement unit, converted to a combatant infantry role.[8] At about this time the depleted Division withdrew further west to an area 20km north of Mariazell.

Early on 8th May, after five years and eight months of fighting, the order came for all Leibstandarte units to destroy their vehicles and equipment and to march west into captivity! The demarcation line agreed between the Russians and Americans was the Enns river at Steyr. No arms could be carried over the line and anyone who was not across by midnight would be a prisoner of the Soviets. From the school at St Anton Peiper sent his last message on the evening of the 7th May: 'The dream of Empire is shattered – tonight . . . we face the last enemy!'[9] Most of the weapons and certainly the four remaining tanks of the old 7th SS Panzer Company ended up in the Enns river; SS Lieutenant Karl-Heinz Pulvermüller later described how they blew up the 105mm guns of the 4th Battery before they crossed.[10]

In the rush to reach the Americans the cohesion of the Leibstandarte began to break up; unit commanders were all trying to find separate ways of escape. SS Lieutenant Leidreiter of the 1st SS Reconnaissance Battalion told how, after crossing to the south of Steyr, they burnt their uniforms and made their way into the mountains.[11] The survivors of Max Hansen's Regiment were lucky to escape – they were twelve hours late when they reached the stone bridge at Losenstein and the Americans said they could not cross – 'with the help of a few tanks we crossed the bridge without firing!'[12]

Despite the problems and chaos of those last few hours, Dietrich's 'boys' mostly marched together into captivity; the amazing survival rate of the Leibstandarte officers had been maintained. Although many, like Diefenthal, had been seriously wounded, only von Westernhagen, Poetschke and Krause were missing from those who had formed Kampfgruppe Peiper on 16th December 1944; inevitably the panzer-grenadiers of Hansen and Sandig had suffered much more – ten of their officers were dead. This is hardly surprising though; in the shock tactics of quick and violent frontal assault, so favoured by the Waffen SS, the infantry were bound to suffer much more than the tank crews.

After crossing the Demarcation Line the Germans were surprised to be simply waved on to the west by the Americans. Some were able to disperse and Jochen Peiper headed for his home and family in Bavaria. He was arrested on 10th May by an American patrol only some 30km from Sigi and the children – his captors had no idea of what an important 'fish' they had caught!

On 10th May the mass of the 1st SS Panzer Division began its march into captivity and on the 12th the men were placed in a camp at Mauer-kirchen. Estimates put the number of Germans there as high as 300,000. Werner Sternebeck said that, despite the appalling conditions and short-age of food, there were no disciplinary problems since most Leibstan-darte units managed to stay together.

Starting on 20th May the Americans began separating the leaders from the men – the former being sent to a camp at Altheim which they nicknamed the 'Hunger Camp', and many of the men to a camp known as the 'Forest Camp', where there were some 2500 LAH and 2000 HJ soldiers. During June another move came, the worst one of all – to two former Concentration Camps at Ebensee,[13] where many of the original inmates were still present! Most of the Leibstandarte prisoners remained in these 'LAH camps' as they became known until mid-August.

On 21st August Peiper was singled out as a potential war criminal by the XV US Corps. On 22nd August he was brought to the 3rd US Army (General Patton) Intelligence Centre at Freising and on 24th August Major Edmund King, Chief of Section, signed a document showing that Peiper was suspected of: 'Development of aggressive policies and German aims in Germanizing all of Eastern Europe and a large part of Western Europe' and 'Killing of 150 US soldiers near Malmédy'. In the 'Comments and Recommendations' section King wrote: 'Peiper appears to lie continuously. He is very arrogant and tries to give the appearance of a correct professional soldier. He is a typical SS officer and cannot be trusted.'

In September Peiper was moved to the US Forces European Theatre Interrogation Centre at Oberursel. There, on 5th October, he was con-fronted with survivors of the Baugnez shootings but no formal interroga-tion took place. He said afterwards that the Americans seemed more interested in the behaviour of Major McCown and other US prisoners who had been in his hands than in anything he might have done! He was kept in solitary confinement for seven weeks before being transferred to a special annexe of the civilian internment camp at Zuffenhausen, near Ludwigsburg, for detailed questioning. Over a thousand members of the Leibstandarte were being held in the camp. Peiper alleged that whilst there he was kept in a 'nearly completely dark cellar' for five weeks and not allowed to wash or shave for three weeks. In December 1945 he was sent to the American interrogation centre at Schwabisch Hall and on 11th April 1946 his Prisoner of War status was removed and he was told that he was to be charged with war crimes.

NOTES

1. Tiemann, *Die Leibstandarte IV/2*, p. 162.
2. Ibid., p. 165.

3. Ibid., p. 233.
4. Ibid., p. 198.
5. Ibid., p. 233.
6. Ibid., p. 250.
7. Lehmann & Tiemann, *The Leibstandarte IV/1*, p. 286.
8. Tiemann op. cit., p. 373.
9. Ibid., p. 410.
10. Ibid., p. 447.
11. Ibid., p. 448.
12. Ibid., p. 415.
13. Ibid., p. 462.

CHAPTER XXXIX

The Trial and Prison[1]

On 14th, 15th and 16th January 1945 the Americans found the bodies of seventy-one of their soldiers in the area of the Baugnez crossroads south of Malmédy. In a final twist of fate it was a platoon of Dave Pergrin's C Company which uncovered the frozen and snow-covered bodies using mine detectors and shovels. They had lain there for a month! Shortly after the discovery the US War Department promised the American people that the perpetrators of 'this infamous crime' would be brought to justice. On 16th May 1946 seventy-one members of Kampfgruppe Peiper and three generals of the German 6th Panzer Army were arraigned before a US Military Court at Dachau, charged with war crimes. Both the number of defendants selected and the location of the trial were not without significance and it is no accident that in the same year that this book is being written, a German television documentary on the subject of the trial, or 'Der Malmédy Prozess' as it is known in Germany, has appeared titled 'The Law of the Victors'.

Many words have been written on the guilt or otherwise of Peiper and the other defendants for their actions in Belgium in 1944. It is not the intention of this author to go over all the details again, but rather to discuss the trial itself.

The General Military Government Trial at Dachau was held before a court of six American officers presided over by Brigadier General Josiah Dalbey. The officers were Colonels Berry, Watkins, Raymond, Steward, Conder and Rosenfeld, the latter being the legal advisor. The accused were SS General Sepp Dietrich, the Commander of the 6th Panzer Army in December 1944 and his Chief of Staff, SS Major General Fritz Kraemer, SS Major General Hermann Priess, Commander I SS Panzer Corps, and

Jochen Peiper with seventy men of his December 1944 Kampfgruppe. The charge was that these seventy-four defendants 'being together concerned as parties, did in conjunction with other persons not herein charged or named, at or in the vicinity of Malmédy, Honsfeld, Büllingen, Ligneuville, Stoumont, La Gleize, Cheneux, Petit Thier, Trois Ponts, Stavelot, Wanne and Lutrebois, all in Belgium, at sundry times between 16 December 1944 and 13 January 1945, willfully, deliberately and wrongfully permit, encourage, aid, abet and participate in the killing, shooting, ill-treatment, abuse and torture of members of the Armed Forces of the United States of America, then at war with the then Third Reich, who were then and there surrendered and unarmed prisoners of war in the custody of the then Third Reich, the exact names and numbers of such persons being unknown but aggregating several hundred, and unarmed allied civilian nationals the exact names and numbers of such persons being unknown.'

The Defence team, which included a number of German lawyers, had an appointed American Lieutenant Colonel named Willis Everett Jr as its Chief Defence Counsel.

The Prosecution, led by Lieutenant Colonel Burton Ellis, alleged that the accused were responsible between them for the deaths of at least 460 Americans and 106 Belgians, including the Americans at the Baugnez crossroads. One of the defendants, Marcel Boltz, was found to be an Alsatian and was handed over to French jurisdiction before the end of the trial – the French found the evidence against him was entirely circumstantial and set him free. Not so the others – on 16th July the Court, after considering each case for an average of less than three minutes, sentenced forty-three of the accused, including Peiper, Diefenthal, Sickel, Christ, Junker, Klingelhöfer, Preuss, Rumpf, Sievers, Sternebeck, Tomhardt and Hennecke to death by hanging, twenty-two including Dietrich and Coblenz to life imprisonment and the remainder to between ten and twenty years in prison. An example of the rushed and unprofessional way the sentencing was handled can be seen on the actual committal sheet, signed by Dalbey, which shows Peiper condemned to 'Death by Hanging' for the offence of 'Malmédy Massacre'. The following day the Germans were all removed to the fortress of Landsberg, where Hitler had been imprisoned in 1925 and had written *Mein Kampf*. Those sentenced to death were made to wear red track-suit tops – it seemed the survivability of Peiper and his officers was finally at an end.

Why has so much controversy surrounded the so-called 'Malmédy Trial'? Even the name 'Malmédy' is controversial. Of the seventy-four defendants arraigned before the Court less than a third had anything directly to do with the shootings at Baugnez – only twenty-two were accused of actual participation; eleven were brought to trial for allegedly giving instructions to subordinates not to take prisoners of war and were not accused of any active participation, and forty were charged with offences at places other than Baugnez.

There can be little doubt that the single most controversial aspect of the Dachau Trial was that in nearly every case the main evidence offered against the accused was a confession, backed up by corroborative extra-judicial statements made by one or more of the other defendants or by other members of Peiper's Kampfgruppe. This led inevitably to allega-tions that the Germans had been tortured into making these confessions and accusing one another of war crimes. Many prosecution witnesses were interviewed by the defence staff after they had testified on the witness stand and several were returned to the stand as defence wit-nesses. In each case they positively denied any truth in their original testimony and freely admitted perjury, giving as their reason that they had been victims of force, duress, beatings and other forms of torture. When Dietrich, Peiper and others, but by no means all, rescinded their extrajudicial statements, this added to the suspicion that torture had been used at Schwabisch Hall. Nor was the fact that nearly all the US interrogators at Schwabisch Hall were Jews of German origin lost on German observers of the Trial. One of the interrogators, Captain Raphael Schumacker, said later: 'If we wanted to get on, we first had to break down the comradeship.'

Peiper himself did not complain that his Schwabisch Hall statements were induced by physical pressure. In 1948, in a sworn statement, he said they had been made when he was in a state of intense mental depression brought on by what he thought had been the 'treason' of his brother officers. He was referring particularly to statements made by his former Adjutant, Hans Gruhle and friend Doctor Sickel. Referring to an interrogation he had undergone with a Lieutenant Perl in March 1946, Peiper said:

Perl told me that they didn't need the 'Crossroads' anymore as they had collected other prosecution material against me; countless single shootings had been ordered and sometimes personally executed by me. The Hillig case was especially strong [author's note: Hillig had said in an extrajudicial statement that at Stoumont on 19th December 1944 Peiper had ordered him to shoot an American POW] and they already had the confessions of Gruhle and Hillig. As I had no idea what they were talking about, Gruhle was called in. In a pre-fixed question and answer game between Perl and Gruhle the latter stated that I had ordered Hillig to shoot a prisoner of war. From this moment on everything was a matter of indifference to me. My confidence in our comradeship was broken and I felt only physical and mental dis-gust against my Adjutant, Mr Perl and the whole surrounding world. . . . At the next interrogation I was informed that Major Diefenthal had shot many prisoners in La Gleize. My reply was that I was of course, responsible for it, for I had given him adequate powers. This statement formed the basis of the Prosecution's case against Diefenthal.

According to Peiper's 1948 statement the reason that Gruhle testified as he did was because he had been shown a false confession allegedly signed by Peiper. The interrogating team's aim of 'breaking down the comradeship' had certainly been achieved!

The simple reason why the Prosecution resorted to this use of confessions and extrajudicial statements was that they had little else to offer as evidence. Not surprisingly there were no Belgians who could be found who were prepared to say they had seen a particular SS man commit a particular war crime; and an attempt to persuade a citizen of Büllingen to sign a sworn and dictated statement saying his wife had been killed by fire from German tanks ended in disaster when he deleted 'German tanks' and wrote 'American artillery'.[2]

Prosecution attempts to prove that orders had been issued before the offensive for the troops not to take prisoners were far from convincing – it was well known that Peiper's Kampfgruppe had sent scores of American prisoners to the rear during the early part of its advance.

Of the forty-two survivors of the surrendered Americans who were present in the field at Baugnez when, for whatever reason, the Germans had opened fire on them, only five were called to testify – Lary, Daub, Ahrens, Dobyns and Ford. Only Lieutenant Virgil Lary claimed to be able to identify any of the accused. He picked out a tank crewman in the 7th SS Panzer Company named Fleps, as the man who first fired on the Americans. This gave rise to further complaints that Lary could not possibly have recognised someone he had seen for just a few seconds, nearly eighteen months before and who would have been unshaven and huddled up against the cold in a tank turret at the time. The suspicion was that Lary had been told that Fleps, who like all the other defendants wore a large identifying number round his neck in the Courtroom, had already confessed to firing the first shot.

A major witness for the defence was Hal McCown who testified that Peiper and his men treated the American POWs in La Gleize quite reasonably considering the circumstances. The Prosecution tried hard to discredit McCown and in the event his evidence had no positive effect on the Court. Testifying on behalf of Waffen SS men in 1946 was hardly likely to enhance a military career and McCown was perhaps fortunate to end up as a major general in the 1970s.

Like many others Willis Everett, the Chief Defence Counsel, was convinced there had been a miscarriage of justice at Dachau and on 28th December 1946 he filed a petition for the case to be reviewed; he followed this with an application for a stay in the execution of the death sentences until he had been given an opportunity to apply to the US Supreme Court for a writ of Habeas Corpus. On 22nd January 1947 the *New York Herald Tribune* published accounts of pre-trial brutalities inflicted on the defendants and in the same month the US Commander-in-Chief in West Germany, General Lucius Clay, ordered an indefinite stay of execution of all death sentences because of the number of petitions before the US Supreme Court.

In May 1948 Everett applied for leave to file a writ of Habeas Corpus in the US Supreme Court against President Harry Truman; the Secretary of the Army, Kenneth Royall; the Chief of Staff of the Army, General Omar Bradley; and Thomas Clark, the Attorney General of the United States of America. In it he set out the reasons why, in his view, the Malmédy Trial was 'utterly void'. The same reasons are used today in Germany to discredit the Prosecution's case and to claim that none of the defendants should have been found guilty of war crimes. Everett stated that:

1. No defense was possible due to the short period of time, less than two weeks, to prepare the defense of the 74 accused, and
2. the unfamiliar and arduous task of communicating through inexperienced interpreters as well as a lack of assigned stenographers and interpreters so hampered the Defense Staff that it was not even physically possible to interrogate all of the accused, much less plan a defense, prior to the forced commencement of the trial, and
3. the entire plan of this forced trial was calculated to make the whole defense impossible by not allowing time to procure and interview witnesses.

As part of his case Everett accused the American Prosecution Team in Schwabisch Hall of depriving the plaintiffs of food for days, withdrawing their blankets in the middle of winter, giving them severe and frequent beatings and other corporal punishments, forcing them into the 'death cell' for days and weeks, threatening their families with violence, taking them to a 'death chamber' where they were shown bullet holes in the wall where human flesh and hair were embedded and taking them to the 'hangman's room' where they were placed on a high stool and had a rope placed round their necks. Everett went on to allege that all these actions were designed to force confessions and signatures on other prosecution-dictated statements. One of his most serious accusations was that plaintiffs were taken hooded into a completely dark cell which was their 'trial room'. The hood was then removed and the plaintiff would see before him a long table, draped with black cloth touching the floor, with candles burning at both ends of the table and a crucifix in the center. Sitting behind this table were varying numbers of American civilians, members of the Prosecution Team, who were illegally wearing the uniform and rank of US Army Officers. A mock defense council, usually an officer of the US Army on the Prosecution Team, was furnished for these youthful German soldiers, who, although he was not an Attorney, held himself out to the plaintiffs as their defense council. They were informed or led to believe that they were being tried by the Americans for violations of International Law. At the other end of the table would be the Prosecutor who would read the charges, yell and scream and attempt to force confessions from them. If this method of threats failed to force desired false confessions from the plaintiffs the mock trials would proceed by bringing in one false witness after another against them . . . upon conclusion, these sham courts would render death penalties within 24 to 48 hours by hanging.

Everett pointed out that all seventy-four defendants had signed a prosecution-dictated statement.

The application for leave to file the writ of Habeas Corpus before the Supreme Court was turned down.

In many ways it would have been surprising if Peiper and his men had been treated strictly in accordance with either Army or judicial regulations in 1945 and 1946 – it was the time when the world became aware of concentration camps and the worst excesses of Nazi Germany. If someone was known to have been a member of the SS, Waffen or otherwise, he was considered by most people to be guilty of crimes against humanity and deserving of punishment; and so it was with Hitler's Life Guards – the surviving members of the Leibstandarte had been tried and found guilty in the minds of most of the World War II victors long before they appeared at Dachau!

There can be little doubt that today most of the evidence presented at the Dachau Trial would be rejected by any court, civilian or military, in any democratic country. No attempt was made to establish any individual guilt but rather to prove that Hitler, his generals, the Waffen SS, and Peiper and his men in particular, had set out to achieve their military aims by deliberately murdering American soldiers and Belgian civilians. Since the American people had been promised that someone would be made to pay for the seventy-one dead at the Baugnez crossroads, objectivity gave way to prosecution at any price, and justice itself became the victim. John Toland, in his book *Battle*, put it succinctly when he wrote in 1959:

Because of poor preparation, shocking irregularities and impassioned pleas for vengeance rather than facts, the Malmédy Trial pleased no one. Many of the documented atrocities went unpunished; men innocent of atrocities were thrown into prison. . . . Enemies of the United States continue to point out that Malmédy is a good example of American justice.

In all fairness though, it has to be said that had the roles been reversed the accused would probably never have reached a courtroom!

After a series of reviews, hearings and commissions, including an investigation by a United States Senate Sub-Committee with which the infamous Senator Joseph McCarthy became involved, the death sentences handed down at Dachau were gradually commuted and all the prisoners eventually released. With the advent of the Cold War and a resulting fear of Soviet intentions, the climate of hatred against the Germans soon changed. By 1948 thirty-one of the death sentences had been reduced to life imprisonment and on 30th January 1951 the last five death sentences, including Peiper's, were commuted. In May 1954 Peiper's life sentence was reduced to thirty-five years.

His imprisonment was not without incident – one of the more bizarre episodes was an attempt by his former comrades to break him out of Landsberg – at least according to the American authorities. On 12th April 1948 the US 970th Counter Intelligence Corps Detachment in Stuttgart issued a secret report, signed by 'Special Agent CIC' Garry A. Bahrich, of 'a plan to free, by force or trickery the SS Officer Joachim Peiper'. Intelligence activity indicated that the plan was 'being worked out by a circle of former friends of the subject in Munich who are in contact with the subject's wife there.' Information was allegedly later received which revealed that the plan called for five Germans, pretending to be members of a War Crimes Commission, to enter Landsberg before 30th May and ask to interrogate Peiper. As soon as they reached him they were to overpower his guards and force their way out of the prison. The American authorities took the threat seriously enough to alert and arm all American personnel at the prison, secretly position a soldier with a machine gun in a sealed area near the main gate, surreptitiously increase the Polish guard details and forbid entry to anyone who had not been personally identified. In the event no attempt to free Peiper was ever made.

Dietrich was released from Landsberg in October 1955 and the last person to be let out on parole, on 22nd December 1956, was Jochen Peiper. He had spent nearly five years in solitary confinement, wearing the red track suit top, and a total of eleven and a half years as a prisoner. But for some people this was not enough; they felt he had got away with murder. And at the end of the day, many people in three countries

– America, Belgium and Germany – were left with a feeling that justice had not been served. Certainly many innocent people had died and suffered as a result of the events of December 1944 in the Ardennes.

NOTES

1. All documents quoted or referred to in relation to the Dachau Trial are held in the US National Archives and Records Administration in Maryland, USA.
2. Anton Jonsten 26 Jun 1946.

CHAPTER XL

After Prison

Peiper was paroled on 22nd December 1956 on the order of the United States Commander-in-Chief in West Germany, General H. I. Hodes.[1] His parole was to last until 21st May 1980 and he was restricted to the Stuttgart area. He was required to report to his US Parole Officer on the 1st and 15th of each month. Sigi and the children had remained in Rottach am Tegernsee whilst Peiper was in Landsberg but in November 1955 she moved to Sinsheim in Baden-Württemberg to be closer. Until she could move again to join him in Stuttgart, Peiper was only allowed to visit his family at weekends and holidays and then by the most direct route.[2]

Whilst he was in Landsberg Peiper had obtained an interpreter's diploma in English and had worked in the prison garden, the motor pool and done some book binding; at one stage he was placed in charge of the occupational courses being run by the prison authorities. But in real terms, apart from his knowledge of English, Peiper had no qualifications for civilian employment when he was released. His parole supervisor was a Doctor Theodor Knapp and his sponsor was Alfred de Maight, the Personnel Chief of the Porsche Motor Company – at least he had one useful contact! His first post-war home was as a tenant of a Doctor Hartmann in Klagenfurtstrasse 4, Stuttgart.

Peiper was a bitter and disillusioned man in 1956. He had witnessed not only the collapse of his whole world, the Third Reich, but in particular of the 'family' to which he had given his life, the Leibstandarte. The motto of the LAH had been 'My Honour is my Loyalty' and yet this loyalty, which had sustained him and his comrades through nearly six years of fighting, had finally collapsed at Schwabisch Hall; and to add insult to injury, as a former member of the Waffen SS, he was not entitled to a state war pension.

In the early days of his new-found freedom Peiper did not seek, nor was he offered, any help from his former comrades. The conditions of his parole banned him from making contact with any of his co-defendants at Dachau or with an organisation called HIAG (Waffen SS Self-Help Organisation) which had been set up in 1954 with the aim of helping former Waffen SS soldiers. His parole sponsor, de Maight, got him his first job[3] as a clerk in the Vehicle Assembly and Construction Office at the Porsche Motor Company in Zuffenhausen.

On 21st June 1958 Peiper was finally released from parole and by 1961 his obvious talents were recognised when Ferry Porsche, the head of the company, appointed him Company Secretary, the first non-member of the Porsche/Piech family to be selected for the appointment. This proposed promotion brought Peiper to the attention of the union, IG Metall. Ferry Porsche was told that, whilst the union could tolerate a war criminal as a clerk, it could not accept Peiper as part of the management. Porsche had little choice but to cancel Peiper's appointment. Rather surprisingly perhaps, Peiper threatened to sue the company but eventually settled for six months' salary as compensation. IG Metall made it quite plain that Peiper would be similarly hounded in other motor companies, so he moved to Reutlingen where he set up as an independent sales promotor for a Volkswagen dealer, training salesmen. He continued this type of work in Offenburg and later in Freiburg. By April 1967 he was back in Stuttgart at Schnellbachstrasse 32. He explained his feelings at that time in an interview with a French writer:

I was a Nazi and I remain one. . . . The Germany of today is no longer a great nation, it has become a province of Europe. That is why, at the first opportunity, I shall settle elsewhere, in France no doubt. I don't particularly care for Frenchmen, but I love France. Of all things, the materialism of my compatriots causes me pain.

On 11th December 1968 the Italian authorities and nine plaintiffs from Boves in Northern Italy accused Peiper and two of his former officers in the Stuttgart court with murder.[4] The accusations stemmed from the incident in 1943 described in Chapter I. After receiving depositions from seventeen Italians and 126 former members of Peiper's SS Panzer-Grenadier Battalion of that time, the court ruled, in February 1969, that there was insufficient evidence for formal charges to be laid.

As well as maintaining his training functions with various VW dealers, Peiper accepted, in 1969, a position as a liaison officer between the publisher/owner and Editor-in-Chief of *Auto, Motor and Sport*. The Editor was by then his closest friend. It was in this same year that Peiper bought a small plot of land in France – at Traves in the Hautes Saône. He had first heard about the area when on holiday in St Tropez in 1962. A German friend, Herr Moritz, who had been stationed there during the war, had told him of its advantages – peace and tranquillity, beautiful countryside, relatively inexpensive properties and close to Germany.

During the winter of 1970/71 Peiper's editor friend died. The reason for his employment had disappeared and he was released from his appointment in 1972. Deprived of a good salary, Peiper could no longer afford to live in Stuttgart and so he and Sigi moved permanently to their chalet-styled house which had been built by the river Sâone in Traves. The French authorities, who had full knowledge of his identity and background, granted him a residence permit on 27th April 1972 which was initially valid until 27th February 1977.

The Peipers were not well off but their children were grown up and had left home and they could live quite well, if quietly, at 'Le Renfort' (The Reinforcement!) alongside the other 280 inhabitants of Traves. The house was some 1,000m from the centre of the village and their nearest neighbour was about 250m further to the west – he was a former Leibstandarte artillery captain named Erwin Ketelhut; he had joined the LAH in 1936, been captured by the Americans in January 1945 and released in 1947. 'Le Renfort' was built on a high bank above the river Saône and lay well back from the country road leading into the village. It was a modest three-bedroomed house, with a living room, library/study and kitchen, and with a terrace at one end and verandah at the other. Trees gave it seclusion and a barbed wire fence separated Peiper's land from a meadow which lay between it and the village road. At this time his son, Hinrich, was a solicitor in Frankfurt, daughter Elke a professor in Munich, and youngest daughter, Silke, lived in Hamburg.

In order to improve his standard of living Peiper undertook translation work with a publication called *Motor Buch Verlag*; he used the pen-name 'Reiner Buschmann'. Most of his work was on military and historical books such as *Arms of the Soviet Army* and *Frederick the Great*. This work, together with a small income from his advisory contract with the VW dealers in Offenburg and Freiburg, allowed Peiper and his wife to live a reasonably comfortable life with their two Drathaar dogs, Tim and Tam. They used to return to Germany about once a month in their BMW car for important shopping, dental appointments and so on. In a letter written in 1989, Peiper's son, who was then living in New York, told the author that his father had enjoyed being master of his own time and had loved 'Le Renfort', France and the French way of life. His mother and father had not mixed very much with the people of Traves since they had little in common, but the contacts they did have were always friendly.

What of Peiper's other comrades? The Waffen SS has been described as 'the most punished Army in history'. Certainly few of its members had an easy time after the war. Sepp Dietrich was paroled in October 1955, tried before a German court in 1957 for his part in the 'Night of the Long Knives' and sentenced to eighteen months in prison. He died in April 1966 and was given a hero's funeral by his 'boys' in Ludwigsberg. Wilhelm Mohnke is still alive, living in Barsbüttel, near Hamburg, and being hounded by the western media as this book is being written. After his release by the Russians in 1955, he worked as a dealer in small trucks and trailers. According to the British Public Record Office, the German Federal Prosecutor has invesigated allegations against him in connection with the deaths of American and Canadian soldiers as well as British, but he has concluded that there is insufficient evidence to bring charges in any of the alleged cases. The British who survived Wormhoudt, Canadians who survived Fontenay-le-Pesnel and Americans who survived Baugnez would not agree.

Hans Gruhle and Werner Sternebeck both died in 1990. The latter had rather surprisingly reached the rank of lieutenant colonel in the Bundeswehr (West German Army) before he retired. His daughter, Sigrid, claimed that the shock of discovering that her father had been in the Waffen SS caused her to become a Red Army Faction terrorist and to play a part in killing a German politician with a car bomb.

Doctor Kurt Sickel was living in Köln in 1990 and still refusing to discuss Peiper's whereabouts in those 'missing' six weeks in early 1945; Jupp Diefenthal returned to his hometown of Euskirchen after release from Landsberg and worked in the local finance office – his wife refuses to let anyone interview him and he has no contact with his former comrades. Georg Preuss died destitute and as a recluse near Lüneberg Heath in 1990, without family, friends, electricity or even running water, and Max Hansen, after running a cleaning shop with his wife in Niebuell, spent his last three or four years as little more than a living corpse – 'his brain and soul already being in Valhalla' as a comrade put it.

Of the Americans, Wallis Anderson and Dave Pergrin both worked for the Pennsylvania Railroad after the war. Since neither had graduated through West Point they were no longer needed in a peacetime US Army and were assigned to the Corps of Engineers Reserve. Wallis Anderson was promoted to Brigadier General and Dave Pergrin to Colonel; Dave lives happily in retirement in Wallingford, Pennsylvania. He worked his way up in the Boy Scouts to District Chairman and is a Master Woodcarver. He and his wife, Peggy, looked after Anderson's widow, 'Aunt Marietta' as she was known to her friends who included Eisenhower's grandson David, until the day she died in 1989 – they were having dinner together in a restaurant at the time. One of the saddest cases is that of Carl Daub, a survivor of the 'Malmédy Massacre', who in 1988, after a mental breakdown, killed his wife with a hammer and attempted to kill his son – he is still being sought by the police. Another deeply affected survivor, Jimmy Mattera, insists he heard someone shout 'Machen alle kaputt' before the shooting started. Virgil Lary died of cancer in 1981 – in one of his last letters he told a friend that he had really died in 1944 in the field at Baugnez. Captain Charles Mitchell of A Company 526th Armored Infantry became a doctor and Lieutenant David Knox of L Company 3/119 Infantry, who had been awarded two Silver and two Bronze Stars during his service in Europe, died in November 1993 after a career in real estate. Hal McCown of the 119th and Robert Frankland of the 117th Infantry both became major generals and William K. Harrison a lieutenant general.

Many Leibstandarte veterans never attended the 1st SS Panzer Corps reunions at Nassau on the river Lahn – the letters 'SS' were, of course, left out and, at least up to 1994, never appeared on memorials. Many found the memories and postwar condemnation by their fellow countrymen too painful. But there are still smaller 'get-togethers', or 'treffs' as they are known, and on more than one occasion a dozen or so of Dietrich's former 'boys' have retraced their December 1944 steps through the Ardennes. They do it quietly for obvious reasons. So of course have the Americans, but in much larger and rather noisier groups! Their memories have dimmed a little and they often fail to recognise many of the places in which they fought – usually because their Tour operators have whisked them across Europe from Normandy to the Danube in just a few days and they are physically and mentally exhausted by it all – just as many of them were in 1944.

But what of Jochen Peiper – the last 'Gefallene' (casualty) of the Leibstandarte, as the comrades still call him? He probably intended to live out his remaining years quietly at 'Le Renfort', but as someone who had 'lived by the sword' for much of his life it was unlikely that he would be left in peace for long – and this was indeed the case.

NOTES

1. Signed by Major Daniel W. Stubbs, Prison Director of Landsberg/Lech Prison on 22 Dec 1956 on behalf of C-in-C.
2. Parole Plan signed by Paul J. Gernert, US Parole Officer.
3. Most of the details of Peiper's life after release from prison were provided by his son Hinrich Peiper, in a letter to the author dated 26 Apr 1989, and by Dr Arndt Fischer, one of Peiper's wartime Adjutants and his dentist at the time of Peiper's death.
4. Lehmann, *The Leibstandarte III*, p. 293.

CHAPTER XLI
Murder[1]

Peiper and his wife did most of their important shopping back in Germany during their monthly visits from Traves. Anything of a minor nature and food was usually bought in the nearest local town – Vesoul. And it was in Vesoul, when Peiper was buying some fencing wire, that someone took more than passing interest in him, as a person of obvious 'Teutonic' character. Peiper was positively identified from details and photographs provided to the French Communist Party by the East German Authorities.

On 21st June 1976 Peiper's peaceful life in Traves was shattered when leaflets were distributed throughout the village which said 'People of Traves, a war criminal, SS Peiper is amongst us!' They went on to call for his expulsion from France. The following day the national daily newspaper *l'Humanité* printed an article along the same lines and within a few days most of the French, and even some international, newspapers joined in the witch-hunt. Walls in Traves and even roads in the area were daubed with swastikas, SS runes and Peiper's name. It was a carefully orchestrated hate campaign. He reported the situation to the French police in Vesoul and they agreed to provide a guard, but in the daytime only. The German Embassy in Paris could offer little other than sympathy and advised him to go away, at least temporarily. Peiper seems to have had some sort of premonition that he was about to fight his last battle. On 22nd June he wrote a letter to his wife which, for obvious reasons, he did not give to her and she would not read until after his death. It read:

My Sigi,
Since the shades of the past are now behind me it looks as though I shall undertake the great adventure – against the stupidity of the repressed masses no living thing can cope. I'd like to thank you once again for everything. You were a great comrade for life and I only regret that I did not provide you with a more carefree existence.

My last thoughts will therefore be about your security, safety and peace of mind. The first of these comes from insurances and pensions and the last I hope you will find in the area of greater Munich.

I think that to sell Traves would be wrong and it would be better to lease it. The children ought to pay for the very small maintenance costs and occasionally see that everything is in order. In good days

264

this particular piece of prime natural land can be a connecting link between us and in bad times a haven, despite all the present harrassments. I would also consider it very important that later on you would not just leave Traves to our three children but leave a part of it to Bettina Wieselmann [Peiper's ward]. She has understood me more than our distinguished children – she is more devoted to Traves than they are.

And then my dogs – they only had a few years but they were good years and I wish them to have a good and completely unexpected leap into the eternal hunting groud, where I hope to find them.

My burial, cremation, or whatever I have, I wish you to carry out without publicity, family taking part or any of my comrades being there, and at least cost.

A final embrace from me and I hope you will still enjoy a few carefree and healthy years in beautiful Bavaria – please remember only the wonderful hours of our life together.

Jo.

By the beginning of July Peiper had become an embarrassment to the French authorities; Giscard d'Estaing, a conservative Independent Republican with an autocratic personal style, was President, and communists and other Government opponents were delighted to be able to claim that a known Nazi war criminal was being given sanctuary and protection in France. Peiper realised his residence permit would probably not be renewed. On 9th July he wrote to his dentist and friend, and former Adjutant in the Leibstandarte, Arndt Fischer – the same Fischer whose Panther tank had been knocked out in Ligneuville on 17th December 1944. In the letter Peiper said he was planning to lease the Traves house and move to a 'green' area like greater Munich; Sigurd would come and look for a property in the autumn. He outlined the current situation and said that although he would like to discuss matters with Fischer, this was impossible as he had to 'hold this position'.

On 13th July Peiper received letters and telephone calls telling him that his house and dogs would be burned. Sigurd left the same day in the BMW. It is not clear exactly where she went. Arndt Fischer told the author in 1991 that the previous May she had arranged to visit an old friend in Strasbourg in July and that Peiper had encouraged her to keep the appointment. This may well be true or she may possibly have gone to her son in Frankfurt – they appeared together in Vesoul the day after Peiper's body was taken there.

After his wife left Peiper wrote to an old friend, Doctor Ernst Klink, in Waldkirch near Freiburg. Klink was a former Waffen SS officer and after the war worked in the Federal Military Archives in Freiburg! In his letter Peiper said that, owing to 'uncertainties in Franco-German relations', he had stopped writing his book and was therefore sending him (Klink) the existing material. He went on to say that if a Miss Bettina Wieselmann came to see him he should give her every assistance.

Erwin Ketelhut, Peiper's nearest neighbour, had arrived in Traves in 1971 and had restored a mill on the river, turning it into what Peiper's wife described as a most beautiful home. He and Peiper were not on especially friendly terms but after the threats began he loaned Peiper a Remington 12-bore shotgun. The only weapons Peiper himself possessed were an old Colt calibre ·38 revolver and ·22 rifle.

On 13th July, after Peiper's wife left, he and Ketelhut discussed the situation and although Peiper said he was not worried because he did not believe the people making the threats were particularly courageous, he agreed to Ketelhut keeping an eye on the area from his balcony. Ketelhut equipped himself with binoculars and two loaded rifles! He told the French police the following day that, at about 2330 hours, having heard and seen nothing suspicious, he took a weak sleeping pill and went to bed. At about 0100 hours on 14th July, Bastille Day, Ketelhut was woken by the sound of the village siren and saw flames coming from Peiper's house.

The Police Judiciaire of Dijon investigated the fire at Peiper's house. The principal Police Commissioner was Monsieur Guichaux and the principal Inspector was named Casseboix. Their report stated that the fire began in Peiper's house sometime in the early hours of 14th July; the fire had started at the back of the house, nearest the road, and the barbed wire fencing between the garden and the meadow had been cut with wire-cutters. When the local fire brigade had been called out their pump was found to be unserviceable; eleven firemen were questioned by the police but the pump was found to be genuinely defective and there were no traces of sabotage.

The police found a badly burned body in the remains of the library/study of Peiper's house. Due to the fire it had shrunk to a length of about 60 centimetres and was barely recognisable as that of a human being. Under the body they found a ·22 calibre rifle, damaged by fire and with an expended case in the chamber. Near the body they found a Colt ·38 revolver with five expended rounds in the cylinder. On the terrace the police found a Remington 12 bore shotgun with an open, empty breech, but with a strong smell of powder. On the ground below the terrace three expended 12 bore shotgun cartridges from the Remington were discovered.

Peiper's two dogs had both been wounded by 6·35mm bullets. Four of these very small bullets were found in the kennel which contained blood stains. (A 6·35mm pistol is a very small weapon indeed, sometimes carried by ladies for self protection.)

An examination of the garden revealed traces of shot at a distance of about 10m from the house, in an oak tree; and at about 10m from the verandah, between a pine tree and the kennel, they found a ·38 bullet.

It further appeared that the victim had tried to save some clothes and papers from the fire. Below the terrace there were some clothes belonging to Frau Peiper and on the verandah there were some personal papers, including Peiper's last letter to his wife.

Thirteen unexpended ·38 rounds were found in the library/study. Peiper's watch, which was found on the body, had stopped at 0100 hours and a clock in the house at 0107 hours.

Two experts in arson, one from Lyon and the other from Marseille, investigated 'Le Renfort' on 15th July. They found three different sources of the fire. The remains of three Molotov cocktails were found in the library/study and one poorly made one outside the house. The fire had apparently taken hold very quickly. All the doors and windows had been closed except for one in Peiper's bedroom and another in the kitchen.

From the projected trajectories of the various weapons fired, and other evidence, the police concluded that the victim had attempted to dissuade his attackers from fire bombing his house by firing all three weapons at them, first from a standing and later from a prone position. There was no evidence of any weapons being fired towards the house, other than the tiny bullets found in the kennel, and therefore no evidence of any direct attempt to kill the victim.

At 0500 hours on the 14th Ketelhut was shown the victim's body and said: 'It is him (Peiper) but he is miniaturised.' The body was then moved to Vesoul. Sigurd and Hinrich Peiper were unable to recognise it before a post mortem was carried out by two French medical examiners on the 15th. The jaw bone was removed for further examination. The French police then made enquiries with the various doctors and dentists who had attended Peiper after his release from Landsberg. The dentists included a Dr Schwartz in Vaihingen, who had attended Peiper between 1964 and 1966, Dr Riede of the same town, who was Peiper's dentist from 1969 to 1972 and Dr Arndt Fischer of Munich who looked after him after he moved to France. He had last seen Peiper on 15th March 1976 and had taken his last X-ray on 19th February 1975. All three provided their records to the French authorities. When the Americans were asked for Peiper's medical records from Landsberg, they replied that these were held in the Washington Archives. For some strange reason the French did not demand that they be sent to France.

After considering the dental records, two French experts declared: 'We conclude without a doubt that the X-rays of the jaw bone and teeth from previous dentists' files are similar to the anatomical piece sent for investigation.'

On 26th July Sigurd Peiper wrote to Ketelhut to thank him for recovering some of their personal effects from the French police and to ask him to look after their boat which was still moored on the river. She mentioned that she and her son were planning to come to Traves in the autumn.

On 19th January 1977 a panel of eight French experts, including a senior policeman, two professors of medicine and three doctors, published a statement concerning the Traves body. They said that in their opinion death had been due to asphyxia but it was possible that this was not the only cause of death. They had no reason to think that the corpse was not that of Peiper. They concluded: 'In consequence the corpse found in the rubbish is certainly the one of Peiper.' Needless to say Sigurd wanted her husband buried in Germany; but, before a German burial certificate for the body found in 'Le Renfort' could be issued, a further autopsy was necessary. Arndt Fischer told the author in June 1991[2] that when the body arrived from France the head was missing. It appeared later but had been sliced up and the only tooth still present was split. The German autopsy was performed by Professor Spann of the Institute for Rechtsmedizin of the University of Munich and Peiper's body was finally laid to rest at Schondorf am Ammersee in Bavaria with those of his mother, father and two brothers. One of the myths which persisted in Germany for many years was that the 'authorities' had refused to release Peiper's body to the family for burial. This story was even repeated in a television documentary programme in the early 1990s. Sigurd Peiper died in Munich on 10th April 1979 and was buried with the rest of the Peiper family.

The police files in the Peiper case are still held in Dijon and have been seen by the author; there are four of them and they are each four inches thick. Follow-up investigations included ballistic tests, house searches of suspects and dozens of interrogations. They all proved fruitless.

Amazing scenes had followed the events of 14th July 1976. Right-wing hooligans in France attacked various Communist Party offices and in Germany a campaign started to have an 'Oberst Peiper Denkmal' (Memorial) erected at, of all places, Dachau. Hinrich Peiper did not support the campaign but tried to persuade various German politicians to have his father's reputation cleared of all ignominy. He failed.

Due to the lack of irrefutable evidence that the body found in the ruins of 'Le Renfort' was definitely that of Peiper, it was inevitable that rumours would soon begin to circulate, particularly in Belgium, that he was still alive and probably living in South America! Odessa, it was said, had spirited him away and murdered some poor person of the correct height, build and colouring to put in the Traves house before it was burned. Much was made of the statement in the police report that a tracker dog had sniffed a trail which ended at the road 50m from Ketelhut's house after crossing two meadows. These theories, which are still current, ignore the fact that such complicated and dangerous actions were totally unnecessary – if Peiper had wanted to start a new life in 1976 on another continent all he had to do was buy a ticket and catch an aeroplane. No, it is much more likely that Jochen Peiper did die in similar circumstances to those in which he found himself so many times in the war – in a 'cauldron', surrounded by enemies. This time, though, there was to be no escape, no 'Long march'. But as he probably saw it, there was one consolation – to paraphrase one of his own expressions – the real outfit was waiting for him in Valhalla!

It is perhaps ironic that on the 18th anniversary of Peiper's murder in France, German soldiers paraded through Paris for the first time since World War II – precisely 52 years previously he had done the same.

NOTES

1. This chapter is based on information set out in the French Police files relating to Peiper's death. They are held in the Police Judiciaire in Dijon.
2. Letter from Fischer to the author dated 27 Jun 1991.

Epilogue

Hitler's last great offensive in the West in general and the attack of I SS Panzer Corps through the Ardennes in December 1944 in particular, beg the same question – did either of them ever have any real chance of success?

It is not the intention of this author to try to answer the first, strategic, question. It would merely entail a repetition of the many theories and theses previously presented in the numerous books written on 'The Battle of the Bulge'. The only thing which is perhaps worth pointing out is that whilst it was, as von Manteuffel called it after the war, a 'brilliant' concept, it surely lacked the necessary logistic backing to make it a realistic proposition at that stage of World War II.

At the tactical level the same logistic weaknesses pertained, but these did not preclude the chance that at least some German forces would reach the Meuse river by D + 3. Given the complete surprise achieved and the strength of the attacking forces, particularly in armour, all that was needed was a bit of luck. Unfortunately for the Germans that element was missing.

The reasons why none of the I SS Panzer Corps Kampfgruppes got anywhere near the Meuse were numerous and cumulative. And only the Leibstandarte KGs will be considered in detail, since the KGs of the 12th SS Panzer Division Hitlerjugend never really got started. In the case of Hitlerjugend, it has to be said that the stubborn and brave resistance put up by the 99th and 1st US Infantry Divisions and the various defenders of Malmédy, was clearly the reason why the German onslaught failed in this important northern area.

But why did the KGs of the Leibstandarte also fail? The following reasons can be deduced:

1. The refusal by Hitler to allow the tank-heavy forces of the 6th Panzer Army to attack further south where the road network was more favourable. This also applies of course to Hitlerjugend.
2. The refusal of 6th Panzer Army to allow I SS Panzer Corps to lead their break-in attack with armour.
3. The initial twelve-hour delay in launching both KGs Peiper and Hansen due to pedantic infantry attacks and the failure to cope quickly with forgotten minefields. This could also be called a failure of intelligence.
4. Peiper's, albeit understandable, decision not to attack Stavelot on the evening of the 17th.

271

5. The decision to halt KG Hansen on 18th December and relieve him with the 9th SS Panzer Division so that he could reinforce KG Peiper.
6. Peiper's decision to use a quarter of his tank force to move on Trois Ponts via Wanne on 18th December.
7. The demolition of the Trois Ponts and Neufmoulin bridges by American engineers on 18th December.
8. The critical delay caused by the air attacks on KG Peiper on the afternoon of 18th December.
9. The failure of 1st SS Panzer Division to resupply Peiper's KG with fuel at any stage during his advance and his own failure to capture sufficient American stocks.

It should be realised, however, that if any one of these factors had not applied, Peiper, or even Hansen, might well have reached the Meuse. For example, if Peiper had attacked Stavelot on the night of the 17th, he would have found no troops to resist him and the Americans would not have had time to prepare the Trois Ponts bridges. Similarly, if his column had not been spotted and attacked from the air on the 18th, he would certainly have crossed the Neufmoulin bridge. But these are the 'ifs' of history and at the end of the day it can be said that the essential element which Peiper lacked, particularly and rather poignantly on 17th December, was luck. That certainly should not detract from the bravery displayed by the American soldiers who stood up to the panzers and panzer-grenadiers of the Leibstandarte and later destroyed Kampfgruppe Peiper.

And Jochen Peiper? Clearly he was a charismatic leader and a very capable soldier – it is easy to become mesmerized by his dashing exploits. But it should never be forgotten that he spent three years in the close service of one of the most notorious and odious men in the history of mankind – Heinrich Himmler. And it is probably only due to the fact that a *Stars and Stripes* reporter, named Hal Boyle, was in Malmédy on 17th December 1944 and was able to publicize the 'Malmédy Massacre' that Peiper has become famous, or infamous, depending on one's nationality and point of view.

The German Kampfgruppes and supporting troops

1st SS Panzer Division (LAH)
Kampfgruppe Peiper

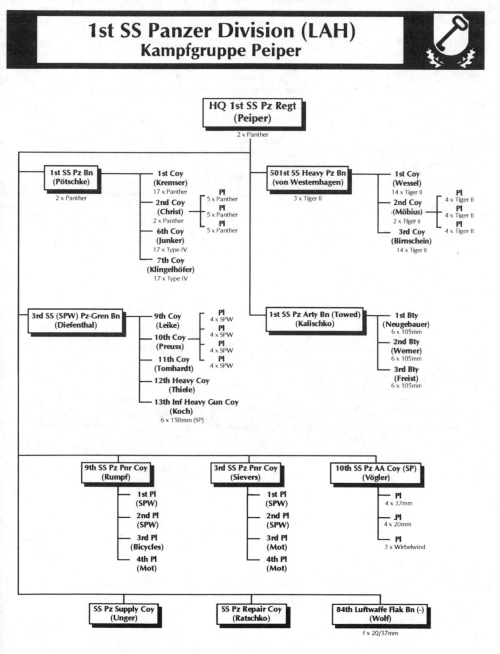

HQ 1st SS Pz Regt (Peiper)
2 x Panther

1st SS Pz Bn (Pötschke)
2 x Panther

- **1st Coy (Kremser)** — 17 x Panther
- **2nd Coy (Christ)** — 2 x Panther
  - Pl — 5 x Panther
  - Pl — 5 x Panther
  - Pl — 5 x Panther
  - Pl — 5 x Panther
- **6th Coy (Junker)** — 17 x Type IV
- **7th Coy (Klingelhöfer)** — 17 x Type IV

501st SS Heavy Pz Bn (von Westernhagen)
3 x Tiger II

- **1st Coy (Wessel)** — 14 x Tiger II
- **2nd Coy (Möbius)** — 2 x Tiger II
  - Pl — 4 x Tiger II
  - Pl — 4 x Tiger II
  - Pl — 4 x Tiger II
- **3rd Coy (Birnschein)** — 14 x Tiger II

3rd SS (SPW) Pz-Gren Bn (Diefenthal)

- **9th Coy (Leike)** — Pl — 4 x SPW
- **10th Coy (Preuss)** — Pl — 4 x SPW
- **11th Coy (Tomhardt)** — Pl — 4 x SPW
  - Pl — 4 x SPW
- **12th Heavy Coy (Thiele)**
- **13th Inf Heavy Gun Coy (Koch)** — 6 x 150mm (SP)

1st SS Pz Arty Bn (Towed) (Kalischko)

- **1st Bty (Neugebauer)** — 6 x 105mm
- **2nd Bty (Werner)** — 6 x 105mm
- **3rd Bty (Freist)** — 6 x 105mm

9th SS Pz Pnr Coy (Rumpf)

- **1st Pl (SPW)**
- **2nd Pl (SPW)**
- **3rd Pl (Bicycles)**
- **4th Pl (Mot)**

3rd SS Pz Pnr Coy (Sievers)

- **1st Pl (SPW)**
- **2nd Pl (SPW)**
- **3rd Pl (Mot)**
- **4th Pl (Mot)**

10th SS Pz AA Coy (SP) (Vögler)

- **Pl** — 4 x 37mm
- **Pl** — 4 x 20mm
- **Pl** — 3 x Wirbelwind

SS Pz Supply Coy (Unger)

SS Pz Repair Coy (Ratschko)

84th Luftwaffe Flak Bn (-) (Wolf)
? x 20/37mm

1st SS Panzer Division (LAH)
Kampfgruppe Hansen

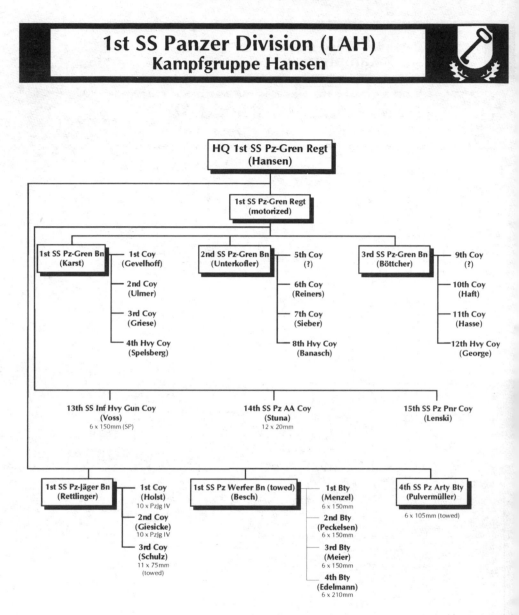

HQ 1st SS Pz-Gren Regt
(Hansen)

1st SS Pz-Gren Regt
(motorized)

1st SS Pz-Gren Bn
(Karst)

1st Coy
(Gevelhoff)

2nd Coy
(Ulmer)

3rd Coy
(Griese)

4th Hvy Coy
(Spelsberg)

2nd SS Pz-Gren Bn
(Unterkofler)

5th Coy
(?)

6th Coy
(Reiners)

7th Coy
(Sieber)

8th Hvy Coy
(Banasch)

3rd SS Pz-Gren Bn
(Böttcher)

9th Coy
(?)

10th Coy
(Haft)

11th Coy
(Hasse)

12th Hvy Coy
(George)

13th SS Inf Hvy Gun Coy
(Voss)
6 x 150mm (SP)

14th SS Pz AA Coy
(Stuna)
12 x 20mm

15th SS Pz Pnr Coy
(Lenski)

1st SS Pz-Jäger Bn
(Rettlinger)

1st Coy
(Holst)
10 x PzJg IV

2nd Coy
(Giesicke)
10 x PzJg IV

3rd Coy
(Schulz)
11 x 75mm
(towed)

1st SS Pz Werfer Bn (towed)
(Besch)

1st Bty
(Menzel)
6 x 150mm

2nd Bty
(Peckelsen)
6 x 150mm

3rd Bty
(Meier)
6 x 150mm

4th Bty
(Edelmann)
6 x 210mm

4th SS Pz Arty Bty
(Pulvermüller)

6 x 105mm (towed)

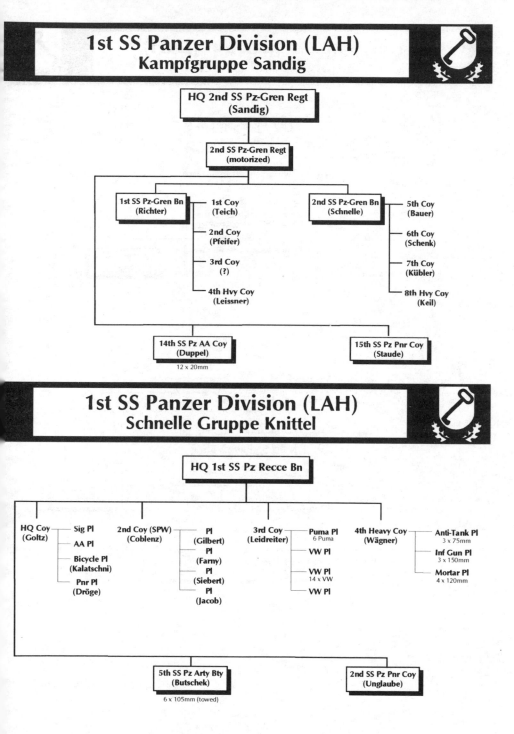

1st SS Panzer Division (LAH)
Kampfgruppe Sandig

HQ 2nd SS Pz-Gren Regt
(Sandig)

2nd SS Pz-Gren Regt
(motorized)

1st SS Pz-Gren Bn
(Richter)

1st Coy
(Teich)

2nd Coy
(Pfeifer)

3rd Coy
(?)

4th Hvy Coy
(Leissner)

2nd SS Pz-Gren Bn
(Schnelle)

5th Coy
(Bauer)

6th Coy
(Schenk)

7th Coy
(Kübler)

8th Hvy Coy
(Keil)

14th SS Pz AA Coy
(Duppel)
12 x 20mm

15th SS Pz Pnr Coy
(Staude)

1st SS Panzer Division (LAH)
Schnelle Gruppe Knittel

HQ 1st SS Pz Recce Bn

HQ Coy
(Goltz)

Sig Pl

AA Pl

Bicycle Pl
(Kalatschni)

Pnr Pl
(Dröge)

2nd Coy (SPW)
(Coblenz)

Pl
(Gilbert)

Pl
(Farny)

Pl
(Siebert)

Pl
(Jacob)

3rd Coy
(Leidreiter)

Puma Pl
6 Puma

VW Pl

VW Pl
14 x VW

VW Pl

4th Heavy Coy
(Wägner)

Anti-Tank Pl
3 x 75mm

Inf Gun Pl
3 x 150mm

Mortar Pl
4 x 120mm

5th SS Pz Arty Bty
(Butschek)
6 x 105mm (towed)

2nd SS Pz Pnr Coy
(Unglaube)

275

1st SS Panzer Divisional Troops

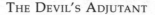

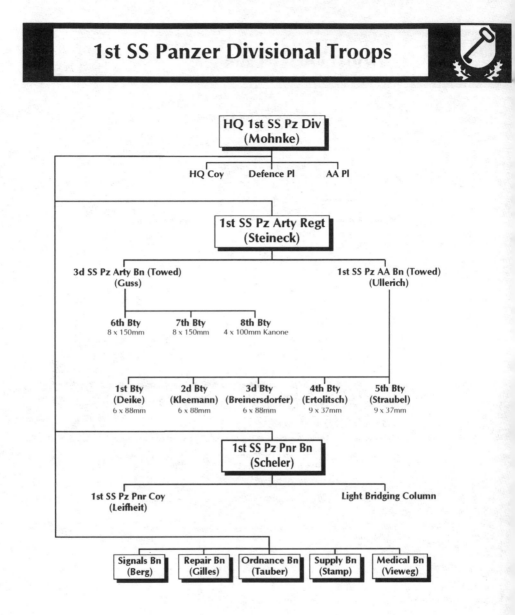

HQ 1st SS Pz Div (Mohnke)

HQ Coy   Defence Pl   AA Pl

1st SS Pz Arty Regt (Steineck)

3d SS Pz Arty Bn (Towed) (Guss)

1st SS Pz AA Bn (Towed) (Ullerich)

6th Bty   **7th Bty**   **8th Bty**
8 x 150mm   8 x 150mm   4 x 100mm Kanone

1st Bty (Deike)   **2d Bty (Kleemann)**   **3d Bty (Breinersdorfer)**   **4th Bty (Ertolitsch)**   **5th Bty (Straubel)**
6 x 88mm   6 x 88mm   6 x 88mm   9 x 37mm   9 x 37mm

1st SS Pz Pnr Bn (Scheler)

1st SS Pz Pnr Coy (Leifheit)   **Light Bridging Column**

Signals Bn (Berg)   **Repair Bn (Gilles)**   **Ordnance Bn (Tauber)**   **Supply Bn (Stamp)**   **Medical Bn (Vieweg)**

150th Panzer Brigade

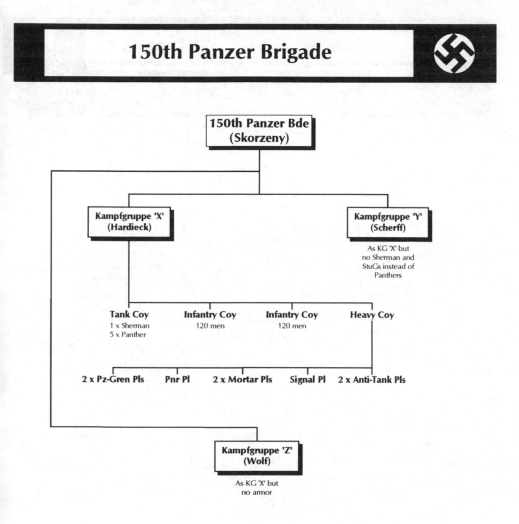

150th Panzer Bde
(Skorzeny)

Kampfgruppe 'X'
(Hardieck)

Kampfgruppe 'Y'
(Scherff)

As KG 'X' but
no Sherman and
StuGs instead of
Panthers

Tank Coy
1 x Sherman
5 x Panther

Infantry Coy
120 men

Infantry Coy
120 men

Heavy Coy

2 x Pz-Gren Pls   Pnr Pl   2 x Mortar Pls   Signal Pl   2 x Anti-Tank Pls

Kampfgruppe 'Z'
(Wolf)

As KG 'X' but
no armor

APPENDIX 2
A Volks-Grenadier Division

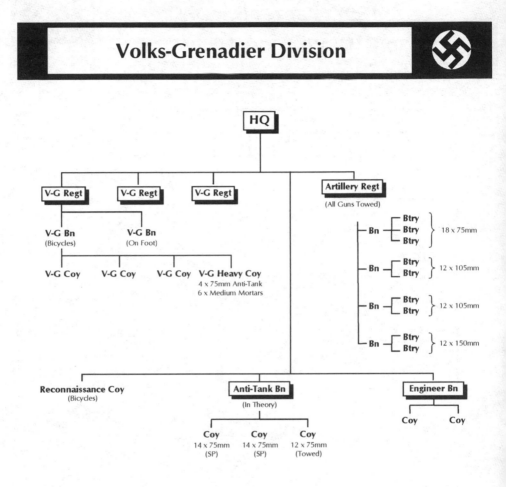

Volks-Grenadier Division

HQ

V-G Regt

V-G Regt

V-G Regt

Artillery Regt
(All Guns Towed)

V-G Bn
(Bicycles)

V-G Bn
(On Foot)

V-G Coy

V-G Coy

V-G Coy

V-G Heavy Coy
4 x 75mm Anti-Tank
6 x Medium Mortars

Bn — Btry / Btry / Btry } 18 x 75mm

Bn — Btry / Btry } 12 x 105mm

Bn — Btry / Btry } 12 x 105mm

Bn — Btry / Btry } 12 x 150mm

Reconnaissance Coy
(Bicycles)

Anti-Tank Bn
(In Theory)

Engineer Bn

Coy
14 x 75mm
(SP)

Coy
14 x 75mm
(SP)

Coy
12 x 75mm
(Towed)

Coy

Coy

The 30th US Infantry Division

30th (US) Infantry Division

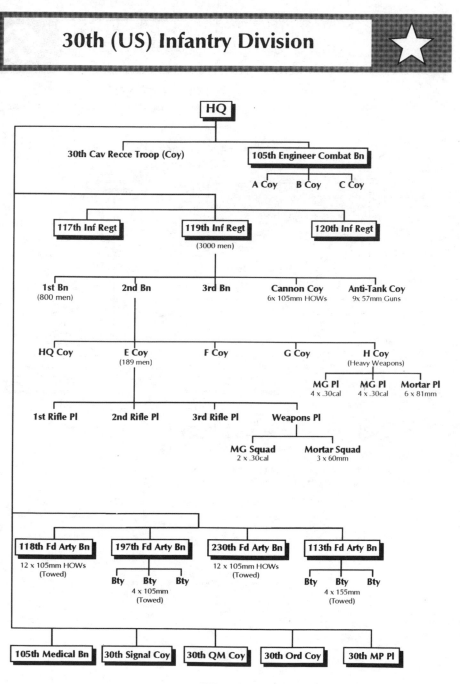

APPENDIX 4

30th US Infantry Division attached units – the 743rd Tank, 823rd Tank Destroyer and 541st AAA Battalions

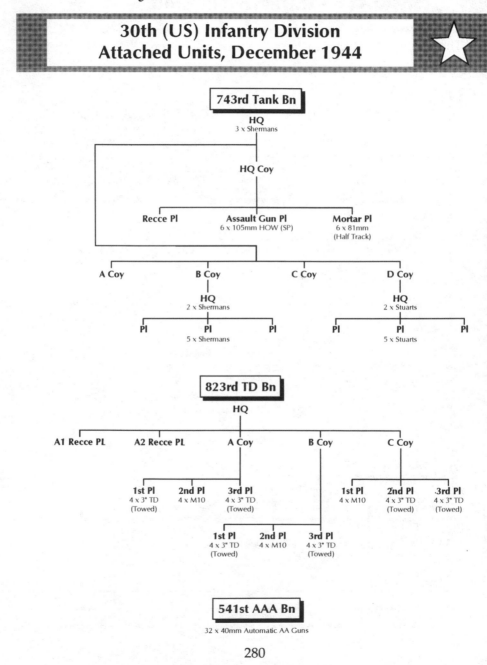

**30th (US) Infantry Division
Attached Units, December 1944**

743rd Tank Bn

HQ
3 x Shermans

HQ Coy

Recce Pl

Assault Gun Pl
6 x 105mm HOW (SP)

Mortar Pl
6 x 81mm
(Half Track)

A Coy

B Coy

HQ
2 x Shermans

Pl

Pl

Pl
5 x Shermans

C Coy

D Coy

HQ
2 x Stuarts

Pl

Pl

Pl
5 x Stuarts

823rd TD Bn

HQ

A1 Recce PL

A2 Recce PL

A Coy

B Coy

C Coy

1st Pl
4 x 3" TD
(Towed)

2nd Pl
4 x M10

3rd Pl
4 x 3" TD
(Towed)

1st Pl
4 x 3" TD
(Towed)

2nd Pl
4 x M10

3rd Pl
4 x 3" TD
(Towed)

1st Pl
4 x M10

2nd Pl
4 x 3" TD
(Towed)

3rd Pl
4 x 3" TD
(Towed)

541st AAA Bn

32 x 40mm Automatic AA Guns

APPENDIX 5

Those present in the 'Massacre Field' at Baugnez, 17th December 1944

The following list shows those Americans who were assembled in the field just south of the Café Bodarwé at Baugnez on 17th December 1944.

Rank	Name	Unit	Remarks
Sgt	K Ahrens	B Bty	Wounded; escaped.
Cpl	C Appman	,,	Unharmed; escaped.
T/5	H Billow	,,	Unharmed; escaped.
Pvt	D Bloom	,,	Killed; see note (a)
T/5	C Blouch	,,	Killed; body in field.
T/5	C Breon	,,	Killed; body west of field.
Cpl	J Brozowski	,,	Killed; body north of field.
T/5	S Burkett	,,	Killed; body in field.
Pfc	M Butera	,,	Wounded; escaped.
T/5	P Carr	,,	Killed; body in field.
Pfc	H Carson	,,	Killed; see note (a).
Pvt	J Coates	,,	Killed; see note (a).
Pvt	J Cobbler	,,	Wounded; escaped; died of wounds in Malmédy.
Pfc	R Cohen	,,	Killed; body in field.
T/5	J Collier	,,	Killed; body in field.
T/5	C Daub	,,	Unharmed; escaped.
T/Sgt	P Davidson	,,	Killed; body in field.
Pvt	D Day	,,	Wounded; escaped.
Pfc	H Desch	,,	Killed; body in field.
Pvt	W Dunbar	,,	Killed; body in field.
Cpl	C Fitt	,,	Killed; body west of field.
Pfc	D Flack	,,	Killed; body in field.
Cpl	T Flechsig	,,	Wounded; escaped.
Cpl	G Fox	,,	Unharmed; escaped.
Sgt	W Franz	,,	Killed; body in field.
Pfc	C Frey	,,	Killed; body west of field.
T/5	P Garstka	,,	Unharmed; escaped.
S/Sgt	D Geisler	,,	Killed; body in field.
T/5	C Haines	,,	Killed; body in field.
Pfc	C Hall	,,	Killed; body at road intersection.
Pvt	S Hallman	,,	Killed; body north-west of field.

Pfc	A Hardiman	B Bty (cont)	Wounded; escaped.
T/4	S Herchelroth	,,	Killed; body in field.
Pfc	H Horn	,,	Wounded; escaped.
Cpl	R Indelicato	HQ Bty 285th	Killed; body in field.
Cpl	O Jordan	B Bty	Killed; body in field.
Pvt	J Kailer	,,	Wounded; escaped.
T/5	K Kingston	,,	Wounded; escaped.
Sgt	A Kinsman	,,	Killed; body north-west of field.
Lt	V Lary	B Bty	Wounded; escaped.
T/5	H Laufer	,,	Killed; see note (a).
Pfc	R Law	,,	Wounded; escaped.
T/5	A Lengyel	,,	Killed; body in field.
T/4	S Leu	,,	Killed; body in field.
T/5	J Leurs	,,	Killed; body in field.
Cpl	L Martin	,,	Killed; body in field.
Pfc	P Martin	,,	Wounded; escaped.
Pvt	J Mattera	,,	Unharmed; escaped.
T/Sgt	W McGovern	HQ Bty 285th	Killed; body in field.
T/5	R McKinney	B Bty	Killed; body north-west of field.
T/4	R Mearig	,,	Unharmed; escaped.
S/Sgt	W Merriken	,,	Wounded; escaped.
Cpl	H Miller	,,	Killed; body in field.
Capt	R Mills	HQ Bty 285th	Killed; body north of field.
T/5	C Moucheron	B Bty	Wounded; escaped.
Lt	J Munzinger	,,	Killed see note (a).
T/5	J O'Connell	,,	Wounded; escaped.
Cpl	D O'Grady	,,	Killed; see note (a)
Pfc	T Oliver	,,	Killed; body in field.
S/Sgt	J Osborne	,,	Killed; body north-west of field.
T/5	T Paluch	,,	Unharmed; escaped.
Pvt	S Piasecki	,,	Killed; body north-west of field.
Pfc	P Piscatelli	,,	Unharmed; escaped.
Pvt	G Pittman	,,	Killed; body in field.
Pvt	A Propanchik	,,	Unharmed; escaped.
Lt	P Reardon	,,	Killed; body in field.
Pvt	W Reem	,,	Unharmed; escaped.
T/5	G Rosenfeld	,,	Killed; body in field.
Cpl	C Rullman	,,	Killed; body north of field.
Pvt	O Saylor	,,	Killed; body in field.
T/5	M Schwitzgold	,,	Killed; body in field.
T/5	M Sciranko	,,	Wounded; escaped.
T/4	I Sheetz	,,	Killed; body in field.
T/5	J Shingler	,,	Killed; body in field.

T/5	M Skoda	B Bty (cont)	Wounded; escaped; later captured and became POW.
Sgt	C Smith	,,	Unharmed; escaped.
Pvt	R Smith	,,	Unharmed; escaped.
Sgt	R Snyder	,,	Killed; body in field.
Sgt	A Stabulis	,,	Escaped; killed later and body found 1km south of field in April 1945.
T/4	G Steffy	,,	Killed; body in field.
Cpl	C Stevens	,,	Killed; see note (b).
T/5	W Summers	,,	Unharmed; escaped.
T/5	L Swartz	,,	Killed; body in field.
Pfc	E Thomas	,,	Killed; body never found.
Pvt	L Vairo	,,	Killed; body found 18km away at Neuhof in Germany in February 1945.
T/5	A Valenzi	,,	Wounded; escaped.
Pfc	R Walker	,,	Killed; body in field.
T/4	T Watt	,,	Killed; body in field.
Pvt	R Werth	,,	Wounded; escaped.
T/5	V Wiles	,,	Killed; body in field.
Pvt	R Anderson	575th Amb Coy	Wounded; escaped.
Pfc	L Burney	,,	Killed; body in field.
Pvt	S Dobyns	,,	Wounded; escaped.
Pfc	S Donitrovich	,,	Unharmed; escaped.
Lt	C Genthner	,,	Killed; body in field.
Pfc	J McKinney	,,	Unharmed; escaped.
Pfc	P Paden	,,	Killed; body north-west of field.
Pvt	W Scott	,,	Killed; body in field.
Pvt	K Mullen	546th Amb Coy	Killed; body north-west of field.
T/5	D Wusterbarth	,,	Killed; body in field.
Pfc	H Ford	518th MP Bn	Wounded; escaped.
Cpl	E Bojarski	32nd Armd Recce Coy	Unharmed; escaped; had been captured between Ondenval and Thirimont.
2nd Lt	L Iames	,,	Killed; body in field; had been captured between Ondenval and Thirimont.
Pvt	J Klukavy	,,	Killed; body north of field; had been captured between Ondenval and Thirimont.

Lt	T McDermott	32nd Armd Recce Coy (cont)	Killed; body in field; had been captured between Ondenval and Thirimont.
T/3	J McGee	,,	Killed; body in field; had been captured between Ondenval and Thirimont.
Sgt	M Lewis	,,	Wounded; escaped; had been captured between Ondenval and Thirimont.
Cpl	W Wendt	,,	Wounded; escaped; had been captured between Ondenval and Thirimont.
S/Sgt	H Zach	,,	Wounded; escaped; had been captured between Ondenval and Thirimont.
Pfc	J Clymire	86th Engrs	Killed; body in field.
S/Sgt	H Johnson	23rd Inf Regt	Wounded; escaped; had been captured east of Waimes.
Sgt	B Lindt	200th FA Bn	Killed; body in field; place of capture unknown. Military Government Police.
Pfc	E Wald	,,	Killed; body in field; Military Government Police.

Note (a)
On arrival at the 44th Evacuation Hospital in Malmédy six of the bodies, including this one, were without numbered tags. However, from sketch maps made by the US recovery teams in January 1945 and still held in the US Archives, it is clear that five of the bodies were recovered from within the field where the prisoners were assembled and one from a few metres to its north.

Note (b)
Recovered from the immediate vicinity of the Baugnez crossroads but exact position not recorded.

Other Americans present at Baugnez, 17th December 1944

Apart from the 113 Americans in the field at Baugnez, there were others who were involved in this clash with Peiper's Kampfgruppe and who are part of the total picture. The following list shows their names, units and what happened to them.

Rank	Name	Unit	Remarks
T/5	T Bacon	B Bty	Unharmed; became normal POW.
Pvt	D Bower	,,	Unharmed; escaped from front of convoy before the surrender.
Pfc	F Clarke	,,	Killed; there is evidence to show he died before the shooting of the men in the field; body found February 1945.
T/5	R Conrad	,,	Unharmed; escaped from front of convoy before surrender.
Pfc	W Davis	,,	Killed; time and place unknown; body found February 1945.
Cpl	E Garrett	,,	Unharmed; escaped from front of column.
2nd Lt	S Goffman	,,	Killed; time and place unknown; body found in February 1945.
Cpl	G Greaff	,,	Unharmed; escaped from front of convoy before surrender.
T/4	W Jones	,,	Killed; body found 1km south of Baugnez in April 1945.
M/Sgt	E Lacy	,,	Unharmed; made normal POW.
Cpl	R Lester	,,	Killed; time and place unknown; body found February 1945.
T/5	R Logan	,,	Unharmed; made normal POW.
T/4	A Lucas	,,	Killed; time and place unknown; body found February 1945.
Cpl	D Lucas	,,	Unharmed; made a normal POW and died in captivity.

Cpl	W Moore	B Bty (cont)	Killed; time and place unknown; body found 1km south of field in April 1945.
Pfc	D Murray	,,	Killed; time and place unknown; body found in February 1945.
Pvt	W Perkowski	,,	Killed; time and place unknown; body found February 1945.
Pvt	P Phillips	,,	Killed; evidence to show he was killed before main shooting at men in the field; body found south of the field.
T/5	C Reding	,,	Unharmed; managed to hide and later escaped.
T/4	J Rupp	,,	Killed; time and place unknown; body found February 1945.
T/5	W Schmitt	,,	Unharmed; escaped from front of convoy before surrender.
Sgt	V Anderson	32nd Armd Recce Coy	Unharmed; made normal POW.
Pvt	W Barron	,,	Unharmed; made normal POW.
Cpl	J Cummings	,,	Unharmed; made normal POW.
T/4	C Cash	197th AAA Bn	Killed before shooting at the men in the field; body found 200 metres east of the crossroads.
T/5	R Heitmann	,,	Killed before shooting at the men in the field; body found 200 metres east of the crossroads.
Pvt	V McKinney	86th Engrs	Wounded; escaped before shooting at men in the field.

Bibliography

It will be clear from the text that the main sources of information used in the compilation of this book have been the direct statements, both written and verbal, of soldiers and civilians who took part in, or witnessed, the actions described, and Formation and Unit After Action Reports, Logs and Diaries. All individual statements were carefully analysed and cross-checked and only those supported by other sources and found to be free of exaggeration have been included. They have been attributed to their authors throughout. American After Action Reports, Logs and Unit Diaries were obtained, in the majority of cases, from the National Archives of the United States of America. No equivalent records exist on the German side since the war diary of the 1st SS Panzer Division (LAH) was destroyed before the end of the war; however, much useful information was gained by studying *The Leibstandarte*, Parts I to III by Rudolf Lehmann, Part IV/I, by Rudolf Lehmann and Ralf Tiemann, all published by J. J. Fedorowicz Publishing Inc, Winnipeg, Canada, and Part IV/II by Ralf Tiemann, published by Munin Verlag GmbH, Osnabrück. Further valuable information was gleaned from strength returns held by the Bundesarchiv, Germany and from interviews with senior German officers carried out after the war on behalf of the US Army Historical Branch. Use was also made of British Royal Air Force records held by the Public Record Office at Kew, near London.

Books quoted and other sources consulted were:

Bastin Dr, *Borgoumont and the von Rundstedt Offensive*, University of Liège, 1951.

Bennett, Ralph, *Ultra in the West*, Hutchinson, 1979.

Blakeslee, Clarence, *A Personal Account of WWII by Draftee # 36887149*, Rockford, Michigan, 1989.

Breitman, Richard, *The Architect of Genocide*, The Bodley Head, 1991.

Broszat, M, *Commandant of Auschwitz, Autobiographical Notes of Rudolf Höss*, Stuttgart, 1958.

Cole, Hugh M, *United States Army in World War II, ETO, The Ardennes: Battle of the Bulge*, Washington, 1965.

Commission des Crimes des Guerre, 1946, *Les Crimes de Guerre commis pendant la contra-offensive von Rundstedt dans les Ardennes*, Ministère de la Justice, Thone, Liège, 1948.

Ellis, Chris, *Tanks of World War 2*, Octopus Books Ltd, 1981.

Fontaine, Serge, *Stoumont, La Gleize, Cheneux, Décembre 1944*, Journal Publicité Idéale, 1970.

Fontaine, Serge, *Trois Ponts Décembre 1944 Quand les Ponts Volaient en Eclats*, Editions Cadusa, 1992.

Frühbeisser, Rudi, *Fallschirmjäger im Einsatz*, St Vith, 1971.

Gavin, James, *On to Berlin*, Leo Cooper, Pen & Sword Books Ltd, London, 1978.

Graves, Clifford L, *Front Line Surgeons*, 1950.

Graves, George D, *Blood and Snow – the Ardennes*.

Grégoire, Gérard, *Les Panzer de Peiper face à l'US Army*, Printed by J. Chauveheid, Stavelot, Belgium.

Grégoire, Gérard, *Feu-Fire-Feuer-Vuur*, as above.

Hammer, Charles A, *History of the 285th Field Artillery Observation Battalion*, 1978.

Hechler, Ken, *Holding The Line*, Office of History US Army Corps of Engineers, Fort Belvoir VA, 1988.

Henlet, Abbé, *The Tragedy of St Edouard's*, University of Liège.

Hewitt, R L, *Work Horse of the Western Front*, The Story of the 30th Infantry Division, Infantry Journal, 1946.

Holt Giles, Janice, *The Damned Engineers*, Houghton Mifflin Company, 1970.

Holt Giles, Janice, *The G.I. Journal of Sergeant Giles*, Houghton Mifflin Company, 1988.

Jung, Hermann, *Die Ardennen Offensive*, Musterschmidt Verlag, 1971.

Kauffman, Robert, *The Red and White Path – One Soldier's Odyssey*.

Lyman, William J. Jr. *Curlew History*, The Story of the 1st Battalion of the 117th Infantry.

MacDonald, Charles B, *A Time for Trumpets*, The Untold Story of the Battle of the Bulge, William Morrow & Co, New York, 1985.

Merriam, Robert E, *The Battle of the Ardennes*, Souvenir Press, London, 1958.

Messenger, Charles, *Hitler's Gladiator*, Brassey's, 1988.

Officers of the Regiment, *Combat History of the 119th Infantry Regiment*.

Officers of the Regiment, *History of the 120th Infantry Regiment*.

Pallud, Jean Paul, *The Battle of the Bulge, Then and Now*, Battle of Britain Prints International Limited, 1984.

Pergrin, David E, with Eric Hammel, *First Across the Rhine*, Atheneum, New York, 1989.

Pulver, Murray, *Longest Year*, Pine Hill Press, South Dakota.

Quarrie, Bruce, *Hitler's Samurai*, The Waffen-SS in Action, Patrick Stephens, Cambridge, 1983.

Reichelt, Dr Walter E, *Phantom Nine*, The 9th Armored (Remagen) Division, 1942–1945, Presidial Press, Austin, 1987.

Roberts, A Eaton, *Five Stars to Victory*, Atlas Printing & Engraving Co, Birmingham, Alabama, USA, 1949.

Rubel, George Kenneth, *Daredevil Tankers*, The Story of the 740th Tank Battalion, US Army.

Sayer, Ian, & Douglas Botting, *Hitler's Last General*, The Case Against Wilhelm Mohnke, Bantam Press, London, 1989.

Skorzeny, Otto, *Skorzeny's Special Missions*, Robert Hale, 1947.

Tiemann, Ralf, *Der Malmedyprozess*, Munin Verlag GmbH, Osnabrück, 1990.

Toland, John, *Battle, The Story of the Bulge*, Severn House Publishers Ltd, Sutton, England, 1977.

Vandervoort, B H, *Trois Ponts*.

The Histories, Narratives, Unit Journals, Logs and After Action Reports (AARs) of the following:

History of the 3rd Armored Division.
Narrative of the 82nd Airborne Division.
AAR 14th Cavalry Group.
AAR CCB/3rd Armored Division.
AAR CCB/9th Armored Division.
History 49th AAA Brigade.
Log 117th Infantry Regiment.
AAR 119th Infantry Regiment.
History 504th Parachute Infantry Regiment.
History 505th Parachute Infantry Regiment.
Official Interview S-3/394th Infantry Regiment.
AAR 18th Cavalry Squadron (Mech).
AAR 32nd Cavalry Squadron (Mech).
AAR 14th Tank Battalion.
AAR 743rd Tank Battalion.
History and Journal 612th TD Battalion.
History and AAR 644th TD Battalion.
Unit Report and Journal 801st TD Battalion.
AAR 820th TD Battalion.
AAR 823rd TD Battalion.
AAR 825th TD Battalion.
AAR 16th Armored FA Battalion.
AAR 110th AAA Battalion.
History 143rd AAA Battalion.
AAR and Log 1111th Engineer Group.
AAR 51st Engineer Combat Battalion.
AAR 105th Engineer Combat Battalion.
AAR 202nd Engineer Combat Battalion.
AAR 254th Engineer Combat Battalion.
AAR 291st Engineer Combat Battalion.

AAR 27th Armored Infantry Battalion.
AAR 99th (Separate) Infantry Battalion.
Official Interview CO 1/394th Infantry Battalion.
Official Interview CO 3/394th Infantry Battalion.
Unit Journal 1/504th Parachute Infantry Battalion.
Unit Journal 2/504th Parachute Infantry Battalion.
Unit Journal 3/504th Parachute Infantry Battalion.
AAR 526th Armored Infantry Battalion.
Report No 19 of 2nd Tactical Air Force Operational Research Section dated 9 Jun 1945 (MOD London DOAE Registry).

Every effort has been made to obtain permission to quote from personal letters to the author and from specific books. In some cases the authors are known to have passed away and in others publishing companies have ceased to exist.

The copyright on all original photographs is indicated where known.

Index

291

Index

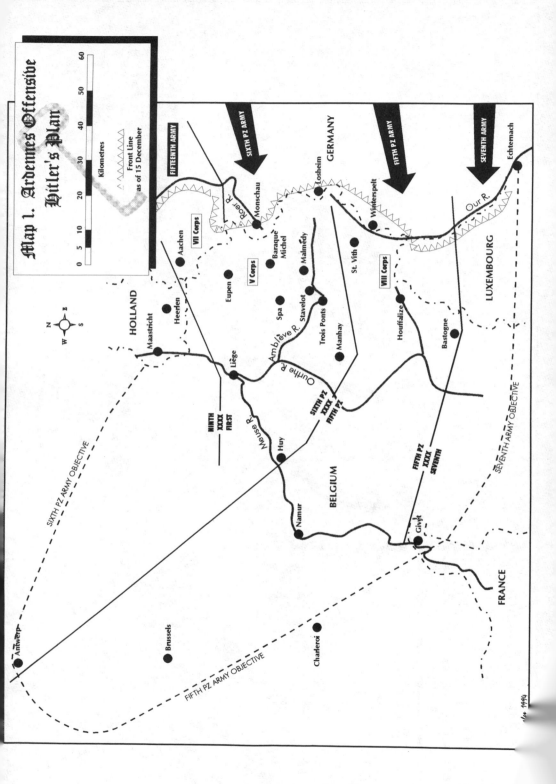

Map 1. Ardennes Offensive
Hitler's Plan

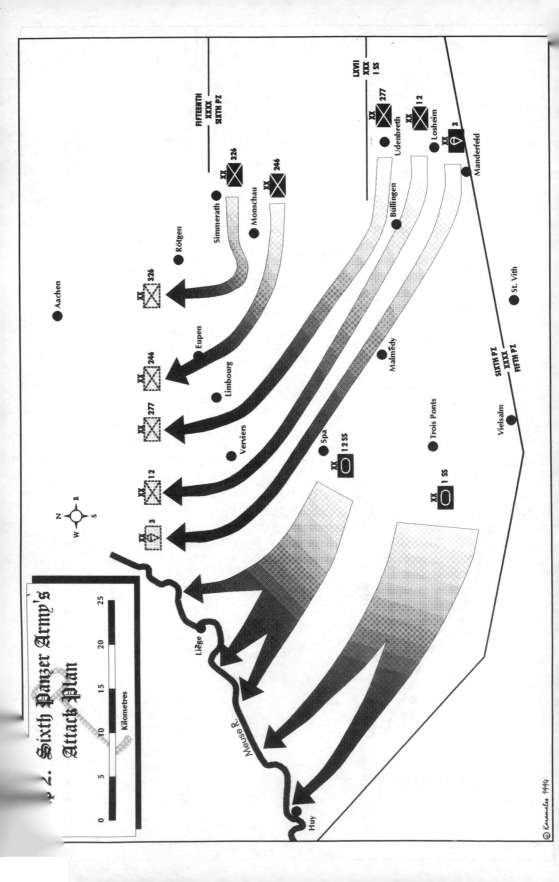

2. Sixth Panzer Army's Attack Plan

Kilometres
0 5 10 15 20 25

© Kessondee 1994

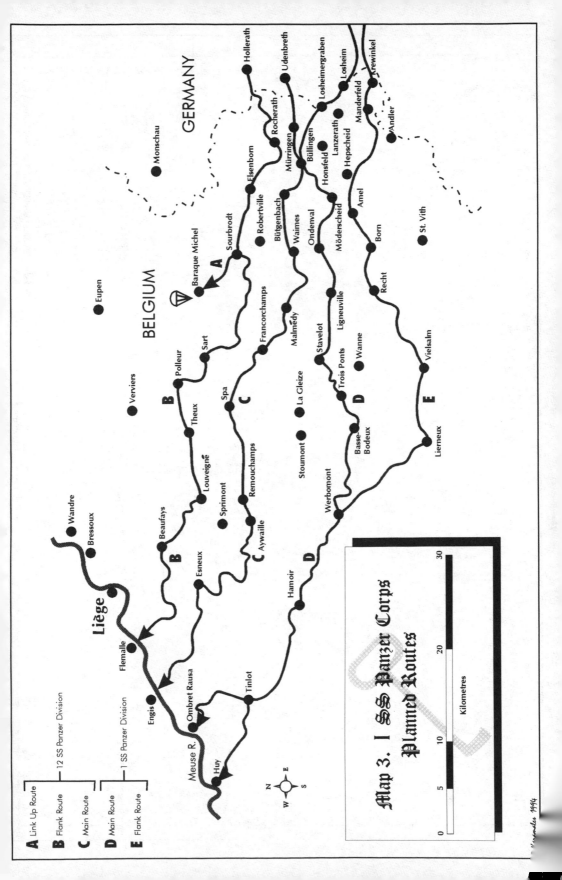

Map 3. I SS Panzer Corps
Planned Routes

A Link Up Route

B Flank Route ⎤
C Main Route ⎦ 12 SS Panzer Division

D Main Route ⎤
E Flank Route ⎦ 1 SS Panzer Division

Kilometres

0   5   10   20   30

GERMANY

BELGIUM

Liège

Meuse R.

N
W — E
S

Monschau

Eupen

Verviers

Wandre
Bressoux

Engis
Ombret Rausa
Flemalle
Tinlot
Huy

Beaufays
Esneux
Louveigné
Sprimont
Aywaille
Remouchamps
Hamoir
Theux
Spa
Stoumont
Werbomont
La Gleize
Basse-
Bodeux

Polleur
Sart
Baraque Michel
Sourbrodt
Francorchamps
Malmédy
Stavelot
Trois Ponts
Wanne
Vielsalm
Lierneux

Hollerath
Udenbreth
Losheimergraben
Losheim
Krewinkel

Elsenborn
Rocherath
Mürringen
Büllingen
Lanzerath
Manderfeld
Andler

Robertville
Bütgenbach
Waimes
Ondenval
Honsfeld
Hepscheid
Möderscheid
Amel
Born
Recht
Ligneuville
St. Vith

B
C

D
E

A

'Vemilee 1994

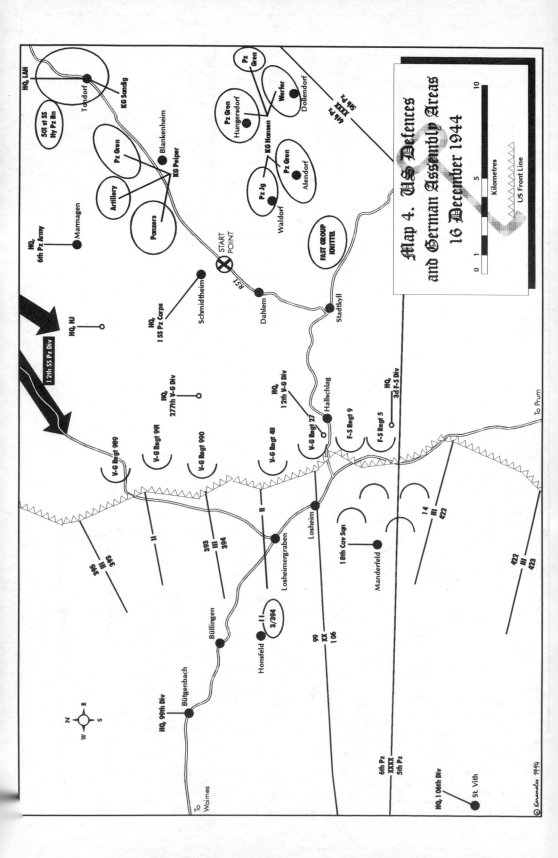

Map 4. US Defences and German Assembly Areas 16 December 1944

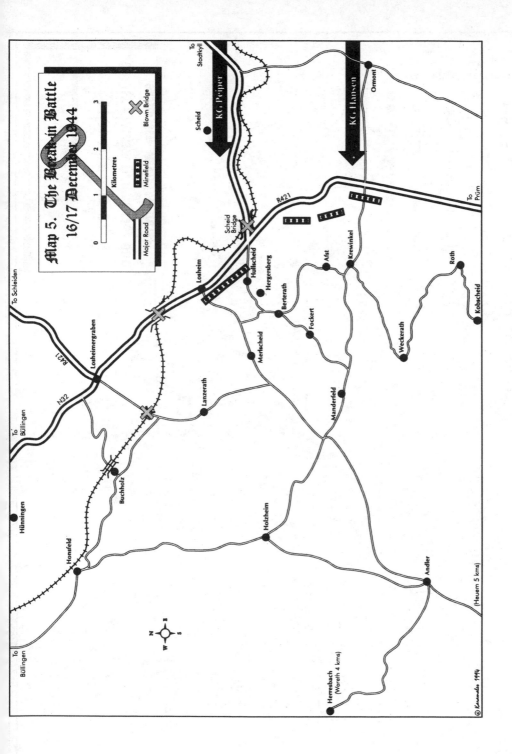

Map 5. The Break-in Battle
16/17 December 1944

Kilometres

Major Road
Minefield
Blown Bridge

KG Peiper

KG Hansen

To Stadtkyll

Scheid

To Prüm

R421

Scheid Bridge

Losheim

Hüllscheid

Hergersberg

Berterath

Afst

Krewinkel

Fockert

Weckerath

Roth

Kobscheid

Mertscheid

Lanzerath

Manderfeld

R421

N32

Losheimergraben

To Schleiden

To Büllingen

Hünningen

Honsfeld

Buchholz

Holzheim

Andler

(Heuem 5 kms)

Herresbach
(Woreth 4 kms)

To
Büllingen

N
W   E
S

© Kasavubu 1994

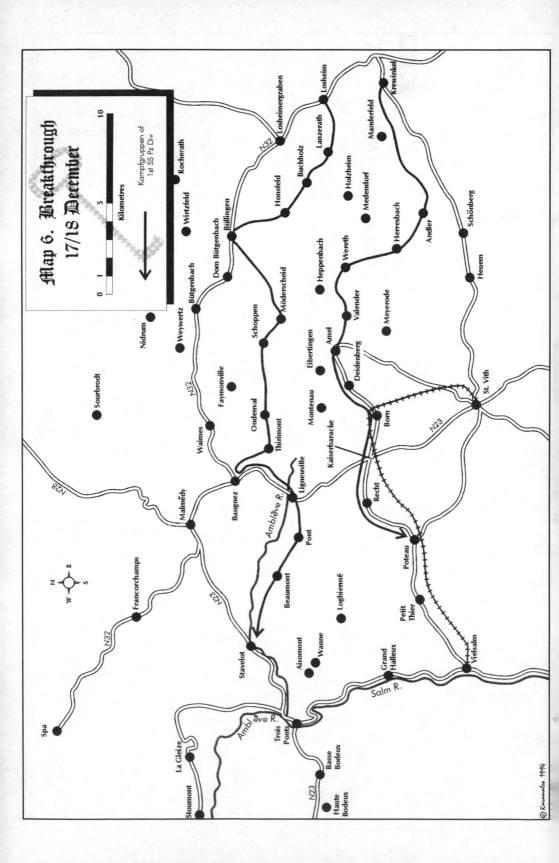

Map 6. Breakthrough
17/18 December

Kampfgruppen of
1st SS Pz Div

Kilometres

0   1   5   10

Rocherath
Wirtzfeld
Bütgenbach
Dom Bütgenbach
Büllingen
Weywertz
Nidrum
Sourbrodt
N32
Waimes
Faymonville
Ondenval
Schoppen
Möderscheid
Thirimont
Honsfeld
Buchholz
Lanzerath
Losheim
Losheimergraben
Krewinkel
Manderfeld
Holzheim
Medendorf
Herresbach
Andler
Schönberg
Heuem
St. Vith
Wereth
Valender
Meyerode
Heppenbach
Eibertingen
Montenau
Amel
Deidenberg
Born
N23
Recht
Kaiserbaracke
Ligneuville
Baugnez
Ambleve R.
Pont
Beaumont
Logbiermé
Poteau
Petit Thier
Grand Halleux
Vielsalm
Salm R.
Malmédy
N28
Francorchamps
N32
Spa
La Gleize
Stoumont
Stavelot
Aisomont
Wanne
Trois Ponts
Ambleve R.
Basse Bodeux
Haute Bodeux
N23

N
W   E
S

© Kasandee 1994

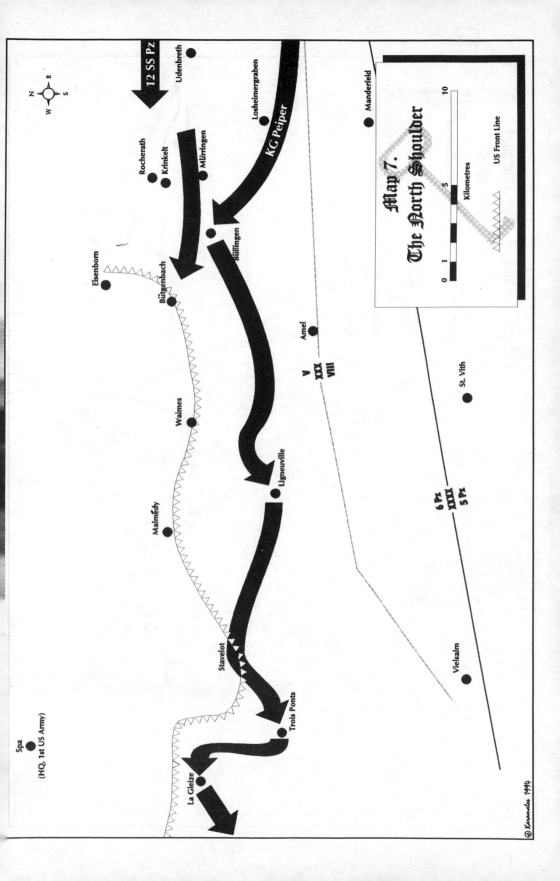

Map 7.
The North Shoulder

Spa
(HQ, 1st US Army)

La Gleize

Trois Ponts

Stavelot

Malmédy

Walmes

Elsenborn

Bütgenbach

Rocherath

Krinkelt

Mürringen

Büllingen

Losheimergraben

Udenbreth

12 SS Pz

KG Peiper

Ligneuville

Amel

V XXX VIII

St. Vith

6 Pz XXXX 5 Pz

Vielsalm

Manderfeld

Kilometres

US Front Line

0 1 5 10

© Kinnear 1994

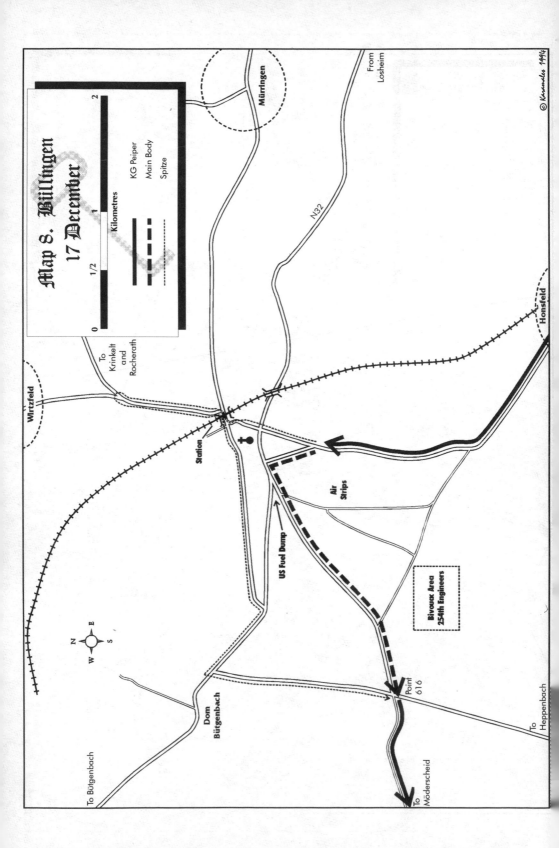

Map 8. Büllingen
17 December

Kilometres
0   1/2   1   2

KG Peiper
Main Body
Spitze

Mürringen

From
Losheim

N32

Honsfeld

To
Krinkelt
and
Rocherath

Wirtzfeld

Station

Air
Strips

US Fuel Dump

Bivouac Area
254th Engineers

N
W   E
S

Point
616

Dom
Bütgenbach

To Bütgenbach

To
Möderscheid

To
Heppenbach

© Kessander 1994

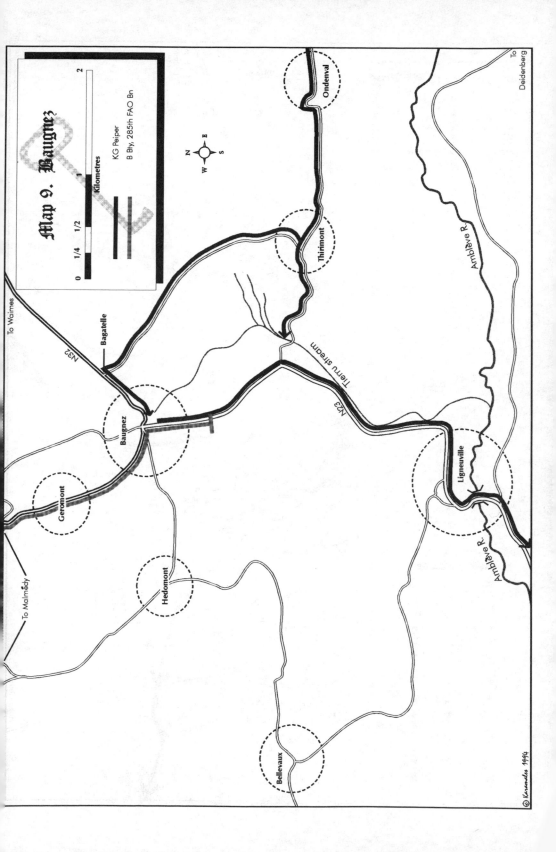

Map 9. Baugnez

Kilometres

KG Peiper

B Bty, 285th FAO Bn

0   1/4   1/2   1   2

To Waimes

N32

Bagatelle

Baugnez

Geromont

To Malmédy

Hedomont

Thirimont

Ondenval

Tierru stream

N23

Ligneuville

Amblève R.

Amblève R.

Bellevaux

To Deidenberg

© Karandus 1994

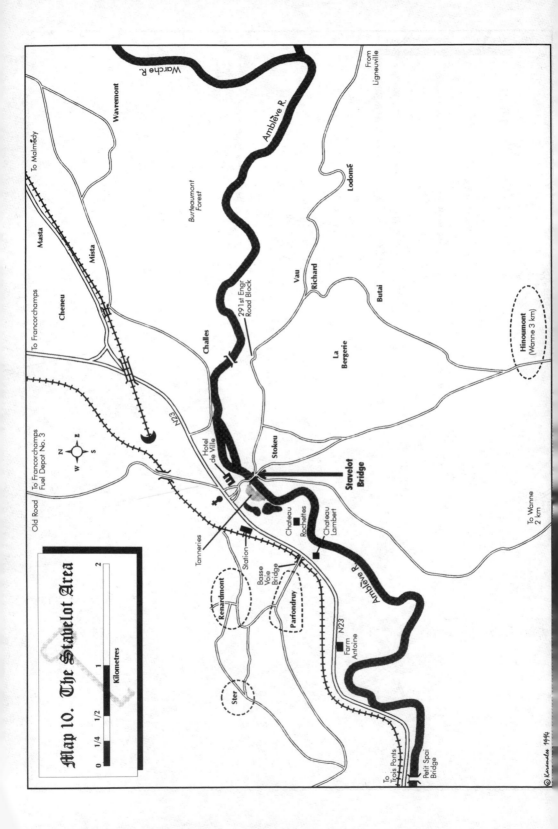

Map 10. The Stavelot Area

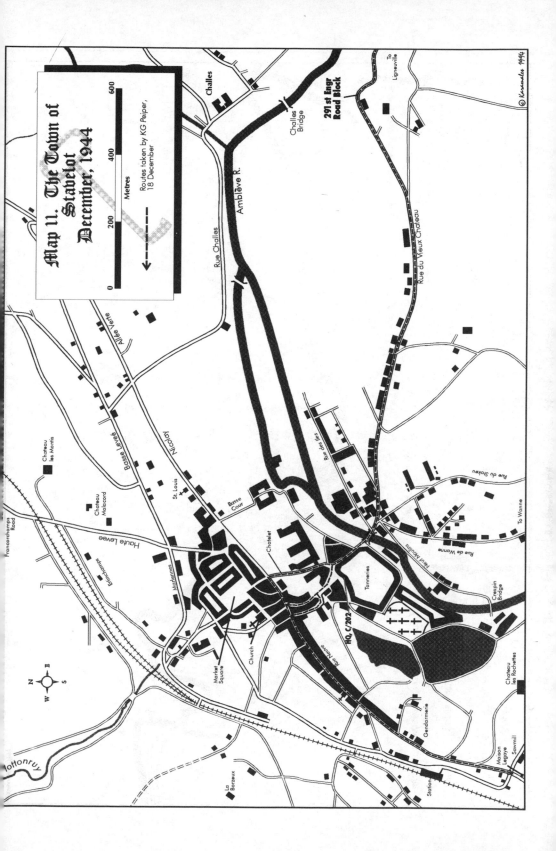

Map 11. The Town of Stabelot December, 1944

Metres

0   200   400   600

Routes taken by KG Peiper, 18 December

N
W — E
S

© Karsander 1994

Challes

Challes Bridge

291st Engr Road Block

To Ligneuville

Ambléve R.

Rue Challes

Rue du Vieux Château

Allée Verte

Basse Levée

Nicolay

St. Louis

Basse Cour

Châtelet

Rue des Îles

Rue du Stokeu

To Wanne

Neuf Moulins

Rue de Wanne

Château les Montis

Château Malacord

Haute Levée

Enhichamps

Madennes

Church

Market Square

Rue Notre

Tanneries

HQ, C/202?

Crespin Bridge

Château les Rochettes

Gendarmerie

Maison Legaye

Sawmill

Station

La Borzeaux

Francorchamps Road

Hottonruy

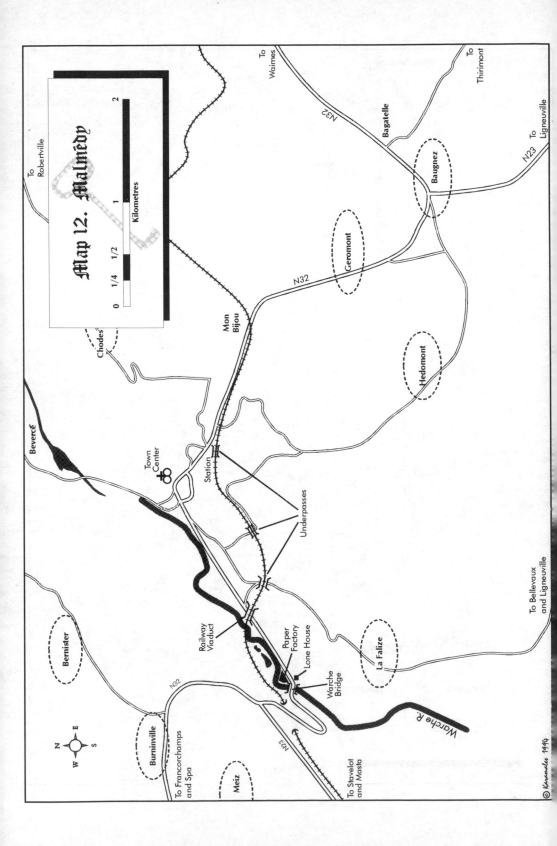

Map 12. Malmédy

Kilometres

0   1/4   1/2   1   2

To Robertville
To Waimes
To Thirimont
Chodes
Bagatelle
N32
Geromont
Baugnez
N23
To Ligneuville
Mon Bijou
N32
Hedomont
Bevercé
Town Center
Station
Underpasses
Bernister
Railway Viaduct
Paper Factory
Lone House
Warche Bridge
La Falize
Burninville
N32
Meiz
N23
To Francorchamps and Spa
To Stavelot and Masta
To Bellevaux and Ligneuville
Warche R.

N
W   E
S

© Karameles 1994

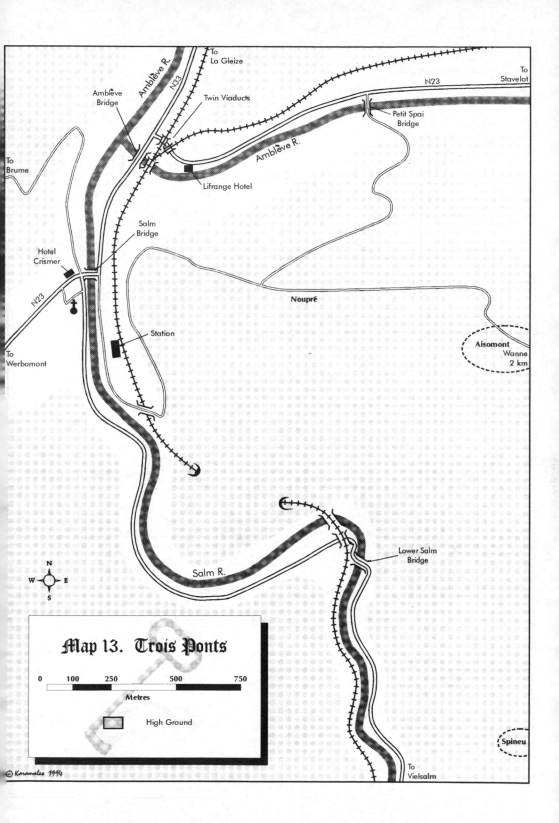

To La Gleize

To Stavelot

N23

Amblève R.

N33

Amblève Bridge

Twin Viaducts

Petit Spai Bridge

Amblève R.

To Brume

Lifrange Hotel

Salm Bridge

Hotel Crismer

Noupré

N23

Aisomont
Wanne
2 km

To Werbomont

Station

Salm R.

Lower Salm Bridge

N

W   E

S

Map 13. Trois Ponts

0   100   250   500   750

Metres

High Ground

Spineu

To Vielsalm

© Karamales 1994

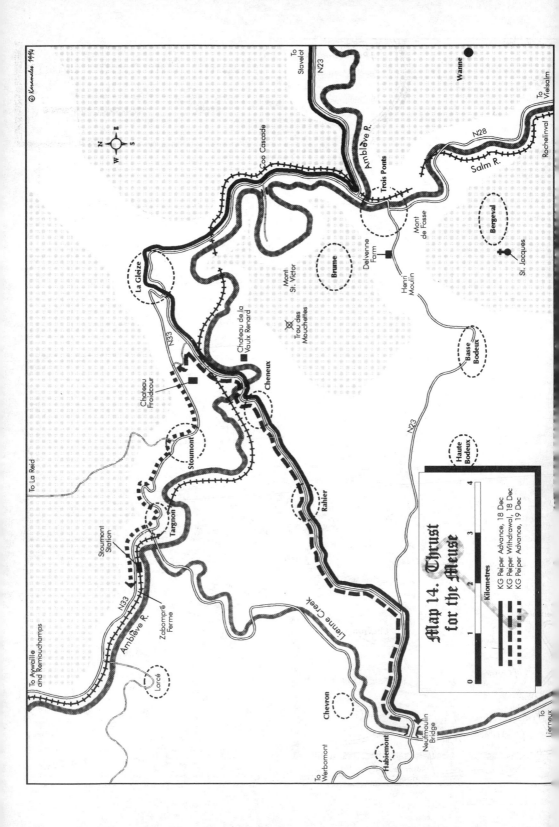

© Karamalos 1994

N
W · E
S

To La Reid

To Aywaille and Remouchamps

N33

Ambléve R.

Lorcé

To Werbomont

Chevron

Habiemont

Neufmoulin Bridge

To Liierneux

Lienne Creek

Zabompré Ferme

N33

Stoumont Station

Targnon

Stoumont

Rahier

Haute Bodeux

N23

Chateau Froidcour

Chateau de la Vaulx Renard

Cheneux

Trou des Mouchettes

Mont St. Victor

Brune

Basse Bodeux

Delvenne Farm

Henri Moulin

Mont de Fosse

La Gleize

N33

Coo Cascade

Trois Ponts

Ambléve R.

To Stavelot

N23

Salm R.

N28

Bergeval

St. Jacques

Wanne

To Vielsalm

Rochelinval

Map 14. Thrust for the Meuse

Kilometres

0   1   2   3   4

KG Peiper Advance, 18 Dec
KG Peiper Withdrawal, 18 Dec
KG Peiper Advance, 19 Dec

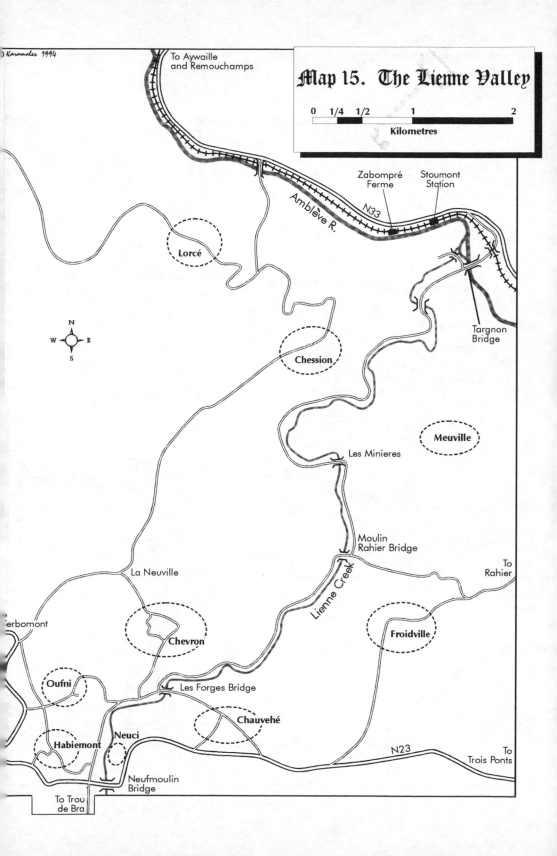

To Aywaille
and Remouchamps

© Karamales 1994

Map 15. The Lienne Valley

0   1/4   1/2   1   2
Kilometres

Zabompré
Ferme

Stoumont
Station

Amblève R.

N33

Lorcé

N
W   E
S

Chession

Meuville

Targnon
Bridge

Les Minieres

Moulin
Rahier Bridge

To
Rahier

La Neuville

Lienne Creek

erbomont

Chevron

Froidville

Oufni

Les Forges Bridge

Chauvehé

Neuci

Habiemont

N23

To
Trois Ponts

Neufmoulin
Bridge

To Trou
de Bra

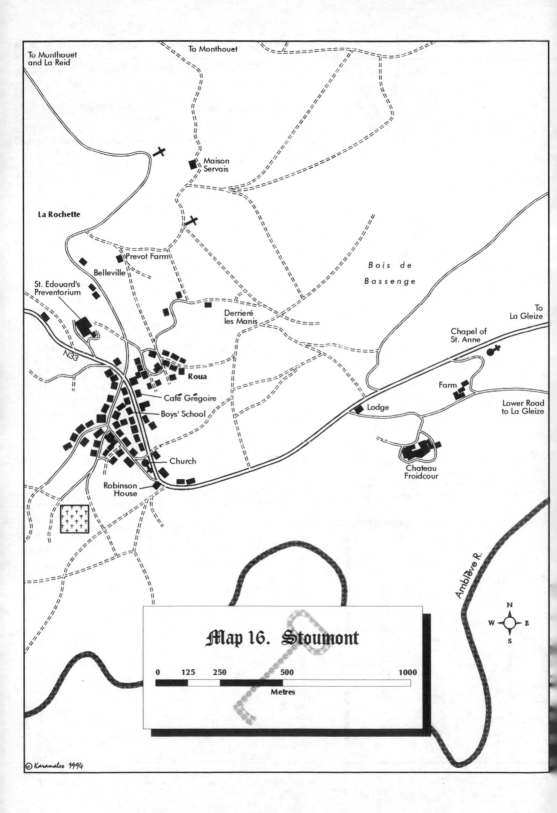

To Monthouet
and La Reid

To Monthouet

Maison
Servais

La Rochette

Prevot Farm

Belleville

St. Edouard's
Preventorium

Derrieré
les Manis

*Bois de
Bassenge*

Chapel of
St. Anne

To
La Gleize

N33

Roua

Farm

Café Grégoire

Boys' School

Lodge

Lower Road
to La Gleize

Church

Chateau
Froidcour

Robinson
House

Ambléve R.

N
W   E
S

Map 16. Stoumont

0   125   250   500   1000

Metres

© Karamales 1994

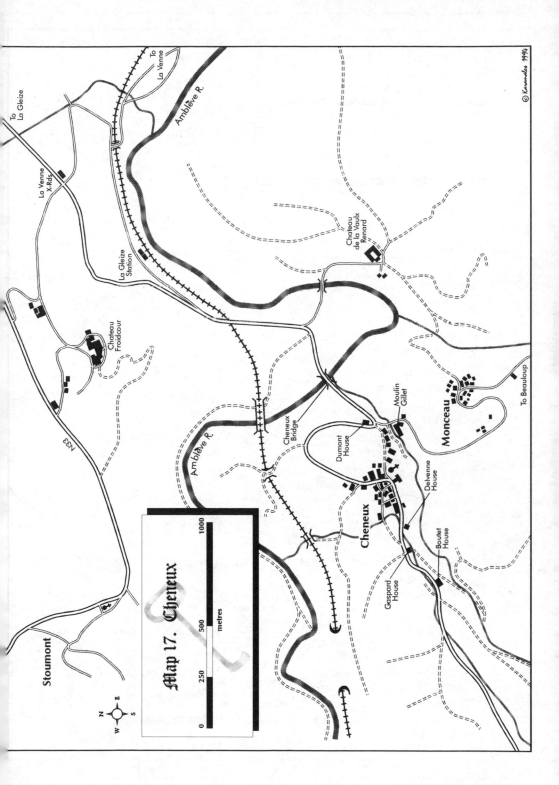

Stoumont

To Gleize
To La Gleize

To La Venne
To La Venne

Amblève R.

La Venne X-Rds

La Gleize Station

N33

Château Froidcour

Amblève R.

Château de la Vaulx Renard

Cheneux Bridge

Dumont House

Moulin Gillet

Monceau

To Beauloup

Cheneux

Delvenne House

Gaspard House

Boulet House

© Karondas 1994

Map 17. Cheneux

metres

0   250   500   1000

N
W E
S

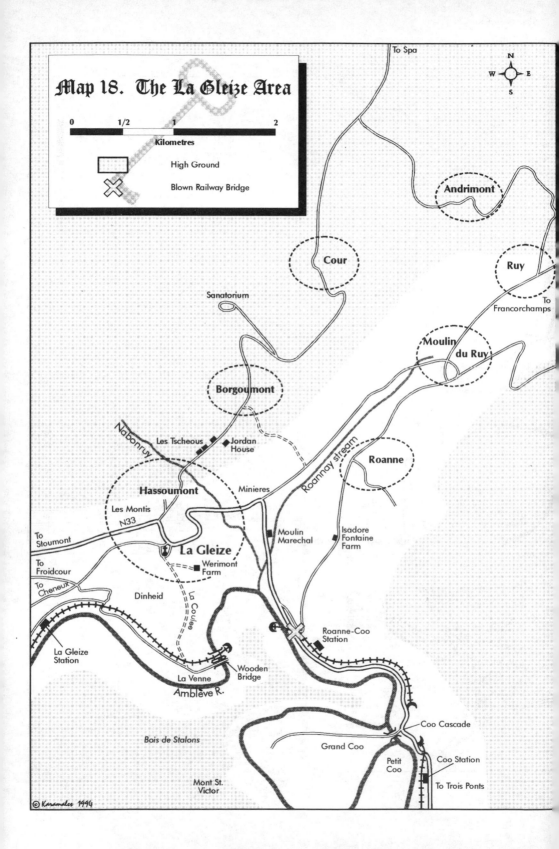

Map 18. The La Gleize Area

0   1/2   1   2

Kilometres

High Ground

Blown Railway Bridge

N
W E
S

To Spa

Andrimont

Cour

Ruy

To Francorchamps

Sanatorium

Moulin du Ruy

Borgoumont

Nabonruy

Les Tscheous   Jordan House

Roannay stream

Roanne

Minieres

Hassoumont

Les Montis

N33

To Stoumont

Moulin Marechal

Isadore Fontaine Farm

La Gleize

To Froidcour

Werimont Farm

To Cheneux

Dinheid

La Coulee

Roanne-Coo Station

La Gleize Station

Wooden Bridge

La Venne

Amblève R.

Bois de Stalons

Coo Cascade

Grand Coo

Petit Coo

Coo Station

To Trois Ponts

Mont St. Victor

© Karamales 1994

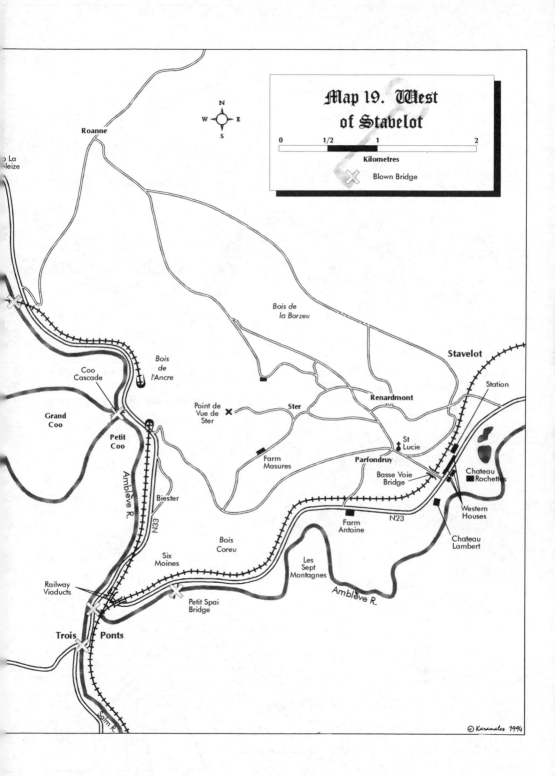

Map 19. West of Stabelot

0   1/2   1   2

Kilometres

✗ Blown Bridge

Roanne

To La
Gleize

Bois de
la Borzeu

Stavelot

Bois
de
l'Ancre

Coo
Cascade

Station

Grand
Coo

Point de
Vue de
Ster

Ster

Renardmont

Petit
Coo

St
Lucie

Chateau
Rochettes

Biester

Farm
Masures

Parfondruy

Basse Voie
Bridge

Amblève R.

N33

Western
Houses

N23

Bois
Coreu

Farm
Antoine

Chateau
Lambert

Six
Moines

Les
Sept
Montagnes

Railway
Viaducts

Amblève R.

Trois   Ponts

Petit Spai
Bridge

Salm R.

© Karamales 1994

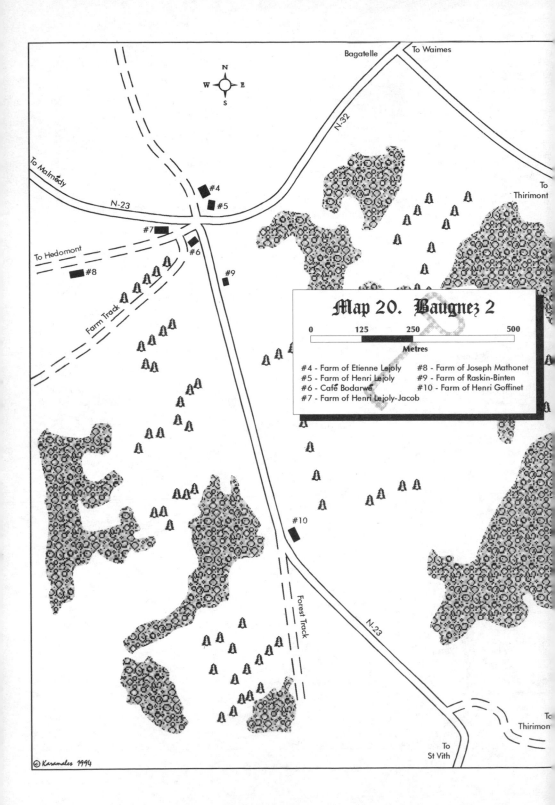

Map 20. Baugnez 2

0   125   250   500
Metres

#4 - Farm of Etienne Lejoly   #8 - Farm of Joseph Mathonet
#5 - Farm of Henri Lejoly   #9 - Farm of Raskin-Binten
#6 - Café Bodarwé   #10 - Farm of Henri Goffinet
#7 - Farm of Henri Lejoly-Jacob

To Waimes
Bagatelle
N-32
To Thirimont
To Malmedy
N-23
#4
#5
To Hedomont
#7
#6
#8
Farm Track
#9
#10
Forest Track
N-23
To Thirimont
To St Vith

© Karamales 1994